A
Century
of
Early
Ecocriticism

EDITED BY DAVID MAZEL

A
Century
of
Early
Ecocriticism

The University of Georgia Press

ATHENS AND LONDON

© 2001 by the University of Georgia Press

Athens, Georgia 30602

Designed by Kathi Dailey Morgan

Set in 10.2 on 13.5 Electra by G&S Typesetters

Printed and bound by Maple-Vail Book Manufacturing Group

The paper in this book meets the guidelines for
permanence and durability of the Committee on
Production Guidelines for Book Longevity of the
Council on Library Resources.

Printed in the United States of America

05 04 03 02 01 C 5 4 3 2 1

05 04 03 02 01 P 5 4 3 2 1

Library of Congress Cataloging-in-Publication Data

A century of early ecocriticism / edited by David Mazel.

p.   cm.

Includes bibliographical references (p.) and index.

ISBN 0-8203-2221-0 (alk. paper)

ISBN 0-8203-2222-9 (pbk. : alk. paper)

1. American literature — History and criticism.
2. Nature in literature.   3. Conservation of natural resources
in literature.   4. Environmental protection in literature.
5. Philosophy of nature in literature.   6. Forests and forestry
in literature.   7. Wilderness areas in literature.
8. Outdoor life in literature.   9. Landscape in literature.
10. Ecology in literature.   I. Mazel, David.

PS163 .C46   2001

810.9'355 — dc21

00-030216

British Library Cataloging-in-Publication Data available

This book is dedicated to my students.

Contents

Acknowledgments

Many people helped make this book possible. I would like especially to thank David Taylor, Roy Underwood, and the Division of Arts and Letters at the University of West Alabama; Gregor Smith and the Julia Tutwiler Library; John Frazee, Joseph Kolupke, and the School of Arts and Letters at Adams State College; Phil Jones and Adams State College's Neilsen Library; and my friends and colleagues SueEllen Campbell, Cheryll Glotfelty, Stephen and Cindy Slimp, Phyllis Ann Thompson, Christopher Healy, and Barbara Griego. Particular thanks go to Irene Marquez and Heather Goodstein Milton, who transcribed the bulk of this book's text, and to Amy Bauer and the servers at Alamosa's legendary Campus Café.

A
Century
of
Early
Ecocriticism

Introduction

That which was unconscious truth, becomes, when
interpreted and defined in an object, a part of the domain
of knowledge, — a new weapon in the magazine of power.
—Ralph Waldo Emerson, *Nature*

Ecocriticism — the study of literature as if the environment mattered — has
only recently come to recognize itself as a distinct critical enterprise. The
term itself apparently dates no further back than 1978, when it was coined by
William Rueckert.[1] Of course, in such a rapidly changing field as literary
studies, 1978 can seem like a long time ago, and a twenty-year history can
confer a quite respectable pedigree. This is the sense I got when Cheryll
Glotfelty wrote, in *The Ecocriticism Reader* (1996), that "individual literary
and cultural scholars have been developing ecologically informed criticism and theory since the seventies" and that therefore the "origin of ecocriticism . . . predates its recent consolidation by more than twenty years."[2]
It was as if those twenty years lent the field the sort of legitimacy *The Ecocriticism Reader* itself has done so much to establish.

Many of us have suspected, however, that ecocriticism actually boasts a
much longer history. After all, the environment has mattered to Americans,
in many of the same ways it matters today, for more than a century. Surely
among the nation's numerous early environmentalists there must have been
an occasional literary critic whose concern for nature was reflected in an
occasional essay or book. Nature writing itself is even older — more than two
centuries old, if we date it from the 1789 publication of Gilbert White's *Natural History of Selborne* — and surely it must have come now and then to the
attention of a literary critic and prompted a de facto ecocriticism.

Just as nature writing and environmentalism predate Earth Day, so must a
kind of ecocriticism predate the essays of Glen Love, William Rueckert,

1

Joseph Meeker, and Lynn White Jr. In searching for such work, and in deciding whether to include it in this collection, I quickly realized that I would
need a working definition. Just what *is* ecocriticism? I have already offered
one formulation above, but there are others. In *The Ecocriticism Reader,* for
example, Glotfelty defines it as "the study of the relationship between literature and the physical environment." In much the same way that "feminist
criticism examines language and literature from a gender-conscious perspective," she continues, "and Marxist criticism brings an awareness of modes of
production and economic class to its reading of texts, ecocriticism takes an
earth-centered approach to literary studies." No matter how it is defined,
ecocriticism seems less a singular approach or method than a constellation
of approaches, having little more in common than a shared concern with the
environment. It can address itself to a wide range of questions, including but
hardly limited to these: "How is nature represented in this sonnet? What role
does the physical setting play in the plot of this novel? Are the values expressed in the play consistent with ecological wisdom? . . . How has the concept of wilderness changed over time?"[3]

Clearly, a broad range of work may legitimately be thought of as ecocriticism. In compiling this anthology I have thus tried to be as inclusive as possible, counting as "ecocriticism" any material that might be of special interest not only to scholars but to all who share a love for both literature and the
environment. I have not limited the collection to professional, peer-reviewed
academic writing, nor even to "the best that has been thought and said" on
the matter. As Glotfelty notes, ecocriticism necessarily encompasses both a
"broad scope of inquiry and disparate levels of sophistication,"[4] and too fussy
a definition would have excluded much of interest. The bottom line was that
I'd rather have readers find this collection useful and interesting than defin-
itionally pristine. The result, as I hope readers will discover, is a varied anthology of works that are well written, highly original, and full of provocative,
strikingly relevant ideas about literature and the natural environment.

Should it be alleged that I have adopted such an expansive definition in
order to appropriate as much work as possible as "early ecocriticism," I can
only plead guilty. In addition to making early ecocritical work available to
contemporary scholars, I am also attempting to create for ecocriticism a history, a tradition, where thus far there has been none. Even in a culture such
as ours, which fetishizes the new, a sense of tradition can still confer legitimacy and power; it can still function as what Van Wyck Brooks perceptively

termed "a usable past." I want this anthology to begin constructing just such a past for the field of literature and environment.

I searched for early ecocriticism in two broad categories. It seemed reasonable to look first for instances in which professional or academic critics had written specifically about nature writing, or at least about the green aspects of works in today's environmental-literature canon. It also made sense to seek critical work by nature writers — instances where nature writers took time out from writing about *nature* in order to write about *writing*. As it turned out, many of this collection's de facto ecocritics fit both of these categories — Joseph Wood Krutch, for example, excelled as both nature writer and professional critic — while others, such as D. H. Lawrence, seem to belong in neither.

Prior to the emergence of environmental literary studies as an academic field in the late 1980s, there was no discourse of ecocriticism per se. What ecocriticism there was necessarily appeared elsewhere, typically as part of the more general discourses of nature writing, scholarship and criticism, and environmentalism. Unlike today's ecocriticism, which seems so clearly an offshoot of the environmental awareness of the 1960s and 1970s, the early ecocriticism of this collection seems to have been prompted only indirectly by environmentalism itself. In the United States, at least, it was much more directly a response to two separate developments. Outside the colleges and universities, ecocriticism appeared in response to the burgeoning popularity of nature writing; within the academy, it arose largely out of what might be termed disciplinary politics, a by-product of the emergence of American literature as an academic discipline.

In the United States a recognizable ecocriticism first arose in the latter half of the nineteenth century, as criticism in general was beginning to undergo two major changes. Academic criticism at the time was dominated by "men of letters," genteel critics such as Harvard's James Russell Lowell — writers who were broadly "cultured" rather than narrowly specialized. Their work, like that of their nonacademic but equally genteel counterparts, appeared in a small cluster of highbrow magazines, most notably the *Atlantic*. The dominant mode of criticism was a Matthew Arnold–style humanism, and Boston was its geographical center. Toward the end of the century, however, fundamental demographic and economic changes tilted the balance of cultural power away from an increasingly provincial Boston — which had given us writers such as Emerson and Thoreau in addition to such critics as

Lowell — toward a more cosmopolitan New York, which could boast of such writers as Walt Whitman and John Burroughs, and later of such critics as Van Wyck Brooks and H. L. Mencken.[5]

At the same time, the American university was being modernized along the lines of the increasingly prestigious German "research model." Where once the mission of the university had been the preservation and transmission of knowledge (and, less officially, the reproduction of existing social hierarchies), that mission more and more emphasized the *production* of knowledge. One result of the ensuing professionalization of academic letters was a profound split between the older, belletristic "critic" and the new, objectively scientific "scholar." As an academic discipline, literary scholarship came to concern itself primarily with etymology and literary history, with the painstaking accumulation of linguistic and literary-historical facts.

Such scholarship was in step with the new emphasis on scientific rigor, but it gave short shrift to what we think of today as *criticism*. The academic scholar did not make and defend judgments about the meaning and value of literary works or examine the unspoken underpinnings of such judgments, much less use literature as a springboard for reflecting critically on culture and society. The scholar was likely to consider such criticism hopelessly subjective, a kind of dilettantism unworthy of the true academic. When the Modern Language Association was chartered in 1883 as part of this professionalizing of literary studies, it reflected the literary-historical bias of the new research model. Criticism rarely appeared in its flagship journal, *Publications of the Modern Language Association*.

By the turn of the century, literary criticism had nearly been expunged from the universities. It took refuge in the classier commercial magazines, which venue continued for a time to be dominated by the Arnoldian "men of letters." Increasingly, however, and from both sides of the political spectrum, their traditional humanism would be challenged. On the right were the so-called New Humanists, which included disaffected academics like Harvard's Irving Babbitt and Princeton's Paul Elmer More. These traditionalists disdained what they saw as the sterile positivism of the research university and championed a renewed emphasis on the classics, believing, as David Shumway has put it, that the only worthwhile literary tradition "began with the Greeks and ended in the Renaissance." On the left were the "literary radicals," critics like Van Wyck Brooks and Randolph Bourne who hoped to enlist literature — including the most contemporary of American works — in the aid of a progressive politics. Where the New Humanists might champion Virgil, Spenser, and Milton, the radicals were more likely to weigh in on behalf of Stephen Crane and Upton Sinclair.[6]

What united these two groups, and set them apart from the academic scholars, was their concern with contemporary culture, mores, and politics. (The latter could include environmental politics, though at this time it rarely did so.) For both groups, and for those who belonged to neither, the authority to pontificate on such issues typically derived not from an academic post but from a literary reputation or a position as an editor.[7] The ecocritical pronouncements of John Burroughs, for example, carried weight primarily because of his status as a best-selling nature writer; those of Hamilton Wright Mabie were underwritten both by the popularity of his books and by his clout as an editor at magazines like the *Christian Century* and *Ladies' Home Journal.*

By the turn of the century there was a small but growing body of de facto ecocriticism, but for the most part it was rooted outside the American academy. This was the situation in 1921, when Norman Foerster and several other university professors formed the American Literature Group as one of the new divisions of the Modern Language Association. Even at this late date the idea that the United States even *had* a literature was not self-evident—at least to the professional scholars of the MLA—and one of the first tasks of the ALG was to establish just what comprised "American literature" to begin with. The subject could not be taken seriously as an academic discipline without an American literature as a discrete object of study, a recognizably *American* literature that was more than just a minor branch of English letters.

The academic scholarship of the day was ill-suited for legitimizing the nascent field of American literature. What was needed was not the accumulation of more facts but the demonstration of some distinctive cultural pattern in American writing that set it apart from its British antecedents. As a member of the New Humanist group—a university professor, but a critic at heart—Foerster *was* qualified for this task, capable of asking questions that transcended the narrowly positivistic confines of scholarly research: Is our national literature recognizably American in some way? If it is, what makes it so? Crucial to answering those questions, Foerster argued, were the American experience of the frontier and the closely related experience of New World nature. It was only by reading literature *as if nature mattered*—by practicing an early ecocriticism—that American literary criticism came to be professionalized, and it is no coincidence at all that Foerster inaugurated the new academic field with a study titled *Nature in American Literature* (1923).[8]

Though their championing of American literature helped reform a generally conservative academic literary culture, Foerster and the ALG remained decidedly conservative in other ways. For one thing, many Americanists remained methodologically committed to the research model. (In practice the putative "objectivity" of the scholar remained quite valuable, insofar as it permitted what was really the *invention* of an American literary tradition to be presented as the *discovery* of such a tradition.) For another, the profession's newfound receptivity to things American owed less to any liberalizing of the academy than it did to the patriotic atmosphere following World War I. Certainly *Nature in American Literature* did not signal the academy's political engagement with the world at large, nor was the book's focus on nature prompted in any immediate way by environmentalism.

When reading work such as Foerster's today, it is important to remember this essential conservatism. To the extent that Foerster engaged in a bona fide criticism, it was generally in the spirit of the New Humanism, which had long epitomized the "right wing of literary culture."[9] The development of a genuinely hermeneutic approach to criticism in the academy—a criticism concerned with the *significance* of literary works—had to wait for the rise of the New Criticism in the 1930s. The New Critics were critics in the modern sense; they did not consider their central task to be the discovery of facts but the interpretation of texts. Literature was conceived to be the bearer of subtle, complex meanings that were not at all self-evident and whose elucidation required "close reading" of the text itself rather than meticulous research in libraries and archives. New Critics did not so much *prove* their conclusions in the cautious manner of the literary historian; rather they *argued for* them—and in doing so had to justify the underpinnings of their arguments. Thus in addition to moving the academy from scholarship to criticism the New Critics helped introduce the wave of literary theorizing that remains with us.

What is most notable for our purposes about the New Critics is how little attention they paid to the natural environment. After all, one might reasonably have expected something like an ecocriticism to have emerged from this group's deep dissatisfaction with industrialism. The Agrarians—a loosely affiliated group of disaffected Southerners that included such New Critics as Allen Tate and John Crowe Ransom—vigorously bemoaned how the "headlong race for mastery over nature . . . stifled the aesthetic impulse, rendered impotent the religious impulse, and converted man's days into a frantic and frenzied drive for the often tawdry experiences of modernism." [10] Yet they consistently limited the evils of industrialism to the social rather than the ecological, and the famous "Statement of Principles" that opens the Agrarian manifesto, *I'll Take My Stand* (1930), does not list environmental degradation among the many lamentable consequences of the new economic order.

The same environmental indifference characterizes the so-called New York Intellectuals, writers like Lionel Trilling and Alfred Kazin who at this time represented the left wing of literary criticism and who opposed the New Critics on almost every other issue. The New York Intellectuals were also vehement critics of industrial capitalism — but they, too, failed to produce much of anything resembling an environmentally informed criticism. "The world" to which they felt literature to be so profoundly related was again the social and not the natural world.

The situation in the years following *Nature in American Literature* was thus one in which those who attended to nature did not do much criticism, while those who *did* do criticism did not attend much to nature. Not until 1941, with the appearance of F. O. Matthiessen's *American Renaissance*, would the two major strands — a genuinely critical methodology and an attention to nature as a literary theme — be brought together and systematically applied to American writing. Adverting frequently to American writers' treatment of nature, Matthiessen argued brilliantly for the organic unity, and hence for the literary value, of nineteenth-century American literature. In doing so he almost single-handedly established the now-familiar Americanist canon — centered on Hawthorne, Emerson, Thoreau, Melville, Dickinson, and Whitman — that has only recently been contested and revised. *American Renaissance* convinced the academy for the first time to adopt a recognizably modern approach to American literature; as was the case with *Nature in American Literature*, the work that ushered in the new regime featured a good deal of ecocriticism.

The same can be said of the next major advance in the academic study of American literature, the emergence of American Studies out of the patriotic crucible of the Cold War. It is again no coincidence that two of the new discipline's foundational texts — Henry Nash Smith's *Virgin Land* (with chapters such as "The Innocence and Wildness of Nature") and Leo Marx's *The Machine in the Garden* — based their arguments on extended analyses of

American views of nature. Just as American literature had earlier needed to distinguish itself from its English antecedents, so American Studies had to distinguish itself from a nascent cultural studies by establishing the "Americanness" of American culture — and this could most readily be done by foregrounding the nation's reaction to the radical transformation of its once wild environment. As Shumway observes, Marx used this approach to particularly good effect when he argued for an American version of the pastoral: "By placing American works in the context of a tradition that goes back to classical antiquity and includes a great many British poets," he writes, "Marx elevates the status of American literature. By arguing that the impingement of industrialism becomes the particular problem of the American pastoral, Marx demonstrates the distinctiveness of American literature."[11]

What I have been arguing is that, prior to the great upheavals of the 1960s and 1970s, each major development in the academic criticism of American letters has been enabled by a kind of proto-ecocriticism. Though still viewed in many academic circles as a marginal and dubious subfield of professional literary studies,[12] ecocriticism has in fact been central and determinative. Without it, our sense of "American literature" might not exist at all.

During all this time, other strands of ecocriticism were evolving outside the academy, partly in response to the exploding popularity of nature writing, and less directly in response to the growth of environmental awareness. The histories of both nature writing and environmentalism have been treated thoroughly elsewhere;[13] what I wish to discuss briefly here is the degree to which an early sort of ecocriticism closely attended, and in a sense made possible, the birth of modern environmentalism itself. Many date that birth to the 1864 publication of George Perkins Marsh's *Man and Nature*—the book that first documented the scope and seriousness of human degradation of the natural environment and that decisively influenced several early environmentalists, including John Muir.[14] Even a casual reading of *Man and Nature* suggests that Marsh did not reach and probably could not have reached his conclusions by observing nature alone; his argument necessarily hinged also on his reading of texts. To make his environmentalist case, Marsh had to demonstrate long-term ecological *change*, to compare environmental conditions past and present, and the science of his day could not provide the necessary historical data. It was only by scouring a wide variety of classical and historical writings for what they revealed about former ecological conditions — by practicing the sort of ecocriticism later performed on a much

smaller scale by Aldo Leopold in "The Forestry of the Prophets" (1920) —
that Marsh could frame his contemporary observations as evidence of ecological damage.

This proto-ecocriticism suffuses *Man and Nature*, though it is too desultory to excerpt in this collection. Much of it appears in Marsh's notoriously
copious footnotes, in which he cites and analyzes dozens of travel narratives,
natural histories, and literary classics. He industriously ferrets out the ecological data recorded — however incidentally — by such disparate authors as
the ancient Greeks, Raphael Holinshed, Edmund Spenser, Alexander von
Humboldt, Timothy Dwight, George Sand, Henry Thoreau; the list goes on
and on. After noting, for example, that the "most important, as well as the
most trustworthy conclusions with respect to the climate of ancient Europe
and Asia, are those drawn from the accounts given by the classical writers,"
he analyzes Pliny's *Naturalis Historiae* and reveals an early awareness of both
ecological damage and its causes: "Destructive torrents," writes Pliny, "are
generally formed when hills are stripped of the trees which formerly confined and absorbed the rains." [15]

As evidence for the species diversity of sixteenth-century British forests,
Marsh quotes stanzas such as this from the "catalogue of trees" in the first
canto of the "Faerie Queen":

> The laurell, meed of mightie conquerours
> And poets sage; the firre that weepeth still;
> The willow, worne of forlorn paramours;
> The eugh, obedient to the benders will;
> The birch for shaftes; the sallow for the mill;
> The mirrhe sweete-bleeding in the bitter wound;
> The warlike beech; the ash for nothing ill;
> The fruitfull olive; and the platane round;
> The carver holme; the maple seeldom inward
>   sound.

Elsewhere, in a particularly garrulous note, Marsh cites Holinshed's famed
Chronicles of England, Scotland and Ireland. Where Shakespeare had mined
this volume for raw material for his history plays, Marsh examines it for hints
of trouble in England's ecological past: "[William] Harrison, in his curious
chapter 'Of Woods and Marishes' in Holinshed's compilation, complains of

the rapid decrease of the forests"; Harrison adds that because the "woods go so fast to decaie" he would like to require "that auerie man, in whatsoeuer part of the champaine soile enioineth fortie acres of land, and vpwards . . . might plant one acre of wood, or sowe the same with oke mast, hasell, beech, and sufficient prouision be made that it may be cherished and kept.'" Still elsewhere, Marsh bases his argument quite ingeniously on his expertise in etymology, inferring changes in the landscape from changes in the meanings of words. The various Swedish terms for *swamp*, he notes, distinguish finely between lands that "are grass-grown, and overflowed with water through almost the whole summer," those that "are covered with mosses and always moist, but very seldom overflowed," and so on. Tracing the history and geographic distribution of such terms through the local literature provides clues about a region's changing hydrology and ecology.[16]

In each of the examples above, Marsh reads his primary texts *as if nature mattered,* and motivating him to do so is a profound concern for the deteriorating physical environment. Thus he is not only one of our earliest and most influential environmentalists but also one of our first ecocritics. Modern environmentalism owes as much as American literature to the practice of early ecocriticism.

In organizing this collection I wanted to avoid imposing upon it a structure of relationships that in fact never existed. Since any thematic arrangement might do just that, I opted simply to arrange the selections in chronological order. A chronological sequence might itself suggest some sort of straightforward history of ecocriticism's "development"; readers should remember that any such sense of orderly genesis is for the most part merely an effect of the anthologizing process. In fact, one of the striking things I noticed in assembling this collection is the degree to which its authors operated with so little overt reference to each other. I did not find Mabel Osgood Wright quoting Hamilton Wright Mabie, nor Dallas Lore Sharp citing Mary Woolley. During the period covered there is a dawning sense of *nature writing* as an interconnected whole, as a coherent literary tradition — and hence a suitable object of critical reflection — but I detected no sense of *ecocriticism* as such a tradition. A consciousness of ecocriticism as a collective enterprise apparently did not arise until the development of the sort of contemporary work anthologized in *The Ecocriticism Reader.*

Some of the writers collected in this anthology are best characterized as men and women of letters — not narrow specialists but broadly learned cultural avatars who wrote copiously on a wide variety of topics. James Russell Lowell is a good example here, though he can be claimed as an ecocritic only to the extent that his concern with major authors like Henry David Thoreau prompted him to ponder the literary treatment of nature. Lowell had little regard for nature in general, as his 1865 essay "Thoreau" makes clear; he in fact considered nature's influence on Thoreau to have been generally unhealthy. Much more generous in spirit is the assessment made of John and William Bartram by a contemporary of Lowell's, Henry Tuckerman. In *America and Her Commentators* (1864), Tuckerman reserves special praise for the younger Bartram's ability to interest even the most jaded reader in the wonders of the natural world.

D. H. Lawrence is another "man of letters" who can be claimed as an early ecocritic. Like Tuckerman, he takes a more positive view than Lowell of primitive nature and what he saw as its invigorating effect on literature. Like many others of his time, Lawrence was a geographical determinist, and central to his influential *Studies in Classic American Literature* (1923) is the idea that "[d]ifferent places on the face of the earth have different vital effluence." He was also an early practitioner of a "hermeneutics of suspicion," a critic who proceeded on the assumption that there is more to literature than is revealed on its surface, that the text must be decoded to reveal its underlying patterns and true significance. Lawrence thus treats Hector St. Jean de Crèvecoeur, in the essay excerpted herein, as a kind of "liar" who depicted nature as pure and benevolent even though he really knew better. But because Crèvecoeur was a genuine literary artist, Lawrence adds, the much more complex and disturbing truth of nature is deeply woven into the text.

Sharing Lawrence's environmental determinism was Mary Hunter Austin, whose 1932 essay "Regionalism in American Fiction" examines the way physical environment shapes consciousness, and hence literature. Geographical place, she argues, has a more profound cultural influence than either shared language or common political affiliation. Thus there is not and never will be just a single America but rather several Americas, a fact writers ignore at their peril. In her view, the best writers are those who can be shown to be genuinely indigenous — not provincial, but still recognizably a product of their natural environment.

As the author of the desert classic, *Land of Little Rain*, Austin was also an accomplished nature writer, as were several other contributors to this collection. Richard Jefferies, the late-nineteenth-century British author of such books as *Wild Life in a Southern County* and *Red Deer*, was one of the first authors to make a living by writing about nature, and also one of the first to bemoan the rapidly increasing volume of such writing. As early as 1887 he could note acerbically that "there is not a thing that grows that may not furnish a monograph." (Jefferies was perfectly aware that he, too, was abetting this proliferation.) The more he read and wrote the more he became conscious of a fundamental gap between nature and the language we use to depict it — a fissure that became the theme of his essay, "Nature and Books."

Jefferies's counterpart in the United States was the nature-writer-cum-ecocritic John Burroughs. Perhaps best known today as the man who fanned the flames of the "nature faker" controversy of 1902–7, Burroughs was also a bit of a philosopher and a quite passable literary critic. His first book was not explicitly about nature at all but rather a critical study of Walt Whitman, whose poetry he championed for its approximation "to a direct utterance of nature herself." Burroughs would later vouch for the classic status of Gilbert White's *Natural History of Selborne*, terming it "a book I can return to again and again"; in subsequent works, and particularly during the nature faker debate, he would argue strenuously for a Selborne-style nature writing disciplined by a scrupulous adherence to observed fact. In his later years, however, despite his earlier allegiance to science, he came to doubt the ability of mere facts to answer the truly fundamental questions and meet the deepest human needs. His final critical judgments seemed to rest on the conviction that wild nature could bolster the spiritual sensibility enervated by an increasingly secular age — implying of nature writing more or less what Matthew Arnold had said half a century earlier about literature in general.

Contrasting sharply with Burroughs was Charles G. D. Roberts, the famed Canadian poet and novelist. Roberts seems more sophisticated than Burroughs in his understanding of what readers actually do with texts. Where Burroughs fretted that "nature faking" would lead readers astray, Roberts trusted their ability to ascertain the specifically literary forms of truth conveyed by good fiction. Certainly he saw little value in asking literature to replicate the work of science; for the nature writer, he suggests in the introduction to his *Kindred of the Wild* (1902), natural science is valuable primarily for providing a plausible framework upon which to build a "psychological romance" that might liberate the reader, if only for a time, from the "mean tenement of self."

Another popular nature writer, Donald Culross Peattie, shared with the early Burroughs a deep respect for the natural sciences. In "Is Thoreau a Modern?" (1938), Peattie explores what he takes to be Thoreau's rather curious indifference to the best science of his day. If Thoreau, as he so famously claimed, genuinely valued the scientific fact for its ability to "flower into a truth," should he not have paid more attention to such fundamental nineteenth-century discoveries as protoplasm and chlorophyll? After all, Peattie suggests, such discoveries provide a scientific basis for the ultimate unity of all life, just the sort of thing that might have tilted Thoreau's stubborn anthropocentrism toward a genuine biocentrism. In the opinion of Mark Van Doren, a Pulitzer Prize–winning poet and for many years the literary editor for the *Nation,* it was precisely such a biocentrism that made Peattie's own nature writing so remarkable. In his 1937 essay "A New Naturalist," Van Doren notes approvingly that Peattie has a "center" that is "removed" from humankind and located instead at the "center of life."

Joseph Wood Krutch, the author of such nature books as *The Desert Year* and *The Twelve Seasons*—and like Van Doren a widely respected professional critic—is one of several who write in this collection about Thoreau. Unlike Peattie, Krutch is not concerned with Thoreau's attitude toward science but with his place in the broad sweep of intellectual history. Much as Mary Hunter Austin had tried to place literature in the physical space of the natural environment, Krutch attempts to situate Thoreau's nature writing in the abstract matrix of the history of ideas—where he finds Thoreau less absolutely original than others had thought.

Most early ecocritics were concerned in one way or another with literature and *nature;* fewer were concerned with literature and *technology.* One exception was Lewis Mumford, who wrote extensively on the conflict between industrial technology and humane values. In "The Dawn" (1926), Mumford insists that Thoreau was not a hermit but rather a thoroughly social being whose individualism was a profound form of cultural engagement; what Thoreau sought in nature was not solitude per se but a better perspective on society. Another exception was Leo Marx, whose contribution to this collection demonstrates how technology figures repeatedly in American literature as the intrusive "machine in the garden." This motif appears so frequently, argues Marx, as to suggest the persistent desire of an industrializing nation to envision itself as pastoral—and also the inevitable failure to sustain so paradoxical a vision, even within the imaginative precincts of literature.

Like Marx, several other early ecocritics were academic Americanists. The very earliest of these reflected the ethos of the research universities where they worked and were essentially literary historians, the authors of "source and influence" studies concerned with the evolution of particular ideas about or attitudes toward wild nature. In "Nature in Early American Literature" (1893), Selden Whitcomb searches colonial and early national texts for evidence of a developing appreciation for nature, which he considered an index of the nation's growing "literary independence" from British culture. In a similar vein Mary Woolley—the brilliant feminist teacher, administrator, and political activist—painstakingly adduces evidence in "The Development of the Love of Romantic Scenery in America" (1897) to show that the American love of natural scenery grew independently of such changes in Europe.

As I noted above, the writings of Norman Foerster, F. O. Matthiessen, and Leo Marx were pivotal in transforming the academic study of American literature, in moving it from literary-historical research to criticism in the contemporary sense. This collection reprints some of their best work, including *Nature in American Literature*'s perceptive and largely sympathetic readings of John Muir and John Burroughs. Foerster's analyses range from a close reading of Muir's dynamic prose to a searching critique of Burroughs's conflicted philosophy. Matthiessen, deeply influenced by the New Criticism, focuses more narrowly on demonstrating how nature enhances the organicism of the work of Emerson and Thoreau; in this way nature proves central to the groundbreaking synthesis of *American Renaissance*. Another Americanist of note was Perry Miller, whose "Nature and the National Ego" (1955) analyzes the ideological function of nature in an evolving American nationalism, showing how nature helped nineteenth-century America distinguish itself from Europe while simultaneously mediating the conflict between two sets of core American ideals, Puritan spirituality and rationalist materialism.

Similarly concerned with nature's role in the creation of national consciousness is Sherman Paul, whose *The Shores of America* (1958) suggests that Thoreau was not so much interested in nature "itself" as in nature as the source and foundation of civilization, as a sort of raw material with which a young nation might construct a legitimating past. Paul suggests as well that this concern helped prompt Thoreau's early call for the preservation of wilderness in national parks.

Other contributors to this collection practiced "criticism" as it is generally conceived by the public. They were *evaluators* who thought it their job to assist readers in distinguishing good nature writing from bad — and, at times, to champion particular authors such as Muir or Thoreau. John Burroughs did this in his early defense of Walt Whitman, as did Mabel Osgood Wright in periodically evaluating nature books for the popular magazines. As Thoreau's literary stock continued to rise around the turn of the century, other critics seemed to take it as their particular duty to debunk some of his factual errors, and while the worst of this strain merely carps, the best of it — such as Fannie Eckstorm's 1908 essay on *The Maine Woods* — is able to critique Thoreau's natural history while praising his ability to wring significance out of his observations.

Any evaluation must, of course, be based on criteria, and the infamous "nature faker" controversy can ultimately be thought of as a dispute over the principles defining good nature writing. The debate centered on the proper literary use of science, more particularly on the idea that nature's "truth" is best revealed through careful observation. What is generally absent from the debate is any nuanced conception of specifically literary concerns, such as the idea that nature writing's status as *literature* might confer on it a certain kind of license. Such license might not necessarily excuse the sort of invention indulged in by Burroughs's primary nemesis, William J. Long, but it does suggest that the natural fact is merely a beginning, that what ultimately counts are the emotional or psychological effects the writer achieves. This idea might seem obvious, yet of the controversy's many combatants very few made it central to their arguments. One who did so was Britain's William Henry Hudson, in "Truth Plain and Coloured" (1905); another was Mabel Osgood Wright, in "Life Outdoors and Its Effect Upon Literature" (1903) and "Nature as a Field for Fiction" (1905).

Several of this collection's contributors, anticipating today's postmodern turn, suggest that "nature" is not an entity that is simply "out there" — that it is not passively waiting to be objectively observed and analyzed but is instead a highly malleable construct to which scientists and nature writers bring considerable cultural baggage. In the late nineteenth century, some critics were already critiquing our concepts of nature and exploring how it is shaped by the language we use in describing it; they were concerned, that is, with what today might be called the "problematics of nature and language" or nature's "discursive construction." This is the subject of William Benjamin Carpenter's 1872 speech, "Man as the Interpreter of Nature." Carpenter was an accomplished British naturalist, a member of the Royal Society who disputed the widely held view that "the scientific interpretation of Nature represents her not merely as she seems but as she really is"; instead, he argued, the scientist's nature is a construct "framed by the mind itself." A similar concern with language and the world it claims to represent informs Richard Jefferies's "Nature and Books" (1887), in which he despairs of ever finding words that can do justice to even the simplest of natural phenomena.

Alfred Austin, a contemporary of Carpenter and Jefferies, was a British poet whose 1877 essay "The Poetic Interpretation of Nature" stresses the fundamental differences between science and poetry. Against the notion that the two are distinct but equally truthful ways of knowing, Austin demonstrates that while scientific investigation has yielded a self-consistent set of beliefs about nature, poetry has given us at best "an enchanting map of contradictions." Nature can be a vehicle for scientific truth, but to the poet it has absolutely no "theological, spiritual, and moral truths to convey." Nature writing can convey a certain *kind* of truth — not about nature itself, however, but only about the human world that contemplates nature and draws sustenance from it.

D. S. Savage is less concerned with the truth value of nature poetry than with its vitality and immediacy. In his "Poetry and Nature" (1942), he invokes T. S. Eliot's notion of the "dissociation of sensibility" to account for what he sees as a general decline in poetry since the late Middle Ages, when Western consciousness "was forced to objectify nature." Because language arose originally out of humanity's interaction with a sensuous and diverse natural world, Savage argues, language in an increasingly denaturalized environment can only become more and more impoverished. Hamilton Wright Mabie, a writer and magazine editor, makes an altogether different and more optimistic argument about this intimate link between nature and language. He argues in his *Short Studies in Literature* (1891) that the ages in which humans "were making discovery of Nature were the ages in which they were also creating language"; for Mabie, *all* writing is nature writing, because nature inevitably "shines . . . on the surface of all human speech."

Other contributors were what would today be called "interdisciplinary." A good example here is Aldo Leopold, the Forest Service biologist who stepped outside his field of expertise to try his hand at biblical exegesis. In "The Forestry of the Prophets" (1920), Leopold searches the Hebrew Bible for antecedents of what today would be called ecological awareness. His analysis is amateurish but nonetheless highly suggestive — and conducted in a much friendlier spirit than Lynn White Jr.'s famous 1978 essay, "The Historical Roots of Our Ecologic Crisis." Where White saw in scripture the seeds of environmental disaster, Leopold finds at least occasional glimmerings of ecological wisdom. Another interdisciplinarian is Havelock Ellis, best known as the pioneering sexologist. Ellis argues in "The Love of Wild Nature" (1909) that the Western appreciation of wilderness has its roots in what he terms "psychasthenia," a psychological condition that drives its sufferers to seek solitude from what they perceive as the intolerable demands of society. Ellis suggests that many early psychasthenics became Christian ascetics, taking refuge in remote monasteries where they learned to love wilderness even as they learned to love God.

It is probably no coincidence that ecocriticism became a self-conscious enterprise in the late 1980s and early 1990s, a time when environmentalism itself began to undergo profound changes: the realization of the global nature of our most pressing ecological problems, the long-overdue concern with environmental justice and environmental racism, and the troubling realization of the degree to which terms such as "nature" and "environment" are socially constructed.[17] Such developments have forced the environmental movement to critique its contemporary practices and to reexamine its history; ecocriticism will undoubtedly have to do the same. Certainly the field has much to gain from a greater awareness of its own antecedents, and that is one need I hope this collection can meet. Ecocriticism can surely benefit from knowing who has already walked the trails we are beginning anew to explore; similarly, it cannot hurt to know that ecocriticism has a lengthy and occasionally illustrious past — that it has played a crucial role in shaping both the literature we read and the environmentalism we practice. Much as Harold Fromm and Cheryll Glotfelty hoped *The Ecocriticism Reader* would "inspire intellectual adventurers to explore the ecocritical terrain," I hope this collection will encourage further exploration of ecocriticism's considerable history, and help create the kind of "usable past" that can guide us to a more useful future.

NOTES

1. The essay is William Rueckert's "Literature and Ecology: An Experiment in Ecocriticism," *Iowa Review* 9 (Winter 1978): 71–86. Reprinted in *The Ecocriticism Reader: Landmarks in Literary Ecology*, ed. Harold Fromm and Cheryll Glotfelty (Athens: Uni-

versity of Georgia Press, 1996), 105–23. Six years earlier, Joseph Meeker had used the parallel term "literary ecology" in his *The Comedy of Survival: Studies in Literary Ecology* (New York: Scribner's, 1972).

2. Fromm and Glotfelty, xvi and xviii.

3. Ibid., xviii and xix.

4. Ibid., xix.

5. David Shumway, *Creating American Civilization: A Genealogy of American Literature as an Academic Discipline* (Minneapolis: University of Minnesota Press, 1994), 30–31; see also 41–45. The discussion that follows is deeply indebted to Shumway's study of the professionalizing of the criticism of American literature.

6. Ibid., 53–56.

7. Ibid., 120.

8. Ibid., 134. The role of the frontier experience in creating a distinctively American culture is more complex than I've indicated here. Shumway notes Foerster's claim that the frontier experience turned Americans toward a raw materialism and away from the imaginative pursuits needed to create a distinctive national culture; ironically, as more and more writers bemoaned this state of affairs, that lack of culture itself became a distinctively American motif. "In Foerster," writes Shumway, "the problem of a national culture is already on its way to becoming a theme in the American tradition, in other words, an aspect of national culture" (134). The defining theme is less nature itself, that is, than the perceived failure of American letters to respond adequately to nature.

9. Ibid., 227.

10. Louis D. Rubin Jr., introduction to *I'll Take My Stand: The South and the Agrarian Tradition*, by *Twelve Southerners* (New York: Harper, 1962), xiii.

11. Shumway, 330.

12. Many contemporary literary critics suspect—wrongly, in my view—that ecocriticism's focus on "nature" functions to reify various politically obnoxious forms of essentialism. It was not until December 1998, "[a]fter a six year battle" with such critics, that the Association for the Study of Literature and the Environment was accepted as an Allied Group of the Modern Language Association.

13. See, for example, Paul Brooks, *Speaking for Nature: How Literary Naturalists from Henry Thoreau to Rachel Carson Have Shaped America* (Boston: Houghton Mifflin, 1980), and Hans Huth, *Nature and the American: Three Centuries of Changing Attitudes* (Lincoln: University of Nebraska Press, 1972).

14. See Lewis Mumford, *The Brown Decades: A Study of the Arts in America, 1865–1895* (New York: Dover, 1931). Mumford writes that Marsh "was the first man to sense the destruction that was being wrought, to weigh its appalling losses, and to point out an intelligent course of action" (72). In addition Marsh was among the first to consider "man as an active geological agent . . . who upset the harmonies of nature and overthrew the stability of existing arrangements and accommodations, extirpating indigenous vegetable and animal species, introducing foreign varieties, restricting spontaneous growth, and covering

the earth with 'new and reluctant vegetable forms and with alien tribes of animal life'"
(76–77). For all these reasons, Mumford concludes that *Man and Nature* "was the fountainhead of the conservation movement" (78). David Lowenthal, in his introduction to
the book, notes that it was "the beginning of land wisdom in this country" and that it
"directly inspired the 1873 memorial which led Congress to establish a national forestry
commission and government forestry reserves." George Perkins Marsh, *Man and Nature;
Or, Physical Geography as Modified by Human Action* (Cambridge: Harvard University
Press, 1965), xxii.

15. Marsh, 22 and 188.

16. Ibid., 31, 192, and 264.

17. See, for example, William Cronon, ed., *Uncommon Ground: Rethinking the Human Place in Nature* (New York: Norton, 1995); Andrew Ross, *Strange Weather: Culture,
Science and Technology in the Age of Limits* (London: Verso, 1991) and *The Chicago Gang-
ster Theory of Life: Nature's Debt to Society* (London: Verso, 1994); Joni Seager, *Coming to
Feminist Terms with the Global Environmental Crisis* (New York: Routledge, 1993); and
Neil Evernden, *The Social Creation of Nature* (Baltimore: Johns Hopkins University Press,
1992). The environmental implications of globalism and postmodernism are discussed
regularly in the journal *Capitalism Nature Socialism* (Guilford Publications), and on a
less regular basis in *ISLE: Interdisciplinary Studies in Literature and Environment* (University of Nevada, Reno).

Henry Tuckerman on
John and William Bartram
(1864)

Henry Theodore Tuckerman, a cousin of the pioneering lichenologist Edward Tuckerman, was born in Boston in 1813. After dropping out of Harvard because of his poor health, he traveled to Italy in search of a more congenial climate, which trip provided the material for the first of his many books, *The Italian Sketch-Book* (1835). After returning to the United States he briefly edited the *Boston Miscellany of Literature and Fashion*; later he moved to New York, where he consorted with the likes of Washington Irving and wrote prolifically, contributing poems, essays, travel narratives, biographies, and critical essays to the *Atlantic* and the *North American Review*. One of his favorite themes was the crassness of American commercialism — although, as one biographer pointed out, Tuckerman's inherited wealth made it rather easy for him to carp at the nouveau riche. He died in New York in 1871.

Of Tuckerman's many books, the most highly regarded was *America and Her Commentators: With a Critical Sketch of Travel in the United States*, which is excerpted below. His comments on John and William Bartram are mainly biographical but include a fair amount of critical commentary that betrays a dawning sense of nature writing as a discrete genre with its own criteria of literary excellence. He praises the elder Bartram's attentiveness to details that other observers would likely miss, noting approvingly that "[n]o feature or phase of nature seems to escape him." William comes in for praise not only for his attention to detail but also for his eloquence. Tuckerman describes the style of the best-selling *Travels through North and South Carolina* (1791) as "more finished than his father could command, more fluent and glowing, but equally informed with that genuineness of feeling and directness of purpose which give the most crude writing an indefinable but actual moral charm." Tuckerman insists that the occasional "touches of pedantry" do not mar the *Travels*; rather the tremendous variety of natural phenomena recorded by Bartram becomes, "in his fresh and sympathetic description, vivid and interesting even to readers who have no special knowledge of, and only a vague curiosity about nature."

America and Her Commentators was published in 1864.

🥀 🥀 🥀

Among the most interesting of the early native travellers in America, are the two Bartrams. Their instinctive fondness for nature, a simplicity and veneration born of the best original Quaker influence, and habits of rural work and meditation, throw a peculiar charm around the memoirs of these kindly and assiduous naturalists, and make the account they have left of their wanderings fresh and genial, notwithstanding the vast progress since made in the natural sciences. John Bartram's name is held in grateful honor by botanists, as "the first Anglo-American who conceived the idea of establishing a botanic garden, native and exotic." He was lured to this enterprise, and its kindred studies, by the habit of collecting American plants and seeds for his friend, Peter Collinson, of London. Encouraged by him, Bartram began to investigate and experiment in this pleasant field of inquiry. He was enabled to confirm Logan's theory in regard to maize, and to illustrate the sexes of plants. From such a humble and isolated beginning, botany expanded in this country into its present elaborate expositions. The first systematic enumeration of American plants was commenced in Holland, by Gronovius, from descriptions furnished by John Clayton, of Virginia. As early as 1732, Mark Catesby, of Virginia, had published a volume on the "Natural History of Carolina, Florida, and the Bahamas." Colden, of New York, corresponded with European botanists, from his sylvan retreat near Newberg. We have already noticed the visit to America of a pupil of Linnaeus—Peter Kalm. The labors of Logan, Dr. Mitchell, Dr. Adam Kuhn of Philadelphia, the first professor of botany there, the establishment of Hosack's garden in New York, Dr. Schoeffs, Humphrey Marshall, Dr. Cullen of Berlin, the two Michauxs, Clinton, and the Abbé Correa, promoted the investigation and elucidation of this science in America, until it became associated with the more recent accomplished expositors. But with the earliest impulse and record thereof, the name of John Bartram is delightfully associated; and it is as a naturalist that he made those excursions, the narrative of which retains the charm of ingenuous zeal, integrity, and kindliness. . . . [A]ccording to the exigencies of the time and country, Bartram was an agriculturalist by vocation, and assiduous therein; yet this did not prevent his indulging his scientific love of nature: he observed and he reflected while occupied about his farm. The laws of vegetation, the loveliness of flowers, the mysteries of growth, were to him a perpetual miracle. To the thrift and simplicity of life common among the original farmers of America, he united an ardent love of knowledge and an admiration of the processes and the products of nature — partly a sentiment and partly a scientific impulse. Purchasing a tract on the banks of the Schuylkill, three miles from Philadelphia, he built, with his own hands, a commodious dwelling, cultivated five acres as a garden, and made continual journeys in search of plants. The place became so attractive, that visitors flocked thither. By degrees he gained acquaintances abroad, established correspondence and a system of exchanges with botanists, and so laid the foundation of botanical enterprise and taste in America. This hale, benign, and wise man, rarely combining in his nature the zeal and observant habitude of the naturalist with the serene self-possession of the Friend, travelled over a large part of the country, explored Ontario, the domain of the Iriquois, the shores and sources of the Hudson, Delaware, Schuylkill, Susquehanna, Alleghany, and San Juan. At the age of seventy he visited Carolina and Florida. . . .

The journal of his tour was sent to England, and was published "at the instance of several gentlemen." The preface shows how comparatively rare were authentic books of travel from natives of America, and how individual were Bartram's zeal and enterprise in this respect. "The inhabitants of all the colonies," says the writer, "have eminently deserved the character of industrious in agriculture and commerce. I could wish they had as well deserved that of *adventurous inland discoverers*; in this they have been much outdone by another nation, whose poverty of country and unsettled temper have prompted them to such views of extending their possessions, as our agriculture and commerce make necessary for us to imitate."

The region traversed by Bartram a little more than a century ago, and described in this little volume, printed in the old-fashioned type, and bearing the old imprimatur of Fleet Street, is one across and around which many of us have flown in the rail car, conscious of little but alternate meadows, woodland, streams, and towns, all denoting a thrifty and populous district, with here and there a less cultivated tract. Over this domain Bartram moved slowly, with his senses quickened to take in whatsoever of wonder or beauty nature exhibited. He experienced much of the exposure, privation, and precarious resources which befall the traveller to-day on our Western frontier; and it is difficult to imagine that the calm and patient naturalist, as he notes the aspects of nature and the incidents of a long pilgrimage, is only passing over the identical ground which the busy and self-absorbed votaries of traffic and pleasure now daily pass, with scarcely a consciousness of what is around and beside them of natural beauty or productiveness. It is worthwhile to retrace the steps of Bartram, were it only to realize anew the eternal truth of our poet's declaration, that

> To him who in the love of nature holds
> Communion with her visible forms, she speaks
> A varied language.

It was on the 3d of July, 1743, that John Bartram set out, with a companion, from his home on the Schuylkill. His narrative of that summer journey from the vicinity of Philadelphia to Lake Ontario, reads like the journal of some intelligent wayfarer in the far West; for the plants and the animals, the face of the country, the traveller's expedients, the Indian camps, and the isolated plantations, bring before us a thinly scattered people and wild region, whereof the present features are associated with all the objects and influences of civilization. Flocks of wild turkeys and leagues of wild grass are early noted; the variety and character of the trees afford a constant and congenial theme; swamps, ridges, hollows alternate; chestnuts, oaks, pines, and poplars are silent but not unwelcome comrades; snakes, as usual, furnish curious episodes: Bartram observed of one, that he "contracted the muscles of his scales when provoked, and that, after the mortal stroke, his splendor diminished." He remarks, at one place, "the impression of shells upon loose stones"; he is annoyed by gnats; and, in an Indian lodge, "hung up his blanket like a hammock, that he may lie out of fleas." He lingers in an old aboriginal orchard well stocked with fruit trees; swims creeks, coasts rivers, lives on duck, deer, and "boiled squashes cold"; smokes a pipe—"a customary civility," he says, "when parties meet." Here he finds "excellent flat whetstones," there "an old beaver dam"; now "roots of ginseng," and again "sulphurous mud"; one hour he is drenched with rain, and another enraptured by the sight of a magnolia; here refreshed by the perfume of a honeysuckle, and there troubled by a yellow wasp. No feature or phase of nature seems to escape him. He notes the earth beneath, the vegetation around, and the sky above; fossils, insects, Indian ceremonies, flowers; the expanse of the "dismal wilderness," the eels roasted for supper, and the moss and fungus as well as locusts and caterpillars. . . .

It is as delightful as it is rare to behold the best tastes and influence of a man reproduced and prolonged in his descendants; and this exceptional trait of American life we find in the career and character of John Bartram's son William, who was born at the Botanic Garden, Kingsessing, Pennsylvania, in 1739, and died in 1823. One of his early tutors was Charles Thomson, so prominent in the Continental Congress. He began life as a merchant, but was formed, by nature, for the naturalist and traveller he became. . . . He was elected professor of botany in the University of Pennsylvania in 1782, and "made known and illustrated many of the most curious and beautiful plants of North America," as well as published the most complete list of its birds, before Wilson. "The latest book I know," wrote Coleridge, "written in the spirit of the old travellers, is Bartram's account of his tour in the Floridas." It was published in Florida in 1791, and in London the following year. The style is more finished than his father could command, more fluent and glowing, but equally informed with that genuineness of feeling and directness of purpose which give the most crude writing an indefinable but actual moral charm. The American edition was "embellished with copperplates," the accuracy and beauty of which, however inferior to more recent illustrations of natural history among us, form a remarkable contrast to the coarse paper and inelegant type. These incongruities, however, add to the quaint charm of the work, by reminding us of the time when it appeared, and of the limited means and encouragement then available to the naturalist, compared to the sumptuous expositions which the splendid volumes of Audubon and Agassiz have since made familiar. In the details as well as in the philosophy of his subject, Bartram is eloquent. He describes the "hollow leaves that hold water," and how "seeds are carried and softened in birds' stomachs." He has a sympathy for the "cub bereaved of its bear mother"; patiently watches an enormous yellow spider capture a humblebee, and describes the process minutely. The moonlight on the palms; the notes of the mockingbird in the luxuriant but lonely woods; the flitting oriole and the cooing doves; the mullet in the crystal brine, and the moan of the surf at night; the laurel's glossy leaves, the canes of the brake, the sand of the beach, goldfish, sharks, lagoons, parroquets, the cypress, ash, and hickory, Indian mounds, buffalo licks, trading houses, alligators, mosquitos, squirrels, bullfrogs, trout, mineral waters, turtles, birds of passage, pelicans, and aquatic plants, are the themes of his narrative; and become, in his fresh and sympathetic description, vivid and interesting even to readers who have no special knowledge of, and only a vague curiosity about nature. The affluence and variety in the region described, are at once apparent. Now and then something like an adventure, or a pleasant talk with one of his hospitable or philosophical hosts, varies the botanical nomenclature; or a fervid outbreak of feeling, devotional or enjoyable, gives a human zest to the pictures of wild fertility. Curiously do touches of pedantry alternate with those of simplicity; the matter-of-fact tone of Robinson Crusoe, and the grave didactics of Rasselas; a scientific statement after the manner of Humboldt, and an anecdote or interview in the style of Boswell. It is this very absence of sustained and prevalence of desultory narrative, that make the whole so real and pleasant.

James Russell Lowell
on Henry David Thoreau
(1865)

Born in Cambridge, Massachusetts, in 1819—the same year as Melville and Whitman—James Russell Lowell entered Harvard when he was sixteen. He graduated in 1838 and at once began the prolific career that would see him become one of the nation's first bona fide men of letters. He wrote extensively on literature and politics, often satirizing the targets of his criticism with the poetic wit exemplified in his "Biglow Papers," which ridiculed the southern slaveholding aristocracy, and his "Fable for Critics," which among other things poked fun at Henry Thoreau and William Ellery Channing for their slavish devotion to Emerson:

> There comes ————, for instance; to see him's rare sport,
> Tread in Emerson's tracks with legs painfully short;
> How he jumps, how he strains, and gets red in the face,
> To keep step with the mystagogue's natural pace!
> He follows as close as a stick to a rocket,
> His fingers exploring the prophet's each pocket.
> Fie, for shame, brother bard; with good fruit of your own,
> Can't you let Neighbor Emerson's orchards alone?
> Besides, 't is no use, you'll find not e'en a core,—
> ———— has picked up all the windfalls before.

In 1854 Lowell was appointed to the Smith Professorship at Harvard, which previously had been held by William Wadsworth Longfellow. Three years later he became the editor of the newly created *Atlantic Monthly*; still later he would serve as coeditor of the *North American Review*.

Lowell is widely credited with being the United States' first professional man of letters, and (along with Edgar Allan Poe) its first notable literary critic. He had little patience with the romantic view of nature and was not predisposed to look favorably upon Transcendentalism in general and Thoreau in particular. His humanist philosophy had convinced him that to "seek to be natural implies a consciousness that forbids all naturalness forever"; he considered "a great deal of the modern sentimentalism about Nature as a mark of disease" and insisted that to "a man of wholesome constitution the wilderness is well enough for a mood or a vacation, but not for a habit of life." In Thoreau's case, Lowell felt that "[s]olitary communion with Nature does not seem to have been sanitary or sweetening." To make matters worse, he did not consider Thoreau particularly adept as a naturalist. Thoreau "discovered nothing," Lowell wrote, and "was not by nature an observer," generally seeing in the woods only what he set out to find there. He nonetheless approved Thoreau's classical knowledge, his strikingly original prose style, and perhaps most of all his deft movement between matter and spirit, the way he "took nature as the mountain-path to an ideal world." "In outward nature it is still man that interests us," Lowell concluded, "and we care far less for the things seen than the way in which they are seen by poetic eyes like Wordsworth's or Thoreau's, and the reflections they cast there."

The essay excerpted below first appeared in the *North American Review* in 1865.

🌸 🌸 🌸

Among the pistillate plants kindled to fruitage by the Emersonian pollen, Thoreau is thus far the most remarkable; and it is something eminently fitting that his posthumous works should be offered us by Emerson, for they are strawberries from his own garden. A singular mixture of varieties, indeed, there is;—alpine, some of them, with the flavor of rare mountain air; others wood, tasting of sunny roadside banks or shy openings in the forest; and not a few seedlings swollen hugely by culture, but lacking the fine natural aroma of the more modest kinds. Strange books these are of his, and interesting in many ways,—instructive chiefly as showing how considerable a crop may be raised on a comparatively narrow close of mind, and how much a man may make of his life if he will assiduously follow it, though perhaps never truly finding it at last.

I have just been renewing my recollection of Mr. Thoreau's writings, and have read through his six volumes in the order of their production. I shall try to give an adequate report of their impression upon me both as critic and as mere reader. He seems to me to have been a man with so high a conceit of himself that he accepted without questioning, and insisted on our accepting, his defects and weaknesses of character as virtues and powers peculiar to himself. Was he indolent, he finds none of the activities which attract or employ the rest of mankind worthy of him. Was he wanting in the qualities that make success, it is success that is contemptible, and not himself that lacks persistency and purpose. Was he poor, money was an unmixed evil. Did his life seem a selfish one, he condemns doing good as one of the weakest of superstitions. To be of use was with him the most killing bait of the wily tempter Uselessness. He had no faculty of generalization from outside of himself, or at least no experience which would supply the material of such, and he makes his own whim the law, his own range the horizon of the universe. He condemns a world, the hollowness of whose satisfactions he had never had the means of testing, and we recognize Apemantus behind the mask of Timon. He had little active imagination; of the receptive he had much. His appreciation is of the highest quality; his critical power, from want of continuity of mind, very limited and inadequate. He somewhere cites a simile from Ossian, as an example of the superiority of the old poetry to the new, though, even were the historic evidence less convincing, the sentimental melancholy of those poems should be conclusive of their modernness. He had none of the artistic mastery which controls a great work to the serene balance of completeness, but exquisite mechanical skill in the shaping of sentences and paragraphs, or (more rarely) short bits of verse for the expression of a detached thought, sentiment, or image. His works give one the feeling of a sky full of stars, — something impressive and exhilarating certainly, something high overhead and freckled thickly with spots of isolated brightness; but whether these have any mutual relation with each other, or have any concern with our mundane matters, is for the most part matter of conjecture, — astrology as yet, and not astronomy.

It is curious, considering what Thoreau afterwards became, that he was not by nature an observer. He only saw the things he looked for, and was less poet than naturalist. Till he built his Walden shanty, he did not know that the hickory grew in Concord. Till he went to Maine, he had never seen phosphorescent wood, a phenomenon early familiar to most country boys.

At forty he speaks of the seeding of the pine as a new discovery, though one should have thought that its gold-dust of blowing pollen might have earlier drawn his eye. Neither his attention nor his genius was of the spontaneous kind. He discovered nothing. He thought everything a discovery of his own, from moonlight to the planting of acorns and nuts by squirrels. This is a defect in his character, but one of his chief charms as a writer. Everything grows fresh under his hand. He delved in his mind and nature; he planted them with all manner of native and foreign seeds, and reaped assiduously. He was not merely solitary, he would be isolated, and succeeded at last in almost persuading himself that he was autochthonous. He valued everything in proportion as he fancied it to be exclusively his own. He complains in "Walden" that there is no one in Concord with whom he could talk of Oriental literature, though the man was living within two miles of his hut who had introduced him to it. This intellectual selfishness becomes sometimes almost painful in reading him. He lacked that generosity of "communication" which Johnson admired in Burke. De Quincey tells us that Wordsworth was impatient when any one else spoke of mountains, as if he had a peculiar property in them. And we can readily understand why it should be so: no one is satisfied with another's appreciation of his mistress. . . .

. . . I once had a glimpse of a genuine solitary who spent his winters one hundred and fifty miles beyond all human communication, and there dwelt with his rifle as his only confidant. Compared with this, the shanty on Walden Pond has something the air, it must be confessed, of the Hermitage of La Chevrette. I do not believe that the way to a true cosmopolitanism carries one into the woods or the society of musquashes. Perhaps the narrowest provincialism is that of Self; that of Kleinwinkel is nothing to it. The natural man, like the singing birds, comes out of the forest as inevitably as the natural bear and the wildcat stick there. To seek to be natural implies a consciousness that forbids all naturalness forever. It is as easy — and no easier — to be natural in a *salon* as in a swamp, if one do not aim at it, for what we call unnaturalness always has its spring in a man's thinking too much about himself. "It is impossible," said Turgot, "for a vulgar man to be simple."

I look upon a great deal of the modern sentimentalism about Nature as a mark of disease. It is one more symptom of the general liver-complaint. To a man of wholesome constitution the wilderness is well enough for a mood or a vacation, but not for a habit of life. Those who have most loudly advertised their passion for seclusion and their intimacy with nature, from Petrarch down, have been mostly sentimentalists, unreal men, misanthropes on the spindle side, solacing an uneasy suspicion of themselves by professing contempt for their kind. They make demands on the world in advance proportioned to their inward measure of their own merit, and are angry that the world pays only by the visible measure of performance. It is true of Rousseau, the modern founder of the sect, true of Saint Pierre, his intellectual child, and of Châteaubriand, his grandchild, the inventor, we might almost say, of the primitive forest, and who first was touched by the solemn falling of a tree from natural decay in the windless silence of the woods. It is a very shallow view that affirms trees and rocks to be healthy, and cannot see that men in communities are just as true to the laws of their organization and destiny; that can tolerate the puffin and the fox, but not the fool and the knave; that would shun politics because of its demagogues, and snuff up the stench of the obscene fungus. The divine life of Nature is more wonderful, more various, more sublime in man than in any other of her works, and the wisdom that is gained by commerce with men, as Montaigne and Shakespeare gained it, or with one's own soul among men, as Dante, is the most delightful, as it is the most precious, of all. In outward nature it is still man that interests us, and we care far less for the things seen than the way in which they are seen by poetic eyes like Wordsworth's or Thoreau's, and the reflections they cast there. To hear the to-do that is often made over the simple fact that a man sees the image of himself in the outward world, one is reminded of a savage when he for the first time catches a glimpse of himself in a looking-glass. "Venerable child of Nature," we are tempted to say, "to whose science in the invention of the tobacco-pipe, to whose art in the tattooing of thine undegenerate hide not yet enslaved by tailors, we are slowly striving to climb back, the miracle thou beholdest is sold in my unhappy country for a shilling!" If matters go on as they have done, and everybody must needs blab of all the favors that have been done him by roadside and riverbrink and woodland walk, as if to kiss and tell were no longer treachery, it will be a positive refreshment to meet a man who is as superbly indifferent to Nature as she is to him. By and by we shall have John Smith, of No. —12—12th Street, advertising that he is not the J. S. who saw a cowlily on Thursday last, as he never saw one in his life, would not see one if he could, and is prepared to prove an alibi on the day in question.

Solitary communion with Nature does not seem to have been sanitary or sweetening in its influence on Thoreau's character. On the contrary, his letters show him more cynical as he grew older. While he studied with respectful attention the minks and woodchucks, his neighbors, he looked with utter contempt on the august drama of destiny of which his country was the scene, and on which the curtain had already risen. He was converting us back to a state of nature "so eloquently," as Voltaire said of Rousseau, "that he almost persuaded us to go on all fours," while the wiser fates were making it possible for us to walk erect for the first time. Had he conversed more with his fellows, his sympathies would have widened with the assurance that his peculiar genius had more appreciation, and his writings a larger circle of readers, or at least a warmer one, than he dreamed of. We have the highest testimony to the natural sweetness, sincerity, and nobleness of his temper, and in his books an equally irrefragable one to the rare quality of his mind. He was not a strong thinker, but a sensitive feeler. Yet his mind strikes us as cold and wintry in its purity. A light snow has fallen everywhere in which he seems to come on the track of the shier sensations that would elsewhere leave no trace. We think greater compression would have done more for his fame. A feeling of sameness comes over us as we read so much. Trifles are recorded with an over-minute punctuality and conscientiousness of detail. He registers the state of his personal thermometer thirteen times a day. We cannot help thinking sometimes of the man who

> "Watches, starves, freezes, and sweats
> To learn but catechisms and alphabets
> Of unconcerning things, matters of fact,"

and sometimes of the saying of the Persian poet, that "when the owl would boast, he boasts of catching mice at the edge of a hole." We could readily part with some of his affectations. It was well enough for Pythagoras to say, once for all, "When I was Euphorbus at the siege of Troy"; not so well for Thoreau to travesty it into "When I was a shepherd on the plains of Assyria." A naïve thing said over again is anything but naïve. But with every exception, there is no writing comparable with Thoreau's in kind, that is comparable with it in degree where it is best; where it disengages itself, that is, from the tangled roots and dead leaves of a second-hand Orientalism, and runs limpid and smooth and broadening as it runs, a mirror for whatever is grand and lovely in both worlds.

George Sand says neatly, that "Art is not a study of positive reality," (*actuality* were the fitter word,) "but a seeking after ideal truth." It would be doing very inadequate justice to Thoreau if we left it to be inferred that this ideal element did not exist in him, and that too in larger proportion, if less obtrusive, than his nature-worship. He took nature as the mountain-path to an ideal world. If the path wind a good deal, if he record too faithfully every trip over a root, if he botanize somewhat wearisomely, he gives us now and then superb outlooks from some jutting crag, and brings us out at last into an illimitable ether, where the breathing is not difficult for those who have any true touch of the climbing spirit. His shanty-life was a mere impossibility, so far as his own conception of it goes, as an entire independency of mankind. The tub of Diogenes had a sounder bottom. Thoreau's experiment actually presupposed all that complicated civilization which it theoretically abjured. He squatted on another man's land; he borrows an axe; his boards, his nails, his bricks, his mortar, his books, his lamp, his fish-hooks, his plough, his hoe, all turn state's evidence against him as an accomplice in the sin of that arti-ficial civilization which rendered it possible that such a person as Henry D. Thoreau should exist at all. *Magnis tamen excidit ausis.* His aim was a noble and a useful one, in the direction of "plain living and high thinking." It was a practical sermon on Emerson's text that "things are in the saddle and ride mankind," an attempt to solve Carlyle's problem (condensed from Johnson) of "lessening your denominator." His whole life was a rebuke of the waste and aimlessness of our American luxury, which is an abject enslavement to tawdry upholstery. He had "fine translunary things" in him. His better style as a writer is in keeping with the simplicity and purity of his life. We have said that his range was narrow, but to be a master is to be a master. He had caught his English at its living source, among the poets and prose-writers of its best days; his literature was extensive and recondite; his quotations are always nuggets of the purest ore; there are sentences of his as perfect as any-thing in the language, and thoughts as clearly crystallized; his metaphors and images are always fresh from the soil; he had watched Nature like a detective who is to go upon the stand; as we read him, it seems as if all-of-out-doors had kept a diary and become its own Montaigne; we look at the landscape as in a Claude Lorraine glass; compared with his, all other books of similar aim, even White's "Selborne," seem dry as a country clergyman's meteorological journal in an old almanac. He belongs with Donne and Browne and Novalis; if not with the originally creative men, with the scarcely smaller class who are peculiar, and whose leaves shed their invisible thought-seed like ferns.

John Burroughs on Walt Whitman, Gilbert White, and Henry David Thoreau
(1867, 1902, and 1919)

John Burroughs was born in 1837 in Delaware County, New York, and grew up on a farm in the Catskill Mountains. He taught school for a decade, then worked as a treasury clerk and bank examiner for more than twenty years. In 1874 he bought a farm, which he named Slabsides, on the Hudson River. There he lived for the remainder of his life, cultivating fruit trees, observing the wildlife around him, reading widely, entertaining a stream of admiring and often quite prominent visitors (including Walt Whitman and Theodore Roosevelt), and writing some two dozen books on literary criticism and the natural world. He died in 1921, a decade after receiving an honorary doctorate from Yale University.

Burroughs's literary career began with a book of criticism, *Notes on Walt Whitman as Poet and Person* (1867). His first book of nature writing, *Wake Robin*, appeared in 1871; the last, *Field and Study*, would be published in 1919. In his nature writing, Burroughs quickly grew beyond an early, rather Emersonian approach to nature to a more modern style grounded in scientific observation. This attachment to scientific rigor is most evident in the vehemence with which he attacked his less fastidious peers in the so-called nature faker debate of 1902–7. (Some of his contributions to the nature faker controversy are excerpted elsewhere in this anthology.) Later in life, however, Burroughs became disenchanted with science, believing instead that nature's most important truths revealed themselves not to the scientist but rather to the mystic and the poet.

In the first of the selections below, adverting to Emerson and "the great German philosopher" Goethe, Burroughs employs material nature as a bedrock literary criterion for evaluating the work of Whitman and Wordsworth. The poems of Whitman must be appreciated as "the most important literary event of our time," insists Burroughs, because they do not merely describe nature but "approximate to a direct utterance of Nature herself." Wordsworth, by contrast, dwelt only on "the healthful moral influence of the milder aspects of rural scenery," because "to have spoken in the full spirit of the least fact which he describes would have rent him to atoms."

In Burroughs's praise of Gilbert White's *Natural History of Selborne* we see the objectivist warrior of the nature faker controversy. Burroughs champions White as "a type of the true observer, the man with the detective eye" whose writing is grounded firmly in the close observation of nature. But what makes White's *Selborne* a classic, capable of being read again and again, is not only its scientific objectivity but also its reserved style, its organicism, and its authenticity. As Burroughs puts it in comparing later nature writers to White: "They choose their theme; the theme does not choose them." In the final essay, Burroughs takes issue with James Russell Lowell's severe criticism of Henry David Thoreau. Though he agrees with Lowell on a few points and adds several criticisms of his own, he insists that what Thoreau does well he does so well as to make "all our other nature-writers seem tame and insipid."

🪷 🪷 🪷

From *Notes on Walt Whitman as Poet and Person* (1867)

What is the reason that the inexorable and perhaps deciding standard by which poems, and other productions of art, must be tried, after the application of all minor tests, is the standard of absolute Nature? The question can hardly be answered, but the answer may be hinted at. The standard of form, for instance, is presented by Nature, out of the prevailing shapes of her growths, and appears to perfection in the human body. All the forms in art, sculpture, architecture, etc., follow it. Of course the same in colors; and, in fact, the same even in music, though more human and carried higher.

But a nearer hint still. The same moral elements and qualities that exist in man in a conscious state, exist, says the great German philosopher, in manifold material Nature, and all her products, in an unconscious state. Powerful and susceptible men—in other words, poets, naturally so—have an affiliation and identity with material Nature in its entirety and parts, that the majority of people (including most specially intellectual persons) cannot begin to understand; so passionate is it, and so convertible seems to be the essence of the demonstrative human spirit, with the undemonstrative spirit of the hill and wood, the river, field, and sky.

I know that, at first sight, certain works of art, in some branches, do not exhibit this identity and convertibility. But it needs only a little trouble and thought to trace them. I assert that every true work of art has arisen, primarily, out of its maker, apart from his talent of manipulation, being filled fuller than other men with this passionate affiliation and identity with Nature. Then I go a step further, and, without being an artist myself, I feel that every good artist of any age would join me in subordinating the most vaunted beauties of the best artificial productions, to the daily and hourly beauty of the shows and objects of outward Nature. I mean inclusively, the objects of Nature in their human relations.

To him that is pregnable, the rocks, the hills, the evening, the grassy bank, the young trees and old trees, the various subtle dynamic forces, the sky, the seasons, the birds, the domestic animals, etc., furnish intimate and precious relations at first hand, which nothing at second hand can supply. Their spirit affords to man's spirit, I sometimes think, its only inlet to clear views of the highest Philosophy and Religion. Only in their spirit can he himself have health, sweetness, and proportion; and only in their spirit can he have any essentially sound judgment of a poem, no matter what the subject of it might be. . . .

. . . Who is the great poet, and where the perfect poem? Nature itself is the only perfect poem, and the Kosmos is the only great poet. The Kosmos:

"Who includes diversity, and is Nature,
Who is the amplitude of the earth, and the coarseness and sexuality of the
    earth, and the great charity of the earth, and the equilibrium also,
Who has not look'd forth from the windows, the eyes, for nothing, or whose
    brain held audience with messengers for nothing;
Who contains believers and disbelievers—Who is the most majestic lover;
Who holds duly his or her triune proportion of realism, spiritualism, and of the
    aesthetic, or intellectual,
Who, having consider'd the Body, finds all its organs and parts good;

Who, out of the theory of the earth, and of his or her body, understands by
     subtle analogies all other theories,
The theory of a city, a poem, and of the large politics of These States."

The image Walt Whitman seems generally to have in his mind is that of
the Earth, "round, rolling, compact," and he aims to produce effects analogous to those produced by it; to address the mind as the landscape or the
mountains, or ideas of space or time, address it; not to excite admiration by
fine and minute effects, but to feed the mind by exhibitions of power; to
make demands upon it, like those made by Nature; to give it the grasp and
wholesomeness which come from contact with realities; to vitalize it by
bringing to bear upon it material forms, and the width of the globe, as the
atmosphere bears upon the blood through the lungs; working always by in-
directions, and depending on a corresponsive working of the mind that reads
or hears, with the mind that produces, as the female with the male; careless
of mere art, yet loyally achieving the effects of highest art; not unmindful of
details, yet subordinating everything to the total effect.

Yet no modern book of poems says so little about Nature, or contains so
few compliments to her. Its subject, from beginning to end, is MAN, and whatever pertains to or grows out of him; the facts of mechanics, the life of cities
and farms, and the various trades and occupations. What I describe, therefore, must be sought in its interior. The poet is not merely an observer of
Nature, but is immersed in her, and from thence turns his gaze upon people,
upon the age, and upon America. Heretofore, we have had Nature talked of
and discussed; these poems approximate to a direct utterance of Nature
herself.

From this comes, in a sense, the male principle of the book, which gives
that erect, proud, aggressive, forenoon character, the opposite of dallying, or
sentimentalism, or poetic sweetness, or reclining at ease — but which tallies
a man's rude health and strength, and goes forward with sinewy life and action. From the same source also comes that quality of the book which makes
it, on the surface, almost as little literary or recondite as the rocks and the
trees are, or as a spring morning is. Yet a careful analysis shows that the author
has certainly wrought with all the resources of literary composition at command. In the same degree that the book is great in a primordial, aboriginal
sense, is it great in a Goethean, Emersonian literary sense. It touches and

includes both extremes; not only is the bottom here, but the top also; not only all that science can give, but more besides. No doubt this fact greatly misled the critics, who failed to discriminate between mere wildness and savagery, as waiting for science and culture, and that vital sympathy with Nature, and freedom from conventional literary restraint, which comes only with the fullest science and culture, and which is one of the distinguishing features of our author. . . .

. . . The poet, like Nature, seems best pleased when his meaning is well folded up, put away, and surrounded by a curious array of diverting attributes and objects. Perhaps the point may be conveyed by the term elliptical. A word or brief phrase is often, or usually, put for a full picture or idea, or train of ideas or pictures. But the word or phrase is always an electric one. He never stops to elaborate, never explains.

Does it seem as if I praised him for making riddles? That is not it; he does not make riddles, or anything like them. He is very subtle, very indirect, and very rapid, and if the reader is not fully awake will surely elude him. Take this passage from the poem *Walt Whitman*:

> "Of the turbid pool that lies in the autumn forest,
> Of the moon that descends the steeps of the soughing twilight,
> Toss, sparkles of day and dusk! toss on the black stems that decay in the muck!
> Toss to the moaning gibberish of the dry limbs.
> I ascend from the moon, I ascend from the night;
> I perceive that the ghastly glimmer is noonday sunbeams reflected;
> And debouch to the steady and central from the offspring great or small."

A picture of death and a hint of immortality, and that the shows of things never stop at what they seem to the sight. The pale and ghastly glimmer of the moon in the midnight pool is, when viewed truly, the light of the ever-glorious sun. . . .

. . . Dating mainly from Wordsworth and his school, there is in modern literature, and especially in current poetry, a great deal of what is technically called Nature. Indeed it might seem that this subject was worn threadbare long ago, and that something else was needed. The word Nature, now, to most readers, suggests only some flower bank, or summer cloud, or pretty scene that appeals to the sentiments. None of this is in Walt Whitman. And it is because he corrects this false, artificial Nature, and shows me the real article, that I hail his appearance as the most important literary event of our times.

Wordsworth was truly a devout and loving observer of Nature, and perhaps has indicated more surely than any other poet the healthful moral influence of the milder aspects of rural scenery. But to have spoken in the full spirit of the least fact which he describes would have rent him to atoms. To have accepted Nature in her entirety, as the absolutely good and the absolutely beautiful, would have been to him tantamount to moral and intellectual destruction. He is simply a rural and metaphysical poet whose subjects are drawn mostly from Nature, instead of from society, or the domain of romance; and he tells in so many words what he sees and feels in the presence of natural objects. He has definite aim, like a preacher or moralist as he was, and his effects are nearer akin to those of pretty vases and parlor ornaments than to trees or hills.

In Nature everything is held in solution; there are no discriminations, or failures, or ends; there is no poetry or philosophy — but there is that which is better, and which feeds the soul, diffusing itself through the mind in calm and equable showers. To give the analogy of this in the least degree was not the success of Wordsworth. Neither has it been the success of any of the so-called poets of Nature since his time. Admirable as many of these poets are in some respects, they are but visiting-card callers upon Nature, going to her for tropes and figures only. In the products of the lesser fry of them I recognize merely a small toying with Nature — a kind of sentimental flirtation with birds and butterflies.

I am aware, also, that the Germanic literary "storm and stress periods," during the latter part of the last century, screamed vehemently for "Nature" too; but they knew not what they said. The applauded works of that period and place were far from the spirit of Nature, which is health, not disease.

If it appears that I am devoting my pages to the exclusive consideration of literature from the point of view of Nature and the spirit of Nature, it is not because I am unaware of other and very important standards and points of view. But these others, at the present day, need no urging, nor even a statement from me. Their claims are not only acknowledged — they tyrannize out of all proportion. The standards of Nature apply just as much to what is called artificial life, all that belongs to cities and to modern manufactures and machinery, and the life arising out of them. Walt Whitman's poems, though entirely gathered, as it were, under the banner of the Natural Universal, include, for themes, as has been already stated, all modern artificial combinations, and the facts of machinery, trades, &c. These are an essential part of his chants. It is, indeed, all the more indispensable to resume and apply to these, the genuine standards.

Our civilization is not an escape from Nature, but a mastery over, and following out of, Nature. We do not keep the air and the sunlight out of our houses, but only the rain and the cold; and the untamed and unrefined elements of the earth are just as truly the sources of our health and strength as they are of the savages'. In speaking of Walt Whitman's poetry, I do not mean raw, unreclaimed Nature. I mean the human absorption of Nature like the earths in fruit and grain, or in the animal economy. The dominant facts of his poetry, carried out strictly and invariably from these principles, are Life, Love, and the Immortal Identity of the Soul. Here he culminates, and here are the regions where, in all his themes, after treating them, he finally ascends with them, soaring high and cleaving the heavens.

From *Literary Values and Other Papers* (1902)

One of the few books which I can return to and re-read every six or seven years is Gilbert White's *Selborne*. It has a perennial charm. It is much like country things themselves. One does not read it with excitement or eager avidity; it is in a low key; it touches only upon minor matters; it is not eloquent, or witty, or profound; it has only now and then a twinkle of humor or a glint of fancy, and yet it has lived an hundred years and promises to live many hundreds of years more. So many learned and elaborate treatises have sunk beneath the waves upon which this cockle-shell of a book rides so safely and buoyantly! What is the secret of its longevity? One can do little more than name its qualities without tracing them to their sources. It is simple and wholesome, like bread, or meat, or milk. Perhaps it is just this same unstrained quality that keeps the book alive. Books that are piquant and exciting like condiments, or cloying like confectionery or pastry, it seems, have much less chance of survival. The secret of longevity of a man—what is it? Sanity, moderation, regularity, and that plus vitality, which is a gift. The book that lives has these things, and it has that same plus vitality, the secret of which cannot be explored. The sensational, intemperate books set the world on fire for a day, and then end in ashes and forgetfulness.

White's book diffuses a sort of rural England atmosphere through the mind. It is not the work of a city man who went down into the country to write it up, but of a born countryman, — one who had in the very texture of his mind the flavor of rural things. Then it is the growth of a particular locality. Let a man stick his staff into the ground anywhere and say, "This is home," and describe things from that point of view, or as they stand related to that spot, — the weather, the fauna, the flora, — and his account shall have an interest to us it could not have if not thus located and defined. . . .

. . . When one reads the writers of our own day upon rural England and the wild life there, he finds that they have not the charm of the Selborne naturalist; mainly, I think, because they go out with deliberate intent to write up nature. They choose their theme; the theme does not choose them. They love the birds and flowers for the literary effects they can produce out of them. It requires no great talent to go out in the fields or woods and describe in graceful sentences what one sees there, — birds, trees, flowers, clouds, streams; but to give the atmosphere of these things, to seize the significant and interesting features and to put the reader into sympathetic communication with them, that is another matter.

Hence back of all, the one thing that has told most in keeping White's book alive is undoubtedly its sound style — sentences actually filled with the living breath of a man. We are everywhere face to face with something genuine and real; objects, ideas, stand out on the page; the articulation is easy and distinct. White had no literary ambitions. His style is that of a scholar, but of a scholar devoted to natural knowledge. There was evidently something winsome and charming about the man personally, and these qualities reappear in his pages.

He was probably a parson who made as many calls afield as in the village, if not more. An old nurse in his family said of him, fifty years after his death, "He was a still, quiet body, and that there was not a bit of harm in him."

White was a type of the true observer, the man with the detective eye. He did not seek to read his own thoughts and theories into Nature, but submitted his mind to her with absolute frankness and ingenuousness. He had infinite curiosity, and delighted in nothing so much as a new fact about the birds and the wild life around him. To see the thing as it was in itself and in its relations, that was his ambition. He could resist the tendency of his own mind to believe without sufficient evidence. Apparently he wanted to fall in with the notion current during the last century, that swallows hibernated in the mud in the bottoms of streams and ponds, but he could not gather convincing proof. It was not enough that a few belated specimens were seen in the fall lingering about such localities, or again hovering over them early in spring; or that some old grandfather had seen a man who had taken live swallows out of the mud. Produce the man and let us cross-question him, — that was White's attitude. Dr. Johnson said confidently that swallows did thus pass the winter in the mud "conglobulated into a ball," but Johnson had that literary cast of mind that prefers a picturesque statement to the exact fact. White was led astray by no literary ambition. His interest in the life of nature was truly a scientific one; he must know the fact first, and then give it to the humanities. How true it is in science, in literature, in life, that any secondary motive vitiates the result! Seek ye the kingdom of truth first, and all things shall be added. . . .

. . . He learned, as every observer sooner or later learns, to be careful of sweeping statements, — that the truth of nature is not always caught by the biggest generalizations. After speaking of the birds that dust themselves, earth their plumage —*pulveratrices*, as he calls them — he says, "As far as I can observe, many birds that dust themselves never wash, and I once thought that those birds that wash themselves would never dust; but here I find myself mistaken," and he instances the house sparrow as doing both. White seems to have been about the first writer upon natural history who observed things minutely; he saw through all those sort of sleight-o'-hand movements and ways of the birds and beasts. He held his eye firmly to the point. He saw the swallows feed their young on the wing; he saw the fern-owl, while hawking about a large oak, "put out its short leg while on the wing, and by a bend of the head deliver something into its mouth." This explained to him the use of its middle toe, "which is curiously furnished with a serrated claw." He timed the white owls feeding their young under the eaves of his church, with watch in hand. He saw them transfer the mouse they brought, from the foot to the beak, that they might have the free use of the former in ascending to the nest.

In his walks and drives about the country he was all attention to the life about him, simply from his delight in any fresh bit of natural knowledge. His curiosity never flagged. He had naturally an alert mind. His style reflects this alertness and sensitiveness. In his earlier days he was an enthusiastic sportsman, and he carried the sportsman's trained sense and love of the chase into his natural history studies. He complained that faunists were too apt to content themselves with general terms and bare descriptions; the reason, he says, is plain, — "because all that may be done at home in a man's study; but the investigation of the life and conversation of animals is a concern of much more trouble and difficulty, and is not to be attained but by the active and inquisitive, and by those that reside much in the country." He himself had the true inquisitiveness and activity, and the loving, discriminating eye. He saw the specific marks and differences at a glance.

From "A Critical Glance into Thoreau" (1919)

The most point-blank and authoritative criticism within my knowledge that Thoreau has received at the hands of his countrymen came from the pen of Lowell about 1864, and was included in *My Study Windows*. It has all the professional smartness and scholarly qualities which usually characterize Lowell's critical essays. Thoreau was vulnerable, both as an observer and as a literary craftsman, and Lowell lets him off pretty easily — too easily — on both counts.

The flaws he found in his nature-lore were very inconsiderable: such as his ignorance of the fact, until he built his Walden shanty, that the hickory grew near Concord; also, that he did not know there was such a thing as phosphorescent wood until he went to Maine; or, until he was forty years old, that the pine had seeds. If there were no more serious flaws than these in his nature observations, we could pass them by without comment.

As regards his literary craftsmanship, Lowell charges him only with having revived the age of *Concetti* while he fancied himself going back to a pre-classical nature, basing the charge on such a far-fetched comparison as that in which Thoreau declares his preference for "the dry wit of decayed cranberry vines and the fresh Attic salt of the moss-beds" over the wit of the Greek sages as it comes to us in the *Banquet* of Xenophon — a kind of perversity of comparison all too frequent with Thoreau.

But though Lowell lets Thoreau off easily on these specific counts, he more than makes up by his sweeping criticism, on more general grounds, of his life and character. Here one feels that he overdoes the matter.

It is not true, in the sense which Lowell implies, that Thoreau's whole life was a search for the doctor. It was such a search in no other sense than that we are all in search of the doctor when we take a walk, or flee to the mountains or to the seashore, or seek to bring our minds and spirits in contact with "Nature's primal sanities." His search for the doctor turns out to be an escape from the conditions that make a doctor necessary. His wonderful activity, those long walks in all weathers, in all seasons, by night as well as by day, drenched by rain and chilled by frost, suggest a reckless kind of health. A doctor might wisely have cautioned him against such exposures. . . .

Lowell's criticism amounts almost to a diatribe. He was naturally antagonistic to the Thoreau type of mind. Coming from a man near his own age, and a neighbor, Thoreau's criticism of life was an affront to the smug respectability and scholarly attainments of the class to which Lowell belonged. Thoreau went his own way, with an air of defiance and contempt which, no doubt, his contemporaries were more inclined to resent than we are at our distance. Shall this man in his hut on the shores of Walden Pond assume to lay down the law and the gospel to his elders and betters, and pass unrebuked, no matter on what intimate terms he claims to be with the gods of the woods and mountains? This seems to be Lowell's spirit. But all this is a divergence from my main purpose. I set out to criticize Thoreau, not Lowell, and to look a little more closely into him than Lowell looked. In doing so, I shall treat him with the frankness that he himself so often employed; not that I love Thoreau less, but that I love the truth more.

I can hold my criticism in the back of my head while I say with my forehead that all our other nature-writers seem tame and insipid beside Thoreau. He was so much more than a mere student and observer of nature; and it is this surplusage which gives the extra weight and value to his nature-writing. He was a critic of life, he was a literary force which made for plain living and high thinking. His nature-lore was an aside; he gathered it as the meditative saunterer gathers a leaf, or a flower, or a shell on the beach, while he ponders on higher things. He had other business with the gods of the woods than taking an inventory of their wares. He was a dreamer, an idealist, a fervid ethical teacher, seeking inspiration in the fields and woods. The hound, the turtle-dove, and the bay horse which he said he had lost, and for whose trail he was constantly seeking, typified his interest in wild nature. The natural history in his books is quite secondary. The natural or supernatural history of his own thought absorbed him more than the exact facts about the wild life around him. He brings us a gospel more than he brings us a history. His science is only the handmaid of his ethics; his wood-lore is the foil of his moral and intellectual teachings. His observations are frequently at fault, or wholly wide of the mark; but the flower or specimen that he brings you always "comes laden with a thought." There is a tang and a pungency to nearly everything he published; the personal quality which flavors it is like the formic acid which the bee infuses into the nectar he gets from the flower, and which makes it honey.

I feel that some such statement about Thoreau should precede or go along with any criticism of him as a writer or as an observer. He was, first and last, a moral force speaking in the terms of the literary naturalist. . . .

Walden is probably our only, as it is certainly our first, nature classic. It lives because it has the real breath of life; it embodies a fresh and unique personality, and portrays an experiment in the art of living close to nature, in a racy and invigorating style. It is a paean in praise of that kind of noble poverty which takes the shine out of wealth completely. All the same, most of its readers would doubtless prefer the lot of the young men, his townsmen, to whom Thoreau refers, "whose misfortune it is to have inherited farms, houses, barns, cattle, and farming tools" — things, he added, that "are more easily acquired than got rid of."

It is this audacious gift which Thoreau has, of suddenly turning our notions topsy-turvy, or inside out, that gives spice to his page and makes *Walden* irritate while it charms. We note such things more easily than we do the occasional lapses in his science. For instance, what can he mean when he says, "Once it chanced that I stood in the very abutment of a rainbow's arch, which filled the lower stratum of the atmosphere, tingeing the grass and leaves around, and dazzling me as if I looked through a colored crystal"? Is it possible, then, to reach the end of the rainbow? Why did he not dig for the pot of gold buried there? How he could be aware that he was standing at the foot of one leg of the glowing arch is to me a mystery. When I see a rainbow, it is always just in front of me: I am standing exactly between the highest point of the arch and the sun, and the laws of optics ordain that it can be seen in no other way. You can never see a rainbow either to the right of you or to the left. Hence, no two persons see exactly the same bow, because no two can occupy exactly the same place at the same time. The bow you see is directed to you alone. Move to the right or the left, and it moves as fast as you do. You cannot flank it or reach its end. It is about the most subtle and significant phenomenon that everyday nature presents to us. Unapproachable as a spirit, like a visitant from another world, yet the creation of the familiar sun and rain! How Thoreau found himself standing in the bow's abutment will always remain a mystery to me.

Thoreau was not a great philosopher, he was not a great naturalist, he was not a great poet, but as a nature-writer and an original character, he is unique in our literature. His philosophy begins and ends in himself, or is entirely subjective, and is frequently fantastic, and nearly always illogical. His poetry is of the oracular kind, and is only now and then worth attention. There are crudities in his writings which make the conscientious literary craftsman shudder; there are mistakes of observation which make the serious naturalist wonder; and there is often an expression of contempt for his fellow country-men, and the rest of mankind, and their aims in life, which makes the judi-cious grieve. But at his best there is a gay symbolism, a felicity of description, and a freshness of observation that delight all readers. . . .

Thoreau called himself a mystic, and a transcendentalist, and a natural philosopher to boot. But the least of these was the natural philosopher. He did not have the philosophic mind, or the scientific mind; he did not inquire into the reason of things, or the meaning of things; in fact, he had no disin-terested interest in the universe apart from himself. He was too personal and illogical for a philosopher. The scientific interpretation of things did not in-terest him at all. He was interested in things only so far as they related to Henry Thoreau. He interpreted Nature entirely in the light of his own idiosyncrasies.

Thoreau was not a born naturalist, but a born supernaturalist. He was too intent upon the bird behind the bird always to take careful note of the bird itself. He notes the birds, but not too closely. . . .

Channing quotes Thoreau as saying that sometimes "you must see with the inside of your eye." I think that Thoreau saw, or tried to see, with the inside of his eye too often. He does not always see correctly, and many times he sees more of Thoreau than he does of the nature he assumes to be looking at. Truly it is "needless to travel for wonders," but the wonderful is not one with the fantastic or the far-fetched. Forcible expression was his ruling pas-sion as a writer. Only when he is free from its thrall, which in his best mo-ments he surely is, does he write well. When he can forget Thoreau and remember only Nature, we get those delightful descriptions and reflections in *Walden*. When he goes to the Maine woods, or to Cape Cod, or to Can-ada, he leaves all his fantastic rhetoric behind him and gives us sane and refreshing books. In his walks with Channing, one suspects that he often let himself go to all lengths, did his best to turn the world inside-out, as he did at times in his journals, for his own edification and that of his wondering disciples.

Thoreau was in no sense an interpreter of Nature: he did not draw out her meanings or seize upon and develop her more significant phases. Seldom does he relate what he sees or thinks to the universal human heart and mind. He has rare power of description, but is very limited in his power to translate the facts and movements of nature into human emotion. His passage on the Northern Lights which Channing quotes from the journals, is a good sample of his failure in this respect: —

> Now the fire in the north increases wonderfully, not shooting up so much as creeping along, like a fire on the mountains of the north, seen afar in the night. The Hyperborean gods are burning brush, and it spread, and all the hoes in Heaven could not stop it. It spread from west to east over the crescent hill. Like a vast fiery worm it lay across the northern sky, broken into many pieces; and each piece, with rainbow colors skirting it, strove to advance itself toward the east, worm-like, on its own annular muscles. It has spread into the choicest wood-lots of Valhalla; now it shoots up like a single, solitary watch-fire, or burning brush, or here it runs up a pine tree like powder; and still it continues to gleam here and there like a fat stump in the burning, and is reflected in the water. And now I see the gods by great exertions have got it under, and the stars have come out without fear, in peace.

Do we get any impression of the mysterious, almost supernatural, character of the Aurora from such a description in terms of a burning wood-lot or a haystack? It is no more like a conflagration than an apparition is like solid flesh and blood. Its wonderful, its almost spiritual, beauty, its sudden vanishings and returnings, its spectral, evanescent character—why, it startles and awes one as if it were the veils around the throne of the Eternal. And then his mixed metaphor—the Hyperborean gods turned farmers and busy at burning brush; then a fiery worm; and then the burning wood-lots of Valhalla! But this is Thoreau—inspired with heavenly elixir one moment, and drunk with the brew in his own cellar the next! . . .

If he sees anything unusual in Nature, like galls on trees and plants, he must needs draw some moral from it and indulge his passion for striking expression and fantastic comparisons, usually at the expense of the truth. For instance, he implies that the beauty of the oak-galls is something that was meant to bloom in the flower; that the galls are the scarlet sins of the tree, the tree's Ode to Dejection—another example of the *Concetti*, to which Lowell referred. Yet he must have known that they are the work of an insect, and are as healthy a growth as is the regular leaf. The insect gives the magical touch that transforms the leaf into a nursery for its young. Why deceive ourselves by believing that fiction is more interesting than fact? But Thoreau is full of this sort of thing; he must have his analogy, true or false. . . .

Wordsworth was about the first poet-walker—a man of letters who made a business of walking, and whose study was really the open air. But he was not a Holy-Lander in the Thoreau sense. He did not walk to get away from people, as Thoreau did, but to see a greater variety of them, and to gather suggestions for his poems. Not so much the wild, as the human and the morally significant, were the objects of Wordsworth's quest. He haunted waterfalls and fells and rocky heights and lonely tarns, but he was not averse to footpaths and highways, and the rustic half-domesticated nature of rural England. He was a nature-lover; he even calls himself a nature-worshiper; and he appears to have walked as many or more hours each day, in all seasons, as did Thoreau; but he was hunting for no lost paradise of the wild; nor waging a crusade against the arts and customs of civilization. Man and life were at the bottom of his interest in nature.

Wordsworth never knew the wild as we know it in this country—the pitilessly savage and rebellious; and, on the other hand, he never knew the wonderfully delicate and furtive and elusive Nature that we know; but he knew the sylvan, the pastoral, the rustic-human, as we cannot know them. British birds have nothing plaintive in their songs, and British woods and fells but little that is disorderly and cruel in their expression, or violent in their contrasts.

Wordsworth gathered his finest poetic harvest from common nature and common humanity about him—the wayside birds and flowers and waterfalls, and the wayside people. Though he called himself a worshiper of Nature, it was Nature in her half-human moods that he adored,—Nature that knows no extremes, and that has long been under the influence of man,—a soft, humid, fertile, docile Nature, that suggests a domesticity as old and as permanent as that of cattle and sheep. His poetry reflects these features, reflects the high moral and historic significance of the European landscape, while the poetry of Emerson and of Thoreau is born of the wildness and elusiveness of our more capricious and unkempt Nature.

William Benjamin Carpenter on Science's Representation of Nature

(1872)

William Benjamin Carpenter has been called one of the last of the classical British naturalists. Born in Exeter in 1813, he entered University College, London, in 1833 as a medical student; after graduating in 1835 he began conducting research in physiology at Edinburgh Medical School, and just four years later published his influential *Principles of General and Comparative Physiology.* After moving to London in 1844 he became a professor of physiology at the Royal Institution and a member of the Royal Society. Before his death in 1885 he would conduct groundbreaking research in microbiology, physiology, zoology, and oceanography. Interested in natural phenomena on both the smallest and the largest scales, he was one of the first to systematically utilize the microscope in examining microorganisms and to theorize the existence of worldwide oceanic circulation.

In 1872, Carpenter was named president of the British Association for the Advancement of Science. The excerpt below is part of his inaugural address, "Man as the Interpreter of Nature," which was published later that year in *Popular Science Monthly.* Carpenter's topic is the "intellectual arrogance" that holds that "the scientific interpretation of Nature represents her not merely as she seems but as she really is." He argues instead that science constructs an "intellectual representation of Nature," "a representation framed by the mind itself." In comparing the scientist's "interpretation" of the natural world with that of the artist and poet, he invokes the durable trope of Nature "as a vast book lying open," a book of which the would-be interpreter "has merely to learn the characters, then to master the language, and finally to apprehend the ideas which that language conveys." Though Carpenter concludes that science's conception of

48

Nature "is a representation framed by the mind itself," he rejects the more radical notion that this representation is no more than "a projection of our own intellect into what surrounds us."

తక తక తక

It has been customary with successive occupants of this chair to open the proceedings of the meetings over which they respectively presided with a discourse on some aspect of Nature in her relation to man. But I am not aware that any one of them has taken up the other side of the inquiry — that which concerns man as the "Interpreter of Nature"; and I have therefore thought it not inappropriate to lead you to the consideration of the mental processes by which are formed those fundamental conceptions of matter and force, of cause and effect, of law and order, which furnish the basis of all scientific reasoning, and constitute the *Philosophia prima* of Bacon. There is a great deal of what I cannot but regard as fallacious and misleading philosophy — "oppositions of science, falsely so called" — abroad in the world at the present time. And I hope to satisfy you that those who set up their own conceptions of the orderly sequence which they discern in the phenomena of Nature as fixed and determinate laws, by which those phenomena not only are, but always have been, and always must be, invariably governed, are really guilty of the intellectual arrogance they condemn in the systems of the ancients, and place themselves in antagonism to those real philosophers by whose grasp and insight that order has been so far disclosed. For what love of the truth, as it is in Nature, was ever more conspicuous than that which Kepler displayed in his abandonment of each of the conceptions of the planetary system which his imagination had successively devised, so soon as it proved to be inconsistent with the facts disclosed by observation? In that almost admiring description of the way in which his enemy Mars, "whom he had left at home a despised captive," had "burst all the chains of the equations, and broke forth from the prisons of the tables," who does not recognize the justice of Schiller's definition of the real philosopher — as one who always loves truth better than his system? And when at last he had gained the full assurance of a success so complete that (as he says) he thought he must be dreaming, or that he had been reasoning in a circle, who does not feel the almost sublimity of the self-abnegation with which, after attaining what was in his own estimation such a glorious reward of his life of toil, he abstains from claiming the applause of his contemporaries, but leaves his fame to after-ages in these noble words: "The book is written; to be read either now or by posterity, I care not which. It may well wait a century for a reader, as God has waited 6,000 years for an observer."

And when a yet greater than Kepler was bringing to its final issue that grandest of all scientific conceptions, long pondered over by his almost superhuman intellect—which linked together the Heavens and the Earth, in the *nexus* of a universal attraction, establishing the truth for whose utterance Galileo had been condemned, and giving to Kepler's Laws a significance of which their author had never dreamed—what was the meaning of that agitation which prevented the philosopher from completing his computation, and compelled him to hand it over to his friend? That it was not the thought of his own greatness, but the glimpse of the grand universal order thus revealed to his mental vision, which shook the soul of Newton to its foundations, we have the proof in that comparison in which he likened himself to a child picking up shells on the shore of the vast ocean of truth—a comparison which will be evidence to all time at once of his true philosophy and of his profound humility.

Though it is with the intellectual representation of Nature which we call science that we are primarily concerned, it will not be without its use to cast a glance in the first instance at the other two principal characters under which man acts as her interpreter—those, namely, of the artist and of the poet.

The artist serves as the interpreter of Nature, not when he works as the mere copyist, delineating that which he sees with his bodily eyes, and which we could see as well for ourselves, but when he endeavors to awaken within us the perception of those beauties and harmonies which his own trained sense has recognized, and thus impart to us the pleasure he has himself derived from their contemplation. As no two artists agree in the original constitution and acquired habits of their minds, all look at Nature with different (mental) eyes; so that, to each, Nature is what he individually sees in her.

The poet, again, serves as the interpreter of Nature, not so much when by skilful word-painting (whether in prose or verse) he calls up before our mental vision the picture of some actual or ideal scene, however beautiful, as when, by rendering into appropriate forms those deeper impressions made by the Nature around him on the moral and emotional part of his own nature, he transfers these impressions to the corresponding part of ours. For it is the attribute of the true poet to penetrate the secret of those mysterious influences which we all unknowingly experience; and, having discovered this to himself, to bring others, by the power he thus wields, into the like sympathetic relation with Nature, evoking with skilful touch the varied response of the Soul's finest chords, heightening its joys, assuaging its griefs, and elevating its aspirations. While, then, the artist aims to picture what he sees in Nature, it is the object of the poet to represent what he feels in Nature; and to each true poet Nature is what he individually finds in her.

The philosopher's interpretation of Nature seems less individual than that of the artist or the poet, because it is based on facts which any one may verify, and is elaborated by reasoning processes of which all admit the validity. He looks at the universe as a vast book lying open before him, of which he has in the first place to learn the characters, then to master the language, and finally to apprehend the ideas which that language conveys. In that book there are many chapters, treating of different subjects; and, as life is too short for any one man to grasp the whole, the scientific interpretation of this book comes to be the work of many intellects, differing not merely in the range but also in the character of their powers. But while there are "diversities of gifts," there is "the same spirit." While each takes his special direction, the general method of study is the same for all. And it is a testimony alike to the truth of that method and to the unity of Nature that there is an ever-increasing tendency toward agreement among those who use it aright — temporary differences of interpretation being removed, sometimes by a more complete mastery of her language, sometimes by a better apprehension of her ideas — and lines of pursuit which had seemed entirely distinct or even widely divergent being found to lead at last to one common goal. And it is this agreement which gives rise to the general belief — in many, to the confident assurance — that the scientific interpretation of Nature represents her not merely as she seems but as she really is.

When, however, we carefully examine the foundation of that assurance, we find reason to distrust its security; for it can be shown to be no less true of the scientific conception of Nature than it is of the artistic or the poetic, that it is a representation framed by the mind itself out of the materials supplied by the impressions which external objects make upon the senses, so that, to each man of science, Nature is what he individually believes her to be. And that belief will rest on very different bases, and will have very unequal values, in different departments of science. . . .

But, it may be said, Is not this view of the material universe open to the imputation that it is "evolved out of the depths of our own consciousness" — a projection of our own intellect into what surrounds us — an ideal rather than a real world? If all we know of matter be an "intellectual conception," how are we to distinguish this from such as we form in our dreams, for these, as our Laureate no less happily than philosophically expresses it, are "true while they last." Here our "common-sense" comes to the rescue. We "awake, and behold it was a dream." Every healthy mind is conscious of the difference between his waking and his dreaming experiences, or, if he is now and then puzzled to answer the question, "Did this really happen or did I dream it?" the perplexity arises from the consciousness that it might have happened. And every healthy mind, finding its own experiences of its waking state not only self-consistent, but consistent with the experiences of others, accepts them as the basis of his beliefs, in preference to even the most vivid recollections of his dreams. . . .

Alfred Austin on the
Poetic Interpretation of Nature
(1877)

Alfred Austin was born in Headingley, Leeds, in 1835. After graduating from London University he began a career in law, but in 1858, after publishing his first novel, *Five Years of It*, he devoted himself exclusively to writing. He would go on to publish two more novels and several volumes of poetry, none of which was considered particularly great; when he was named Britain's poet laureate in 1896, the choice was derided as a reward not for his literary merit but for his partisan political journalism.

The selection below, published in 1877 in the *Contemporary Review*, is excerpted from a lengthy book review of J. C. Shairp's *On the Poetic Interpretation of Nature*. Austin disputes Shairp's contention that the poetic view of the natural world is just as truthful as the scientific. He suggests instead that, in contrast to the self-consistent worldview put forth by science, the poetic treatment of Nature has produced at best an "enchanting map of contradictions." He insists that "Nature is a dumb oracle, who, of herself, says nothing, but will most obligingly emit any voice the poet chooses to put inside her," and that assertions to the contrary are not only wrong but dangerous. He argues convincingly against "the theory, apparently flattering to poets, but in reality ruinous and degrading to them, that Nature has theological, spiritual, and moral truths to convey, and that it is the business of the poet to expound them. Examined closely, it will be found only an ingenious device for chaining the poet to the theologian or the moralist, and making him hymn the glories of his captor."

Somewhat paradoxically, however, Austin suggests that the poet's attention to

nature *can* facilitate a certain sort of truth — if only by providing poets a degree
of detachment from society that helps them see the human world more clearly
than their fellows.

🕸 🕸 🕸

The phrase that gives the name to this paper, as many readers of the CONTEM-
PORARY doubtless know, is not mine. It is the title of a work recently published
by the new occupant of the Chair of Poetry at Oxford, and I fear I can borrow
it only for the purpose of challenging its appropriateness. Professor Shairp is
one of the most genial and, in the largest sense of the word, most generous
of writers. He is in a striking degree what the Italians call sympathetic. He is
always on the side of the angels; and, however much the more than Christian
charity of our time may have led people to "pity the puir de'il," a celestial
bias is always an advantage to a writer, and sorely tempts our neutrality to
show him something more than benevolence. The key-note of all his discourses is "*Sursum corda!*" His prejudices are prejudices of kindliness; his
prepossessions are in favour of what is noble and elevating; and we might say
of him, as a critic even, that his very failings lean to virtue's side. Such a
writer cannot possibly provoke antagonism by the nature of his opinions or
by his manner of expounding them; and dissent from him must therefore be
based on fundamental and genuine divergence of view. That he is eminently
well qualified to instil into the rising generation of Oxford those *bonos mores*
which Horace, in the "Carmen Seculare," beseeches the Gods to bestow on
the youth of Rome, his writings abundantly prove. But whether he will
prompt them to think with as much accuracy as fervour, the contents of this
volume may lead us to doubt.

   If language be intended, not to veil, but to convey thought, the phrase "the
poetic interpretation of Nature" implies that Nature means something, and
has something to say. I must venture to affirm, in contravention of this impli-
cation, that Nature is a dumb oracle, who, of herself, says nothing, but will
most obligingly emit any voice the poet chooses to put inside her. It will be
understood that the Nature whereof Professor Shairp discourses is what is
commonly called visible external Nature, and comprises, roughly speaking,
all that is not Man, nor the exclusive production of man. It is perhaps as well

to say this much; though there is no danger of ambiguity in the present employment of a word which too often lends itself to a labyrinth of ambiguities.

Lest it should be thought that my quarrel is with a phrase, and that injustice may be done by putting too literal a construction on the mere title of a book, I will set forth, with as much fulness as a reasonable regard for brevity allows, the author's doctrine in his own words. According to him, then, it is not true that Nature is a blank or unintelligible scroll, with no meaning of its own, save that which we put into it from the light of our own transient feelings. Each of the physical sciences attempts to explain the outer world in one of its aspects, to interpret it from one point of view; and the whole circle of the physical sciences explains the appearances of the material world by reducing what seems complex and manifold to the operation of a few simple but all-pervading laws. But there are other aspects of Nature, with which physical science does not deal, other questions suggested by natural phenomena, which it cannot and does not attempt to answer. It is the province of poetry to explain and account for these. In fact, poetry has to do with truth as really as science has, though with a different order of truth; and poetry is as "true" a form of thinking as any other. Physical science explains the appearances of the material world by the properties of matter; poetry explains their meaning by the properties of the soul. As the poet looks on the face of the earth, sea, and sky, the thought whence come they? whither tend they? what is their origin, meaning, and end? are the questions which the poet asks, and is able to answer. Thus the poet is the highest, best, and truest interpreter of Nature.

It must be allowed that this is a pretty plain and categorical collection of statements, each corroborating the other in the opinion that Nature means something, has something of her own to say, and contains a certain body of truth; and that poets, by a special power of interpretation, can tell us what it is.

I should think it will occur to many persons besides myself to make the preliminary remark, that, if this be so, the amount of truth arrived at by poets in interpreting Nature must by this time be considerable, and that, furthermore, this body of truth, like any other body of truth, must be consistent with itself. Poetry was, perhaps, the earliest form of literature, and has certainly proved as enduring as any other. There has been no period of intellectual activity during which poets, more or less distinguished, have not existed, and there is no reason to fear that the race is becoming extinct. Moreover, they have, with rare exceptions, lived much with Nature, and discoursed much of Nature. The phrase *gaudentes rure Camoenae,* has passed into a proverb. Where, then, is this poetic interpretation of Nature, this truth, as sure and true as the interpretations of physical science, to be found? Presumably, in their poetry.

To their poetry, then, let us turn. I do so, and what do I find? A most enchanting map of contradictions. I find that Nature is gentle, that Nature is cruel; that she sympathizes with man, that she is utterly indifferent to him; that he is in harmony with her and that he is in hopeless discord with her. One poet tells me that Fate, blind, immoral, inexorable, rules all things. Another assures me that there is a beneficent Creator of the Universe; that He upholds the mountains and ruffles the sea, and that by Him the heavens are kept pure from wrong. A third sings with exquisite modulations of many and multiform gods that cannot die; while a fourth mournfully predicts that man's gods shall go down to him dead, and that the waves shall be upon even our deities at last. By one melodious interpreter I am carried through hell, purgatory, and heaven; by another I am warned that these are the hideous inventions of tyrants and hypocrites, or the distempered dreams of servile natures. *Timor primus fecit Deos,* exclaims one of the greatest of poets. To war against the throne and monarchy of God, exclaims another, possibly yet greater, is impious, and challenges adamantine chains, penal fire, and bottomless perdition. One interpreter informs me that death is the sable smoke where vanishes the flame of life and of the soul; another bids me hope that death's dark door, upon the other side, upon a more than living brightness looks. Let not the soul that suffers, says one poet in a tone of warning, turn unto Nature where she sits solitary and aloft in the majesty of the mountains, for her face is cold and stern, and looks not with compassion on her sad and erring child. Before the sound of the sentence has quitted my ears, a more sonorous voice arises, chanting—

"Where rose the mountains, there to him were friends;"

and the "he" of this passage was sad and suffering enough in all conscience; when he sought his solace among them. He watched the stars, he says, and the lakes, and the lofty places, till earth, and earth-born jars, and human frailties were forgotten quite. By one bard Nature is hailed as "Maternal Nature;" by another she is described as a murderess and assassin, and the slayer of her own offspring. When we approach the "origin and end of things," the Babel of poetic voices becomes more and more confused. Homer begs the "Heavenly Goddess" to inspire his muse. Milton calls upon the Spirit that, with mighty wings outspread, sate dove-like on the vast abyss and made it pregnant. Shelley invokes the "Mother of this unfathomable world." I find one cosmogony in the "De Rerum Natura," a quite different one in "Paradise Lost." One bard humbly affirms that wrong and suffering are the consequence of Original Sin; a second fathers them on this very belief, which he denounces as criminal superstition. Obey Nature, says one poet; contend with her and crush her, says a second; while a third bids us take her as we find her, and cease to torment ourselves with her origin or her purpose — content to find her now fair, now foul, to-day beneficent, tomorrow ruthlessly brutal, but always interesting and practically irresistible.

Such are a few of the glaring contradictions to be found in the poets; contradictions for each of which chapter and verse could easily be given, and, as every one familiar with the writers appealed to will perceive, have been in large measure given in the very language I have employed.

Surely, if there be such a thing as a true and sure poetic interpretation of Nature, we are here in presence of a serious difficulty! We are told that poetry has to do with truth as really as science has, though with a different order of truth, and that poetry is as true a form of thinking as any other. I suspect that if scientific writers contradicted each other about the scientific truths of Nature, as the poets contradict each other and themselves about the alleged poetic truths contained in her, they would quickly lose that authority which they have so justly and honourably acquired. If one physicist told us that there is a natural law of gravitation by which bodies are attracted to each other inversely as the square of the distances, while a second assured us that they attract each other with no reference to distance, and a third that they do not attract each other at all, we should lose all faith in their astronomical and cosmical conclusions, and should infallibly infer that there is no such thing as scientific truth. Are we not equally impelled by the foregoing array of clashing poetic statements to conclude that there is no such thing as poetic truth, whether in the interpretation of Nature, or of anything else?

I do not know that it will much help us to escape from the difficulty in which I find myself, by examining the long and interesting chapter in which Professor Shairp enumerates eight different ways in which poets "deal with" Nature; but it will perhaps be fairer to him to do so, and in the process the divergence of view between us will be brought out more distinctly. It will have been observed that another phrase has been introduced. Instead of the word "interpreting" Nature, we have the words "dealing with" Nature. But I must observe either that the two are intended by the author to be synonymous and interchangeable, or that all this chapter is irrelevant to the purpose of his volume. No one would deny that poets "deal with" Nature. The question is, Do they interpret her? do they stand between her and us, and yield authentic account of her significance?

The first of the eight ways in which it is said poets deal with Nature is to express the simple, spontaneous, unreflecting pleasure which all unsophisticated beings feel in free open-air life. The second is using Nature as a background or setting to human action. The third is the associating certain definite portions of Nature, in plainer words certain places, with the human and historic events of which they have been the scene. The fourth is the conferring upon Nature, under the influence of strong emotion, sympathy and kinship with the heart thus moved. The fifth is the contrasting the inhuman indifference of Nature with man's yearning for sympathy and gentleness. The sixth consists in describing Nature phenomenally or just as she appears.

There are two other ways in which poets deal with Nature, enumerated by Professor Shairp, and they shall not be forgotten. But, for the moment, let me pause, in order to inquire how far any of these six ways can in a just sense be said to be an interpretation of Nature.

The first and the sixth disappear from controversy without any effort. Obviously, to describe Nature, as the Italians say, *tale quale*, precisely as she seems to all of us, or to express the delight that all of us feel in her beauty and geniality, is not to interpret her. Otherwise, anybody who, feeling it, exclaimed, "What a delicious day it is!" or any one who accurately described the external appearance of a flower, would be a poet and interpreter. The second and third ways contain a distinction without a difference, save so far as time is concerned; in each case all that is done with Nature being to use her as a convenient and suggestive background. But no one would seriously argue that to make this very proper and judicious use of Nature, is to add anything to our knowledge of her meaning. She is employed in this manner plainly for purposes of effect; and though the person who does this with skill and success may be a great artist, he is in no sense an interpreter.

There remain, of the six ways of dealing with Nature already enumerated, only two, the fourth and the fifth, and these two are in reality one and the same. "Another way," says Professor Shairp, "in which poets and others deal with Nature, is where the heart, under the stress of some strong emotion, colours all Nature with its own hues, sees all things in sympathy with its own mood, making

> 'All melodies an echo of that voice,
> All colours a suffusion from that light.'"

This is the fourth way, and it is only supplemented and enlarged, not really added to, by the fifth, when, again in the author's words, the poet finds that Nature yields no response to him, but that when he smiles she weeps, and when he weeps she smiles. In so dealing with Nature, the poet no doubt is doing something more with her than when he merely expresses a feeling of joy in her comeliness, or of exultation in her sublimity, or than, again, when he strives accurately to describe her, and, in describing her, uses her as a background for human action.

But in doing this something more, is he interpreting her? For this is the question; and we have reached the point at which I can propound it with the hope of extorting a definite answer.

My own answer shall be definite enough. The poet never gets any nearer to an interpretation of Nature than he reaches when employing the two methods I have last named; but, in employing these, he could far more justly be said to be interpreting himself than to be interpreting Nature. He is appealing to her to lend him language for his own passion, tropes for his own grief, similitudes for his own sentiment. It is not she that feels, but he. It is not Nature that is asking for sympathy, but the poet himself; not Nature that has got anything to say to him, but he that has got much to say to her. It is true that Nature has ears no more than lips; but his transcendental egotism not only transfers his own speech to her mouth, but he actually forms a sort of double personage of her, and makes her the deferential recipient of what he first makes her say for him. So egotistical is he that he is surprised when ever and anon—though this happens rarely—he cannot get her to listen to him! and he construes her indifference or inert antagonism into intentional disdain or opposition.

Let us see if we cannot make out how this attitude of his, this dealing on his part with Nature, arises. Every poet has an intense love of beauty, and an insatiable craving for sympathy. These are the two most striking and most operative idiosyncrasies of the poetic temperament. He has the sensuous eye, and the restless heart. Beauty is his joy; love and what follow from love, or rather what accompany it, sympathy and agreement, are what he eternally craves. Other people, no doubt, are alive to beauty, and prefer it to ugliness; and other people, too, like to be agreed with. But they can dispense with both beauty and sympathy better than with several other things that could be named; comfort, success, society, position, home, domestic alliances, a good outlook for offspring, in fact everything that is commonly held to constitute life. It could not be maintained, even with speciousness, that the quest and worship of beauty, and a hunger for sympathy, are prominent in the lives of the bulk of mankind. They may start with some such desires, but they get completely cured of these long before they reach the meridian of life.

Now love of beauty and thirst for sympathy are the central and the enduring passions of the poet. He never ceases to cherish them; he never grows reconciled to their renunciation. Where is he to find a fitting field for their indulgence? It is not necessary to inveigh against society here; for I am labouring to state facts, not to expound prejudices, or even to give rein to moral indignation. But who will say that beauty and sympathy on a large scale, or of a delicate sort, are to be found in society? Beauty, no doubt, is not utterly banished from it, nor is sympathy unknown in its domain. But the beauty one finds there is invariably alloyed with much that is the opposite of beautiful; and the poet experiences from the contemplation of it a feeling of mixed and doubtful pleasure. The same may be said of such sympathy as society has to offer to the mind of keen and various susceptibilities. Even if society did its best to be sympathetic, it is far too busily occupied with objects and ends that demand a selfish concentration of purpose, to succeed in the endeavour. But there is nothing less observant, less meditative, or less self-examining, than society. It acts roughly, robustly, effectively, but without much consideration. This is not to accuse it; it is only to say that it acts as it must act. But to one who perpetually craves for sympathy, it must prove a sorry companion. It is rather ugly; and it cares little or nothing for individual feelings, more especially when they are of the tantalizing and irrelevantly sentimental or exalted sort.

Shall we wonder if persons of poetic temperament turn away with a mixture of repugnance and terror from a medium of existence in which, it seems to them, there is little else save noise, uncomeliness, and cruelty? I am speaking of course of the poetic temperament in the early stages of its experience, of the poet in his youth and early manhood. Later on, if his faculties develop as they should, he contrives to extract some music from the noise, as to hear, as Wordsworth beautifully puts it, the still sad music of humanity; to discover some faint relics of beauty in its uncomeliness; and to press even its cruelty into the service of tenderness and pathos. But, as Goethe remarks, no youth can be a master; and the reason why he cannot be a master is that he himself has not yet learnt. But in order that he should learn so as to be able, at some future time, to teach others, you must not dry up the sources of his sensibility too soon. If you do, you kill the poet, and you leave only a man — like another. I think it is Saint-Beuve who observes that many men of forty are dead poets. They became reconciled to the world too soon. They succumbed to the stern conditions of life without a struggle, either from cowardice, from lassitude, or from self-interest, and they henceforth swell the densely packed ranks of so-called practical people. Ever and anon in their lives they catch the sound of the pathetic minor, though usually it has to be struck for them by some poet or other; but for the most part their lives are attuned to the chord, and worked out in the major key, of direct self-interest.

The poet, afflicted by the ugliness and unconcern of society, flies to the lap of Nature. There he finds beauty, perfect and undefiled; the golden exhalations of the dawn, dewy eve, fair woods, placid water, sweet shy spring, frank voluptuous summer, and autumn's meditative haze. His craving for sensuous beauty is fully fed; and he encounters nothing to remind him that sensuous beauty may be allied to much moral ugliness. This beautiful Nature is as good as she is beautiful. The lilies of the field do not contradict, the stars of heaven do not thwart him. He craves for music that has no discord in it; and, lo! the lark mounts, the linnet sings. He yearns for colour, and odour, and delicate forms; and, behold, the year puts on its beauty, the tassels of the larch rock in the light south wind, the briony reddens or yellows, or the violet, without being seen, scents all the air. He too can contribute to the beauty of the scene; for he can people it with such beings as he will. He is not afraid to think his thoughts, and give rein to his own feelings, in such company as this. There is no one here who will laugh at him, no one who will stare a moment, and then turn away. He can strike no chord that has not got its echo somewhere in the sympathetic lonely places.

This, I submit, is the genesis and explanation of the feeling of the poet for Nature. It may seem to give it a selfish origin; but I do not know that it is less accurate on that account. It is egotism, no doubt, that drives the young poet from society to solitude; but it is the egotism which prefers its own love of beauty to the insensibility of others to ugliness, and its own soaring thoughts to a grovelling want of thought in its neighbours. Fortunately, in these others, in many of those neighbours, there lingers some of the original craving for beauty, some residuum of preference for the noble over the base; or the poet's musical egotism would always be, what it too often is, a voice crying in the wilderness.

The time comes when, after having thoroughly steeped himself in Nature, the poet returns to society. Not that he ever abandons himself to it; or, if he does, he does so at his peril. But just as a lover, when first mated, cares for no companionship save that of his beloved, but by degrees begins to be willing to divide his time between her and others, yet ever, to the last, reverts to her with a sense of solace and refreshment; so the poet, in the days of his honey-moon, will consort with Nature only; and though, afterwards, he moves in society, *in* it but scarcely *of* it, scanning it, understanding it, but more or less detached from it, he perpetually reverts to his one sweet mistress, to Nature, his first, last, and only love. And as a man will always, in moments of excite-ment, speak the language he knows the best and learned the earliest, — in other words, will always turn him to his mother tongue, — the poet, when he wants to explain himself in moments of keen emotion, speaks the language of Nature, treats her, so to speak, as his dictionary, and uses her as his store-house, nearest at hand, of explanation, simile, metaphor, and analogy. Na-ture furnishes his terminology. If he thinks of death, he sees last year's leaves upon the ground. If he talks of youth, the sounds of spring fill his ears, the language of spring rushes to his lips. If he tells of sadness, bereavement, and regret, he hears the moaning of the wintry wind. If he muses on eternity, he hears the mighty waters rolling evermore. These are trite examples; but I purposely make them trite, for they equally well exhibit what the poet does whenever he glitters with apposite weapons, borrowed from the inexhaust-ible armoury of Nature.

But though Nature has thus done so much for him, what has he done for Nature? I humbly submit, nothing, unless it be to win others over to love her with a love something like his own. But has he interpreted her? By no man-ner of means. As I said before, she has interpreted him, and he blesses her from his heart for her translation of his perplexed and ambiguous spirit.

But I must not run the risk, through indulgence in enthusiasm and metaphorical language, of being mistaken. I do not want to write a rhapsody; I seek to expose an error, and to establish a conclusion. Of course, Nature has not interpreted him in the strict sense of the word. He has interpreted himself in terms of Nature, and in interpreting himself he has interpreted the human heart. When his powers ripen, and he becomes freed from thraldom to her and to his own individual emotions, then the vocabulary and the images with which she furnished him while he studied only himself, become available for expounding the thoughts, feelings, and passions of a wider humanity. The cardinal business of the poet is with the human heart and human life. It is these which he has got to interpret, not Nature; and she helps him in the task by providing him with a world of imagery and illustration that are as familiar to him as to others are household words, by reason of his long and assiduous residence with her. Not less than Professor Shairp am I ready to exclaim, of the poets and the visible world —

> "They took the whole earth for their toy,
> They played with it in every mood;
> A cell for prayer, a hall for joy,
> They treated Nature as they would."

But that these lines should be quoted in support of the theory that Nature has got something to say, and that poets interpret this something, I own, surprises me. "They treated Nature as they would." Precisely. "They played with her in every mood." Most unquestionably. But is it not obvious that, in doing so, it is not she, but they, who are the real oracle? As Antonio says in "Twelfth Night,"

> "In Nature there's no blemish but the mind."

"There is another way in which the poet deals with the external world," says Professor Shairp (and here we reach the two remaining ways he enumerates, and of which I promised not to lose sight) —

> "when he enters into the life and the movement of Nature by a kind of imaginative sympathy, and brings it home to us by one stroke, flashing upon our hearts by one touch, one inspired line, a sense of the inner life of things, and a conviction that he has been allowed for a moment to penetrate into their secret. This, which has been called in a special way the interpretative power of

poetry, is that in which it reaches its highest function, and exercises one of its finest offices of mediation between the soul of man and Nature."

This is very nicely and eloquently written, and seems highly complimentary to poets. But I am not quite certain that I know what it means. Neither am I sure that it represents anything very definite to the author himself. He says, "I have dwelt too long on this aspect of poetry;" yet I find that he has dedicated to it scarcely four and a-half short pages; and of these nearly two contain a quotation from Mr. Matthew Arnold, who seems to me to say something very different from what Professor Shairp fancies he says, while the rest consists, for the most part, of quotations from the poets, illustrating this specially interpretative power of poetry. I will therefore cite one of these:—

> "The silence that is in the starry sky,
> The sleep that is among the lonely hills."

Two lovely lines, of a certainty. But when we are asked, "Who has not felt as though he had a new revelation made to him about the starry sky and the mountain-stillness, after reading them for the first time?" I at least feel compelled to reply that I do not feel as though a new revelation had been made to me, in any accurate sense, but only that what I knew and felt before has here been put in a perfect manner, for which everybody who can feel it at all must be profoundly grateful.

I suspect, however, that this seventh way of dealing with Nature is only a precursor to the eighth way, of which it is said:—

> "The last and highest way in which Nature ministers to the soul and spirit of man is when it becomes to him a symbol translucent with the light of the moral and the spiritual world. In other words, the highest use to which imagination can put this visible world is to gather from it some tidings of the world invisible."

For in what does this eighth way differ from the seventh, when, in illustration of it, it is said, "Does not Keats bring home to us the meaning, the inner secret, of the ocean, and the impression it makes on the human heart, when he speaks of

> 'The voice mysterious, which whoso hears
> Must think on what will be, and what has been'?"

Thus, just as the second and third ways of dealing with Nature were shown to be one and the same, and as the fourth and fifth were seen to be practically identical, so between the seventh and eighth there is no perceptible distinction; and they may both be regarded as ways by which the poet brings home to us the moral and spiritual meaning of Nature, and by a proper interpretation of the visible world gives us authentic tidings of that which is invisible.

There we are, at last! We have Nature erected into an altar, behind which is dimly inscribed the Decalogue, and before which the poet stands transformed into an arch-priest and a theologian.

I trust I should not be guilty of such trifling as to pile page upon page only in order to discover precisely what Professor Shairp means by the word interpretation, if he means anything at all, if he used the word in an accurate sense, or if he employs it now in one sense and now in another. I have been led to my present task by no love of carping or of criticism. My object is to unmask and protest against a dangerous doctrine, which they who hold it cannot set forth in plain intelligible terms, but to which they cloudily cling because they half-consciously feel it will buttress other doctrines which they think it behoves them to support in every possible manner. They want to call the poet into court as a witness to certain theological tenets and to certain moral and spiritual truths in the sense in which they themselves employ those words, meaning thereby certain crystallized and definite opinions concerning conduct and speculation.

But what a bold attempt! If they call one poet into court, they must call every poet in turn. If they produce the page of one inspired bard in corroboration of their views, I must ask them to turn over the leaf and read the other side as well. Which poet, I ask, gives us tidings of the invisible after looking at the visible? Is it Wordsworth, or Shelley? Is it Byron, or Milton? Is it Dante, or Shakespeare? Professor Shairp can tell us; let us listen to him: —

"It cannot but affect even the poet's feeling about the most common material things, what may be his regards towards that Unseen Presence on which, not Nature only, but the spirit of man reposes? As he looks on the face of earth, sea, and sky, the thought whence come these things? whither tend they? what is their origin and their end? must habitually enter in and colour that which the eye beholds. It can hardly be but that a man's inner thoughts about these things will find their way out and colour the observation of his eye. Even the ethereal beauty of Shelley's descriptions—his perception of the motion of clouds, and shadows, and sunbeams—his delight in all skyey and evanescent things too delicate for grosser eyes—you cannot read them long without being crossed by some breath blown from his own distempered atmosphere. The 'sky-cleaving crags' suggest to him heaven-defying minds, and his mountains have a voice 'to repeal large codes of fraud and woe.' Byron, though his later poetry contains noble passages on mountain scenery, even the high Alps are hardly strong enough to lure him into forgetfulness of his own unhappy self and his quarrel with mankind. In fact, so closely and deeply united are all the parts of the universe that no one can apprehend the full compass of its manifold harmonies whose own heart is not filled with that central harmony which sets it right with God and man."

Habemus confitentem, we may well exclaim. In this passage the author not only betrays what, in the compliments he pays to poets for their power of interpreting Nature, he is really aiming at, but he cuts off the bough on which he is sitting, by loudly complaining that the greatest poets often interpret her wrongly and amiss.

Who is to decide that question? The theologian. Then clearly it is the theologian that interprets, not the poet, since it is the theologian who decides whether the poet's interpretation is correct. So long as the poet finds a central harmony in the world, he is an interpreter. The moment he finds a central, centrifugal, and all-permeating discord, he is not an interpreter at all. Is he a poet? If he is not, then whether a man is a poet depends upon whether he takes what the theologian considers the correct view of the universe. If he is, then a man may be a poet and yet not be able to interpret Nature—indeed, to do nothing but interpret her wrongly! He may employ the sky-cleaving crags as silent fingers pointing up to heaven, but he must on no account use them as heaven-defying minds. Why not? I find either figure equally poetical. But one represents a physical and moral truth, while the other represents a physical and moral falsehood. Who says so? The theologian. Then be satisfied with the theologian's interpretation of the matter. But don't appeal to poets to interpret it for you, for they will leave you in the lurch, or, still worse, in hopeless perplexity, since one poet will interpret it in one way, another in another. Nay, the same poet will offer you one interpretation to-day, and a precisely opposite one tomorrow. Lear exclaims:—

"I tax ye not, ye elements, with unkindness."

On the other hand, Pericles says: —

> "A terrible childbed hast thou had, my dear!
> No fire, no light. The unfriendly elements
> Forgot thee utterly."

Which interpretation of the elements is the correct one? In which play is Shakespeare an interpreter, and in which no interpreter at all? Are the elements to be taxed with unkindness or not? Are they really unfriendly, or utterly incapable of friendliness and unfriendliness alike? In poetry, either view will do equally well; but in plain prose, and in criticism that seeks, not to establish some foregone theological conclusion, but the facts of the matter as they really are, to maintain that the elements care one jot about man or woman, about discrowned kings, unfilial daughters, or rough childbeds, seems to me little better than nonsense.

I hope it will not be supposed that these remarks are made in a spirit of hostility to theology. Professor Shairp appears to be anxious lest the inroads of Science should limit the sphere within which the poet works. The conclusions of Science trouble the poet very little if at all more than the conclusions of Theology. I suppose every poet during the last two hundred years has been aware that the earth goes round the sun, and not the sun round the earth. Has that prevented any poet during the last two hundred years talking of the sunrise or the sunset? I suppose most poets are aware that the dew does not fall, but rises. I should think Wordsworth was aware of the fact. Yet that did not prevent him from beginning a poem with the line —

> "The dew was falling fast, the stars began to blink."

I might likewise observe that Science might object to the statement that the stars blink. But a man of science who made that objection to a poet would only show himself to be exceedingly stupid, and a poet to whom the objection seemed to be of any consequence would not be likely to give the world much valuable poetry. Mr. Bailey says, in "Festus,"

> "It is the eye that twinkles, not the star."

I am not so sure of that either, and should require to consult an oculist and an astronomer before satisfying myself as to the fact. But I admire the line greatly, and I should think no one will require to be told why. When flashed upon Campbell the line,

A CENTURY OF EARLY ECOCRITICISM

"Coming events cast their shadows before,"

he is said to have jumped out of bed with delight and written it down. I scarcely think he need have made such a fuss about it. Still, it is a happy thought; and its felicity is not destroyed by the scientific fact that things coming towards us often have their shadows behind them — invariably, if the sun is in front of them. Mr. Tennyson, in an incautious moment, and too enamoured of a supposed astronomical fact, talked of "moonless Mars." And, lo! the astronomy of to-day contradicts the astronomy of yesterday, and Mars has got a couple of moons, and the poet who trusted to his scientific friends is left to look a little foolish. When the same exquisite poet trusts to his own astronomical observations, and exclaims of the wild hyacinths of spring,

"It seemed the Heavens upbreaking through the earth,"

he not only writes a divinely beautiful line, but he is on safe ground, from which neither theology nor science can ever dislodge him, and the line would be no more beautiful if theology demonstrated that there is a heaven, or less so if science proved that there is not. The world has seen many theologies, and not a few philosophies and sciences. I do not mean to say that there are not several conclusions of science which seem to be more solidly established than any conclusions of theology. But what are called scientific ideas, are perhaps regarded only as provisional by the truly scientific mind, and I can feel no certainty that even the Development Theory, for which I entertain great respect, will not, by virtue of its own nature, in due course develop another; and I should be exceedingly sorry to use its conclusions as the machinery of a poem upon the Universe, or so to absorb them as to be unable to look at Nature except from their point of view. The poet will make some use of them, I daresay, as he has made some use of various theological and scientific conclusions. But he will not suffer himself to be bound adscript to either master. For they are not his master at all, but his servants and handmaids, as everything is, from the pebble to the star, that will help him to interpret, not Nature, but the human heart. Science and theology keep shifting, Nature and the human heart are always the self-same, and their years do not fail. They are the two that remain while the others change and pass. Explain yourself, and what you feel, in terms of theology or science, and a thousand years hence you may not be understood, or may be thought to be talking nonsense. Say it in terms of Nature, and your heart using that language will be understood through all time.

"Back unto life, ye living. Nothing new
Under the sun? Say rather, nothing old.
Have the winds lost their freshness, or the spring
One dimple of her beauty? Looks the moon
One hour less young than when, o'er Trojan plains,
To Trojan eyes, she shepherded the stars?
Hero's true lamp is out; Leander's arms
No longer breast the barricading surge,
And seas of separation moan unseen
'Twixt love and locked embraces, salter far
Than e'er embittered sweet Abydos' shore.
Though Delphi's fires be quenched, fresh vapours rise
From burning hollows in the human heart,
Inspiring riddles only verse can read.
Who understand not, ne'er had understood."

Therefore, I, for one, lift up my voice, and protest with all the force in my power, against the theory, apparently flattering to poets, but in reality ruinous and degrading to them, that Nature has theological, spiritual, and moral truths to convey, and that it is the business of poets to expound them. Examined closely, it will be found only an ingenious device for chaining the poet to the chariot-wheels of the theologian or the moralist, and making him hymn the glories of his captor. Thank God, poets have long since given up glorifying tyrants or patrons; and I will not believe that it is reserved for them, in these latter days, to return to a narrower slavery. . . .

It is Man, therefore, and not Nature, as I said at starting, who is the real voice — the real oracle. It is not she who is sublime, or tender, or contemplative, but he who is all these things, and many more, and who finds in her a storehouse of language and symbols by which better to express and expound what he feels. If Nature has anything to say to us, it is certainly not the poets who have found out what it is; for they are perpetually making her contradict herself. But in truth she is not a song, but an instrument, and the poet fingers the stops as he pleases. . . .

Richard Jefferies on the
Shortcomings of Language
(1887)

Richard Jefferies, a popular English nature writer and novelist, was born in 1848 in Wiltshire. He ran away at the age of sixteen to France, with plans to walk to Moscow. When that didn't pan out he and his companion hoped to proceed to America, but instead wound up back in Wiltshire. Jefferies then learned shorthand and became a reporter for a local paper, the *North Wilts Herald*; about this time he began writing fiction as well. His first three novels were commercial failures, and he was unable to find a publisher for his fourth. His first successful book was a collection of natural history essays, *Gamekeeper at Home*, published originally in 1877 in the *Pall Mall Gazette*. Two years later he published a similar collection of articles, *Wild Life in a Southern County*. In the 1880s he wrote four novels that combined fiction with natural history, and these, along with *Wild Life*, were the mainstay of his literary reputation. One of his novels, *After London*, features a depopulated England that has relapsed into wilderness—what once was the Thames has become a lake, and London is depicted as a swamp. Jefferies died in 1887.

   The essay below, "Nature and Books," is an extended meditation on the incommensurability of nature and the language with which we attempt to describe it. Jefferies notes that even in his day there was a profusion of writing about nature—"there is not a thing that grows," as he puts it, "that may not furnish a monograph." Yet they are all, somehow, inadequate; in spite of this "endless, endless botany," and in spite of the considerable "power of language," all the nature books "are yet to be written": "So many, many books," he laments, "and such a very, very little bit of nature in them! . . . There are a million books, and yet with all their aid I cannot tell you the colour of the May dandelion."

"Nature and Books" appeared in the *Fortnightly Review* in 1887.

🪷 🪷 🪷

What is the colour of the dandelion? There are many dandelions: that which I mean flowers in May, when the meadow grass has started and the hares are busy by daylight. That which flowers very early in the year has a thickness of hue, and is not interesting; in autumn the dandelions quite change their colour and are pale. The right dandelion for this question is the one that comes about May with a very broad disc, and in such quantities as often to cover a whole meadow. I used to admire them very much in the fields by Surbiton (strong clay soil), and also on the towing-path of the Thames where the sward is very broad, opposite Long Ditton; indeed I have often walked up that towing-path on a beautiful sunny morning, when all was quiet except the nightingales in the Palace hedge, on purpose to admire them. I daresay they are all gone now for evermore; still, it is a pleasure to look back on anything beautiful. What colour is this dandelion? It is not yellow, nor orange, nor gold; put a sovereign on it and see the difference. They say the gipsies call it the Queen's great hairy dog-flower — a number of words to one stalk, and so, to get a colour to it, you may call it the yellow-gold-orange plant. In the winter on the black mud under a dark, dripping tree, I found a piece of orange peel, lately dropped — a bright red orange speck in the middle of the blackness. It looked very beautiful, and instantly recalled to my mind the great dandelion discs in the sunshine of summer. Yet certainly they are not red-orange. Perhaps if ten people answered this question they would each give different answers. Again, a bright day or a cloudy, the presence of a slight haze, or the juxtaposition of other colours, alters it very much; for the dandelion is not a glazed colour, like the buttercup, but sensitive. It is like a sponge, and adds to its own hue that which is passing, sucking it up.

The shadows of the trees in the wood, why are they blue? Ought they not to be dark? Is it really blue, or an illusion? And what is their colour when you see the shadow of a tall trunk aslant in the air like a leaning pillar? The fallen brown leaves wet with dew have a different brown to those that are dry, and the upper surface of the green growing leaf is different to the under surface. The yellow butterfly, if you meet one in October, has so toned down his spring yellow that you might fancy him a pale green leaf floating along the road. There is a shining, quivering, gleaming; there is a changing, fluttering, shifting; there is a mixing, weaving—varnished wings, translucent wings, wings with dots and veins, all playing over the purple heath; a very tangle of many-toned lights and hues. Then come the apples: if you look upon them from an upper window, so as to glance along the level plane of the fruit, delicate streaks of scarlet, like those that lie parallel to the eastern horizon before sunrise; golden tints under bronze, and apple green, and some that the wasps have hollowed, more glowingly beautiful than the rest; sober leaves and black and white swallows: to see it you must be high up, as if the apples were strewn on a sward of foliage. So have I gone in three steps from May dandelion to September apple; an immense space measured by things beautiful, so filled that ten folio volumes could not hold the description of them, and I have left out the meadows, the brooks, and hills. Often in writing about these things I have felt very earnestly my own incompetence to give the least idea of their brilliancy and many-sided colours. My gamut was so very limited in its terms, and would not give a note to one in a thousand of those I saw. At last I said, I will have more words; I will have more terms; I will have a book on colour, and I will find and use the right technical name for each one of these lovely tints. I was told that the very best book was by Chevreul, which had tinted illustrations, chromatic scales, and all that could be desired.

Quite true, all of it; but for me it contained nothing. There was a good deal about assorted wools, but nothing about leaves; nothing by which I could tell you the difference between the light scarlet of one poppy and the deep purple-scarlet of another species. The dandelion remained unexplained; as for the innumerable other flowers, and wings, and sky-colours, they were not even approached. The book, in short, dealt with the artificial and not with nature. Next I went to science—works on optics, such a mass of them. Some I had read in old time, and turned to again; some I read for the first time, some translated from the German, and so on. It appeared that, experimenting with physical colour, tangible paint, they had found out that red, yellow, and blue were the three primary colours; and then, experimenting with light itself, with colours not tangible, they found out that red, green, and violet were the three primary colours; but neither of these would do for the dandelion. Once upon a time I had taken an interest in spectrum analysis, and the theory of the polarisation of light was fairly familiar; any number of books, but not what I wanted to know. Next the idea occurred to me of buying all the colours used in painting, and tinting as many pieces of paper a separate hue, and so comparing these with petals and wings, and grass, and trifolium. This did not answer at all; my unskilful hands made a very poor wash, and the yellow paper set by a yellow petal did not agree, the scientific reason of which I cannot enter into now. Secondly, the names attached to many of these paints are unfamiliar to general readers; it is doubtful if bistre, Leitch's blue, oxide of chromium, and so on would convey an idea. They might as well be Greek symbols: no use to attempt to describe hues of heath or hill in that way. These, too, are only distinct colours. What was to be done with all the shades and tones? Still there remained the language of the studio; without doubt a master of painting could be found who would quickly supply the technical term of anything I liked to show him; but again no use, because it would be technical. And a still more insurmountable difficulty occurs: in so far as I have looked at pictures, it seems as if the artists had met with the same obstacle in paints as I have in words — that is to say, a deficiency. Either painting is incompetent to express the extreme beauty of nature, or in some way the canons of art forbid the attempt. Therefore, I had to turn back, throw down my books with a bang, and get me to a bit of fallen timber in the open air to meditate.

Would it be possible to build up a fresh system of colour language by means of natural objects? Could we say pine-wood green, larch green, spruce green, wasp yellow, humble-bee orange; and there are fungi that have marked tints, but the Latin names of these agarics are not pleasant. Butterfly blue — but there are several varieties; and this plan is interfered with by two things: first, that almost every single item of nature, however minute, has got a distinctly different colour, so that the dictionary of tints would be immense; and next, so very few would know the object itself that the colour attached to it would have no meaning. The power of language has been gradually enlarging for a great length of time, and I venture to say that the English language at the present time can express more, and is more subtle, flexible, and, at the same time, vigorous, than any of which we possess a record. When people talk to me about studying Sanscrit, or Greek, or Latin, or German, or, still more absurd, French, I feel as if I could fell them with a mallet happily. Study the English, and you will find everything there, I reply. With such a language I fully anticipate, in years to come, a great development in the power of expressing thoughts and feelings which are now thoughts and feelings only. How many have said of the sea, "It makes me feel something I cannot say"? Hence it is clear there exists in the intellect a layer, if I may so call it, of thought yet dumb — chambers within the mind which require the key of new words to unlock. Whenever that is done a fresh impetus is given to human progress. There are a million books, and yet with all their aid I cannot tell you the colour of the May dandelion. There are three greens at this moment in my mind: that of the leaf of the flower-de-luce, that of the yellow iris-leaf, and that of the bayonet-like leaf of the common flag. With admission to a million books, how am I to tell you the difference between these tints? So many, many books and such a very, very little bit of nature in them! Though we have been so many thousand years upon the earth we do not seem to have done any more as yet than walk along beaten footpaths, and sometimes really it would seem as if there was something in the minds of many men quite artificial, quite distinct from the sun, and trees, and hills — altogether house people, whose gods must be set in four-cornered buildings. There is nothing in books that touches my dandelion.

It grows, ah yes, it grows! How does it grow? Builds itself up somehow of sugar and starch, and turns mud into bright colour and dead earth into food for bees, and someday perhaps for you, and knows when to shut its petals and how to construct the brown seeds to float with the wind, and how to please the children, and how to puzzle me. Ingenious dandelion! If you find out that its correct botanical name is *Leontodon teraxacum*, or *Leontodon dens-leonis*, that will bring it into botany; and there is a place called Dandelion Castle in Kent, and a bell with the inscription: —

> "John de Dandelion with his great dog,
> Brought over this bell on a mill cog,"

which is about as relevant as the mere words *leontodon taraxacum*. Botany is the knowledge of plants according to the accepted definition; naturally, therefore, when I began to think I would like to know a little more of flowers than could be learned by seeing them in the fields, I went to botany. Nothing could be more simple. You buy a book which first of all tells you how to recognise them, how to classify them; next instructs you in their uses, medical or economical; next tells you about the folk-lore and curious associations; next enters into a lucid explanation of the physiology of the plant and its relation to other creatures; and finally, and most important, supplies you with the ethical feeling, the ideal aspiration to be identified with each particular flower. One moderately thick volume would probably suffice for such a modest round as this. . . .

I remember taking sly glances when I was a very little boy at an old Culpepper's Herbal, heavily bound in leather and curiously illustrated. It was so deliciously wicked to read about the poisons; and I thought perhaps it was a book like that only in papyrus rolls, that was used by the sorceress who got ready the poisoned mushrooms in old Rome. Youth's ideas are so imaginative, and bring together things that are so widely separated. Conscience told me I had no business to read about poisons; but there was a fearful fascination in hemlock, and I recollect tasting a little bit — it was very nasty. At this day, nevertheless, if anyone wishes to begin a pleasant, interesting, unscientific acquaintance with English plants he would do very well indeed to get a good copy of Culpepper. Grey hairs had insisted in showing themselves in my beard when, all those weary years afterwards, I thought I would like to buy the still older Englishman, Gerard, who had no Linnaeus to guide him, who walked about our English lanes centuries ago. What wonderful scenes he must have viewed when they were all a tangle of wild flowers, and plants that are now scarce were common, and the old ploughs, and the curious customs, and the wild red-deer — it would make a good picture, it really would, Gerard studying English orchids! Such a volume! — hundreds of pages, yellow of course, close type, and marvellously well printed. The minute care they must have taken in those early days of printing to get up such a book — a wonderful volume both in bodily shape and contents. Just then the only copy I could hear of was much damaged. The cunning old bookseller said he could make it up; but I have no fancy for patched books, they are not genuine; I would rather have them deficient; and the price was rather long, and so I went Gerardless. Of folk-lore and medicinal use and history and associations here you have hints. The bottom of the sack is not yet; there are the monographs, years of study expended upon one species of plant growing in one locality, perhaps; some made up into thick books and some into broad quarto pamphlets, with most beautiful plates, that, if you were to see them, would tempt you to cut them out and steal them, all sunk and lost like dead ships under the sand: piles of monographs. There are warehouses in London that are choked to the beams of the roof with them, and every fresh exploration furnishes another shelf-load. The source of the Nile was unknown a very few years ago, and now, I have no doubt, there are dozens of monographs on the flowers that flourish there. Indeed, there is not a thing that grows that may not furnish a monograph. The author spends perhaps twenty years in collecting his material, during which time he must of course come across a great variety of amusing information, and then he spends another ten years writing out a fair copy of his labours. Then he thinks it does not quite do in that form, so he snips a paragraph out of the beginning and puts it at the end; next he shifts some more matter from the middle to the preface; then he thinks it over. It seems to him that it is too big, it wants condensation. The scientific world will say he has made too much of it; it ought to read very slight, and present the facts while concealing the labour. So he sets about removing the superfluous, — leaves out all the personal observations, and all the little adventures he has met with in his investigations; and so, having got it down to the dry bones and stones thereof, and omitted all the mortar that stuck them together, he sends for the engraver, and the next three years are occupied in working up the illustrations. About this time some new discovery is made by a foreign observer, which necessitates a complete revision of the subject, and so having shifted the contents of the book about hither and thither till he does not know which is the end and which is the beginning, he pitches the much-mutilated copy into a drawer and turns the key. Farewell, no more of this; his declining days shall be spent in peace. A few months afterwards a work is announced in Leipsic which "really trenches on my favourite subject, and really after spending a lifetime I can't stand it." By this time his handwriting has become so shaky he can hardly read it himself, so he sends in despair for a lady who works a type-writer, and with infinite patience she makes a clean manuscript of the muddled mass. To the press at last, and the proofs come rapidly. Such a relief! How joyfully easy a thing is when you set about it, but by-and-by this won't do. Sub-section A ought to be in a foot-note, family B is doubtful; and so the corrections grow and run over the margin in a thin treble hand, till they approach the bulk of the original book — a good profit for the printer; and so after about forty years the monograph is published — the work of a life is accomplished. Fifty copies are sent round to as many public libraries and learned societies, and the rest of the impression lies on the shelves till dust and time and spiders' webs have buried it. Splendid work in it too. Looked back upon from to-day with the key of modern thought, these monographs often contain a whole chest of treasure. And still there are the periodicals, a century of magazines and journals and reviews and notices that have been coming out these hundred years and dropping to the ground like dead leaves unnoticed. And then there are the art works—books about shape and colour and ornament, and a naturalist lately has been trying to see how the leaves of one tree look fitted on the boughs of another. Boundless is the wealth of Flora's lap; the ingenuity of man has been weaving wreaths out of it for ages, and still the bottom of the sack is not yet. Nor have we got much news of the dandelion. For I sit on the thrown timber under the trees and meditate, and I want something more: I want the soul of the flowers.

The bee and the butterfly take their pollen and their honey, and the strange moths so curiously coloured, like the curious colouring of the owls, come to them by night, and they turn towards the sun and live their little day, and their petals fall, and where is the soul when the body decays? I want the inner meaning and the understanding of the wild flowers in the meadow. Why are they? What end, what purpose? The plant knows, and sees, and feels; where is its mind when the petal falls? Absorbed in the universal dynamic force, or what? They make no shadow of pretence, these beautiful flowers, of being beautiful for my sake, of bearing honey for me; in short, there does not seem to be any kind of relationship between us, and yet—as I said just now—language does not express the dumb feelings of the mind any more than the flower can speak. I want to know the soul of the flowers, but the word soul does not in the smallest degree convey the meaning of my wish. It is quite inadequate; I must hope that you will grasp the drift of my meaning. All these life-laboured monographs, these classifications, works of Linnaeus, and our own classic Darwin, microscope, physiology, and the flower has not given us its message yet. There are a million books; there are no books: all the books have to be written. What a field! A whole million of books have got to be written. In this sense there are hardly a dozen of them done, and these mere primers. The thoughts of man are like the foraminifera, those minute shells which build up the solid chalk hills and lay the level plain of endless sand; so minute that, save with a powerful lens, you would never imagine the dust on your fingers to be more than dust. The thoughts of man are like these: each to him seems great in his day, but the ages roll, and they shrink till they become triturated dust, and you might, as it were, put a thousand on your thumb-nail. They are not shapeless dust for all that; they are organic, and they build and weld and grow together, till in the passage of time they will make a new earth and a new life. So I think I may say there are no books; the books are yet to be written.

Hamilton Wright Mabie on
Hebrew Poetry, John Burroughs, and
Nature's Record in Language
(1891 and 1897)

Hamilton Wright Mabie was born in Cold Spring, New York, in 1845 or 1846. He earned bachelor's and master's degrees from Williams College, where he did editorial work for the *Williams Quarterly*. He later received a law degree from Columbia and spent eight years at the bar. In 1879 he signed on as an editor for Lyman Abbott's *Christian Union*, which four years later was renamed the *Outlook*; in 1902 he became a contributing editor for the *Ladies' Home Journal*, where for most of his editorial career he labored to provide reading material appropriate for the proper "young lady." As one contemporary put it, "the distinguishing characteristic of his taste was that it was 'correct,' rather than good; he conducted young women into the suburbs of literature and left them there."

Among Mabie's many books, of particular interest here are *Nature in New England* (1890), *Short Studies in Literature* (1891), *Under the Trees and Elsewhere* (1891), *Essays in Literary Interpretation* (1892), and *Nature and Culture* (1897). As a critic he was indebted to Hyppolite Taine's philosophy of environmental determinism (an idea we will encounter again, notably in the work of D. H. Lawrence and Mary Hunter Austin). Mabie asserts that not only culture but language itself is inextricably bound up with nature:

> The impress of Nature upon man is not only discoverable in the deeps of consciousness and in the bases of character; it shines also on the very surface of all human speech. Men could not, in the nature of things, absorb through their senses and imagination the beauty and significance of the world about them

without reproducing this pervasive influence in every form of speech. The ages in which they were making discovery of Nature were the ages in which they were also creating language,—that most marvellous of all the things they have made.

Thus, Mabie insists, "Man is incomprehensible without Nature, and Nature is incomprehensible apart from man."

The essays below are excerpted from two of Mabie's books—*Short Studies in Literature* (1891) and *Nature and Culture* (1904)—and an article, "John Burroughs," which appeared in *Century Magazine* in 1897.

଼ ଼ ଼

"Nature in Hebrew Poetry," from *Short Studies in Literature*

A very interesting illustration of the development of idea, the broadening and deepening conception of life which, with character, forms the highest achievement of humanity, is to be found in the enlargement of the thought of Nature discoverable in literature. The three great themes of literature are God, Man, and Nature. About these fundamental conceptions all thought has organised itself, and in them all the arts have had their roots. The real history of the world has not been written in dynasties, constitutions, campaigns, and diplomacy; it is to be found in the record of changes of thought concerning these dominant facts. Religions of all kinds have had their origin in conceptions of Deity; and as these conceptions have changed, religious reformations or revolutions have followed. Every form of government has represented an idea of man; and as that idea has changed, governmental overturnings and reconstructions have registered the change. The real difference between monarchy, aristocracy, and democracy is a difference not only of form, but of idea; a difference of conception of the character and position of man in the world.

As a middle ground between God and Man, Nature has been an object of intense interest to men. Her function and influence in the making of civilisation and its arts, have already been indicated; hardly less important has been her appeal to the intelligence and imagination, and the interpretation of her being, which different ages and races have accepted. The Hebrew regarded Nature in a profoundly religious spirit, as the garment of deity; he barely paused to reflect upon the impressive phenomena which he saw about him, or to receive the full disclosure of their beauty, because through them, as through an open window, his eyes sought and found God. In the Book of Job the sublimest aspects of Nature are brought before the mind with a majesty and vividness never paralleled in later literature, but one hardly perceives that he is looking at Nature, so near and awful is the presence of God. These appalling visions of cloud and storm hold one's attention only as the mist through which the mountain is swiftly breaking into view.

The 104th Psalm is perhaps the most adequate and impressive picture of the universe that has ever been made, and it breathes the very genius of the Hebrew race:

> Who coverest thyself with light as with a garment;
> Who stretchest out the heavens like a curtain;
> Who layeth the beams of his chambers in the waters;
> Who maketh the clouds his chariot;
> Who walketh upon the wings of the wind;
> Who maketh winds his messengers,
> His ministers a flaming fire;
> Who laid the foundations of earth,
> That it should not be moved forever.
> Thou coveredst it with the deep as with a vesture;
> The waters stood above the mountains.
> At thy rebuke they fled;
> At the voice of thy thunder they hasted away;
> They went up by the mountains, they went down by the valleys,
> Unto the place which thou hadst founded for them.
>
> . . . .
>
> He appointed the moon for seasons:
> The sun knoweth his going down.
> Thou makest darkness, and it is night;
> Wherein all the beasts of the forest do creep forth.
> The young lions roar after their prey,
> And seek their meat from God.
> The sun ariseth, they get them away,

And lay them down in their dens.
Man goeth forth unto his work
And to his labour until the evening. . . .
These wait all upon thee,
That thou mayest give them their meat in due season.

The sustained sublimity of this poetry is matched only in the Book of Job, and in the words of that prophet of glowing imagination, Isaiah. These great spirits hardly see Nature at all, so near and real is God to them; all visible things are but a mist between them and the Invisible, are but a flowing stream rushing from his hand. "Break forth into singing, ye mountains, O forest and every tree therein," says Isaiah in an ecstasy of adoration. The limitation of this poetry as a representation of Nature lies in the fact that Nature is, in a way, lost in God; it is all profoundly true, infinitely deeper and truer than a great deal of modern thought about Nature; and yet, while it remains un-approached as an expression of the thought of God in Nature, the very clear-ness and majesty with which it sets forth this thought relegates Nature to a secondary place, and makes her an illustration instead of a theme.

There are two ways of bringing the thought of God to the imagination: by making Nature a transparent medium which is consumed in the vision of deity and rolled away like a curtain; and by dwelling upon and spreading out the glory of the visible world with all its phenomena, its forces, its laws, its ma-jestic harmony, and its perfect adjustment of parts so that a deep and beautiful sense of the infinity of divine resource and range and beauty is borne in upon the soul. The first method was that of the Hebrew poets; it consumes the sym-bol in searching for its truth; the very earth goes up in flame before the pres-ence of the Lord. There is another and not less spiritual way, which deepens and broadens the impression of Nature until it is pervaded by the conscious-ness of an unseen presence. The garden is not consumed; it blooms with a beauty deep as the soul of man, and at the eventide God walks in it. This is the poetry of Nature; the Hebrew poetry, notwithstanding the glory with which it crowns Nature for the moment, was the poetry of God. The idea of God shines through Hebrew literature and gives it its unique place. In the development and illustration of that idea it remains unapproached. To that idea all other ideas are subordinated; in the endeavour to receive that idea, and give it fit utterance, the Hebrew genius was absorbed. It was left to other literatures to conceive of Nature as distinct from God, and yet instinct with divine force, radiant with divine beauty, and so charged with divine truth that it becomes a new revelation.

From "John Burroughs"

John Burroughs, like Thoreau, is strictly indigenous; he could not have grown in any other soil. Our literature betrays, in almost every notable work, the presence of foreign influences; but Thoreau and Burroughs have been fed by the soil, and have reproduced in flower and fruit something of its distinctive quality. Of the two, Thoreau had the more thorough formal education; but Burroughs shows keener susceptibility to formative influences of all kinds. Thoreau had the harder mind, the nature of greater resisting power; Burroughs is more sensitive to the atmosphere of his time, to the proximity of his fellows, and to the charms of art. Thoreau would have devoted more time to a woodchuck than to Carlyle, Arnold, or Whitman; Burroughs emphasized his indebtedness to Wordsworth, Arnold, Emerson, and Whitman. He has the more open mind, the quicker sympathies, the wider range. If he sometimes strikes us as less incisive and original than Thoreau, he is not less distinctively American, and there is a riper and saner quality in him. In Thoreau one is constantly aware of the element of wild life which still survives on this new continent. In Burroughs one feels the domesticity of nature; one is aware at all times of the simple, natural background of American life. In nothing is Burroughs's freedom from academic and literary tradition more evident than in the quality of homeliness which runs through his work. He writes in his shirt-sleeves, and is not ashamed of it; on the contrary, he believes that the only real writing is done by men who speak unaffectedly out of the conditions which form their natural environment. He can admire an academician who is an academician by nature; but he has no sympathy with the man who exchanges his native dialect for a speech which has greater precision and eloquence, but which is not a part of himself. . . .

To look at nature with the inward as well as with the outward eye is the distinctive gift of the writer, who not only sees what other men fail to observe, but who gives his record of what he sees the quality of his personality. It is a significant fact in Mr. Burroughs's early history that he tapped the maple-trees, and secured the earliest market for his sugar, in order that he might buy text-books. Thus early did he lay nature under contribution for his education; and from the days when he whipped the brooks, as his grandfather had done before him, to these days when he has come to hold the foremost place among living American writers about nature, that education has been uninterrupted and productive. He has not only steadily broadened his own vision, but he has shared his divinations and discoveries with an increasing number who find Thoreau a little too aboriginal and remote. For Thoreau often treats nature like a peasant proprietor whose love of the soil has a touch of fanatical exclusiveness, and sets up prohibitory notices and spring-guns at all approaches. He makes the conditions of acquaintance with nature so hard that we are constantly tempted to ask whether an entire surrender of civilization is not too great a price to pay, even for so great a privilege. There is something exclusive and divisive in the attitude of the recluse of Walden, which provokes the doubt as to whether a man cannot pay his taxes *and* learn all that nature has to impart for his discipline, instruction, and enrichment. We find ourselves asking what shall we gain if we make a new schism. Nature was long under the ban. Now that the two sides of life have been brought together, must civilization go to the wall in order that men may live again in complete and vital relation with nature? In Thoreau individualism runs to extremes, and he pays the penalty imposed on puritanism in a partial and one-sided view of life. He is a schismatic, as his fathers were before him, because he divides the human activities and resources instead of conceiving of them as constituting an organic whole. Genuine fellowship with nature does not involve renunciation of the gains and resources of civilization; a man need not strip himself bare and revert to a savage type in order to get back to nature. It is natural to live the free, joyous life of the instincts and the senses, to seek silence and solitude, to love the smell of the earth and the sweep of the sky; but it is equally natural to live the life of thought, knowledge, taste, culture. It is natural to be born in "a state of nature"; but it is equally natural to grow out of that state into something fuller and higher, and civilization, in its essential quality, is nothing but growth. The seed and the blade are natural, and so also are the flower and the fruit.

This saner and deeper, if less striking, view of nature is presented by John Burroughs. He is not a schismatic; he is a harmonizer. He has no great love for cities, but he does not lose his poise and fall to cursing when he thinks of London or Boston or New York. He sees clearly enough the shams, the hypocrisies, the artificialities, which flourish among men organized into society; but he does not therefore leap to the conclusion that civilization is a

sham or an artifice. He knows the supreme value in education of the solitude, the silence, the detachment of nature from all personal ties and all
individual life; but he knows also that what one learns in the woods finds its
closest readers in cities; that the spring of inspiration is hidden in the personality, but that it misses its great function of fertilization unless its current
flows into organized human life; that man cannot be wholly sane and complete apart from nature, but that sanity and perfection are also conditional
upon human relationship. Burroughs is less radical than Thoreau, but he is
more fundamental; his point of view is less striking, but it is sounder.

"The Record in Language," from *Nature and Culture*

The impress of Nature upon man is not only discoverable in the deeps of
consciousness and in the bases of character; it shines also on the very surface
of all human speech. Men could not, in the nature of things, absorb through
their senses and imagination the beauty and significance of the world about
them without reproducing this pervasive influence in every form of speech.
The ages in which they were making discovery of Nature were the ages in
which they were also creating language,—that most marvellous of all the
things they have made. Words are so familiar that we have largely lost their
first associations, their primary meanings; but when we recover these for a
moment, the "faded metaphor" glows again with the light of its earliest poetic substance. Indeed, it is only when we rescue language from the insensibility to its far-reaching relationships brought about by constant use that we
realize how poetic the language-makers were, and how great a part the imagination played in the making of language. For language is not only largely
faded metaphor, but it is largely a product of man's thought about Nature.
The more closely it is studied the more intimate the intercourse between
men and Nature is seen to have been, and the more distinct becomes the
fact that Nature not only educated men in all manner of skills and arts, but
that she furnished them with complete illustration of their inward life by
analogy, symbol, and vital processes of every kind.

So closely do we stand to the material order about us, and so fundamental
is the correspondence between that order and the facts and processes of our
lives, that primeval men did not separate them in thought. Nature was divine
to them, as she will become again to their later descendants, because she was

part of themselves; without her they could not have understood what was going on within their own souls; without the aid she offered them they would have been powerless to express themselves. They had not made that distinction between matter and spirit, which, as commonly understood, has brought so much confusion into thought by making spirit vague and unreal, and matter dead and sensual.

Science has been radically changing this conception of matter of late years, until the materialistic idea of the world is swiftly fading in the presence of a conception which has not only spiritualized matter, but is fast bringing back the world to the place given it by the earliest men. They rested unconsciously in that unity to which we are slowly working our way back through more intimate and exact knowledge. In the childhood of the race, when all things were explained by the imagination, and men projected themselves into Nature as freely and as unconsciously as they looked at the stars or listened to the sea, the outward material fact seemed the necessary picture or symbol of the inward spiritual process, and Nature was the great parable by which man explained himself and fashioned an adequate instrument of expression of himself.

In Nature he found the constant illustration of his intellectual, moral, and emotional life. His language was, therefore, a series of metaphors suggested by natural facts or by his relations to them. To do right was not, in his thought, an abstract thing; it was going in a straight line: and to do wrong was similarly concrete, for it was to take a crooked course. Spirit, so often elusive and intangible to modern men, was the wind to him; something unseen, but unmistakably real; invisible, but of vast range of power; intangible, but all-pervasive.

The words which are borrowed from natural phenomena or processes, to express spiritual phenomena or processes, are numberless; they form the base of every language. But the intimacy of men with Nature is evidenced not less impressively by the great series of metaphors which bring before the mind the spirit or character of a man, a thought, a feeling, or an action, by reference to some appearance or fact of Nature. The world over, in figure, fable, and parable, Nature is drawn upon to set in clear, strong light human character and action. The wolf is everywhere the synonym for hunger and want, the fox for cunning, the ox for patience, the eagle for audacity, the lion for strength, the serpent for malice. In like manner, the higher and subtler ideas find their most striking and effective illustrations in natural phenomena. In all languages the sky is the symbol of purity, vastness, inclusiveness; the sea, of restlessness; the mountain, of solidity and majesty; the stars, of clearness and fixity; light and darkness, of good and evil, of ignorance and knowledge. So general and so constant is the use of these figures that they form a kind of universal element in all languages; and the more we study them, the more clearly do we perceive that Nature has furnished man with a complete commentary on himself, and that language is a sublime registry of an intimacy once so close and so long continued as to constitute a substantial unity between those who shared it.

As thought clarifies, and deals more and more definitely with the spiritual aspects of man's life, Nature does not recede, but advances with still deeper and more wonderful illustration of these higher phases of the life of her children. Homer had a notable gift for vivid illustration from Nature, and the "Iliad" especially is lighted from beginning to end with bold or beautiful metaphors. But it is in the Bibles of the race, in the Old Testament and the Vedic Hymns, that Nature matches the loftiest thought of man. In these great revelations of the human spirit the obvious illustrations, which children still discover in their games, give place to the perception of that profounder meaning in phenomena and process which makes Nature one great and luminous symbol of the life of man. When the mind has passed through the earlier stages of observation by the senses and discovery through the imagination, there dawns on man a vaster and deeper conception of the world about him and of his relation to it. The order, the force, the beauty, the sublimity of that world become the garment of God to him; and in this unspeakable splendor which enfolds him he sees the sublime pageant of a life not less divine than his own, and flooding him on every side with light on his own nature and destiny. In this stage of his growth Nature enters his speech in a thousand forms, to help him express the highest thought that is in him. Stars, mountains, seas, the infinite heavens, become then the obvious symbols of the life of the spirit. In the book of Job the universe moves before the imagination as with the breath of God; and in the New Testament, when Paul — that great poet struggling with the prose of a dialectic period — would picture man in the mysterious and awful transformation from the earthly to the heavenly, he invokes the aid of Nature, and carries conviction in the familiar image of one of the most familiar natural processes, — "it is sown a natural body; it is raised a spiritual body."

Selden Whitcomb on
Nature in Early American Literature
(1893)

Born in Grinnell, Iowa, in 1866, Selden Lincoln Whitcomb earned a bachelor's degree from Iowa College (now Grinnell) and a master's from Columbia University. He later studied at Cornell, Harvard, and the University of Chicago. After teaching at a series of small midwestern colleges — including Grinnell and what was then called Iowa State Teachers College — he settled in at the University of Kansas, where he edited the journal *Humanistic Studies*. He wrote two scholarly monographs, *Chronological Outlines of American Literature* (1894) and *The Study of the Novel* (1905), as well as several books of poetry.

In the essay below, which appeared in the *Sewanee Review* in 1893, Whitcomb searches early American literature for "indications that our slowly awakening literary personality was coming to consciousness." Taking for granted that the "comparatively minute distinction of different emotional and ethical values in the phenomena of nature is in the course of true progress," a harbinger of "genuine culture as distinguished from a merely haphazard intelligence," he approaches the treatment of nature in early Anglo-American literature as an indicator of the nation's "literary independence" — of the existence of a genuinely *American* literature freed from British models and sensibilities. "As our national life has deepened," he writes, "as it has grown away from the restraints of false and foreign domination, more and more the nobler yearnings of man's spirit have asserted themselves" — and for Whitcomb, as for such later critics as Norman Foerster, what most engaged the "American spirit" was an acute sensitivity to American nature.

87

The subject of the present paper is not one of a dozen that might be selected as equally illustrative of the development of our literature. The spirit in which an author looks upon external nature reveals in a peculiar way the delicacy of his perception in general and particularly his relations to the literary standards which have been accepted by other men under other circumstances. In a word, it is as good a single test as can easily be found, of the most essential and undying power of literature — its sincerity. It is proposed here to apply this test to the early literature of our own country, and it should be noted that literature in one of its noblest aspects may be best regarded as a social institution, having its origin and growth among the people who are to utilize it as a means of progress and of a common spiritual life. In America the order of development has been political independence, commercial independence, social independence, and lastly literary independence, not even yet entirely achieved.

It may be possible to distinguish certain steps or gradations in the early development of our observation of nature. There was first a growth leading from the more material, business point of view, to that in which the free spirit of man finds in nature something partaking of his own rich emotional and intellectual life, something which he may not utilize, perhaps, or fully understand, but which yields him sympathy and inspiration. The principal purpose of the early travellers and explorers was to enlighten the world, to advance men's knowledge concerning the distinguishing features and characteristic flora and fauna of newly discovered regions. This noble motive was, however, too often contaminated by the desire for mere commercial or territorial gains. Travellers were tempted to exaggerate, because much was expected by those who awaited the returns at home; there was a tendency to be somewhat inaccurate, because so much must be done in a short time and because there was no one at hand to contradict. Very frequently they underwent the most severe experiences; what they yield us is won after suffering, fatigue, distrust, and perplexity. Books of travel can, then, rarely be considered literature in the higher sense of the word, but it is not out of place to include them in a general survey of what people wrote and read in some past period. Naturally enough the traveller with his book is very prominent in the early history of America.

But the class just mentioned were wayfarers in the land. Their abiding place was elsewhere, and the more fruitful intimacies with nature were denied them. Time passed and into the new regions came bands of men who

made their home there, who labored to understand the mysteries surrounding them, not for the sake of giving information or profit to a distant people,
but in order to subdue nature and compel her to yield them the wherewithal
to exist. Their relations with the weather, with animal and vegetable life, with
rock, river and soil, were close and continuous, but they selected for closest
examination only those phenomena that were important in the solution of
pressing problems. They tested the soil to find whether it would yield its
productive powers to certain kinds of seed; they rooted out the plant that was
noxious to agricultural processes, however attractive it might have been to
the man in search of the beautiful. Nature was indeed in many respects more
familiar to them than to the ordinary traveller, but it was a familiarity which
too often bred contempt — a professional intercourse, not fruitful in literature, because it had no ulterior and universal meaning.

With the next step our forefathers passed from a merely professional and
necessary acquaintance with nature to one which is for all men and all time,
and embraces every phenomenon, however minute, however ugly, however
difficult to examine — the step which the scientist makes. It is not always easy
to indicate the exact point where the observation of nature ceases to be scientific and becomes artistic or poetic. The scientist, pure and simple, seems
to stand (in a scale of aesthetic or emotional values), next to the old-school
naturalists, these being followed by the writers whom we have learned to call
poet-naturalists, then by the poets themselves, and finally by a small, select
group whose absorption in nature is even deeper than that of the ordinary
poet. We may, perhaps, call this last class nature-mystics. Among their number are a few rare, hardly healthy minds, like Thoreau and Jones Very.

The distinction between a scientific and a poetic observation of nature is
generally said to rest in the personal quality of the poet's experience, the
absolutely objective and unbiased attitude of the scientist. Certainly in all
the higher forms of art produced under a direct inspiration from nature, the
emotional element is a strong one, and the whole personality of the observer
is awakened, not his intellect merely. But if it is to be an emotion that awak-
ens a sympathetic throb in other men, in distant times and places, it must
rest upon no freakish, sudden, and untested experience. Hamerton, in his
Intellectual Life, speaks of that class of amateur artists who wake up some
fine, sunshiny day, and feeling the quickening influence in their veins, go
forth with easel and brush to sit by the stream's side and paint their inspiration upon canvas. Great artists are not so made; they require the experience

of a thousand preparative days of toil and common-place results before the day of success arrives. There was need, then, for a class of men and women who should live more or less habitually with nature; who should have as close and permanent a contact with it as the pioneers, but in a different mood, and with a different purpose and result. Out-of-door life becomes to such people a daily influence, a recognized element in thought and emotion, and they are willing to partake of the dullness of nature as well as of her inspiration in the days when "the genius of God doth flow." Nature has been transformed for them and for us through them, and we perceive her uncovered face, worthy of eternal study and eternal reverence. She is no longer an enemy, no longer a mere teacher or chance acquaintance, but a friend who shares the inner life with us.

In order to contrast the scientific, or semi-scientific record of a single phenomenon in nature with that form of description in which the artistic quality — the personal, emotional element — is strong, let us examine the following verses. About 1690, Thomas Makin, a school teacher of Pennsylvania, described the singing of the mocking-bird in these words:

> Hic avis est quaedam dulci celeberrima voce,
> Quae variare sonos usque canendo solet.

In "Evangeline," Longfellow has, with the same event of nature before him, given us the lines:

> Then from a neighboring thicket, the mocking-bird, wildest of singers,
> Swinging aloft on a willow spray that hung o'er the water,
> Shook from his little throat such floods of delicious music,
> That the whole air and the woods and the waves seemed silent to listen.
> Plaintive at first were the trees and sad; then soaring to madness
> Seemed they to follow or guide the revel of frenzied Bacchantes.
> Single notes were heard in sorrowful, low lamentations;
> Till, having gathered them all, he flung them abroad in derision,
> As when, after a storm, a gust of wind through the tree-tops,
> Shakes down the rattling rain in a crystal shower on the branches.

A second series of steps may be further distinguished, progressing from the observation of the plainer features of nature — such as the coloring of the autumn foliage — to the contemplation of those natural phenomena that are revealed only to the careful student and the genuine lover. If the first series

indicated a growing purification of motive, the second marks the approach
to a true and reliable method. Very early in the history of American literature
we find the great streams enrolled — the Hudson, the James, and the Mississippi. The uncertainty of our weather, the severity and long duration of the
New England winter, at once found mention in annals and poems, or attempts at poems. The humming-bird by its beauty and marvelously built
frame, the whippoorwill by its strange, foreboding evening note, the robin by
his nest-building on every tree in the village, the passenger-pigeons by their
multitudinous migrations — all were very soon well known to the settlers. But
let us take a still more definite example of what is meant by progress in detailed observation. A German traveller in our country wrote near the beginning of this century:

> In the thrush kind America is poor; there is only the red-breasted robin, which
> is very common, that can be accounted of that number. There are no sparrows.
> Very few birds nest in the woods; a solemn stillness prevails throughout them,
> interrupted only by the screaming of crows.

Now any lover of birds at the present day, who pretends to familiarity with
them in their haunts, recognizes at least three thrushes besides the robin,
which are beautiful singers, and whose quality of song is strongly individual.
He can mention several, stopping to think, from twelve to twenty distinct
species of sparrows, (i.e., of the sparrow family), all of which he knows not
merely as one in search of scientific facts, but as a lover of the finer shadings
in nature's harmony. The comparatively minute distinction of different emotional and ethical values in the phenomena of nature is in the course of true
progress. It marks genuine culture as distinguished from a merely haphazard
intelligence, and becomes objectionable only at the point where all analysis
does — when in the attention to details the larger outlines are obscured, when
the means becomes an end, and the method a cult.[1]

It has been customary with many writers, though I believe the latest historians question somewhat the utility of the tradition, to indicate a strong
contrast between the colonists of Massachusetts and those of Virginia. Certain differences are, however, well established, and they are of great importance in the treatment of our topic. Let us turn for a moment to the conditions in Virginia. Society there was not so democratic as it was in Plymouth
and neighboring towns. The higher aristocratic circles looked upon nature

as English country gentlemen are inclined to view it—as a portion of the vast estate which Providence has kindly given into their keeping as a pleasure ground; a region for fox hunting and sport generally. The background of the life of a Virginia squire was society and politics, as the background of existence to a New England divine was the Church and scholarly industry. The love of the chase and of horse racing, even the zeal of Jefferson in promoting scientific exploration, though most valuable in their way, were very far removed from the mental attitude toward *out-doordom* of Thoreau or Burroughs. The hero of Jamestown's early history recorded many an event of those pioneer days, possibly gave place to one or two that happened only in his own stalwart imagination. Here is a touch of local color which may serve to illustrate the way in which John Smith opened his eyes along the banks of the Chickahominy:

> On both sides in the very neck of the Maine are high hills and dales, yet much inhabited, the Ile declining in a plaine fertile corne field, the lower end a marsh; more plentie of swannes, cranes, geese, duckes, and mallards, and diverse sorts of fowles none would desire.

The Pilgrims and Puritans believed that they had found the *unum necessarium* for which the Anglo-Saxon mind is always searching, in a religious life directed by a free conscience. They regarded the body and its material environment as dust and ashes, enemies of the soul, phenomena which the breath of God would one day wipe away. They explored the innermost recesses of their consciousness to find some germ of rebellion against God, but they did not so readily explore the branches of a tree to see if they might find there the nest of some tiny warbler. To the Puritan mind Thoreau gathering berries with the children along the Concord roadside, Audubon standing for hours up to his waist in a swamp, watching a tiny bird build its nest, are ridiculous figures; it learns with difficulty the lesson of deep wisdom conveyed in a sentence of La Fontaine's, "One needs the lesser being." The moralizing tone of one who is professing simply to examine the operations of nature, does not necessarily offend us; only it must be sincere and personal, not the mere echo of a convention, the insertion of something for the sake of answering the expectations of the pious. Even in reading Bryant, we do not always feel that the moral grows naturally and inevitably out of the events of nature which have produced in him a poetic exaltation. We are inclined to suspect most men of insincerity or of dull vision, if in every slight observation they make of nature, they perceive at once a special dispensation of Providence. The old "argument from design" is not yet lost, but it rests upon far broader and deeper grounds than it did even at the beginning of the century.

Yet with all this restriction it has been the New Englander who has done the most to record and explain the life of bird and plant and insect in the spirit of the poet and the poet-naturalist. In "Our Forefather's Song" which has been traced as far back as 1630, there are several references to the relations of the colonists with nature. They may not be considered very poetical, but they give us a great deal of solid information. Of the maize it is said:

> And when it is come to full corn in the ear
> It is often destroyed by raccoon and by deer.

And here are a few lines in which every person with New England blood in his veins will see a vision of Thanksgiving time:

> Our pumpkins and parsnips are common supplies,
> We have pumpkins at morning, pumpkins at
>   noon,
> If it was not for pumpkins we should be undone.
> If barley be wanting to make into malt
> We must be contented and think it no fault,
> For we can make liquor to sweeten our lips
> Of pumpkins and parsnips and walnut tree chips.

There appeared, also, in New England very soon after the founding of Plymouth, a woman poet who was so fortunate as to win the title of "The Tenth Muse." Mrs. Anne Bradstreet seems to have aimed at making a universal encyclopædia of her book of poetry. In fact, it is a liberal education to read even the title. Yet in the midst of long, pedantic dissertations on the four monarchies of antiquity, and summaries of all that was known about the four elements, we find slight but genuine touches of nature. The poetess appears sometimes to have forgot that she was not upon the soil of Old England, and yet it was probably from her own observations that she wrote:

> I heard the merry grasshopper then sing,
> The black-clad cricket bear a second part;
> They kept one tune and played on the same string,
> Seeming to glory in their little art.

She noted also that:

> The primrose pale and azure violet
> Among the verdurous grass hath nature set. . . .
> The fearful bird his little house now builds
> In trees and walls, in cities and in fields;
> The outside strong, the inside warm and neat.

Omitting all mention of numerous minor writers who flourished in the seventeenth century and in the early part of the eighteenth, I pass to one whose name is familiar, at least to all lovers of botany. John Bartram, from the importance of his historical position, and no less from the inherent interest of his career, deserves to be considered a classical figure among our early naturalists. He began, in 1734, a correspondence with Peter Collinson, of London, which continued for over a generation, and at various times he was in communication with many of the most learned men of science in America and in Europe. Franklin was his personal friend and Linnaeus called him the greatest self-taught botanist in the world. The good Quaker's interest in plants was largely a practical one. His letters reveal little that has the charm of White's "Natural History of Selborne," which was being written about the same time that John Bartram was coming into prominent notice. . . .

But there was living in America at the time when Franklin and other sober minded men were listening with intense anxiety to the mutterings of the coming Revolution, a genuine man of letters and one who had deep sympathy with the life of nature, Hector St. John de Crevecoeur, born a Frenchman, the author of *Letters from an American Farmer*. No man in America who has left any records to posterity from the eighteenth century, reveals a spirit more akin to that of the poet-naturalists of our own day. Yet he was entirely a man of his own times, breathing the atmosphere of *Paul and Virginia* and *Studies from Nature*, and showing the unmistakable influence of Rousseau. In a singularly charming style he idealizes the agricultural life in the colonies just prior to the separation from the mother country — idealizes and yet pictures with a fidelity growing out of actual and long continued acquaintance. He says of his letters: "If they be not elegant, they will smell of the woods and be a little wild," and he is, in general, true to his promise. He wishes to put "on paper a few American wild cherry trees, such as nature forms them here, in all her unconfined vigor, in all the amplitude of their extended limbs and spreading ramifications." When Burns was but a lad entering his teens, this husbandman of New York declared the possibility of a union of plowman and man of letters: "After all why should not a farmer be allowed to make use of his mental faculties as well as others? Because a man works is he not to think, and if he thinks usefully why should he not in his leisure hours set down his thoughts? I have composed many a good sermon as I followed my plow," and he proceeds to give the highest praise to the art of tilling as an aid to reflection. In beautiful and adequate language he gives many of the picturesque details of the farmer's life; shows us his little boy seated gleefully upon a chair which is attached to the swaying plow; shares with us his doubt as to whether he ought to consider the kingbirds friends or enemies. The severities of winter drive the quails to his barn door, where he permits them to search for grain in security. While his less sympathizing neighbors are perhaps trapping the defenceless birds, he is carrying food to them as they stand almost freezing "in the angles of the fences where the motion of the wind prevents the snow from settling," and for this trouble he is well repaid by the merry whistlings of the thankful birds which resound across his fields in spring. He traces the vagrant bees to their storehouse of honey in some tree hidden in the depths of the forest, and gives us a relation of the hunt with a picturesqueness which will bear comparison with the corresponding description of Burroughs. He rises regularly in the dim dawn, and it is not the "feathered tribes" which give a charm to the morning hours; it is "the sweet love tales of our robins told from tree to tree," the shrill notes of the catbird, and the melodious voice of the thrush singing from the swaying tree tops. In his piazza, it is not the old-world swallow alone that builds, but also the phoebe bird, as she builds yet, after the lapse of a century and a quarter, after the cannonadings of three great wars. The birds in which he is interested are those that nest, scold, preen their feathers, and teach their young to fly, about his own domicile. A score of writers had already pictured the marvelous tints of the hummingbird, but Crevecoeur does not rest content with what were already commonplaces. He has noticed that "this insect-bird . . . will tear and lacerate flowers into a hundred pieces"; that two humming birds will fight as furiously as wild beasts until one falls a sacrifice to this strange ferocity. And wasps and snakes he has observed with the same accurate and steady eye. . . .[2]

Near the beginning of our century the forces of new, vigorous life which were fermenting in the Old World began to have a wide influence in America. In the decade from 1790 to 1800 Wordsworth had published "An Evening Walk" and "Lyrical Ballads"; Carlyle, Keats, and Shelley had been born; while Cowper's "Task," and the first volume of Burns's poems came in the middle years of the eighties. In America the publication of Brown's early novels, the establishment of Dennie's *Portfolio* in the first year of the new century, and of the Boston *Monthly Anthology*, in 1803, were indications that our slowly awakening literary personality was coming to consciousness.

As editor of the *Portfolio* Dennie gave place to a vast number of pastoral pieces of entirely British tone, but only grudgingly and under a sense of compulsion. He knew what he was about. He accepted, in 1806, a stinging burlesque upon the popular pastoral conventions, and in the first volume of the *Portfolio* he wrote to a contributor: "The pastoral dialogue between two shepherds of Schuylkill we are obliged to reject with some degree of loathing. Nothing can be more insipid than this style of writing. 'The oaten reed' and 'the skipping lamb,' the 'brawling brook' and the 'whispering breeze' are images of most egregious triteness. It is an established rule with the editor when he finds an epitaph upon a "Departed Patriot," "Elegy upon a Dead Girl," or a pastoral, to twirl over the leaf with a sort of instinctive abhorrence." This was unjust to pastoral poetry as a legitimate form of writing, but it was a wholesome dose for the crude and careless versifiers who sent spring effusions to the office in Philadelphia. In inserting a prose or poetical piece which had value because it was distinctively American, Dennie very often pointed out that merit; frequently the author himself noted it. The "Rural Wanderer" in the very first number of the magazine assures us that he is "really a rambler over hills and through glades, along the banks of rivers and in the borders of villages."

After a more or less close study of the *Portfolio* from 1801 to the date of "Thanatopsis," and of the *Anthology* for about half that period, I note three facts which it may be well to specify as evidence of our growing interest and independence in the study of out-door life.

First: There is a noticeable awakening on the part of the more intelligent writers to the facts of our American nature. They had learned that there was a literary and a personal, as well as a scientific meaning in the simple statement of White of Selborne: "It is, I find, in zoology as it is in Botany, all nature is so full that that district produces the greatest variety that is the most examined."

Second: There had arisen a small class of writers who more or less *habitually* reported nature as they personally observed her. They did not, indeed, retire into a semi-seclusion from society as Thoreau did, but out-door life permanently interested them; it was that which gave health and tone to their mental operations, and they found it a source of private and literary inspiration. . . .

Third: About 1807 or 1808, the *Portfolio* began to give its readers an occasional view of American scenery, sketched and engraved by home talent and intended to foster a love for the natural beauty and sublimity lying at our own doors. For a long time previous the claim had been constantly made that our rivers, cataracts, forests, and mountains were as noble as those of foreign lands, and that they were commonly neglected and despised.

The two men whose names stand out most prominently from the oblivion which has kindly covered most of the literary work of the first decade of our century, Charles Brockden Brown and Alexander Wilson, were radically different in their relation to nature, though both were undoubted geniuses, breaking their way through the mists of convention into the sunlight of independence and original effort. Regarding the novelist, the criticism of Richard Henry Dana remains an essentially true one: "Of all men of imagination we know of none who appear from their writings to have looked less at nature or to have been less open to her influences. . . . A power of his kind knows no association with nature; for in the gloomiest and the wildest and the barrenest scenes of nature there is something enlarging and elevating—something that tells us there is an end to all unmixed sorrow."

The story of Alexander Wilson has been told many times and the main outlines of his life are familiar to most reading Americans. But his fame and labor as an ornithologist have unfortunately tended to obscure the fact that he was, as "Christopher North," (in *Blackwood's*) declared him to be, "absolutely a man of literature." His poetry is not so good as his prose, but he continued to write it as long as he lived. In his youth he drank in the spirit of Burns, of nature in Scottish moor and brae. He wandered over many a mile of Scottish sea-coast and mountain, noting the ways of bird and man, the mists on the highlands and the storied ruins of castles. In the year in which Bryant was born, Alexander Wilson landed on the coast of Delaware, a young man not yet thirty, with all the enthusiasm of youth and the incalculable resources of genius. His career from beginning to end will bear an examination such as that of few other men could undergo. Wilson developed in his great work considerable scientific power; as a teacher and as a man of steady intellectual appetite, he did not disdain the labored analyses of the classifiers. But it cannot be too distinctly remembered that what he loved was nature herself. Before the conception of a study of all the birds of this country had matured in his mind, he had written a long descriptive poem, called "The Foresters," which had grown out of his own observations made upon a pedestrian journey to the Falls of Niagara. The trip gave to this man of wide open eyes the possibility of picturing truly many of the most characteristic scenes and customs of what was then a pioneer region.

Wilson was a patriot, a scientist, a poet, something of an artist, but more than all these a lover of nature. It was fitting that a man of his particular passions and achievements should have very early received the distinctive appellation of poet-naturalist.[3] Yet he was still more than poet-naturalist, for he revealed the essential qualities of genius? It is, says Dr. Elliott Coues, creating a definition which would be true of Alexander Wilson, "that union of Passion and Patience, which bears fruit unknown to Passion alone, to Patience alone impossible."

The year after Wilson had published his prospectus for the *American Ornithology*, there appeared in the *Monthly Anthology* (June, 1808) a criticism of a poem, called "The Embargo" and purporting to have been written by a lad of thirteen. The reviewer is in general favorable and is kind enough to say: "If the young bard has met with no assistance in the composition of the poem, he certainly bids fair, should he continue to cultivate his talent, to gain a respectable station on the Parnassian mount and to reflect credit on the literature of his country." But it was by no mere cultivation of the muse which gave birth to "The Embargo," a political satire after the manner of Pope, that five years later the boy of seventeen was able to write "Thanatopsis." Mighty influences were at work upon Bryant. He began to feel the throb of the new and higher spirit of poetry that ruled in the "Lyrical Ballads."

Nature also, whom he had loved from childhood and with whom he lived at peace, in a growing sympathy, overpowered the monarch of the Augustan Age. The transition from "The Embargo" to "Thanatopsis" is not a development; it is a revolution, a new birth; the declaration of a spiritual being. Though still moralizing and retaining to some extent a conventional tone, Bryant in "Thanatopsis" threw off the yoke of academic authority and ecclesiasticism. He looked upon the endless procession journeying to the silent halls, under the limitations of the Anglo-Saxon race, if you will, but no longer as a literary feigner, no longer merely as a Puritan. "Thanatopsis" was composed under the influences of actual New England skies and forests, yet it has a trace more of subservience to British tradition than "The Yellow Violet" which was written in 1814. With that poem we may well begin a new era in the influence of nature upon our literature. Bryant was the giant among his compeers, but he was not alone in his studies afield. A host of minor singers flourished about this time, who felt the breath of the wind on their brows — Wilcox, Sprague, Drake, Hillhouse, Percival, Prentice, and Fitz-Greene Halleck among them. The old era had passed away, both in England and in America. Brown, Dennie, and Wilson, the three men who had made Philadelphia a literary centre of no mean significance, died within a few years of each other, at just the time when "Childe Harold" and "Queen Mab" appeared. The year of "The Yellow Violet" saw "Waverly" and "The Excursion."

The results of this study of the early development of the observation of nature in America are not extensive, yet the progress of the investigation itself may not have been valueless. Over and over again it is necessary to learn the lesson that the true evolution of literature and of society knows no real cataclysm. From the beginning of colonization until the present day, there have been writers in America seeing with interest and with pleasure what nature has set before their eyes; whose conscious life has been, to a greater or less extent, molded by her constant presence. As our national life has deepened, as it has grown away from the restraints of false and foreign domination, more and more the nobler yearnings of man's spirit have asserted themselves. All that was genuine in our early poetry and prose, however humble and imperfect, had a share in the influences which made possible Bryant, Emerson, Thoreau, Whitman, and gave to each a loving, understanding audience. We need have no regrets for the loss of so much of the literature of nature as lacked sincerity. It is not dead. It is simply non-existent, for as Thoreau said, "in order to die, it is necessary first *to have lived*."

NOTES

1. See the very admirable explanation of what a "love of nature" ought to mean, in Mrs. Van Rensselaer's *Art Out of Doors*, chapter xv.

2. Hazlitt contributed an excellent criticism of Crevecoeur to the *Edinburgh Review* for 1829. I regret that considerations of space prevent citation from it as well as any description of the pathos of Crevecoeur's last years.

3. I have the impression that this name was first used in characterizing him; it was certainly given to him before Thoreau had won it.

Mary Woolley on the
Love of Romantic Scenery in America
(1897)

The early feminist and activist Mary Emma Woolley was born in 1863 in South Norwalk, Connecticut. In 1882 she entered what was then Wheaton Seminary; after graduating in 1884, she returned as a member of the faculty and taught there for several years. In 1891 she became the first woman to enroll at Brown University, where she received a bachelor's degree in 1894 and a master's the following year. She taught for the next several years at Wellesley. In 1900, at the age of just thirty-seven and after declining an offer to become dean of what by then had become the Women's College at Brown, she was named president of Mount Holyoke College.

During her long tenure at Mount Holyoke, Woolley proved both an able administrator and a politically engaged academic. She increased the school's endowment nearly tenfold, liberalized regulations governing student life, expanded graduate programs, and significantly increased the size, educational level, and salaries of the faculty. She served as an officer of the American Civil Liberties Union, working in that capacity to help defend Sacco and Vanzetti; she was also a member of the advisory council of the American Association for Labor Legislation, which urged women to boycott goods produced in sweatshops. An early peace activist, Woolley publicly supported American membership in the League of Nations, served as a vice-president of the American Peace Society, and chaired the People's Mandate to End War. In 1932, she was named by President Hoover an official delegate to the Conference on Reduction and Limitation of Armaments — becoming perhaps the first woman to represent the United States at such a high-level diplomatic event.

Woolley was also a prominent feminist. In 1906 she delivered a speech before the National American Woman's Suffrage Association at a fete honoring Susan B. Anthony; two years later she helped form the National College Women's Equal Suffrage League. For five years she served as president of the American Association of University Women. Later she was a prominent member of the National Women's Party and an early supporter of the proposed Equal Rights Amendment.

Woolley's three published scholarly studies are meticulously researched and cautiously argued, exemplars of the literary-historical model then favored in the academy. The essay excerpted below, which appeared in 1897 in the *American Historical Review,* attempts to pin down just when Anglo-Americans developed the romantic feeling for wild nature. Woolley concludes that this change took place "within a definitely limited time," roughly around the time of the Revolution, and that it "was spontaneous or indigenous," relatively independent of similar changes in sensibility in Europe.

🪷 🪷 🪷

Friedländer and others have made it a familiar thought that admiration and affection for wild and romantic scenery are modern feelings, belonging chiefly to the period since the middle of the last century. Among the ancients, isolated instances of such feelings may be found, but are certainly extremely rare. Their admiration was reserved for cultivated scenery, mild and gentle, meadows and orchards and lawns and springs. A characteristic passage is that in which Cicero notes as remarkable, that we take pleasure in places where we have long sojourned, *even though* they be mountainous and wooded. The medieval writers were, almost without exception, subject to the same limitations. Indifference to wild and mountainous scenery, abhorrence even, continued to be almost universal throughout the sixteenth and seventeenth centuries, and indeed until after the middle of the eighteenth. Montaigne and Addison passed over the Alps without recorded sign of pleasure. Goldsmith, after visiting the Highlands of Scotland, wrote in disgust that "every part of the country presents the same dismal landscape," while soon afterward he wrote of Holland that "nothing can equal its beauty. Wherever I turned my eye, fine houses, elegant gardens, statues, grottos, vistas presented themselves. Scotland and this country bear the highest contrast; there, hills and rocks intercept every prospect; here it is all a continued plain." If a few passages in certain poems be left out of account, it may fairly be said that the modern feeling with respect to wild scenery was virtually non-existent at the time when these words were written (1754). It was in the next year that the youthful Gibbon made the tour of Switzerland, and the manner in which, writing his autobiography thirty years later, he speaks of these travels, is plain evidence that the great change came about, substantially, within a generation. In every place he visited the churches, arsenals, libraries, and all the most eminent persons; he examined Switzerland after the same manner in which he would have examined a country that had no scenery. "The fashion of climbing the mountains and reviewing the glaciers," he says, "had not yet been introduced by foreign travellers who seek the sublime beauties of nature." The *Nouvelle Héloise* was published in 1759. A generation later, before Gibbon had died, came that time in Wordsworth's youth which he has described in the lines written near Tintern Abbey, when

> The sounding cataract
> Haunted me like a passion: the tall rock,
> The mountain, and the deep and gloomy wood,
> Their colours and their forms, were then to me
> An appetite; a feeling and a love,
> That had no need of a remoter charm,
> By thought supplied, nor any interest
> Unborrowed from the eye.

And Wordsworth, and others like-minded with him, have taught to all subsequent generations a passionate love of wild and romantic scenery which sharply differentiates the modern feeling for nature from that of earlier times.

The history of this development has been traced in English and other European literatures. It is of some interest to examine its course in America. Shall we find such a change supervening, here also, within a limited time? Shall we find it proceeding spontaneously or by imitation? If the former, we may find in it some confirmation of that opinion which seems wisest in the European case, that this modern attitude toward nature arose not by the influence of Rousseau or any one writer, but that the change was one phase of that general "modulation of key" which we call the romantic movement. To the questions thus put, the travellers and the poets will furnish the best answers; and among travellers it is plain that those who are distinctively American will deserve the greatest weight.

Travellers to the colonies in the seventeenth and eighteenth centuries were fond of recording their experiences in the new country, but most of them confined their descriptions to the social, economic, political and religious characteristics, with an occasional digression into the fields of geography or natural history. If they spoke of the land, it was generally with reference to its productive capacity, the wheat or tobacco which a given region yielded. There were chapters devoted to the climate, the soil, rivers and navigation, but not to scenery. Nor did many of them penetrate into the interior, where the wild scenery was to be found. But even those who braved the difficulties of inland discovery seem little impressed by anything save the horror and desolation of the region.

The first visit to the White Mountains, then called the Crystal or White Hills, seems without doubt to have been made in 1642, when Darby Field, an Irishman, in company with several others, ascended them, hoping to find minerals of value. The account as given by Winthrop in his history of New England is as follows.

"In the same year, 1642, one Darby Field, an Irishman, with some others travelled to an high mountain, called the White Hills, an hundred miles or near upon to the west of Saco. It is the highest hill in these parts of America. They passed there many of the lower and rainy clouds as they ascended up to the top thereof, but some that were there afterwards saw clouds above them. There is a plain of sixty feet square on the top, a very steep precipice on the west side, and all the country round about them seemed like a level and much beneath them. There was a great expectation of some precious things to be found, either on the top or in the ascent, by the glistering of some white stones. Something was found like crystal, but nothing of value."

There is not a word of the grandeur of the scenery, no reference to that which is romantic or picturesque, only a bare statement of facts as to situation, the dimensions of the plain and the steepness of the precipice.

Travellers to this region were not numerous during the seventeenth century. The Indians had a superstitious veneration for the summit, as the habitation of invisible beings, and not only never ventured to ascend it themselves, but also endeavored to dissuade everyone from the attempt. They were most earnest in their entreaties to Darby Field not to undertake the daring feat and thus stir up the wrath of the gods. The first visitor to leave an account of his journey in print was John Josselyn, the naturalist, who visited the mountains between 1663 and 1671, and from whom, in another age, we might expect a glowing account, or at least some allusion to the impression produced upon him by their grandeur. In his *New England Rarities Discovered* he says: "From this rocky hill you may see the whole country round about; it is far above the lower Clouds and from hence we beheld a vapor (like a great Pillar) drawn up by the Sun Beams out of a great Lake or Pond into the Air, where it was formed into a Cloud. The country beyond these Hills northward is daunting terrible, being full of rocky Hills, as thick as mole-hills in a meadow and clothed with infinite thick woods." It is plain that the wilderness impressed him, but not with feelings of admiration.

In his *Relation of Two Voyages to New England* Josselyn tells of a "neighbour" who "rashly wandered out after some stray'd cattle, lost his way, and coming as we conceived by his Relation near to the head spring of some of the branches of the Black Point River or Saco River did light into a Tract of land for God knows how many miles full of delfes and dingles and dangerous precipices, rocks and inextricable difficulties which did justly daunt, yea, quite deter him from endeavoring to pass any further; many such like places are to be met with in New England." Only once is the writer betrayed into an expression which borders upon appreciation of such scenes, and that is a mild reference to "one stately mountain . . . surmounting the rest."

Lahontan, writing of his voyage to America in 1688, speaks of a cataract as "fearful." In the same year John Clayton, a Yorkshire rector, sent to the Royal Society a *Letter giving Account of Several Observables in Virginia*, which contains chapters on the air, water, earth and soil, birds and beasts of Virginia, but not one word describing the natural scenery of the colony. Robert Beverley, who published his history of that colony in 1705, had certainly a vivid feeling for the beauties of nature as he saw them; but as for the mountains, he regards them from a strictly utilitarian point of view. "A little farther backward there are mountains which indeed deserve the Name of Mountains for their Height and Bigness; which by their difficulty in passing may easily be made a good Barrier of the country against Incursions of the Indians, etc., and shew themselves over the Tops of the Trees to many Plantations at 70 or 80 Miles distance very plain. These Hills are not without their Advantages; for out of almost every riseing Ground throughout the Country there issue abundance of most pleasant Streams of pure Chrystal Water, than which certainly the World does not afford any more delicious . . . where the finest water works in the World may be made, at a very small expence."

Daniel Neal, in his *History of New England*, published at London in 1719, in a description of New Hampshire, says: "The Inland part of the country is high and mountainous and consequently barren," a concise, but hardly an appreciative way of disposing of the White Mountains. That mountain scenery had not been reported to him with high laudations may be inferred from a casual remark in his description of Connecticut: "The East parts of this Country are pleasant and fruitful, but the Western are swampy and mountainous." Swamps and mountains were equally undesirable features of a landscape in the minds of our early forefathers. In 1729 Burton's *English Empire in America* appeared. It contains a description of Virginia, but no mention of the Natural Bridge, nor anything to denote an interest in the picturesque and romantic scenery of the colony. Except for the Rev. Andrew Burnaby (1759, 1760), there is perhaps no praise of the American mountains by foreign travellers until the time of the Revolution.

Meanwhile, in sporadic instances we find native expressions of appreciation of wild scenes. In the New York *Colonial Documents* one finds *The Journal and Relation of a New Discovery made behind the Apuleian Mountains to the West of Virginia*, written in 1671, in which we are assured that "In a clear place on the top of a hill [the discoverers] saw over against them to the southwest a curious prospect of hills, like waves raised by a gentle brize, riseing one behind another. . . . They then returned homewards again, but when they were on the Top of the Hill they took a prospect as far as they could view and saw westerly over certain delightful hills." More conclusive in its bearing is the following phrase from the same account: "They had here a pleasing but dreadful sight to see Mts. and Hills piled one upon another." Here is an unmistakable instance of admiration for the grand, the awful — "pleasing but dreadful" is precisely the note of romanticism — and an illustration the more striking because it is the only one which the present writer has discovered in seventeenth-century descriptions of America.

Early in the eighteenth century another instance occurs, again a sporadic one, but explicit. Passages from Col. William Byrd's *History of the Dividing*

Line run in the Year 1728 clearly show that that vivacious writer shared the modern spirit. First, as to the admiration of mountains. "The smoke continued still to veil the mountains from our sight, which made us long for rain, or a brisk gale of wind, to disperse it. Nor was the loss of this wild prospect all our concern." "In the afternoon we marched up again to the top of the hill to entertain our eyes a second time with the view of the mountains, but a perverse fog arose that hid them from our sight." "In the evening a brisk northwester swept all the clouds from the sky, and exposed the mountains, as well as the stars, to our prospect. That which was the most lofty to the southward . . . we called the Lover's Leap." Perhaps even more striking exhibitions of the modern spirit will be thought to lie in the two extracts which follow: "The Irvin runs into the Dan about four miles to the southward of the line, and seemed to roll down its waters from the N.N.W. in a very full and limpid stream, and the murmur it made, in tumbling over the rocks, caused the situation to appear very romantic and had almost made some of the company poetical, though they drank nothing but water." "As we passed along, by favor of a serene sky, we had still, from every eminence, a perfect view of the mountains, as well to the north as to the south. We could not forbear now and then facing about to survey them, as if unwilling to part with a prospect which at the same time, like some rake's, was very wild and very agreeable." This last phrase, whimsically as it is framed, is of precisely the sort we are seeking, strangely as it sounds from a contemporary and friend of Pope. . . .

From the Revolution on, there is little doubt of the general existence of the new sentiment in the cultivated American mind. If it were not impossible to fix upon a definite date for the beginning of movements in the history of mind, one would be tempted to select the years from 1780 to 1785 as the time when this new spirit of admiration for wild and romantic scenery became fully established. Before this, its manifestations had been exceptional; henceforth they are abundant in the writings of both natives and foreigners. Many of the foreign travellers of this period were Frenchmen, and it is perhaps to be expected that they would be among the first to exhibit this tendency. Chastellux's expression (1780–1782) is characteristic: "all this apparatus of rude and shapeless Nature, which Art attempts in vain, attacks at once the senses and the thoughts and excites a gloomy and melancholy admiration." Smyth's *Tour in America* (1784) shows the new tendency even on its title page, "An account of the present situation of the Country . . . Mountains, Forests,

Rivers, and the most beautiful, grand and picturesque Views throughout that vast Continent." If no date were given for the publication of the book this title-page would almost prove that its date was not earlier than the latter half of the eighteenth century. The heading of one of the chapters is: "Description of a most extensive, grand and elegant perspective. Ideas raised in the mind." Before this time most travellers in America had not been burdened by ideas raised in the mind by the scenery.

More interesting to the present purpose, no doubt, are the expressions of American observers in these years. Take, for instance, Jefferson's remarks on the Natural Bridge, in his *Notes on Virginia* (1781–1784). He declares it "the most sublime of Nature's works." "It is impossible," he says, "for the emotions arising from the sublime to be felt beyond what they are here: so beautiful an arch, so elevated, so light, and springing as it were up to Heaven. The rapture of the spectator is really indescribable." The Reverend Archibald Alexander, who as a youth visited it about 1789, speaks of it as exciting in him "an emotion entirely new," "a genuine emotion of the sublime"; and adds, "I never saw one of any class, who did not view the object with considerable emotion." Evidently the taste for such scenery was becoming endemic.

If we turn again to the White Mountains, so little thought of in colonial times, we find the *Belknap Papers* of 1784 a mine of suggestion. In his diary of this year (July 28) Dr. Belknap says of a meadow in the Notch, "This meadow, surrounded on all sides with mountains, some of them perpendicular, is a singularly romantic and picturesque scene." Again, in describing the Notch, he calls it "a most sublimely picturesque and romantic scene." We have already noticed in Smyth's *Tour* a reference to "ideas raised in the mind" by the scenery. This suggestion of a psychological effect we find still more pronounced in Dr. Belknap's descriptions. "These beauties of nature gave me inexpressible delight. The most romantic imagination here finds itself surprised and stagnated. Everything which it had formed an idea of, as sublime and beautiful, is here realized. Stupendous mountains, hanging rocks, chrystal streams, verdant woods, the cascade above, the torrent below, all conspire to amaze, to delight, to soothe, to enrapture; in short to fill the mind with such ideas as every lover of Nature and every devout worshipper of its Author would wish to have." He thinks that "a poetic fancy may find full gratification amidst these wild and rugged scenes, if its ardor be not checked by the fatigue of the approach"; but would caution the observer to "curb the imagination and exercise judgment with mathematical precision, or the temptation to romance will be invincible."

John Eliot, writing to Dr. Belknap, says: "Brother Cutler is romantic in his description, as well as you, in the short touch you gave me in your letter." It was during this year, 1784, that the Reverend Manasseh Cutler, in company with several others, made the first scientific expedition to the White Mountain region, and one is not surprised to find in his journals such memoranda as: "we had here a grand view of ranges of mountains. . . . arising one above another"; "the country to the north very mountainous, and its appearance has a most noble effect."

In the closing decade of the century there is no dearth of expressions of admiration for the picturesque and romantic; indeed they are so common as to give the impression of their being somewhat of a "fad" at the time. . . .

The *Travels* of President Dwight (1797, 1803) show the love of romantic scenery fully developed. It is hard to choose from such a wealth of material, when almost every page of the description of the White Mountains abounds in expressions of admiration for their rugged grandeur. "Mountains in immense ranges, bold spurs and solitary eminences . . . are everywhere dispersed with delightful successions of sublimity and grandeur." Former travellers had carefully avoided the region because of the mountains; Dr. Dwight says, "The scenery in the Notch of the White Mountains . . . was one of the principal objects which had allured us into the region." He is impressed by the "wild and solemn appearance." He personifies the "hoary cliffs" which, "rising with proud supremacy, frowned awfully on the world below." He speaks of the "sprightly murmurs" of the cascade, of the "wild, tumultuous and masterly workmanship of nature," and of her "wild and awful majesty." It would be impossible to find more conclusive evidence of admiration for the romantic in nature than expressions such as "The eye finds here everything which can gratify its wishes for rude, wild and magnificent scenery"; "The scene excelled every conception which they had hitherto formed of awfulness and grandeur"; "bidding adieu, therefore, to the singular combination of wild and awful magnificence, we set out on our return."

We have traced the development of the love of romantic scenery among travellers; a glance at the poets of the eighteenth century will show that its development was certainly not earlier among them. There was no lack of what was called poetry before the Revolution, but it reveals little or no love of romantic scenery. There were poems to Phyllis, Daphne and Amanda, verses political and patriotic, metaphysical and religious, elegies and satires; but poems in praise of nature were few, unless of a much-adorned and cultivated nature in the form of "groves and fertile lawns," of "purling rills" and "prattling streams." It is distinctly the "pleasing landscape" and

> the lawn
> Beaut'ous at morn, at noonday and the dawn;
> Rural shades and groves e'er attract the mind,
> And lead the thoughts to those things that's divine.

A poem read at the Yale commencement of 1784 speaks of Niagara, but as the

> stupendous Niagarian falls
> Which to behold the affrighted heart appalls,

with no sign of pleasure. Early visitors to the falls speak of them in much the same way. Father Hennepin (1697) describes them as a "vast and prodigious cadence of water, which falls down after a surprising and astonishing manner, in so much that the universe does not afford its parallel." The feeling aroused is one of wonder rather than of admiration and pleasure.

As late as 1797, Josias Arnold, tutor in Rhode Island College, published a collection of poems from which a stanza may be quoted to show the old feeling as to romantic nature still surviving.

> Where ancient forests their tall branches bend,
> And o'er the wild a horrid gloom extend,
> There shall appear a variegated scene,
> Of fields and gardens in perennial green.

On the other hand, before the close of the Revolution the new feeling for nature in her more majestic moods begins to find poetical expression, as, for instance, in a poem read at the Yale Commencement in 1781,

> What various grandeur strikes the gladdening eyes;
> Bays stretch their arms and mountains lift the skies;
> And all the majesty of nature smiles.

More distinctly of the sort we are seeking, an inscription to *The Prospect of America* (1786) speaks of

> Those deep forests, where the eye is lost,
> With beauteous grandeur mingling in the sight;
> All these conspire to give the soul delight.

Barlow's *Vision of Columbus* (1787) shows a still more marked love of romantic scenery. The poet sings of the "majesty of nature," of her "nobler prospects" and "sublimest scenes," of the hills "that look sublime o'er Hudson's winding bed."

> A dread sublimity informs the whole,
> And wakes a dread sublimity of soul.

The writer of a *Rhapsody*, published in 1789, exclaims:

> How oft, delighted with the wild attire
> Of nature, in her recesses, thro' scenes
> Like these, in roving childhood have I strayed,
> Aw'd with the gloom and desert solitude
> That environed me . . . . .
> There is a rude disorder in these wilds,
> A native grandeur, that, unaffected
> By the touch of art, transcends its graces,
> And strikes some finer sense within the soul.

Quite Wordsworthian is this point of view, and far removed from that of the admirer of "purling rills" and "verdant lawns." One more illustration may be taken from poems published in 1792 by a Mr. Edwards:

> . . . where sublime
> Yon wond'rous mountains rise, whose shaggy sides
> Invests th' ethereal azure and whose brows
> Th' eternal vapour shrouds. Great Nature there
> Reigns in dread majesty and unshorn strength.
> . . . .
> Musing, I wander, and admiring trace
> Old ocean's abdicated Empire there.

The writer of an essay on poetry, published in 1795, says, "Almost every person is delighted with the prospect of Nature. The sublimity of the heavens, the towering mountain, the unfathomable and wide extended ocean, the blooming gardens and level vallies inspire the mind with elevation and contemplative reflection." The author of the *Poetical Wanderer*, which appeared the next year, 1796, writes, "Everyone is sensible of the impression made by viewing the sublime objects of nature. . . . The blazing sun, the spacious firmament, the spangled heavens, the towering mountains, variegated landscapes, the expanded ocean, are all grand and beautiful and we contemplate them with delight." The quotations are significant, for by the words of contemporary writers they show that the love of the romantic and grand in nature was no longer an undeveloped element of American character.

Recurring to the questions suggested at the beginning of this article, we may certainly conclude that the change of mind, in America also, came about within a definitely limited time, and namely, so far as most instances show, at about the time of the Revolution. That it was spontaneous or indigenous will not be thought to have been so clearly proved, yet it is not without evidence.

Exchanges from the
"Nature Faker" Controversy
(1902–1907)

By the beginning of the twentieth century, the American public's appetite for nature was enormous. Nature study was becoming part of the public school curriculum, nature writing was increasingly profitable for both writers and publishers, and social critics were becoming increasingly skeptical of what they viewed as a burgeoning "cult" of nature. Such critics were sometimes joined by natural scientists, who bemoaned the sentimentality and lack of rigor of many of the most popular nature books, particularly those of Charles G. D. Roberts and William J. Long. In such an atmosphere it was perhaps inevitable that something like the "nature faker" controversy of 1902–7 would emerge.

The selections below begin with John Burroughs attacking the work of William Long. Burroughs champions what he considers to be his own strict adherence to observed fact, and ridicules Long for his sentimentality and gullibility. In response, Long defends the validity of his observations and—pursuing a more interesting line of argument—points out that even the most rigorous science is not necessarily as objective as it claims to be. He points out that science often makes a priori choices that can predetermine the outcome of its research—as, for example, in deciding to limit its ethological observations to generalities characteristic of an entire species rather than focusing, as Long claims to do, on the idiosyncratic behavior of individual animals.

Long was no slouch intellectually and turned out to be a more articulate and rhetorically gifted opponent than Burroughs had perhaps anticipated. Born in North Attleboro, Massachusetts, in 1866, he graduated with a teaching certificate from State Teachers College in Bridgewater. He went on to earn degrees from Harvard University and Andover Theological Seminary, then to study history,

philosophy, and theology in several European cities before earning his Ph.D. at
the University of Heidelberg in 1897. In 1899 he was appointed pastor of the
Congregational Church in Stamford, Connecticut, but his real vocation was
writing. He would eventually author some nineteen books—several of which
were translated and republished abroad—on topics ranging from nature to
American history and literature. He was by no means a scientist, but he was a
capable observer and, as Ralph Lutts points out in *The Nature Fakers*, his understanding of animals was at times better than that of the professional scientists.

Of Long's nature books, it was *School of the Woods* (1902) that provoked Burroughs into beginning the nature faker debate. By the time the controversy sub-
sided, dozens of articles and tens of thousands of words would be published in
some of the nation's most prestigious venues; even the president of the United
States would weigh in (Theodore Roosevelt, who took the side of his friend Burroughs). At no other time until the emergence of contemporary ecocriticism
would so much ink be spilled on the topic of writing about nature. Sustaining
the debate was the conflict between two irreconcilable views of animals: the Cartesian, scientific view that sees animals as inert objects of study, and the more
empathetic view that sees even wild animals the way people see their pets, as
individuals with unique behaviors and personalities. Also at issue, of course, were
the literary criteria of good nature writing, including such ancient questions as
that of "truth" in fiction. Unfortunately, these literary questions only rarely informed the nature faker debate (as they do, for example, in William Henry Hudson's "Truth Plain and Coloured").

The selections below are arranged chronologically.

🌸 🌸 🌸

John Burroughs, from "Real and Sham Natural History," published in March 1903 in the *Nation*.

I suppose it is the real demand for an article that leads to its counterfeit,
otherwise the counterfeit would stand a poor show. The growing demand for
nature-books within the past few years has called forth a very large crop of
these books, good, bad, and indifferent,—books on our flowers, our birds,

our animals, our butterflies, our ferns, our trees; books of animal stories, animal romances, nature-study books, and what not. There is a long list of them. Some of these books, a very small number, are valuable contributions to our natural history literature. Some are written to meet a fancied popular demand. The current is setting that way; these writers seem to say to themselves, Let us take advantage of it, and float into public favor and into pecuniary profit with a nature-book. The popular love for stories is also catered to, and the two loves, the love of nature and the love of fiction, are sought to be blended in the animal story—books, such as Mr. Charles G. D. Roberts's Kindred of the Wild, Mr. William Davenport Hulbert's Forest Neighbors, Mr. Thompson Seton's Wild Animals I Have Known, and the Rev. William J. Long's School of the Woods. Only the last two writers seem to seek to profit by the popular love for the sensational and the improbable, Mr. Long, in this respect, quite throwing Mr. Thompson Seton in the shade. It is Mr. Long's book, more than any of the others, that justifies the phrase "Sham Natural History," and it is to it and to Mr. Thompson Seton's Wild Animals I *Alone* Have Known, if I may be allowed playfully to amend his title to correspond with the facts, that I shall devote the major part of this article. . . .

Of all the nature-books of recent years, I look upon Mr. [Dallas Lore] Sharp's as the best; but in reading it, one is keenly aware of the danger that is always lurking near the essay naturalist,—lurking near me as well as Mr. Sharp,—the danger of making too much of what we see and describe,—of putting in too much sentiment, too much literature,—in short, of valuing these things more for the literary effects we can get out of them than for themselves. This danger did not beset Gilbert White. He always forgets White, and remembers only nature. His eye is single. He tells the thing for what it is. He is entirely serious. He reports directly upon what he sees and knows without any other motive than telling the truth. There is never more than a twinkle of humor in his pages, and never one word of style for its own sake. Who in our day would be content to write with the same moderation and self-denial? Yet it is just these sane, sincere, moderate books that live.

In Mr. Charles G. D. Roberts's Kindred of the Wild one finds much to admire and commend, and but little to take exception to. The volume is in many ways the most brilliant collection of animal stories that has appeared. It reaches a high order of literary merit. Many of the descriptive passages

in it of winter in the Canadian woods are of great beauty. The story called
A Treason of Nature, describing the betrayal and death of a bull moose by
hunters who imitated the call of the cow moose, is most striking and effective. True it is that all the animals whose lives are portrayed—the bear, the
panther, the lynx, the hare, the moose, and others—are simply human beings disguised as animals; they think, feel, plan, suffer, as we do; in fact,
exhibit almost the entire human psychology. But in other respects they follow
closely the facts of natural history, and the reader is not deceived; he knows
where he stands. Of course it is mainly guesswork how far our psychology
applies to the lower animals. That they experience many of our emotions
there can be no doubt, but that they have intellectual and reasoning processes like our own, except in a very rudimentary form, admits of grave
doubt. But I need not go into that vexed subject here. They are certainly in
any broad generalization our kin, and Mr. Roberts's book is well named and
well done.

Yet I question his right to make his porcupine roll himself into a ball when
attacked, as he does in his story of the panther, and then on a nudge from
the panther roll down a snowy incline into the water. I have tried all sorts of
tricks with the porcupine and made all sorts of assaults upon him, at different
times, and I have never yet seen him assume the globular form Mr. Roberts
describes. . . .

The father of the animal story as we have it to-day was doubtless Charles
Dudley Warner, who, in his A-Hunting of the Deer, forever killed all taste
for venison in many of his readers. The story of the hunt is given from the
standpoint of the deer, and is, I think, the most beautiful and effective animal
story yet written in this country. It is true in the real sense of the word. The
line between fact and fiction is never crossed.

Neither does Mr. William Davenport Hulbert cross this line in his Forest
Neighbors, wherein we have the life stories of the porcupine, the lynx, the
beaver, the loon, the trout, made by a man who has known these creatures
in the woods of northern Michigan from his boyhood. The sketches are sympathetically done, and the writer's invention is called into play without the
reader's credulity ever being overtaxed. But in Mr. Thompson Seton's Wild
Animals I Have Known, and in the recent work of his awkward imitator, the
Rev. William J. Long, I am bound to say that the line between fact and fiction
is repeatedly crossed, and that a deliberate attempt is made to induce the
reader to cross, too, and to work such a spell upon him that he shall not know

that he has crossed and is in the land of make-believe. Mr. Thompson Seton says in capital letters that his stories are true, and it is this emphatic assertion that makes the judicious grieve. True as Romance, true in their artistic effects, true in their power to entertain the young reader, they certainly are; but true as natural history they as certainly are not. Are we to believe that Mr. Thompson Seton, in his few years of roaming in the West, has penetrated farther into the secrets of animal life than all the observers who have gone before him? There are no stories of animal intelligence and cunning on record, that I am aware of, that match his. Gilbert White, Charles St. John, Waterton, Wallace, Darwin, Jefferies, and others in England, — all expert students and observers; Bates in South America, Audubon roaming the whole country, Thoreau in New England, John Muir in the mountains of California and in the wilds of Alaska have nothing to report that comes within gunshot of what appear to be Mr. Thompson Seton's daily experiences. Such dogs, wolves, foxes, rabbits, mustangs, crows, as he has known, it is safe to say, no other person in the world has ever known. Fact and fiction are so deftly blended in his work that only a real woodsman can separate them. . . .

Since Mr. Thompson Seton took his reader into his confidence at all, why did he not warn him at the outset against asking any questions about the literal truth of his stories? Why did he not say that their groundwork was fact and their finish was fiction, and that if the reader find them entertaining, and that if they increase his love for, and his interest in, our wild neighbors, it were enough?

It is always an artist's privilege to heighten or deepen natural effects. He may paint us a more beautiful woman, or a more beautiful horse, or a more beautiful landscape, than we ever saw; we are not deceived even though he outdo nature. We know where we stand and where he stands; we know that this is the power of art. But when he paints a portrait, or an actual scene, or event, we expect him to be true to the facts of the case. Again, he may add all the charm his style can impart to the subject, and we are not deceived; the picture is true, perhaps all the more true for the style. Mr. Thompson Seton's stories are artistic and pleasing, but he insists upon it that they are true to the fact, and that this is the best way to write natural history. "I believe," he says in his preface, "that natural history has lost much by the vague general treatment that is so common." Hence he will make it specific and individual. Very good; but do not put upon our human credulity a greater burden than it can bear. His story of the pacing mustang is very clever and spirited, but the endurance of the horse is simply past belief. What would not one give for the real facts of the case; how interesting they would be, no matter how much they fell short of this highly colored account! There should be nothing equivocal about sketches of this kind; even a child should know when the writer is giving him facts and when he is giving him fiction, as he does when Mr. Thompson Seton makes his animals talk; but in many of the narrations only a real woodsman can separate the true from the false. Mr. Thompson Seton constantly aims to convey the idea to his reader that the wild creatures drill and instruct their young, even punishing them at times for disobedience to orders. His imitator, the Rev. Mr. Long, quite outdoes him on this line, going so far as to call his last book the School of the Woods.

Mr. Long doubtless got the hint of his ridiculous book from Mr. Thompson Seton's story of the crow, wherein he speaks of a certain old pine woods as the crows' fortress and college: "Here they find security in numbers and in lofty yet sheltered perches, and here they begin their schooling and are taught all the secrets of success in crow life, and in crow life the least failure does not simply mean begin again. It means *death*." Now the idea was a false one before Mr. Long appropriated it, and it has been pushed to such length that it becomes ridiculous. There is not a shadow of truth in it. It is simply one of Mr. Thompson Seton's strokes of fancy. The crows do not train their young. They have no fortresses, or schools, or colleges, or examining boards, or diplomas, or medals of honor, or hospitals, or churches, or telephones, or postal deliveries, or anything of the sort. Indeed, the poorest backwoods hamlet has more of the appurtenances of civilization than the best organized crow or other wild animal community in the land!

Mr. Long deliberately states as possibly a new suggestion in the field of natural history "that animal education is like our own, and so depends chiefly upon teaching." And again: "After many years of watching animals in their native haunts [and especially after reading Thompson Seton] I am convinced that instinct plays a much smaller part than we have supposed; that an animal's success or failure in the ceaseless struggle for life depends, not upon instinct, but upon the kind of training which the animal receives from its mother." This is indeed a new suggestion in the field of natural history. What a wonder that Darwin did not find it out, or the observers before and since his time. But the honor of the discovery belongs to our own day and land!

Now let us see if this statement will bear examination. Take the bird with its nest, for instance. The whole art of the nest builder is concealment,—both by position and by the material used,—blending its nest with and making it a part of its surroundings. This is the way to safety. Does the mother bird teach her young this art? When does she do it, since the young do not build till they are a year old? Does she give them an object lesson on their own nest, and do they remember it till the next season? . . .

The question I am here arguing is too obvious and too well established to be considered in this serious manner, were it not that the popularity of Mr. Long's books, with their mock natural history, is misleading the minds of many readers. No pleasure to the reader, no moral inculcated, can justify the dissemination of false notions of nature, or of anything else, and the writer who seeks to palm off his own silly inventions as real observations is bound sooner or later to come to grief.

There is a school of the woods, as I have said, just as much as there is a church of the woods, or a parliament of the woods, or a society of united charities of the woods, and no more; there is nothing in the dealings of animals with their young that in the remotest way suggests human instruction and discipline. The young of all the wild creatures do instinctively what their parents do and did. They do not have to be taught; they are taught by nature from the start. . . .

Why should any one palm off such stuff on an unsuspecting public as veritable natural history? When a man, writing or speaking of his own experience, says without qualification that he has seen a thing, we are expected to take him at his word. Mr. Long says his sketches were made in the woods with the subjects themselves living just outside his tent door; and that "they are all life studies, and include also some of the unusual life secrets of a score of animals and birds." We are not, therefore, to regard him as playing with natural history material for the amusement of his reader, or, like Mr. Thompson Seton, seeking to make up an artistic whole out of bits and fragments of the lives of the animals, gathered here and there, and heightened and intensified by a fertile fancy, but as an actual recorder of what he has seen and known. What the "life secrets" are that he claims to have discovered, any competent reader can see. They are all the inventions of Mr. Long. Of the real secrets of wild life, I do not find a trace in his volume.

The only other book of Mr. Long's I have looked into is his Beasts of the

Field, and here he is for the most part the same false prophet that he is in the School of the Woods. His statements are rarely convincing; rarely do they have the verisimilitude of real observations. His air is that of a witness who is trying to mislead the jury. . . .

Charles Prescott Daniels, from "Discord in the Forest:
John Burroughs vs. William J. Long," published
in the March 7, 1903, *Boston Evening Transcript.*

Honest, absolutely honest, and yet not quite telling the truth — that is a seeming paradox, but a real paradox only as many a poetic temperament is itself a paradox, and any poetic temperament, any temperament to which imagination is all but reality, and to which the thing loved and therefore, the thing sought, is by a natural consequence the thing believed — any such temperament will prepare bitter grief for itself when it enters the world of natural science. Scientists have always to guard against the personal equation. This is well illustrated in the disappearance from scientific use of the pencil sketch and its replacement by the photograph. Let me draw the strata in yonder rocks, and nine chances in ten I shall unconsciously draw into them the theory which I intend them to illustrate. The camera, on the other hand, tells no lies, and very plainly Mr. Long is some other thing than a camera. His finished product is art, not science; it is the forest plus Mr. Long, it is the woodland folk introduced, interpreted, beloved — I had almost said at the first, created by Mr. Long. And I wonder whether, after all, Mr. Burroughs is not equally writing his own delightful personality into his own charming pages. The world-wide difference comes in at one point only. Mr. Burroughs is temperamentally fitted to interpret nature through the forms of literature; Mr. Long is not so fitted.

It would seem, therefore, that he should seek other avenues of approach to his desired haven. As a poet, and he has written some very charming verses, as a master of fiction, and many of his stories have given pleasure, he would rid himself of the bitter criticism of Mr. Burroughs.

Mr. Burroughs has written a very entertaining paper on "Birds and Poets," in which, after taking Longfellow to task for his ornithological blunders, he adds with sweet courtesy, "It is an ungracious task thus to cross-question the gentle muse of Longfellow": but let a William J. Long so much as lift the top of his head out of oblivion and our friend Mr. Burroughs is for rapiers, bludgeons and blunderbusses. . . .

What, then, is Mr. Long to do next? Word already comes from Stamford, Conn., that Mr. Long has resigned his parish, where he has been greatly beloved, and intends to devote himself entirely to writing and lecturing on nature. I am tempted, though this is surely no affair of mine, to offer him a suggestion, and to do it publicly. Let Mr. Long engage a collaborator, let him strike up a jolly partnership with the most accurate, painstaking, laborious student of natural history he can find. Mr. Long will bring to the literary and scientific firm large funds of enthusiasm and a most devoted love for the forest folk, endless powers of observation, the inspiration that comes to fine imaginative temperaments, and a rare literary gift, for whatever his failings, he puts charm into all he writes. The junior member of the proposed combination will serve constantly as a check upon rash, half-formed opinion and excited reasoning. Together they may give us nature books such as will undoubtedly please Mr. John Burroughs, and which certainly ought to be read for instruction by the forest folk themselves.

Just a word more. It seems that Mr. John Burroughs ought also to take a friendly suggestion from a sincere admirer. The next time he finds an inaccurate nature book, I think that in common fairness he ought to be sure of his man before he slaughters him in the pages of the parlorly *Atlantic* after his brutal fashion. It is not such a very vicious thing in Mr. Long that he is a clergyman, and certainly it should be a very happy thing for this world if all clergymen were as faithful and useful and inspiring in their pulpits as Mr. Long has been. It is unfair for Mr. Burroughs to charge Mr. Long with pecuniary rapacity. He is not that kind of person. It is certainly extremely unjust for Mr. Burroughs to brand as mendacious the superficial and inaccurate statements which result from the peculiar education and far more peculiar personality of their writer. Indeed, I question whether Mr. Burroughs's ferocity does have an effect quite opposite to that he desired; whether, indeed, it does not leave the reader with a kinder feeling for Mr. Long than for Mr. Burroughs, and leave him, too, with a suspicion that, after all, the beasts and birds will forgive Mr. Long for having so amiably misrepresented them.

William J. Long, from "The Modern School of Nature-Study and Its Critics," published in the *North American Review* in May 1903.

Two things should be borne in mind if one would understand the present in Nature-study, or classify the large number of books which minister to that interest:

First, the study of Nature is a vastly different thing from the study of Science; they are no more alike than Psychology and History. Above and beyond the world of facts and law, with which alone Science concerns itself, is an immense and almost unknown world of suggestion and freedom and inspiration, in which the individual, whether animal or man, must struggle against fact and law to develop or keep his own individuality. It is a world of *appreciation*, to express it in terms of the philosophy of professor Royce, rather than a world of *description*. It is a world that must be interpreted rather than catalogued, for you cannot catalogue or classify the individuality for which all things are struggling. Here the "flower in the crannied wall" is analyzed, indeed, but not according to the principles of Gray's Manual; "the eagle that stirreth up her nest, fluttereth over her young, and beareth them on their wings," sweeps into our hearts without the might of a Latin name added; and the "poor, cowerin', timorous beastie" runs away and leaves us with a question that cannot be answered by telling us whether this mother mouse belongs to the long-tailed or jumping variety. This upper world of appreciation and suggestion, of individuality interpreted by individuality, is the world of Nature, the Nature of the poets and prophets and thinkers. Though less exact, it is no less but rather more true and real than Science, as emotions are more real than facts, and love is more true than Economics —

> "Und wenn Natur Dich unterweist
> Dann geht die Scelenkraft Dir auf,
> Wie spricht ein Geist zum andern Geist."

That is the word which Goethe, himself a scientist and philosopher, put into the mouth of Faust, a man who knew all the sciences, but who cried out for the life of Nature. "I study facts and law; they are enough," says the scientist. "We know the tyranny of facts and law too well," answer the naturestudents. "Give us now the liberty and truth of the spirit."

Let me illustrate this difference clearly and simply by reference to two animals that I have followed, under difficulties, for many years. They are the beaver and the otter, both wonderful swimmers, more at home in the water than on the land. The beaver uses only his hind feet in swimming; the otter, except when playing on the surface, uses only his forefeet for the same purpose; when chasing a trout under water, the hind legs are trailed behind him with his tail. Why this difference in two powerful swimmers of the same waters? Again, both these animals are unusually peaceable at all seasons. Of all the wood-folk that mind their own business, the beaver is the most exemplary; and the otter, though a powerful fighter and belonging to the quarrelsome weasel family, is gentle and playful, lets the other animals severely alone, and makes the most docile of pets when you catch him. Yet these two peaceable animals fight like Kilkenny cats whenever they cross each other's path. Why?

Science has no answer here. It is not her field; and long ago she classified both animals and finished with them. The work of the nature-student, on the other hand, has hardly more than begun. Following these shy animals summer and winter, entering into their struggles, he has learned to interpret how, in their dim way, they think and feel, and how their interests are bound to clash. And he understands perfectly both their swimming and their animosities; for he sees the individuality which the scientist, with other interests, must always miss.

In a word, the difference between Nature and Science is the difference between a man who loves animals, and so understands them, and the man who studies Zoology; it is the difference between the woman who cherishes her old-fashioned flower-garden and the professor who lectures on Botany in a college class-room.

The second thing to remember is this: that the field of natural history has changed rapidly of late, and in the schools and nature clubs the demand is for less Science and more Nature. Formerly, the writer of natural history, working on the scientific plan, simply catalogued his facts and observations. Animals were assumed to be creatures of instinct and habit. They were described in classes, under the assumption that all animals of the same class are alike. Style and living interest were both alike out of place; for it was, and still is, asserted that a personal interest destroys the value of an observation.

The modern nature-student has learned a different lesson. He knows that animals of the same class are still individuals; that they are different every one, and have different habits; that they are not more alike than men and women of the same class, and that they change their habits rapidly—more so, perhaps, than do either governments or churches—when the need arises. When a student at the Theological Seminary, I watched a toad that lived under the stone door-step. Now, toads are not supposed to have much individuality; yet, though I have watched toads since I was a child, when I made pets of them, I recorded a dozen things of this one toad that I had never seen before, and that have never been observed, so far as I know, by any other naturalist.

The truth is, that he who watches any animal closely enough will see what no naturalist has ever seen. This is the simple secret of the wonderful cat story, or the incredible dog story, to be heard in almost every house. It means that, after you have catalogued dogs perfectly, you still have in every dog a new subject with some new habits. Every boy who keeps a pet has something to tell the best naturalist. . . .

There is one other thing that the modern nature-writer has learned, namely, that in this, as in every other field of literature, only a book which has style can live. And style is but the unconscious expression of personality. Not only may the personal element enter into the new nature-books; it must enter there if we are to interpret the facts truthfully. Every animal has an individuality, however small or dim; that is certain. (I know not how much farther one may safely go in the line of Leibnitz's philosophy and find the development of individuality below the animal). And the nature-student must seek from his own individuality, which is the only thing that he knows absolutely (this is the centre of the philosophy of both Hume and Descartes) to interpret truthfully and sympathetically the individual before him. For this work he must have not only sight but vision; not simply eyes and ears and a note-book; but insight, imagination, and, above all, an intense human sympathy, by which alone the inner life of an animal becomes luminous, and without which the living creatures are little better than stuffed specimens, and their actions the meaningless dance of shadows across the mouth of Plato's cave.

With these general considerations in mind, it is a simple matter to estimate Mr. Burroughs's astounding criticism in a recent number of the *Atlantic Monthly*. Aside from the unwarranted personal attacks, which those who like him best will most deplore, the article has two evident faults that destroy the force of his criticism: (1) it overlooks entirely the individuality of animals and the adaptiveness of nature; (2) it weighs the universe with the scales of his own farm and barnyard. What the animals do there is the absolute measure and limit of what they will do in the Maine wilderness and the Canadian Rockies. From the mice and woodchucks of his pasture, where he is at home, he affirms what is true and false of the bear and caribou of the great forest where he has never been. One must deny at the outset the very grounds of his opposition.

These two faults are glaringly manifest in Mr. Burroughs's specific denials and assertions. He accuses Mr. Thompson-Seton of deliberate falsehood and misrepresentation, on the sole ground that he himself has not seen the things recorded and that, therefore, they cannot be true. Frankly, I differ radically from Mr. Thompson-Seton in many of his theories and observations of animals. That is either because I have seen less, and less sympathetically, than he has, or because I have watched bears and wolves with different individual habits. But Mr. Thompson-Seton is a gentleman. When he tells that he has seen a thing that is new and wonderful to me, though I know his animals well as a class, I shall simply open my own eyes wider, and question Indian hunters more closely, to know whether his observation is in error, or whether he saw some peculiar trait of some one animal, or whether the same thing has been seen by others in different places. For me to question his veracity, and deny what he has seen because I have not seen it, would be simply to show my own lack of courtesy, and arouse suspicion that I might be jealous of his hard-won and well-deserved success. . . .

There are more things in heaven and earth, and in the heart of the wild things, evidently, than are seen on Mr. Burroughs's farm or dreamed of in his philosophy. Many will remember his cutting criticism of the poets in which he ridicules Lowell for having buttercups and dandelions in the same field, and Bryant for giving fragrance to the yellow violet, and both poets for many other things which they had seen. Yet the poets were perfectly right; and Mr. Burroughs's quarrel was with the Almighty, not with the servants who did but interpret His works. Thomas Wentworth Higginson showed how arrogant and inaccurate was this whole criticism; but, though the article was modified in its book-form, it still takes the poets to task most unjustly for seeing many things as they are. The fault was, not that Mr. Burroughs did not know his buttercups, but that he overlooked the fact that his farm does not set bounds to the universe, and that the New England fields raised a crop of their own, of whose habits, even of whose species, he was unwittingly quite ignorant.

Indeed, whenever Mr. Burroughs leaves his own field for criticism, those of us who have been most delighted with what he has seen and recorded there will most regret his limitations. One recalls his harsh criticism of Maurice Thompson, a scholar and a gentleman, anent the classics. But how shall a man criticise the classics who does not read them? One remembers his criticism of Victor Hugo, in which, to borrow the great writer's own figure, "he confounds the constellations of profundity with the stars which a duck's feet leave in a puddle." One reads this arbitrary criticism of modern nature-writers, in which he hath put down the mighty from their seats and hath exalted them of low degree. No mention of Rowland Robinson, every one of whose pages is a clear photograph; no allusion to Dr. Lockwood, the friend of Agassiz, who of all the nature-writers that America has produced was best fitted to write her natural history, and who, in his lectures and notes, has recorded more marvels of animal life than all the rest of us put together. He commends White, who is invariably dry as a stuffed owl, and has no word for Jefferies, who is fresh and inspiring as a morning in the English fields with the hawthorn all ablow. And as to those whom he foreordains and elects, one must take even more exceptions, and say frankly: this is not the voice of authority, as it was meant to be. For, in a word, criticism is not dogmatism. It is not bald assertion or denial: "this is so, sir, and that is false, upon my word and authority." Criticism is an art with a continuous historical development; and he who would criticise must first learn courtesy, and then he must understand the canons of criticism that prevail from Homer to Heine and from Bede to Balzac.

William J. Long, from "Science, Nature and Criticism," published in the May 13, 1904, issue of *Science*.

The question naturally arises, and has indeed been asked with some irritation, why, with all these facts at hand, a man does not write as a scientist and produce his evidence. The answer is threefold: (1) I am accustomed to be believed when I speak. Knowing my subject, and with the evidence of my own eyes before me, it has hardly seemed necessary, for the sake of a few critics who will not believe, to refer to supplementary evidence, of which I have a plenty; to 'cross my throat,' boy fashion, as an evidence of sincerity, and to state after every observation: Mr. So-and-so saw that same thing in Such-a-place; if you don't believe it, ask him. (2) I have gone into the outdoor world as a nature lover, not as a scientist; for recreation, not for work; and my aim, as that of other nature writers, is chiefly to influence other people to go out of doors themselves, and by telling the whole truth, so far as I can see it, to open their eyes to the facts of animal life which the scientist, as well as the vacationist, has overlooked, under the supposition that birds and animals are governed solely by instinct and reflex impulses. And (3) while the scientist deals with laws and generalizations and works largely with species, I have dealt always with individuals, and have tried to understand every animal from moose to woodmouse that I have met in the wilderness.

That birds and animals (and even the insects, especially the solitary wasps and spiders) differ greatly among themselves in individual characteristics and habits, is now beyond a question. Sooner or later science will collect these individual differences and go to work upon new laws and generalizations; but at the present moment when one goes into animal individuality he crosses the borderland of science into a realm where our present laws and classifications apply only in the most general way. Every animal he studies closely is different from every other animal, for nature seems to abhor repetition as she abhors a vacuum. As among men, the differences, which lie deep, are much harder to detect than the resemblances, which are mostly on the surface. All the men of a city street are alike from a third-story window, which is nearer than we generally get to wild animals. There are even women who declare that the generalization holds true at a closer inspection—but that is another matter. Two men in dress suits will pass the same general social muster at a dance or reception, and may be indistinguishable across a small room; but it will take some intimate acquaintance to discover that they are as far apart as Beelzebub and Gabriel. And any one who has ever learned to know intimately a litter of pups or a litter of fox cubs will recognize instantly that the same differences in character and disposition which prevail among men prevail also, though in less degree, among the beasts of the field, and are the last things to be discovered.

Though the field is an immense one, and practically unknown so far as wild animals are concerned, there are as yet only a few pioneers scattered over it. The facts are plenty enough, but the observers who have the patience and sympathy for the work are very few, and it will be years before they make any impression upon our general ignorance about birds and animals. It must be said also, of the nature students as distinct from the scientists, that they go into the field for pure love of it, rather than from any desire to make a book, or a theory, or to be enrolled among the discoverers of science. The element of personal taste also is a factor against them; they hate to kill and destroy, to stuff and label and put into a museum.

The ornithologists, for instance — and I have known many of them intimately — have been busy for years making collections of nests and eggs and bird skins; they have determined the range and distribution of species fairly accurately, and have gathered much interesting information as to food and breeding places of our native birds. These are the acknowledged 'scientists' of the bird world; and we have watched their work with interest, though at times with regret at the enormous and unnecessary amount of killing which generally accompanies their investigation. They deal with species and general habits, and their work, so far, covers little more than the surface of bird life. Meanwhile the individual bird, with his own thoughts and feelings, his own life to live and his own problems to solve, has remained almost unknown till a few nature lovers and students entered the field and, leaving behind the gun and the egg-case and the 'identification of species' as the one thing to seek after, have hidden and watched and followed and loved the bird, and have understood exactly in proportion as they have loved him. The derisive cry of 'interested observer' raised against them by certain professed scientists has no reasonable foundation. No man watches and no man records in any field except he be interested. His observations are valuable exactly in proportion as love impels him to find out about things. Scientist and nature student are both seeking truth, and finding the particular manifestations of truth that they seek after. The difference is something like this, that the ornithologist loves specimens and the identification of species and other superficial things, while the nature student loves birds and the life that is akin to our own. The latter may prove, in the end, to be more scientific than the former.

At present the nature student is simply trying, without prejudice, to understand and record life as he sees it, and asks no scientific consideration beyond that suggested by common honesty and courtesy. When his record is written, his facts may be collected, and the comparative-psychologist, who now knows almost nothing of the life of the wild bird or animal, will then be able to finish the work which the ornithologist only began. Not till then shall we have anything like an adequate picture of bird life; and till then it may be well for critics to remember that truth is a large proposition and, like honesty, is not subject to monopoly. . . .

John Burroughs, from "The Literary Treatment of Nature," published in the July 1904 issue of the *Atlantic Monthly*.

The literary treatment of natural history themes is, of course, quite different from the scientific treatment, and should be so. The former, compared with the latter, is like free-hand drawing compared with mechanical drawing. Literature aims to give us the truth in a way to touch our emotions, and in some degree to satisfy the enjoyment we have in the living reality. The literary artist is just as much in love with the fact as is his scientific brother, only he makes a different use of the fact, and his interest in it is often of a nonscientific character. His method is synthetic rather than analytic. He deals in general, and not in technical truths,—truths that he arrives at in the fields and woods, and not in the laboratory.

The essay-naturalist observes and admires; the scientific naturalist *collects*. One brings home a bouquet from the woods; the other, specimens for his herbarium. The former would enlist your sympathies and arouse your enthusiasm; the latter would add to your store of exact knowledge. The one is just as shy of over-coloring or falsifying his facts as the other, only he gives more than facts,—he gives impressions and analogies and, as far as possible, shows you the live bird on the bough.

The literary and the scientific treatment of the dog, for instance, will differ widely, not to say radically, but they will not differ in one being true and the other false. Each will be true in its own way. One will be suggestive and the other exact; one will be strictly objective, but literature is always more or less subjective. Literature aims to invest its subject with a human interest, and to this end stirs our sympathies and emotions. Pure science aims to convince the reason and the understanding alone. Note Maeterlinck's treatment of the dog in a late magazine article,—probably the best thing on our four-footed comrade that English literature has to show. It gives one pleasure, not because it is all true as science is true, but because it is so tender, human, and sympathetic, without being false to the essential dog nature; it does not make the dog *do* impossible things. It is not natural history; it is literature; it is not a record of observations upon the manners and habits of the dog, but reflections upon him and his relations to man, and upon the many problems, from the human point of view, that the dog must master in a brief time; the distinctions he must figure out, the mistakes he must avoid, the riddles of life he must read in his dumb dog way. Of course, as a matter of fact, the dog is not compelled "in less than five or six weeks to get into his mind, taking shape within it, an image and a satisfactory conception of the universe." No, nor in five or six years. Strictly speaking, he is not capable of conceptions at all, but only of sense impressions; his sure guide is instinct, — not blundering reason. The dog starts with a fund of knowledge, which man acquires slowly and painfully. But all this does not trouble one in reading of Maeterlinck's dog. Our interest is awakened, and our sympathies moved, by seeing the world presented to the dog as it presents itself to us, or by putting ourselves in the dog's place. It is not false natural history, — it is a fund of true human sentiment awakened by the contemplation of the dog's life and character.

Maeterlinck does not ascribe human powers and capacities to his dumb friend, the dog; he has no incredible tales of its sagacity and wit to relate; it is only an ordinary bull pup that he describes, but he makes us love it, and, through it, all other dogs, by his loving analysis of its trials and tribulations, and its devotion to its god, man. In like manner, in John Muir's story of his dog, Stickeen, — a story to go with *Rab and his Friends*, — our credulity is not once challenged. Our sympathies are deeply moved because our reason is not in the least outraged. It is true that Muir makes his dog act like a human being under the press of great danger; but the action is not the kind that involves reason; it only implies sense perception, and the instinct of self-preservation. Stickeen does as his master bids him, and he is human only in the human emotions of fear, despair, joy, that he shows.

In Mr. Egerton Young's book, called *My Dogs of the Northland*, I find much that is interesting and several vivid dog portraits, but Mr. Young humanizes his dogs to a greater extent than does either Muir or Maeterlinck. For instance, he makes his dog Jack take special delight in teasing the Indian servant girl by walking or lying upon her kitchen floor when she had just cleaned it, all in revenge for the slights the girl had put upon him; and he gives several instances of the conduct of the dog which he thus interprets.

Now one can believe almost anything of dogs in the way of wit about their food, their safety, and the like, but one cannot make them so entirely human as deliberately to plan and execute the kind of revenge here imputed to Jack. No animal could appreciate a woman's pride in a clean kitchen floor, or see any relation between the tracks which he makes upon the floor and her state of feeling toward himself. Mr. Young's facts are doubtless all right; it is his interpretation of them that is wrong.

It is perfectly legitimate for the animal story-writer to put himself inside the animal he wishes to portray, and tell how life and the world look from that point of view; but he must always be true to the facts of the case, and to the limited intelligence for which he speaks.

In the humanization of the animals, and of the facts of natural history which is supposed to be the province of literature in this field, we must recognize certain limits. Your facts are sufficiently humanized the moment they become interesting, and they become interesting the moment you relate them in any way to our lives, or make them suggestive of what we know to be true in other fields and in our own experience. Thoreau made his battle of the ants interesting because he made it illustrate all the human traits of courage, fortitude, heroism, self-sacrifice. Burns's mouse at once strikes a sympathetic chord in us without ceasing to be a mouse; we see ourselves in it. To attribute human motives and faculties to the animals is to caricature them; but to put us in such relations with them that we feel their kinship, that we see their lives embosomed in the same iron necessity as our own, that we see in their minds a humbler manifestation of the same psychic power and intelligence that culminates and is conscious of itself in man, — that, I take it, is the true humanization.

We like to see ourselves in the nature around us. We want in some way to translate these facts and laws of outward nature into our own experiences; to relate our observations of bird or beast to our own lives. Unless they beget some human emotion in me, — the emotion of the beautiful, the sublime, — or appeal to my sense of the fit, the permanent, — unless what you learn in the fields and the woods corresponds in some way with what I know of my fellows, I shall not long be deeply interested in it. I do not want the animals humanized in any other sense. They all have human traits and ways; let those be brought out, — their mirth, their joy, their curiosity, their cunning, their thrift, their relations, their wars, their loves, — and all the springs of their actions laid bare as far as possible; but I do not expect my natural history to back up the Ten Commandments, or to be an illustration of the value of training-schools and kindergartens, or to afford a commentary upon the vanity of human wishes. Humanize your facts to the extent of making them interesting, if you have the art to do it, but leave the dog a dog, and the straddle bug a straddle bug.

Interpretation is a favorite word with some recent nature writers. It is claimed for the literary naturalist that he interprets natural history. The ways and doings of the wild creatures are exaggerated and misread under the plea of interpretation. Now, if by interpretation we mean an answer to the question, "What does this mean?" or, "What is the exact truth about it?" then there is but one interpretation of nature, and that is the scientific. What is the meaning of the fossils in the rocks? or of the carving and sculpturing of the landscape? or of a thousand and one other things in the organic and inorganic world about us? Science alone can answer. But if we mean by interpretation an answer to the inquiry, "What does this scene or incident suggest to you? how do you feel abut it?" then we come to what is called the literary or poetic interpretation of nature, which, strictly speaking, is no interpretation of nature at all, but an interpretation of the writer or the poet himself. The poet or the essayist tells what the bird, or the tree, or the cloud, means to him. It is himself, therefore, that is being interpreted. What do Ruskin's writings upon nature interpret? They interpret Ruskin, — his wealth of moral and ethical ideas, and his wonderful imagination. Richard Jefferies tells us how the flower, or the bird, or the cloud is related to his subjective life and experience. It means this or that to him; it may mean something entirely different to another, because he may be bound to it by a different tie of association. The poet fills the lap of Earth with treasures not her own, — the riches of his own spirit; science reveals the treasures that are her own, and arranges and appraises them.

Strictly speaking, there is not much in natural history that needs interpreting. We explain a fact, we interpret an oracle; we explain the action and relation of physical laws and forces, we interpret, as well as we can, the geological record. Darwin sought to explain the origin of species, and to interpret many palaeontological phenomena. We account for animal behavior on rational grounds of animal psychology; there is little to interpret. Natural history is not a cryptograph to be deciphered, it is a series of facts and incidents to be observed and recorded. If two wild animals, such as the beaver and the otter, are deadly enemies, there is good reason for it; and when we have found that reason, we have got hold of a fact in natural history. The robins are at enmity with the jays in the spring, and the reason is, the jays eat the robins' eggs. When we seek to interpret the actions of the animals, we are in danger of running into all kinds of anthropomorphic absurdities, by reading their lives in terms of our own thinking and consciousness. A man sees a flock of crows in a tree in a state of commotion; now they all caw, then only one master voice is heard, presently two or three crows fall upon one of their number and fell him to the ground. The spectator examines the victim and finds him dead, with his eyes pecked out. He interprets what he has seen as a court of justice; the crows were trying a criminal, and, having found him guilty, they proceeded to execute him. The curious instinct which often prompts animals to fall upon and destroy a member of the flock that is sick, or hurt, or blind, is difficult of explanation, but we may be quite sure that, whatever the reason is, the act is not the outcome of a judicial proceeding in which judge and jury and executioner all play their proper part. . . .

I suppose we should not care much for natural history, as I have before said, or for the study of nature generally, if we did not in some way find ourselves there,—that is, something that is akin to our own feelings, methods, and intelligence. We have traveled that road, we find tokens of ourselves on every hand; we are "stuccoed with quadrupeds and birds all over," as Whitman says. The life history of the humblest animal, if truly told, is profoundly interesting. If we could know all that befalls the slow moving turtle in the fields, or the toad that stumbles and fumbles along the roadside, our sympathies would be touched, and some spark of real knowledge imparted. We should not want the lives of those humble creatures "interpreted" after the manner of "our modern school of nature study," for that were to lose fact in fable; that were to give us a stone when we had asked for bread; we should want only a truthful record from the point of view of a wise, loving, human eye, such as, say, Gilbert White or Henry Thoreau might have given us. How interesting White makes his old turtle, hurrying to shelter when it rains, or seeking the shade of a cabbage leaf when the sun is too hot, or prancing about the garden on tiptoe in the spring by five in the morning, when the mating instinct begins to stir within him! Surely we may see ourselves in the old tortoise.

In fact, the problem of the essay-naturalist always is to make his subject interesting, and yet keep strictly within the bounds of truth.

William Henry Hudson, from "Truth Plain and Coloured,"
published in the December 9, 1905, issue of the *Speaker*.

A good book is a gift to be grateful for, and here we have two, both very good;
yet it is enough to make even the weariest and saddest man smile to receive
these same two wrapped up together in one piece of brown paper and tied
round with one piece of string. It is as if your two dear friends, who hate each
other with a fierce hatred, should by an unhappy chance drop in upon you
at the same moment. Fortunately books are in a sense inanimate objects, else
these two on being released from the parcel would certainly rise up and fly
at and buffet one another, upsetting the ink and creating a tremendous confusion among the papers on my writing-table. For it happens that these authors represent the two opposite and just now extremely antagonistic schools
of nature writing in North America. Both are now very well known in this
country, and I am inclined to think that readers at this distance, or on this
side of the Atlantic, are best able to appreciate their respective merits. The
dust is washed off when they reach us. John Burroughs is of the school we
know best—the oldest man among us has known it from his childhood; and
when his first book, *Wake Robin*, was issued in this country thirty or thirty-
five years ago, it found a ready public which he has never lost; on the contrary, it has grown with each succeeding book, most of all perhaps with *Fresh
Fields*, in which he describes his impressions of nature in England so delightfully. He would, and indeed does, describe himself as a literary or "essay"
naturalist, a student of nature in the open air who aims at presenting his facts
in a way to touch the emotions—to produce in some degree the enjoyment
we experience in the living reality. He is scientific, too, since he is devoted
to truth, only he sweetens his science with feeling and gives it literary form.
His nature study, as he aptly says, is only science out of school, happy in the
fields and woods, loving the flowers and animals which it observes, and finding in them something for the sentiments and emotions as well as for the
understanding.

If Gilbert White had analysed his own feelings and aims with reference to
his nature study and set it down, he would probably have anticipated much
that the American naturalist says of himself in this book. And it is a fact, I
think, that Burroughs, notwithstanding his modernity and American spirit,
impatient of old ways, comes nearest in mind to the historian of Selborne of

all living naturalists. In reading him I am often reminded of White's older followers—of Knapp, Jenyns, Moggridge, Jesse, and Knox of the *Ornithological Rambles*, rather than of any literary naturalist of the last fifty years. He is more emotional; he is also a very much better writer—there is no comparison; but he is undoubtedly of their tribe, his whole interest being in things as they are; his keener sympathy with all sentient life, and better gift of expression have never misled him into reading his own mind into that of the lower animals, nor tempted him to colour the simple truth as he finds it. "There is," he says, "but one interpretation of nature, and that is the scientific." And, again: "Jefferies tells how the flower, or the bird, or the cloud is related to his subjective life and experience. It means this or that to him; it may mean something entirely different from another, because he may be bound to it by a different tie of association. The poet fills the lap of earth with treasures not her own—the riches of his own spirit; science reveals the treasures that are her own, and arranges and appraises them."

To this point he returns again and again; the truth that to humanise animal life is to falsify, to caricature it, he ingeminates on page after page, dwelling on it with heat and eloquence. It is an almost angry protest against the new American-made romantic or sentimental school of nature study of which Thompson Seton, Long, and Charles Roberts are the leading exponents. Here in England one is surprised at the amount of feeling displayed in the book; but there is good cause; the trouble is that this new humanised natural history, which makes the beasts and birds a very much more intelligent and nice-minded people than, say, the African pigmies or other low-down savages, is taken with tremendous seriousness on the other side of the water. They prefer it over there to the old sober sort of literary natural history, which dates back to the eighteenth century, and came from the village of Selborne. It is infinitely more interesting to the general reader—and it is truer! Again, it is distinctly flattering to the Transatlantic mind to know that this new method of finding out the truth is their own original invention, and that their soil and electrical atmosphere has produced not one but a whole crowd of writers who, in insight and knowledge of the animal mind, surpass all other naturalists who exist or have existed on the globe. We think a great deal of Professor Owen's feat in reconstructing the entire framework of the gigantic Dinornis, long extinct, from the fragment of a single bone. It is nothing compared to that of the new naturalists, who build you up the entire psychology, and whole life from the cradle to the grave, so to speak, of fox, and caribou, and bobcat, and chipmunk, and forty others from a few isolated facts concerning the habits of those animals.

Possibly the new writers were themselves astonished at the great reputation they had made, or which had been thrust on them; in any case, having got it, they are determined to keep it, and are not taking Mr. Burroughs's punishment lying down. There is not an incident in their animal biographies, they assert, however improbable or even incredible it may seem to those who do not know the mind that is in an animal, which has not been witnessed and put on record by some competent observer. Their critic, they say, has narrowed his point of view to the limits of his own personal experience; and they remind him loftily that they have been in the woods and lonely wildernesses, studying the creatures in their own homes, conversing, too, with Indians and trappers who have a life-long familiarity with the subject, and, finally, they tell him that he judges all animals from those he has seen on his own small farm. His retort is: "Your natural history knowledge of the East will avail you in the West. 'There is no country,' says Emerson, 'in which they do not wash the pans and spank the babies,' and there is no country where a dog is not a dog or a fox a fox, or where a hare is ferocious or a wolf lamb-like."

That is how the matter stands; it is a pretty quarrel, amusing to the looker-on, but it does not concern us. We are a sober-minded people not at all likely to be carried away by anything this romantic school can send us, and this being so we can receive their books without apprehension and read and thoroughly enjoy them. For it must be said that they are delightful, and strike one as something new in literature. We have, it is true, something resembling it in our numerous animal biographies and auto-biographies, the best by far being Fortescue's *Life of a Wild Red Deer on Exmoor*. But these products are comparatively poor; in most cases the subjects are extravagantly over-humanised; they are by inferior writers or else by writers who do not possess all the qualities required to make such work really good.

Of the American writers who have made such a success in this line I should say that Charles Roberts is the foremost, and that *Red Fox*, his latest work, is a worthy successor of the *Kindred of the Wild* and *Watchers by the Trails*. All that the orthodox naturalists, and hunters, and trappers, know of the wild animals, he knows; and to his knowledge he adds a keen sympathy with wild life, and, above all, he possesses imagination and invention. The result is a book which, purely as a story, is as delightful to read as the unforgettable adventures of Brer Rabbit and Brer Fox. At the same time, the author infuses his own into the animal mind with so nice a judgment and so much restraint that we do not regard his life of a fox, or of any other animal, as mere romance, but it does produce the right illusion, and knowing that it was founded on truth, that there is so much truth intermixed with it, we are pleased to take it as all true.

Harold S. Deming, from "Mr. John Burroughs on Fake Natural History," published in the April 1907 *Outing Magazine*.

The *Briartown Sketches* are not treatises upon natural history. They do not attempt to generalize upon plant or animal life. They do not pretend to present results of prolonged scientific research, but are just what they appear to be, outdoor *sketches*, written not from the point of view of the scientific naturalist at all, but composed by casting together into pleasant descriptive form a series of observations made by an interested onlooker at the doings of birds and other creatures. . . .

Though to the ordinary eye it would seem clear enough that these are not scientific monographs, but literary sketches, Mr. Burroughs is unwilling to permit in them any latitude of descriptive phrase, but has demanded of them an exactness of statement and a nicety of description like that in a scientific treatise. Yet, if the reader will place the *Briartown Sketches* side by side with Mr. Burroughs' article, he will notice that Mr. Burroughs himself, in his versions of my statements, certainly shows no scientific exactness. My statements are there in cold type, unchanging. They were facts under Mr. Burroughs' observation. If the reader will contrast his own impression of them with the impression which Mr. Burroughs gives of them in his article, the result will need little comment. Not only does Mr. Burroughs pick out isolated statements and phrases and treat them apart from the context, omitting when he speaks of one statement any mention of another explaining it; he goes farther, he puts unfair construction upon passages as a whole, and as a result attacks not what I have said, but what he reports me to have said; and in one instance at least he invented an extraneous circumstance which threw a false light on what I did say. . . .

Some of his dogmatic generalizations from which he has deduced the falsity of my "invented" statements will perhaps surprise the reader, if he has ever taken a country vacation in New England in the summer. For instance, he lays down this rule as to the race of kingbirds: "As a matter of *fact*, the kingbird only attacks its enemies when they appear in the vicinity of its nest." Has Mr. Burroughs never seen a kingbird pursue a hawk or crow as far as his eye could follow them on some late August day when kingbirds' nests are empty? I venture to say that the reader has. It is worth mention in passing that Mr. Burroughs misreports me as having made the kingbirds "attack . . . a great blue heron."

Again, Mr. Burroughs writes that I "should be told that red-shouldered blackbirds do not nest in colonies of 'countless pairs,' but singly—a pair or two in one locality." Therefore I lied when, in writing of a broad marsh bordering a lake, I put in one of my sketches these words: "In the alders almost countless pairs of red-winged blackbirds built their nests." To begin with, would a fair critic transmute my description above into one of a "colony" (such as herons build)? But waiving that, if Mr. Burroughs has never seen more than a couple of pairs of redwings nesting in one "locality," I feel sure that there are plenty to agree with me that this can go to prove no more than that Mr. Burroughs' experience with redwings has been rather limited, much too limited for him to generalize with assurance as to every group of redwings in the union.

In *The Outing Magazine* for December last Mr. Burroughs states that "the nests (of humming birds) are *always* neatly thatched with lichens"; and with this as his scientific premise, he *deduces* the result that I lie when I write that I saw on a grapevine a hummer's nest thatched with bits of grapevine bark. If he will look in "Birdcraft," by Mrs. Mabel Osgood Wright, a well-known writer, he will find record of a hummer's nest, in a tall spruce, "covered with small flakes of spruce bark, instead of the usual lichens." This accords ill with the omniscience of Mr. Burroughs as to humming birds. . . .

When Mr. Burroughs turns his attention to my report of having found a crow's treasure heap of bright trifles, he is moved to declare a general law of nature broad enough to include all animals. He denounces my statement as a palpable invention, "preposterous and not worthy of a moment's credence. What purpose," queries Mr. Burroughs, "could the habit" of collecting bright objects "serve in the economy of" a crow's life? "None." "That tame crows will carry away bright objects and hide them is no proof that wild crows will do the same." (Nor would it, Mr. Burroughs, appear to be an appropriate argument for the contrary conclusion.) *"The wild creatures have no traits or habits that are not directly related to their needs,"* says Mr. Burroughs. Taking the italicized sentence as an enunciation of an incontrovertible law of science, Mr. Burroughs *deduces* the result that my report of the crow's treasure is a deliberate lie. Does the Australian bower bird build its bowers and ornament them with bright feathers and little heaps of whitened bones to meet an "economic" need in its life? And does the clipping of the wings and the taming of a crow born wild create within it new needs, non-economic, leading it to steal, hide, and then secretly visit (as more than one tame crow is known to have done) various bright objects?

How can even a naturalist of Mr. Burroughs' long experience lay down the law as to what every individual wild creature in this world will do, and hold such a mighty generalization fit basis from which, as if by geometry, to deduce that any one who differs with him is a liar? . . .

My statement that a certain humming bird's nest did not drain dry after a rain sends Mr. Burroughs into an ecstasy of contemptuous incredulity. "How long would a race of birds that built such watertight nests survive?" he cries. "A bird's nest will not hold water as well as a boy's straw hat—not even the mud-lined nest of the robin." I wrote not of a race of birds, but of a single very tiny nest, so unhappily tucked away in the corrugations of the bark on a broad branch, that it did not drain. How long would a race of birds survive if it built nests so carelessly that a mere breeze would shake them down? Yet Mr. Burroughs has doubtless seen here and there a nest so built. How long would a race of birds survive in which the would-be parents hanged themselves in loops from the building nests? Yet many have seen occasionally such catastrophes.

In brief, Mr. Burroughs' method of attack may be thus summed up: Apart from the bad names he calls me, his article consists mainly of three elements. First, he makes unfair, distorted versions of many of my descriptive statements, and then, displaying to the reader the perversions which he himself has created, scoffs at them as clumsy fabrications of mine. Secondly, he lays down dogmatically the law as to the things which every individual member of a given species of animal will (or apparently can) do, wherever found in this broad land—and many of his "laws" it takes no scientific naturalist to recognize as at variance with common experience — then from these "laws" which he himself has made, he deduces the conclusion, which he then asserts as a fact, that my statements inconsistent therewith are deliberate lies. Thirdly, as to my other statements whose verity he denies, his process is simpler. He says in effect: "I don't believe you; therefore you lie." But Mr. Burroughs is not omniscient. That he has not seen a certain thing does not make it *impossible* that another man should see it.

Mr. Burroughs' position is untenable. The *Briartown Sketches* are not the product of a morbid imagination; they are based upon actual observations honestly made and honestly recorded. I may have misobserved or through faulty recollection misreported; and I have no wish to deprecate fair criticism of any of my statements. But, as we have seen, Mr. Burroughs' article is not only not fair criticism, it is not criticism at all, but a blend of faulty logic, frequent misstatements and heated temper, strangely out of tune with the good sense and kindliness which so distinguish his writings when he is not in this curious bellicose mood.

Theodore Roosevelt, from "Nature Fakers,"
published in *Everybody's Magazine* in 1907.

The highest type of student of nature should be able to see keenly and write interestingly and should have an imagination that will enable him to interpret the facts. But he is not a student of nature at all who sees not keenly but falsely, who writes interestingly and untruthfully, and whose imagination is used not to interpret facts but to invent them.

True Nature Lovers

We owe a real debt to the men who truthfully portray for us, with pen or pencil, any one of the many sides of outdoor life; whether they work as artists or as writers, whether they care for big beasts or small birds, for the homely farmland or for the vast, lonely wilderness, whether they are scientist proper, or hunters of game, or lovers of all nature — which, indeed, scientists and hunters ought also to be. John Burroughs and John Muir, Stewart Edward

White, and Frederic Remington, Olive Thorne Miller, Hart Merriam, William Hornaday, Frank Chapman, J. A. Allen, Ernest Ingersoll, Witmer Stone, William Cram, George Shiras — to all of these and to many like them whom I could name, we owe much, we who love the breath of the woods and the fields, and who care for the wild creatures, large or small. And the surest way to neutralize the work of these lovers of truth and nature, of truth in nature-study, is to encourage those whose work shows neither knowledge of nature nor love of truth.

The modern "nature faker" is of course an object of derision to every scientist worthy of the name, to every real lover of the wilderness, to every faunal naturalist, to every true hunter or nature lover. But it is evident that he completely deceives many good people who are wholly ignorant of wild life. Sometimes he draws on his own imagination for his fictions; sometimes he gets them second-hand from irresponsible guides or trappers or Indians.

Yellow Journalists of the Woods

In the wilderness, as elsewhere, there are some persons who do not regard the truth; and these are the very persons who most delight to fill credulous strangers with impossible stories of wild beasts. As for Indians, they live in a world of mysticism, and they often ascribe supernatural traits to the animals they know, just as the men of the Middle Ages, with almost the same child-like faith, credited the marvels told of the unicorn, the basilisk, the roc, and the cockatrice.

Of all these "nature fakers," the most reckless and least responsible is Mr. Long; but there are others who run him close in the "yellow journalism of the woods," as John Burroughs has aptly called it. It would take a volume merely to catalogue the comic absurdities with which the books of these writers are filled. There is no need of discussing their theories; the point is that their alleged "facts" are not facts at all, but fancies. Their most striking stories are not merely distortions of facts, but pure inventions; and not only are they inventions, but they are inventions by men who know so little of the subject concerning which they write, and who to ignorance add such utter recklessness, that they are not even able to distinguish between what is possible, however wildly improbable, and mechanical impossibilities. Be it remembered that I am not speaking of ordinary mistakes, of ordinary errors of observation, of differences of interpretation and opinion; I am dealing only with deliberate invention, deliberate perversion of fact.

"Uncle Remus" Wolves

Now all this would be, if not entirely proper, at least far less objectionable, if the writers in question were content to appear in their proper garb, as is the case with the men who write fantastic fiction about wild animals for the Sunday issues of various daily newspapers. Moreover, as a writer of spirited animal fables, avowed to be such, any man can gain a distinct place of some importance. But it is astonishing that such very self-evident fiction as that which I am now discussing should, when advertised as fact, impose upon any person of good sense, no matter how ignorant of natural history and of wild life. . . .

Fable Weavers and Believers

In one story a woodcock is described as making a kind of mud splint for its broken leg; it seems a pity not to have added that it also made itself a crutch to use while the splint was on. A Baltimore oriole is described as making a contrivance of twigs and strings whereby to attach its nest, under circumstances which would imply the mental ability and physical address of a sailor making a hammock; and the story is backed up by affidavits, as are others of these stories. This particular feat is precisely as possible as that a Rocky Mountain pack rat can throw the diamond hitch. The affidavits in support of these various stories are interesting only because of the curious light they throw on the personalities of those making and believing them.

If the writers who make such startling discoveries in the wilderness would really study even the denizens of a barnyard, they would be saved from at least some of their more salient mistakes. Their stories dwell much on the "teaching" of the young animals by their elders and betters. In one story, for instance, a wild duck is described as "teaching" her young how to swim and get their food. If this writer has strolled into the nearest barnyard containing a hen which had hatched out ducklings, a glance at the actions of those ducklings, when the hen happened to lead them near a puddle would have enlightened him as to how much "teaching" they needed. But these writers exercise the same florid imagination when they deal with a robin or rabbit as when they describe a bear, a moose, or a salmon.

It is half amusing and half exasperating to think that there should be excellent persons to whom it is necessary to explain that books stuffed with such stories, in which the stories are stated as facts, are preposterous in their worthlessness. . . .

The Guilty Ones

Men of this stamp will necessarily arise, from time to time, some in one walk of life, some in another. Our quarrel is not with these men, but with those who give them their chance. We who believe in the study of nature feel that a real knowledge and appreciation of wild things, of trees, flowers, birds, and of the grim and crafty creatures of the wilderness, give an added beauty and health to life. Therefore we abhor deliberate or reckless untruth in this study as much as in any other; and therefore we feel that a grave wrong is committed by all who, holding a position that entitles them to respect, yet condone and encourage such untruth.

Lyman Abbott, from "The Roosevelt-Long Controversy" and "Imagination in Natural History," published in the June 8, 1907, issue of the *Outlook*.

The greater the man, the more likely he is to have the defects of his virtues. Mr. Roosevelt's extraordinary vitality, coupled with his unusual interest in all that concerns human welfare, makes it very difficult for him to keep silence in the presence of anything which he thinks injurious to his fellow-men. So, if the traditional spelling seems to him cumbersome, he wants to help reform it; and if the teaching of natural history in the schools is not to his liking, he wants to set it right. That his public office and the splendid opportunities for influence on any kind of question which it furnishes impose any limits upon him he is not inclined to believe. His latest incursion into fields non-political is a reported interview in *Everybody's Magazine* on "The Nature Fakers." It is true that this title is not his; it is not he, but either the interviewer or the editor, who thus characterizes Dr. William J. Long, the well-known writer for children on animal life. But he does characterize Dr. Long's writing as absurd, a description, not of what he has seen, but of a confused memory of what he has heard or read. That a wolf should tear the heart of a caribou by a wound in the chest, he says, is a "mathematical impossibility." . . . A correspondent of the *New York Times*, apropos of this controversy, calls attention to the fact that the prophet Hosea seems to have observed something like what Dr. Long describes, for he says: "I will meet them as a bear that is bereaved of her whelps, and will rend the caul [covering] of their heart." No one would think of quoting Hosea as an authority on natural history, but it indicates at least that Dr. Long is not the only man who thinks he has witnessed something of this description.

Upon one point of principle *The Outlook* finds itself in disagreement with the president, with whom on most moral questions it is in agreement. It is in the sharp distinction which he undertakes to make between fiction and fact. He enjoys Ruyard Kipling's "Jungle Book" stories, but he does not care for Dr. Long and but little apparently for Mr. Thompson Seton. We quite agree that fiction ought not be palmed off on school-children as fact; but we do not agree with what is implied, that imagination may not be used in interpreting and narrating facts. Men see through their temperaments; the imaginative man sees through his imagination; and he is telling the truth if he tells what he sees as he sees it. Mr. Froude, who had a vivid historical imagination, was bitterly condemned by Mr. Freeman, who had none; but Mr. Froude's history is not only interesting while Mr. Freeman's is dull, but very eminent authorities regard him as the better historian of the two. Whether or not Dr. Long correctly interprets the frolic of the caribou calves which he witnessed when he tells his readers that under the "guise of a frolic the calves were being taught a useful lesson," Dr. Long had a perfect right to give this interpretation, and he is not to be condemned by an observer with less fertile imagination for so doing. His interpretation may be challenged; but he ought not to be accused of bearing false witness. The question whether animals possess a certain measure of *quasi* human reason, or are purely the creatures of a mechanically formed habit, is not to be settled by the short and easy method of denying the possibility of all the phenomena which point to a human kinship in animals. The question is really one rather of psychology than of natural history, and cannot be closed by either an appeal to past tradition or a dogmatic declaration upon the authority of any observer, however wide his observations. *The Outlook* hopes that Dr. Long and Mr. Thompson Seton will continue to write about animal life, and that the children will continue to read their books.

John Burroughs, from "Imagination in Natural History,"
published in the June 29, 1907, issue of the *Outlook*,
followed by Abbott's response.

As a reader of *The Outlook* I could wish that in your editorial of June 8 on the use of the imagination in natural history, wherein you take President Roosevelt to task for his too sharp distinction between fiction and fact in this field, you had set forth a little more explicitly the distinction which you think permissible. You say you "agree that fiction ought not be palmed off on school-children as fact," which is just the sum total of President Roosevelt's contention. He would have no confusion between the two in books of natural history that go into the schools. He enjoys Kipling's "Jungle Book," as you say, but not the animal stories of William J. Long. Is not this because the "Jungle Book" is avowedly fiction and can deceive no one, while in the stories of Mr. Long fact and fiction are constantly confused, and only the practical woodsman can separate them?

I do not agree with you that in insisting on the reality of this distinction the President implies that "imagination may not be used in interpreting and narrating facts." On the contrary, I know that the President would agree with me that the use of imagination is indispensable in all such writing. There can be no good literature without it. But it is one thing to interpret facts and quite another thing to invent them. With Mr. Long's interpretation of the facts of natural history neither the President nor myself has any quarrel; all we contend for is for the fact—we dispute his statement of fact. Mr. Long may find in the croaking of frogs a key to the riddle of the universe if he can, and be entirely within his rights. All that I demand of him is that he be sound upon his frogs. I will not even accept a toad; when he says frog it must be a frog. Spring after spring, as revealed in his journal, Thoreau attributed the song of the toad to the frog, but at last he caught on; he saw his mistake, and thenceforth he rendered to the toad the things that were the toad's, and to the frog the things that were the frog's. I would have Mr. Long and every other nature writer equally honest and exact about his facts. Let the fact set his imagination all aflame if it can, but let him see to it that it is a fact. An imagination tipsy with its own creations is one thing, and an imagination aglow in the interpretation of facts is quite another. In short, there is a legitimate and an illegitimate use of the imagination in writing natural history, as in writing human history. Its legitimate use in nature-writing is in presenting the facts with charm and convincingness, as in the works of Maeterlinck and Thoreau, men who are always loyal to the mere fact, yet throw a charm of poetry and romance about all they write, that less imaginative men cannot attain to. Its illegitimate use is seen in the writings of Mr. Long, where it often takes the form of mere exaggeration, and where it as often supplies the fact which observation alone can yield. . . .

It is this kind of fake natural history that President Roosevelt objects to being put into the hands of school-children or into the hands of children by the fireside. It is vicious, because it is not true. Yet *The Outlook* accepts it and encourages Mr. Long to go on producing it. That a thing is true gives it no additional value; that it is false does not detract from it! . . .

Pardon me for saying that you confuse my mind instead of enlightening it when you say we all see through our temperaments, and when you draw from this fact an excuse and justification for the misseeing Mr. Long. Is there, then, not such a thing as seeing truly and seeing falsely? True it is that the report of every man of what he sees in nature and in life will be colored more or less by his temperament, or by his personal equation — colored, I say, but not necessarily distorted or falsified. The poet and the artist see nature through the imagination, but the natural history observer sees through his eyes, or else his observations have no value as natural history. With him it is not a question of temperament, but a question of accurate seeing and honest reporting. He cannot tell the incredible stories Mr. Long does and then take refuge in the statement, as Mr. Long has, that there is a region beyond the world of fact and law in which he dwells, "an immense and almost unknown world of suggestion and freedom and inspiration," "a world that must be interpreted rather than catalogued." True, there is such a world, but it is not the world of the natural history observer and reporter, it is the world of the poet and prophet and of the ethical teacher, and Mr. Long cannot escape into it when the sticklers for the truth of observation, like the President, get hot upon his trail.

[We acknowledge that both Mr. Burroughs and the President speak on the subject of natural history with far more scientific knowledge, far wider experience, and far greater and more accurate observation than we possess. As to any question of fact concerning the life or history of animals, we should hesitate a long time before contradicting either Mr. Roosevelt or Mr. Burroughs. Our criticism of the President's denunciation of Mr. Long was not based upon a question of fact. If Mr. Burroughs will look again carefully at what *The Outlook* said respecting the Roosevelt-Long controversy, he will see that we distinctly disavowed expressing an opinion regarding the accuracy of Mr. Long's observations. We think it undoubted that he has often made unconscious misstatements of fact, and perhaps not infrequently has been misled by erroneous observation. All men, not even excepting the President and Mr. Burroughs or the editors of *The Outlook*, suffer from these defects. We take issue with the President in this controversy on other grounds, as follows:

First, we regret to see the President of the United States making a personal attack on any individual citizen on a question of this kind, for the simple reason that the private individual stands on uneven terms in any discussion with any man occupying the President's position. It is debatable whether the President might not, in an extreme case for the protection of the public morals of the whole country, publicly denounce a man who, by common consent, was believed to be debauching the morals or poisoning the minds of all the schoolchildren of the country. Mr. Long is not such an individual. Moreover, our own careful observation and experience lead us to believe that his books have, on the whole, done much more good than harm, by interesting the children of this country in the life and welfare of animals. In this respect, in our judgment, he has had wider influence among young children than Mr. Burroughs himself. Mr. Burroughs appeals to the adult mind, Mr. Long to the imagination and curiosity of the child. . . .]

—The Editors of *The Outlook*

Charles G. D. Roberts on the
Evolution of the Animal Story

(1902)

Charles George Douglas Roberts, the famed Canadian poet and novelist, was born in 1860 in New Brunswick. After earning his bachelor's and master's degrees at the University of New Brunswick, he worked as a high school teacher and principal, then edited a newspaper, the *Toronto Week*. For a decade he taught literature at King's College in Windsor, Nova Scotia. He also wrote prolifically, and before his death in 1943 he would be hailed as one of the greatest of Canadian writers, the author of dozens of books of poetry and prose — including such popular nature books as *The Kindred of the Wild* (1902), *The Watchers of the Trails* (1904), and *Red Fox* (1905).

In the excerpt below, which appeared in 1902 as the introduction to *Kindred of the Wild*, Roberts anatomizes the genre at which he excelled, the animal story. He insists that the animal story is most usefully understood as "a psychological romance constructed on a framework of natural science." At its best, he adds, it "is a potent emancipator," capable of liberating readers for a time "from the mean tenement of self of which we do well to grow weary" and returning us "to the old kinship of earth, without asking us to relinquish by way of toll any part of the wisdom of the ages."

Alike in matter and in method, the animal story, as we have it to-day, may be regarded as a culmination. The animal story, of course, in one form or another, is as old as the beginnings of literature. Perhaps the most engrossing part in the life-drama of primitive man was that played by the beasts which he hunted, and by those which hunted him. They pressed incessantly upon his perceptions. They furnished both material and impulse for his first gropings toward pictorial art. When he acquired the kindred art of telling a story, they supplied his earliest themes; and they suggested the hieroglyphs by means of which, on carved bone or painted rock, he first gave his narrative a form to outlast the spoken breath. We may not unreasonably infer that the first animal story—the remote but authentic ancestor of "Mowgli" and "Lobo" and "Krag"—was a story of some successful hunt, when success meant life to the starving family; or of some desperate escape, when the truth of the narrative was attested, to the hearers squatted trembling about their fire, by the sniffings of the baffled bear or tiger at the rock-barred mouth of the cave. Such first animal stories had at least one merit of prime literary importance. They were convincing. The first critic, however supercilious, would be little likely to cavil at their verisimilitude.

Somewhat later, when men had begun to harass their souls, and their neighbours, with problems of life and conduct, then these same animals, hourly and in every aspect thrust beneath the eyes of their observation, served to point the moral of their tales. The beasts, not being in a position to resent the ignoble office thrust upon them, were compelled to do duty as concrete types of those obvious virtues and vices of which alone the unsophisticated ethical sense was ready to take cognisance. In this way, as soon as composition became a *métier*, was born the fable; and in this way the ingenuity of the first author enabled him to avoid a perilous unpopularity among those whose weaknesses and defects his art held up to the scorn of all the caves.

These earliest observers of animal life were compelled by the necessities of the case to observe truly, if not deeply. Pitting their wits against those of their four-foot rivals, they had to know their antagonists, and respect them, in order to overcome them. But it was only the most salient characteristics of each species that concerned the practical observer. It was simple to remember that the tiger was cruel, the fox cunning, the wolf rapacious. And so, as advancing civilisation drew an ever widening line between man and the animals, and men became more and more engrossed in the interests of their own kind, the personalities of the wild creatures which they had once known so well became obscured to them, and the creatures themselves came to be regarded, for the purposes of literature, as types or symbols merely,—except in those cases, equally obstructive to exact observation, where they were revered as temporary tenements of the spirits of departed kinsfolk. The characters in that great beast-epic of the middle ages, "Reynard the Fox," though far more elaborately limned than those which play their succinct rôles in the fables of Æsop, are at the same time in their elaboration far more alien to the truths of wild nature. Reynard, Isegrim, Bruin, and Greybeard have little resemblance to the fox, the wolf, the bear, and the badger, as patience, sympathy, and the camera reveal them to us to-day.

The advent of Christianity, strange as it may seem at first glance, did not make for a closer understanding between man and the lower animals. While it was militant, fighting for its life against the forces of paganism, its effort was to set man at odds with the natural world, and fill his eyes with the wonders of the spiritual. Man was the only thing of consequence on earth, and of man, not his body, but his soul. Nature was the ally of the enemy. The way of nature was the way of death. In man alone was the seed of the divine. Of what concern could be the joy or pain of creatures of no soul, to-morrow returning to the dust? To strenuous spirits, their eyes fixed upon the fear of hell for themselves, and the certainty of it for their neighbours, it smacked of sin to take thought of the feelings of such evanescent products of corruption. Hence it came that, in spite of the gentle understanding of such sweet saints as Francis of Assisi, Anthony of Padua, and Colomb of the Bees, the inarticulate kindred for a long time reaped small comfort from the Dispensation of Love.

With the spread of freedom and the broadening out of all intellectual interests which characterise these modern days, the lower kindreds began to regain their old place in the concern of man. The revival of interest in the animals found literary expression (to classify roughly) in two forms, which necessarily overlap each other now and then, viz., the story of adventure and the anecdote of observation. Hunting as a recreation, pursued with zest from pole to tropics by restless seekers after the new, supplied a species of narrative singularly akin to what the first animal stories must have been, — narratives of desperate encounter, strange peril, and hairbreadth escape. Such hunters' stories and travellers' tales are rarely conspicuous for the exactitude of their observation; but that was not the quality at first demanded of them by fireside readers. The attention of the writer was focussed, not upon the peculiarities or the emotions of the beast protagonist in each fierce, brief drama, but upon the thrill of the action, the final triumph of the human actor. The inevitable tendency of these stories of adventure with beasts was to awaken interest in animals, and to excite a desire for exact knowledge of their traits and habits.

The interest and the desire evoked the natural historian, the inheritor of the half-forgotten mantle of Pliny. Precise and patient scientists made the animals their care, observing with microscope and measure, comparing bones, assorting families, subdividing subdivisions, till at length all the beasts of significance to man were ticketed neatly, and laid bare, as far as the inmost fibre of their material substance was concerned, to the eye of popular information.

Altogether admirable and necessary as was this development at large, another, of richer or at least more spiritual significance, was going on at home. Folk who loved their animal comrades — their dogs, horses, cats, parrots, elephants — were observing, with the wonder and interest of discoverers, the astonishing fashion in which the mere instincts of these so-called irrational creatures were able to simulate the operations of reason. The results of this observation were written down, till "anecdotes of animals" came to form a not inconsiderable body of literature. The drift of all these data was overwhelmingly toward one conclusion. The mental processes of the animals observed were seen to be far more complex than the observers had supposed. Where instinct was called in to account for the elaborate ingenuity with which a dog would plan and accomplish the outwitting of a rival, or the nice judgment with which an elephant, with no nest-building ancestors behind him to instruct his brain, would choose and adjust the teak-logs which he was set to pile, it began to seem as if that faithful faculty was being overworked. To explain yet other cases, which no accepted theory seemed to fit, coincidence was invoked, till that rare and elusive phenomenon threatened to become as customary as buttercups. But when instinct and coincidence had done all that could be asked of them, there remained a great unaccounted-for body of facts; and men were forced at last to accept the proposition that, within their varying limitations, animals can and do reason. As far, at least, as the mental intelligence is concerned, the gulf dividing the lowest of the human species from the highest of the animals has in these latter days been reduced to a very narrow psychological fissure.

Whether avowedly or not, it is with the psychology of animal life that the representative animal stories of to-day are first of all concerned. Looking deep into the eyes of certain of the four-footed kindred, we have been startled to see therein a something, before unrecognised, that answered to our inner and intellectual, if not spiritual selves. We have suddenly attained a new and clearer vision. We have come face to face with personality, where we were blindly wont to predicate mere instinct and automatism. It is as if one should step carelessly out of one's back door, and marvel to see unrolling before his new-awakened eyes the peaks and seas and misty valleys of an unknown world. Our chief writers of animal stories at the present day may be regarded as explorers of this unknown world, absorbed in charting its topography. They work, indeed, upon a substantial foundation of known facts. They are minutely scrupulous as to their natural history, and assiduous contributors to that science. But above all are they diligent in their search for the motive beneath the action. Their care is to catch the varying, elusive personalities which dwell back of the luminous brain windows of the dog, the horse, the deer, or wrap themselves in reserve behind the inscrutable eyes of all the cats, or sit aloof in the gaze of the hawk and the eagle. The animal story at its highest point of development is a psychological romance constructed on a framework of natural science.

The real psychology of the animals, so far as we are able to grope our way toward it by deduction and induction combined, is a very different thing from the psychology of certain stories of animals which paved the way for the present vogue. Of these, such books as "Beautiful Joe" and "Black Beauty" are deservedly conspicuous examples. It is no detraction from the merit of these books, which have done great service in awakening a sympathetic understanding of the animals and sharpening our sense of kinship with all that breathe, to say that their psychology is human. Their animal characters think and feel as human beings would think and feel under like conditions. This marks the stage which these works occupy in the development of the animal story.

The next stage must be regarded as, in literature, a climax indeed, but not the climax in this genre. I refer to the "Mowgli" stories of Mr. Kipling. In these tales the animals are frankly humanised. Their individualisation is distinctly human, as are also their mental and emotional processes, and their highly elaborate powers of expression. Their notions are complex; whereas the motives of real animals, so far as we have hitherto been able to judge them, seem to be essentially simple, in the sense that the motive dominant at a given moment quite obliterates, for the time, all secondary motives. Their reasoning powers and their constructive imagination are far beyond anything which present knowledge justifies us in ascribing to the inarticulate kindreds. To say this is in no way to depreciate such work, but merely to classify it. There are stories being written now which, for interest and artistic value, are not to be mentioned in the same breath with the "Mowgli" tales, but which nevertheless occupy a more advanced stage in the evolution of this genre.

It seems to me fairly safe to say that this evolution is not likely to go beyond the point to which it has been carried to-day. In such a story, for instance, as that of "Krag, the Kootenay Ram," by Mr. Ernest Seton, the interest centres about the personality, individuality, mentality, of an animal, as well as its purely physical characteristics. The field of animal psychology so admirably opened is an inexhaustible world of wonder. Sympathetic exploration may advance its boundaries to a degree of which we hardly dare to dream; but such expansion cannot be called evolution. There would seem to be no further evolution possible, unless based upon a hypothesis that animals have souls. As souls are apt to elude exact observation, to forecast any such development would seem to be at best merely fanciful.

The animal story, as we now have it, is a potent emancipator. It frees us for a little from the world of shop-worn utilities, and from the mean tenement of self of which we do well to grow weary. It helps us to return to nature, without requiring that we at the same time return to barbarism. It leads us back to the old kinship of earth, without asking us to relinquish by way of toll any part of the wisdom of the ages, any fine essential of the "large result of time." The clear and candid life to which it reinitiates us, far behind though it lies in the long upward march of being, holds for us this quality. It has ever the more significance, it has ever the richer gift of refreshment and renewal, the more humane the heart and spiritual the understanding which we bring to the intimacy of it.

Mabel Osgood Wright on
Nature, Gender, Outdoor Life, and Fiction
(1903 and 1905)

The nature writer and conservationist Mabel Osgood Wright was born in 1859 into a decidedly literary family. Her father, a Unitarian minister and author of several essays, biographies, and translations, was part of the prominent New York circle associated with William Cullen Bryant. Her mother was related to Susanna Rowson, author of the popular early American novel, *Charlotte Temple*. Wright's first book, *The Friendship of Nature* (1894), was a collection of newspaper pieces appearing originally in the *New York Evening Post*. A year later she published one of the earliest modern field guides, *Birdcraft* (1895); before her death in 1934 she would go on to write a number of magazine articles — many of them as a contributing editor for the new ornithological magazine, *Bird-Lore* — and at least twenty-five novels and nature books.

As one of the first conservationists to systematically approach the problem of bird protection, Wright was instrumental in the formation of Birdcraft Sanctuary, an early Connecticut refuge that she managed for several years. She also helped found the Connecticut Audubon Society and served for several years as its president; later she would be named a director of the National Association of Audubon Societies.

The first of the two essays below appeared in the *Critic* in 1903. Among other things, it raises an interesting objection to the gendering of nature. Given that "Nature is one and indivisible," Wright asks, "why is Nature always spoken of as feminine — Mother Nature — which indicates the incomplete, the partial?" Wright also recognizes in contemporary nature writing the fundamental distinction, familiar to today's ecocritics, between anthropocentric and biocentric perspectives, noting that there are "two distinct schools of Nature Study," one "which for lack of a better name we may call economic humanity, the preservation of Nature, that we may still have it to enjoy and no type may prematurely perish; and the more ethical one of viewing the wild from its own point of view."

Wright notes that the exploding popularity of outdoor recreation "has within the past ten years opened an entirely new field for authors." With writers rushing to meet this growing demand, she asks, how is the public to tell the good from the bad? Though she is being facetious in suggesting that "the Publisher's Association . . . found a scholarship of Nature-Book criticism," she is serious in pondering the criteria of good nature writing. In this she may well have been prompted by the nature faker controversy, which was then in full force and to which she repeatedly refers — particularly in the second of the two essays below, which appeared in 1905 in the *New York Times*. Like John Burroughs, Wright is critical of the work of William J. Long; she goes further than Burroughs, however, in acknowledging that the natural world affords an appropriate vehicle for fiction and that fiction conveys truths of its own. Where Burroughs sees a question of scientific truth, Wright more perceptively sees a question of literary merit — and it is as a deficient writer, rather than as a purveyor of falsehoods, that she criticizes Long.

🌸 🌸 🌸

From "Life Outdoors and Its Effect Upon Literature" (1903)

We have not always been a Nature-loving people, for if we had, it would have been reflected earlier in our literature and art. The colonists had too severe a hand-to-hand struggle with Nature's ruder elements to stand back from them and get the perspective necessary for the enjoyment of its beauties. The earlier writings were mere inventories, and the values given were of food and meat, not loveliness. We had the explorer, the trapper, and the hunter, — in fact I believe that with man as with other animals the primary instinct is to hunt, and so the distinction between the hunter for pelt and food and the hunter for sport is often only one of degree.

For a hundred years past the well-to-do dwellers in cities have had country places more or less remote, to which they retired for change and relaxation, but the impulse to seek Nature pure and simple, even if it was felt by individuals, had no general leavening force and left no impress.

In early times, when the country looked toward New England for its intellectual stimulus, Nature, one might say, was held in abhorrence. The very backbone of the Puritan cult being that Nature and depravity were interchangeable terms, there could be no hope of an understanding until the ice of prejudice was melted by the gradual thaw, neutralized and finally swept away by the middle-century flood of transcendentalism that broke down the barriers and allowed people to come face to face with Nature and understand what she really means.

By the way, why is Nature always spoken of as feminine — Mother Nature — which indicates the incomplete, the partial? Nature is one and indivisible, the eternal male and female, the teacher whose rule no one may gainsay; who is unchangeable, save through evolution of type, no matter how much humanity and its view-point may alter; the sociologist whose arguments no one can refute, whose penalties no one can alter, for the Creator has bestowed upon His agent limitless power within its own domain, and it is at once adorable and pitiless.

Always excepting the poets, who ever in spirit live the Life Outdoors, our first authors were sermonists and historians, our first artists portrait makers, public sentiment, more than environment, doubtless guiding their choice. Audubon was the firstborn American to approach Nature for her own sake, with brush and pen. Durand did not turn to landscape painting until he had been for some time an engraver, and it was not until Thomas Cole failed as an itinerant painter of portraits that he turned to landscape work, perhaps learning in his wanderings for the first time what American Nature had to offer Art.

It is many years since, when N. P. Willis, seeking health in the valley of the Susquehanna, wrote "Letters from under a Bridge." Emerson's essay on Nature was published about this time; and ten years were to elapse before Thoreau in 1849 bid his countrymen to what Lowell called "his water party," "A Week on the Concord and Merrimac Rivers."

This book marked an era; it was the first clear, decisive call to man to lead the Life Outdoors; it was not written in answer to any demand or need of man in general, but expressed the emotions felt by Thoreau in abandoning the artificial. And though this utterance from its overweight of quotation and comparison lacks the intrinsic value of his later work, it still remains our first example of Nature literature pure and simple. . . .

. . . The present great awakening of the people facing eastward and watching the rising sun is of course a reaction from the intense contraction and brain worry of city life, a striving against artificial conditions, and the wonderful annual pilgrimage to the Life Outdoors is a movement of the greatest importance to all America to-day in securing the perpetuity of the race through the betterment of physical health and mental energy.

That this crusade should have its impulse and rise at the time of the greatest financial prosperity and consequently highest nervous tension that the country has ever known, is fresh proof of the continued presence of the adjusting balance wheel. It is not a "going back to Nature" as it is often called, for any backward movement is to be deplored; not a relapse to insensate savagery, but a stepping forward, with keen understanding eyes and outstretched hands, to meet Nature upon the higher plane of the desire of perfect mental and physical understanding.

Many pens and voices preached the new order. Burroughs was its recording secretary and Hamilton Gibson its noble exponent with both brush and pen, while dry-plate photography stepped in just in time to be recording angel of the almost unbelievable.

This new and wholesome attitude is in itself an appeal—a public appeal from the multitude who do not know, to the few who do, or think they do, for information, so that this condition has within the past ten years opened an entirely new field for authors, and been productive not only of much interesting and instructive reading-matter but a great deal that must take a permanent rank as literature.

Up to 1890, however, it was well-nigh impossible to obtain any inexpensive handbooks upon birds, flowers, trees, stars, or any other of the objects that set the Nature lover's mind at work, that were at once accurate and yet written in a style suited to popular comprehension. The closet scientists shrugged their shoulders and said, "You have your botanys, ornithologies, charts, etc., work your way out, you lack industry," but some were wiser and relented and joined their knowledge with the spontaneous freedom of expression belonging to the non-scientific, and behold "The How to Know Nature" school of writers was inaugurated and its success has been as tremendous as the output has been somewhat overpowering.

The new order has also developed and is being developed by two distinct schools of Nature Study: through that which for lack of a better name we may call economic humanity, the preservation of Nature, that we may still have it to enjoy and no type may prematurely perish; and the more ethical one of viewing the wild from its own point of view, which Kipling approached from the man's point in the Jungle Books and Thompson-Seton from within in "Wild Animals I Have Known." Of the latter writer it may be said as of Frederick II of Swabia, the royal naturalist who was five hundred years ahead of his times, "he observes with his *own* eyes and draws judicious conclusions."

Now by the very nature of the revolt that does away with the hard and fast scientific boundaries and bids all welcome who have anything to say and words wherein to say it. There are originators and there are imitators. There are discoverers and there are guessers, there are seers and there are braggarts. That a distinct line should be drawn between these classes is of the greatest importance to those who wish "to know."

There are public censors of history and of all branches of exact science, but in that wide field of so-called Nature Study, holding sway in school as well as out, and embracing pretty much everything from the simplest fact to profound psychological theories of animal intelligence and transmigration, there seem to be as yet no authoritative and unprejudiced critics to separate sheep from goats.

Perhaps the Nature Study movement is too new and the creative expression too active, for there is a theory that the cult of pure criticism flourishes best when creative literature is in abeyance, which is not the present case with Nature books, for they are in full force even creating new fact-fantasies that if they are to be taken seriously should be seriously criticised.

Every spring the voice of the wailer is heard in the editorial rooms — more Nature books. Why not, pray? For how many centuries have the mysteries of the Human Heart received constant expression? Why then should not the great Heart of Nature, upon which everything else must rest, receive its due?

"Yes, that is all very well," says the editor, who is dividing the new crop among the various reviewers, "but it is so difficult to classify them and put them in hands competent to differentiate between the bad and the merely indifferent, for in no branch of literature perhaps is the supply so uneven and various. The purely sporting book, the gardening manual, etc. are easily disposed of, but all the others?

"After the first rush came the tendency, with people who think it's clever to write but haven't much to say, to undertake the compilation of a certain class of Nature writing, just as there was a period when rural parents with sons too weak for farming concluded they were predestined for the ministry—the results being equally direful. I think the Publishers' Association should found a scholarship of Nature-Book criticism, at the very least."

This is all very true, but at the same time the demand coming from every class in the community the supply must be equally catholic. The idealist may not tolerate the work of the mere reporter, who goes out to make copy and invades Nature as it were. Neither will the shop-girl riding out on her wheel of a Sunday be anything but repelled if forced to read Thoreau's meditations by Walden pond.

There is one school of writing, however, born of the recent pilgrimage to the Life Outdoors which is fraught with danger, in that it tends to provoke the ridicule of the thinking and well-informed, inside the rank of pilgrims as well as of outside scoffers. This might be called the School of the Long Bow, the literature of the braggart, its system and fault being the jumping at conclusions by inference and proclaiming general facts from single instances, after the fashion of the old catch logic—John is a man; John lies; *ergo*, all men are liars.

This sort of Nature writing, born not, as it assumes, of personal observation but of fluent speech and the impulse to do the real the "one better" that makes it unique even if unreal, is pernicious in the extreme, especially to the younger and more impressionable pilgrims, because it is a destroyer of values, and one of the greatest benefits of the Life Outdoors is its perfect balance.

But why worry—all the world is afield; some will gather wild roses, some mushrooms; and some in spite of all warnings will trim their hats with poison ivy; the fact that they are out of doors is the great thing; once being there they will never again dumbly and contentedly remain inside, any more than they will ever abandon shirtwaists and short skirts.

As to the books, let them come, good, bad, and indifferent, the survival will be only for the truest, because in the end they will be found the fittest. Also we should hesitate to brand deductions as untrue because they are not within the range of our own experiences. This attitude stamps the critic as a clock that has stopped. Sensationalism is a fungus of the early morning that appears in the generously fertilized flower-beds of all branches of literature and is generally dispelled by the sun long before noon. Besides, the discovery of an evil often works its cure as well as that of others. Think you that Diogenes would have so vociferously gone about with a lantern at mid-day to find an honest man, if his own father had not been caught debasing the coin of the realm?

"Nature as a Field for Fiction" (1905)

Some time ago when John Burroughs wrote his famous article for *The Atlantic Monthly* attacking the writings of Ernest Thompson Seton and William J. Long, he made one grave error; that of taking the point of view of the quasi scientific observer of nature's methods, instead of that of the naturalist facing a rather new literary phase where nature was seized as a field of fiction. Seton began with virile originality, but worked his lode so greedily that he frequently sidetracked and bored through into sand. Long used as his stock in trade an incomprehensible mixture of enthusiasm, love of the beautiful, inverted observation and folk-lore testimony of guides and halfbreeds, leaven by a weird credulity much broader than the wide but fixed limits of natural law, by which it must be judged, if his claims were to be regarded seriously.

Of course throughout all time natural history has been a setting for mythology, overdrawn conclusions, and errors of observation backed up by curious forms of ignorance such as made John Josselyn, gentleman of Kent, who, in writing his observations made in this country in 1638, states that "in the New World barley commonly degenerates into oats and Summer wheat often changeth into rye."

The difference between the creator of the hero of human fiction and the authentic record of the doings of a specific individual that constitute biography lies in this. The hero of fiction is in more or less degree a composite character, but all his attributes must be of course in accord with the known qualities of man, even though mixed in proportions to suit the author. This latter point some of our creators of this new type of fiction forget, and insist not only upon the introduction of unprovable characteristics for their animal heroes, that do not add but rather detract from the strength of the situations, no matter in what light they are considered, but insist that the composite be considered as an individual pure and simple, whose comings, goings, and thoughts they have personally (or by proxy) watched and fathomed.

This position is foolish from any standpoint, for those who love a good, human story, both for its characterization and literary expression, do not care a pennyworth whether the hero is an actual man known to the author or a creature of his fancy, so long as a rational and convincing probability is maintained. It is when the authors in this new field insist that they are not only telling "the truth and nothing but the truth," which moreover, they have personally touched, tasted, swallowed, and digested, that a halt must be called.

Charles G. D. Roberts, the most consistent writer of this new school, as well as the one having the most artistic temperament, regarded from the literary standpoint, sounds the right note in the preface to his splendid story of "Red Fox," when he says:

> In the following story I have tried to trace the career of a fox of the backwoods district of Eastern Canada. The hero of the story, Red Fox, may be taken as fairly typical, both in his characteristics and in the experiences that befall him, in spite of the fact that he is stronger and cleverer than the average run of foxes. . . . This fact does not detract from his authenticity as a type of his kind. . . . As for any emotions which Red Fox may once in a great while seem to display, these may safely be accepted by the most cautious as fox emotions, not as human emotions. In so far as man is himself an animal, he is subject to and impelled by many emotions which he must share with not a few other members of the animal kingdom. Any full presentation of an individual animal of one of the more highly developed species must depict certain emotions not altogether unlike those which a human being experiences under like conditions. To do this is not by any means, as some hasty critics would have it, to ascribe human emotions to the lower animals.

William J. Long, however, in his latest volume, "Northern Trails," persistently and foolishly, no matter what may be the standpoint, adheres to his old formula, which was made into kindling wood, burned, and the ashes scattered to the four winds by Burroughs's somewhat narrow criticism. This volume, with its spirited illustrations by Charles Copeland, is made up of eight stories. "Wayseeses the Strong One," (a wolf story, following many miles after "Lobo," Seton's first and best achievement,) "In Quest of Weptonk the Wild," the pursuit of the wild goose in its breeding grounds; "Pequam the Fisher," the cunning robber of traps; "The Trail of the Cunning One," "Out of the Deeps," dealing with whales, seals, sharks, and gulls; "Matweeck of the Ice-

bergs," a polar bear; "Where the Salmon Jump," and "The Story of Kopseep," a salmon-colored romance.

Listen to the author's solemn guarantee of absolute veracity, and the completely identified individuality of each animal depicted, with one single exception in the case of Kopseep the Salmon, where, it being impossible to
personally follow the fish under water from the sea to the river sources, the
author was obliged "either to omit that part of his life or to picture it as best
I could from imagination and the records of the salmon hatcheries and deep-
sea travelers."

> The reader who has not followed such trails before will ask at once, How many
> of these things are true? Every smallest incident recorded here is as true as
> careful and accurate observation can make it. In most of the following chap-
> ters, as in all previous volumes, will be found the direct results of my own
> experience among animals; and in the few cases where, as stated plainly in the
> text, I have used the experience of other and wiser men, I have taken the facts
> from first hand and accurate observers, and have then sifted them carefully, so
> as to retain only those that are, in my own mind, without a question as to truth.

Ah, Mr. Long, here is another illustration of the glaring inconsistency of
your methods. We, the reading public, must swallow whole any presentment
you choose to make, but you reserve the right to question the statement born
of the experience of "other and wiser men, firsthand and accurate observers,"
and retain only what appeals to you as being truth, thus confessing to a standard of veracity that, instead of being fixed, is to be wholly controlled by the
personal equation of the author. Against this a priori the pen of criticism is
powerless except to recommend a severe Winter course of pure logic as a
possible cure. Aside from the controversial side as to whether these eight
stories are to be classified as natural history or fiction, these tales of the northern trails are dull and lifeless. A certain entertaining quality that the author's
earlier volumes, probable or improbable, possessed is missing. For some reason, we care very little about the animals portrayed; the stories are too much
worked out; insistence upon truth and verbosity of detail and palpable word
painting are not creative qualities, and nowhere is there a single breath of
the genius such as makes the creatures of the jungle books as vitally probable
to us as the little squirrel that gambols about the porch.

Fannie Eckstorm on
Thoreau's *The Maine Woods*
(1908)

Fannie Pearson Hardy Eckstorm was born in 1865 in Brewer, Maine, on the Penobscot River adjacent to Bangor. Her mother was descended from the owners of one of Maine's earliest lumber mills, and her father traded in furs; the two businesses, as Eckstorm later wrote, kept her family in contact with "most of the hunters, trappers, head lumbermen, head boatmen, and Indian guides in northern and eastern Maine." This wide circle of acquaintances would provide an endless source of material for her many books.

In 1885 Eckstorm entered Smith College, where among her accomplishments was the founding of an Audubon society. In the summer of 1888, canoeing with her father, she made the first of many excursions through the Maine backcountry. From 1889 to 1891 she served as superintendent of the Brewer public schools—perhaps the first woman to hold that office in Maine. Her writing career began with a series of articles for *Field and Stream,* in which she argued for policies that would preserve the state's big game without prejudicing the traditional hunting rights of Native Americans. She went on to write eleven books and numerous articles on topics ranging from Maine folklore to ornithology.

In "Thoreau's Maine Woods," excerpted below from the *Atlantic Monthly* of August 1908, Eckstorm draws on her wide-ranging experience to assess Thoreau's treatment of the Maine wilderness. She handily deflates the myth of Thoreau-as-master-woodsman but nonetheless has high praise for his ability to find poetic significance in the wilds, noting that it "was not as an observer that Thoreau surpassed other men, but as an interpreter." By revealing "the human values of natural objects," she argues, Thoreau's art can "reveal the Me through the Not Me" of nonhuman nature.

۞ ۞ ۞

It is more than half a century since Henry D. Thoreau made his last visit to Maine. And now the forest which he came to see has all but vanished, and in its place stands a new forest with new customs. No one should expect to find here precisely what Thoreau found; therefore, before all recollection of the old days has passed away, it is fitting that some one who knew their traditions should bear witness to Thoreau's interpretation of the Maine woods.

We hardly appreciate how great are the changes of the last fifty years; how the steamboat, the motor-boat, the locomotive, and even the automobile, have invaded regions which twenty years ago could be reached only by the lumberman's batteau and the hunter's canoe; how cities have arisen, and more are being projected, on the same ground where Thoreau says that "the best shod travel for the most part with wet feet," and that "melons, squashes, sweet-corn, tomatoes, beans and many other vegetables, could not be ripened," because the forest was so dense and moist.

Less than twenty years since there was not a sporting camp in any part of the northern Maine wilderness; now who may number them? Yet, even before the nineties, when one could travel for days and meet no one, the pine tree was gone; the red-shirted lumberman was gone; the axe was about to give place to the saw; and soon, almost upon the clearing where Thoreau reported the elder Fowler, the remotest settler, as wholly content in his solitude and thinking that "neighbors, even the best, were only trouble and expense," was to raise one of the largest pulp mills in the world, catching the logs midway their passage down the river and grinding them into paper. And the pine tree, of which Thoreau made so much? Native to the state and long accustomed to its woods, I cannot remember ever having seen a perfect, old-growth white pine tree; it is doubtful if there is one standing in the state to-day.

So the hamadryad has fled before the demand for ship-timber and Sunday editions, and the unblemished forest has passed beyond recall. There are woods enough still; there is game enough, — more of some kinds than in the old days; there are fish enough; there seems to be room enough for all who come; but the man who has lived here long realizes that the woods are being "camped to death;" and the man who is old enough to remember days departed rustles the leaves of Thoreau's book when he would listen again to the pine tree soughing in the wind.

What is it that *The Maine Woods* brings to us besides? The moods and music of the forest; the vision of white tents beside still waters; of canoes drawn out on pebbly beaches; of camp-fires flickering across rippling rapids; the voice of the red squirrel, "spruce and fine;" the melancholy laughter of the loon, and the mysterious "night warbler," always pursued and never apprehended. Most of all it introduces us to Thoreau himself.

It must be admitted in the beginning that *The Maine Woods* is not a masterpiece. Robert Louis Stevenson discards it as not literature. It is, however, a very good substitute, and had Robert Louis worn it next the skin he might perhaps have absorbed enough of the spirit of the American forest to avoid the gaudy melodrama which closes *The Master of Ballantrae*. *The Maine Woods* is of another world. Literature it may not be, nor one of the "three books of his that will be read with much pleasure;" but it is—the Maine woods. Since Thoreau's day, whoever has looked at these woods to advantage has to some extent seen through Thoreau's eyes. Certain it is that no other man has ever put the coniferous forest between the leaves of a book.

For that he came—for that and the Indian. Open it where you will—and the little old first edition is by all odds to be chosen if one is fastidious about the printed page, to get the full savor of it; open where you will and these two speak to you. He finds water "too civilizing;" he wishes to become "selvaggia;" he turns woodworm in his metamorphosis, and loves to hear himself crunching nearer and nearer to the heart of the tree. He is tireless in his efforts to wrench their secrets from the woods; and, in every trial, he endeavors, not to talk *about* them, but to flash them with lightning vividness into the mind of the reader. "It was the opportunity to be ignorant that I improved. It suggested to me that there was something to be seen if one had eyes. It made a believer of me more than before. I believed the woods were not tenantless, but choke-full of honest spirits as good as myself any day."

It is sometimes the advantage of a second-rate book that it endears the writer to us. The Thoreau of *Walden*, with his housekeeping all opened up for inspection, refusing the gift of a rug rather than shake it, throwing away his paperweight to avoid dusting it—where's the woman believes he *would* have dusted it?—parades his economies priggishly, like some pious anchoret with a business eye fixed on Heaven. But when he tells us in the appendix to the *Woods* that for a cruise three men need only one large knife and one iron spoon (for all), a four-quart tin pail for kettle, two tin dippers, three tin plates and a fry pan, his economy, if extreme, is manly and convincing. We meet him here among men whom we have known ourselves; we see how he treated them and how they treated him, and he appears to better advantage than when skied among the lesser gods of Concord. . . .

There is a popular notion that Thoreau was a great woodsman, able to go anywhere by dark or daylight, without path or guide; that he knew all the secrets of the pioneer and the hunter; that he was unequaled as an observer, and almost inerrant in judgment, being able to determine at a glance weight, measure, distance, area, or cubic contents. The odd thing about these popular opinions is that they are not true. Thoreau was not a woodsman; he was not infallible; he was not a scientific observer; he was not a scientist at all. He could do many things better than most men; but the sum of many excellencies is not perfection.

For the over-estimate of Thoreau's abilities, Emerson is chiefly responsible. His noble eulogy of Thoreau has been misconstrued in a way which shows the alarming aptitude of the human mind for making stupid blunders. We all have a way of taking hold of a striking detail—which Mr. Emerson was a rare one for perceiving—and making of it the whole story. We might name it *the fallacy of the significant detail.* Do we not always see Hawthorne, the youth, walking by night? Who thinks of it any less habitual than eating his dinner? And because Stevenson, in an unguarded moment, confessed that "he had played the sedulous ape" to certain authors, no writer, out of respect to our weariness, has ever forborne to remind us of that pleasant monkey trick of Stevenson's youth. Nor are we ever allowed to forget that Thoreau "saw as with a microscope, heard as with ear-trumpet," and that "his power of observation seemed to indicate additional senses." It is because the majority of mankind see no difference in values between facts aglow with poetic fervor and facts preserved in the cold storage of census reports, that Emerson's splendid eulogy of his friend, with its vivid, personal characterizations rising like the swift bubbles of a boiling spring all through it, has created the unfortunate impression that Thoreau made no blunders.

Emerson himself did not distinguish between the habitual and the accidental; between a clever trick, like that of lifting breams guarding their nests, and the power to handle any kind of fish. He even ran short of available facts, and grouped those of unequal value. To be able to grasp an even dozen of pencils requires but little training; to be able to estimate the weight of a pig, or the cordwood in a tree, needs no more than a fairly good judgment; but that "he could pace sixteen rods more accurately than another man could measure them with rod and chain,"—that is nonsense, for it puts at naught the whole science of surveying. Emerson's data being unequal in rank and kind, the whole sketch is a little out of focus, and consequently the effect is agreeably artistic.

Nor is the matter mended by misquotation. Emerson says, "He could find his path in the woods at night, he said, better by his feet than his eyes." There is nothing remarkable in this. How does any one keep the path across his own lawn on a black dark night? But even so careful a man as Stevenson paraphrases thus: "He could guide himself about the woods on the darkest night by the touch of his feet." Here we have a different matter altogether. By taking out that "path," a very ordinary accomplishment is turned into one quite impossible. Because Emerson lacked woods learning, the least variation from his exact words is likely to result in something as absurd or as exaggerated as this.

Thoreau's abilities have been overrated. *The Maine Woods* contains errors in the estimates of distance, area, speed, and the like, too numerous to mention in detail. No Penobscot boatman can run a batteau over falls at the rate of fifteen miles an hour, as Thoreau says; no canoeman can make a hundred miles a day, even on the St. John River. The best records I can discover fall far short of Thoreau's estimate for an average good day's run. Even when he says that his surveyor's eye thrice enabled him to detect the slope of the current, he magnifies his office. Any woman who can tell when a picture hangs straight can see the slant of the river in all those places.

But his worst error in judgment, and the one most easily appreciated on its own merits, is the error he made in climbing Katahdin. He writes that their camp was "broad off Katahdin and about a dozen miles from the summit," whereas we know that his camp was not five miles in an air-line from the top of the South Slide, and not more than seven from the highest peak. The trail from the stream to the slide has always been called four miles, and Thoreau says his boatmen told him that it was only four miles to the mountain; "but as I judged, and as it afterwards proved, nearer fourteen." The only reason why it proved "nearer fourteen" was because he did not go the short way. Instead of climbing by the Slide, where all West Branch parties ascend to-day, he laid a northeast course "directly for the base of the highest peak," through all the débris and underbrush at the foot of the mountain, climbing where it is so steep that water hardly dares to run down. He ought to have reasoned that the bare top of a mountain is easy walking, and the nearest practicable point, rather than the peak itself, was the best place to climb.

But surely he was a competent naturalist? There is no space to go over the text in detail, but we may turn directly to the list of birds in the appendix. After making allowance for ornithology in the fifties being one of the inexact sciences, the list must be admitted to be notably bad. It is worse than immediately appears to the student who is not familiar with the older nomenclature. Thoreau names thirty-seven species, and queries four of them as doubtful. Oddly, the most characteristic bird of the region, the Canada jay, which the text mentions as seen, is omitted from the list. Of the doubtful species, the herring gull is a good guess; but the yellow-billed cuckoo and the prairie chicken (of all unlikely guesses the most improbable) are surely errors, while the white-bellied nuthatch, which he did not see, but thought he heard, rests only upon his conjecture. Mr. William Brewster thinks that it might occur in that region in suitably wooded localities, but I can find no record west of Houlton and north of Katahdin. The tree sparrow, though a common migrant, is more than doubtful as summer resident. The pine warbler must be looked upon with equal suspicion. The wood thrush is impossible — a clear mistake for the hermit. . . .

The list proves that, even according to the feeble light of the day, Thoreau was not an ornithologist. As a botanist he did much better; but that was largely by grace of Gray's *Manual*, then recently published. Of the scientific ardor which works without books and collates and classifies innumerable facts for the sake of systematic knowledge, he had not a particle. His notes, though voluminous and of the greatest interest, rarely furnish material for science. If he examined a partridge chick, newly hatched, it was not to give details of weight and color, but to speculate upon the rare clearness of its gaze. If he recorded a battle between black ants and red, he saw its mock heroic side and wrote an *Antiad* upon the occasion; but he did not wait to see the fight finished, and to count the slain.

It was not as an observer that Thoreau surpassed other men, but as an interpreter. He had the art — and how much of an art it is no one can realize until he has seated himself before an oak or a pine tree and has tried by the hour to write out its equation in terms of humanity—he had the art to see the human values of natural objects, to perceive the ideal elements of unreasoning nature and the service of those ideals to the soul of man. "The greatest delight which the fields and woods minister, is the suggestion of an occult relation between man and the vegetable," wrote Emerson; and it became Thoreau's chief text. It is the philosophy behind Thoreau's words, his attempt to reveal the Me through the Not Me, reversing the ordinary method, which makes his observations of such interest and value.

> Flower in the crannied wall,
> I pluck you out of the crannies;—
> Hold you here, root and all, in my hand,
> Little flower—but *if* I could understand
> What you are, root and all, and all in all,
> I should know what God and man is.

This power to see is rare; but mere good observation is not supernormal. We must not attribute to Thoreau's eyes what was wrought in his brain; to call him uniquely gifted in matters wherein a thousand men might equal him is not to increase his fame.

The Maine Woods also shows clearly that Thoreau knew nothing of woodcraft. Do we realize that his longest trip gave him only ten days actually spent in the woods? or that few tourists to-day attempt to cover the same ground in less than two or three weeks? What his own words proclaim there can be no disputing over, and Thoreau admits frankly, and sometimes naively, that he was incapable of caring for himself in the woods, which surely is the least that can be asked of a man to qualify him as a "woodsman."

In the first place, his mind does not work like a woodsman's. "We had not gone far," he writes, "before I was startled by seeing what I thought was an Indian encampment, covered with a red flag, on the bank, and exclaimed 'Camp!' to my comrades. I was slow to discover that it was a red maple changed by the frost." He ought to have been "slow to discover" that it was anything else. . . .

"The carry-paths themselves," he says again, "were more than usually indistinct, often the route being revealed only by countless small holes in the fallen timber made by the tacks in the drivers' boots, or where there *was* a slight trail we did not find it." This is almost funny. In those days the carries were little traveled except by the river-drivers; in summer they were much choked with shrubbery; but what did the man expect—a king's highway? That spring the whole East Branch drive, probably a hundred men, had tramped the carry for days; and every man had worn boots each of which, in those days, was armed with twenty-nine inch-long steel spikes. The whole carry had been pricked out like an embroidery pattern. Those little "tack-holes" *were* the carry. If Thoreau could have realized that a river-driver never goes far from water, and that his track is as sure as a mink's or an otter's to lead back to water, he would have appreciated how much, instead of how little, those calk-marks were telling him. But Thoreau did not know the facts of woods life, and when he saw a sign he was often incapable of drawing an inference from it.

The proof that Thoreau did not know the alphabet of woodcraft—if further proof is wanted—is that, on Mud Pond Carry, which, in his day, was the most open and well-trodden of all the woods roads beyond North-East Carry, he took a tote-road, used only for winter hauling, showing neither hoof-mark, sled-track, nor footprint in summer, and left the regular carry, worn by human feet, merely because a sign-board on the former pointed to his ultimate destination, Chamberlain Lake. Now in the woods a tote-road is a tote-road, and a carry is a carry; when a man is told to follow one, he is not expected to turn off upon the other; there is no more reason to confuse the two than to mistake a trolley line for a steam-railroad track. No wonder Polis "thought little of their woodcraft."

But aside from this deficiency in woods education, Thoreau never got to feel at home in the Maine wilderness. He was a good "pasture man," but here was something too large for him. He appreciated all the more its wildness and strangeness; and was the more unready to be venturesome. The very closeness of his acquaintance with Concord conspired to keep him from feeling at home where the surrounding trees, flowers, and birds were largely unfamiliar; for the better a man knows one fauna, the more he is likely to be ill at ease under a different environment. No man has expressed so well the timidity which sometimes assails the stranger when surrounded by the Sabbath peace of the wilderness. "You may penetrate half a dozen rods farther into that twilight wilderness, after some dry bark to kindle your fire with, and wonder what mysteries lie hidden still deeper in it, say at the end of a long day's walk; or you may run down to the shore for a dipper of water, and get a clearer view for a short distance up or down the stream. . . . But there is no sauntering off to see the country, and ten or fifteen rods seems a great way from your companions, and you come back with the air of a much-traveled man, as from a long journey, with adventures to relate, although you may have heard the crackling of the fire all the while,—and at a hundred rods you might be lost past recovery, and have to camp out." That is all very true, but most men do not care to own it. "It was a relief to get back to our smooth and still varied landscape," he writes after a week's trip to Chesuncook, which then, as now, was only the selvage of the woods. . . .

[T]hough he was neither woodsman nor scientist, Thoreau stood at the gateway of the woods and opened them to all future comers with the key of poetic insight. And after the woods shall have passed away, the vision of them as he saw them will remain. In all that was best in him Thoreau was a poet. The finest passages in this book are poetical, and he is continually striking out some glowing phrase, like a spark out of flint. The logs in the camp are "tuned to each other with the axe." "For beauty give me trees with the fur on." The pines are for the poet, "Who loves them like his own shadow in the air." Of the fall of a tree in the forest, he says, "It was a dull, dry, rushing sound, with a solid core to it, like the shutting of a door in some distant entry of the damp and shaggy wilderness." Katahdin is "a permanent shadow." And upon it, "rocks, gray, silent rocks, were the silent flocks and herds that pastured, chewing a rocky cud at sunset. They looked at me with hard gray eyes, without a bleat or low." I have seen the rocks on many granite hills, but that belongs only to the top of Katahdin.

Indeed, this whole description of Katahdin is unequaled. "Chesuncook" is the best paper of the three, taken as a whole, but these few pages on Katahdin are incomparable. Happily he knew the traditions of the place, the awe and veneration with which the Indians regarded it as the dwelling place of Pamola, their god of thunder, who was angry at any invasion of his home and resented it in fogs and sudden storms. ("He very angry when you gone up there; you heard him gone *oo-oo-oo* over top of gun-barrel," they used to say.) Thoreau's Katahdin was a realm of his own, in which for a few hours he lived in primeval solitude above the clouds, invading the throne of Pamola the Thunderer, as Prometheus harried Zeus of his lightnings. The gloomy grandeur of Aeschylus rises before him to give countenance, and he speaks himself as if he wore the buskin. But it is not windy declamation. He does not explode into exclamation points. Katahdin is a strange, lone, savage hill, unlike all others—a very Indian among mountains. It does not need superlatives to set it off. Better by far is Thoreau's grim humor, his calling it a "cloud factory," where they made their bed "in the nest of a young whirlwind," and lined it with "feathers plucked from the live tree." Had he been one of the Stonish men, those giants with flinty eyebrows, fabled to dwell within the granite vitals of Katahdin, he could not have dealt more stout-heartedly by the home of the Thunder-God.

The best of Thoreau's utterances in this volume are like these, tuned to the rapid and high vibration of the poetic string, but not resolved into rhythm. It is poetry, but not verse. Thoreau's prose stands in a class by itself. There is an honest hardness about it. We may accept or deny Buffon's dictum that the style is the man; but the man of soft and slippery make-up would strive in vain to acquire the granite integrity of structure which marks Thoreau's writing. It is not poetical prose in the ordinary scope of that flowery term; but, as the granite rock is sifted and threaded with veins of glistening quartz, this prose is fused at white heat with poetical insights and interpretations. Judged by ordinary standards, he was a poet who failed. He had no grace at metres; he had no aesthetic softness; his sense always overruled the sound of his stanzas. The fragments of verse which litter his workshop remind one of the chips of flint about an Indian encampment. They might have been the heads of arrows, flying high and singing in their flight, but that the stone was obdurate or the maker's hand was unequal to the shaping of it. But the waste is nothing; there is behind them the Kineo that they came from, this prose of his, a whole mountain of the same stuff, every bit capable of being wrought to ideal uses.

Havelock Ellis on the Psychological
Roots of the Love of Wilderness
(1909)

In 1865 — just six years after his birth in Croydon, Surrey — Henry Havelock Ellis accompanied his sea-captain father on a voyage to Australia and South America. Ten years later he returned to Australia to teach in a remote country school in New South Wales, which experience provided the material for his only novel, *Kanga Creek*. After teaching for four years in Australia, Ellis returned to Britain to study medicine at St. Thomas's Hospital in London. He practiced for a few years, then abandoned medicine to pursue his literary interests, editing the *Mermaid Series of Old Dramatists* and working on the editorial staff of the prestigious *Westminster Review*.

Ellis is best known for the research in human sexuality that culminated in his monumental and controversial *Studies in the Psychology of Sex*. As his biographers note, his groundbreaking work as a sexologist tends to obscure the fact that he was also a wide-ranging literary and cultural critic. These combined interests in nature, psychology, and sex appear to date at least as far back as his years in Australia, as *Kanga Creek* makes clear. Early in this novel, speaking in a semi-autobiographical third person, the narrator remarks on how frequently

> the dreary heat of that path across the hills, or the toilsome slime of the descent after rain was made sweet and easy by this inner life which rendered him unconscious of the things around him. But yet in spite of himself the things around him formed an inseparable part of his mental process, and some indifferent or unnoticed object, some mere bush or hillock, became linked to an idea and forever recalled it with persistent irritation; and he grew irritated that the free pearls of his thought should be strung and confined by the common-

place line of his path across the hills. Yet, sometimes, under the stress of some peculiarly soft and exhilarating flood of light and air, of some wider pulse of blood, he was called out of such concentrated and abstract moods by more concrete appeals from the large nature around him.

Later, the natural setting of Kanga Creek provides the context in which the narrator ponders his dawning sexual awareness. In one particularly idyllic passage, Ellis's wild surroundings and his newfound lover seem one undifferentiated object of desire, and blend into a single picturesque tableau:

> The moon was bright above; below, a straggling row of pools, each a great pearl, marked the line of the creek; from the delicate boughs of the tall gums the long pale leaves drooped silently; there was no sound but the occasional scamper and cry of some nocturnal animal, or the remote melancholy call of the curlew; to the right loomed the great purple mass of Bambaroo; to the left soft luminous clouds lay on the horizon formed by a distant ridge. Close behind stretched upward the dusky green slope, the background on which rested the bright pale forms, inquisitive, alive, thrilling with a pulse of Nature so swift that the Nature around seemed dead. She sat on the stone, clasping her leg and softly resting his cheek on her knee, while her hands wandered from his hair to his neck. She said nothing and he was very still. . . .

In the essay below, first published in 1909 in the *Contemporary Review,* Ellis traces the development of the love of wilderness to the early Christians, or, more particularly, to "the special temperament of many of those who were most strongly drawn into the fold of Christianity." That special temperament was "psychasthenia," a condition believed to render the "ordinary routine of life" insufferable — a condition, Ellis suggests, that could be ameliorated by life in the ascetic and remotely situated communities of early Christianity. He writes that Rousseau, too, was psychasthenic, and thus "peculiarly fitted to be receptive to natural influences" and to infuse romanticism with the love of wild nature. In making such arguments, Ellis proves perhaps the earliest practitioner of what today is termed "ecopsychology."

The origin of the love of Nature in scenery has been obscured by confused and conflicting statements. We are told, on the one hand, that the beauty of wild Nature was discovered by Rousseau and the leaders of the Romantic movement during the following half-century. We are told, on the other hand, that the love of even the wildest landscape has existed in all ages. There is a certain amount of truth in both these statements, but they are not illuminative, because they fail to bring us to the causes of the love of Nature. It is useless to pile up miscellaneous quotations showing the appreciation, or the lack of appreciation, of natural scenery. We may, perhaps, reach the root of the matter, and reconcile opposing assertions, by analysing the significance of our accumulated facts.

By the love of wild Nature we properly mean the attraction to any kind of scenery — sky, mountain, ocean, forest, desert — untouched by man. Scenery mixed with man, to some extent moulded by him, and so presenting a suitable home, cannot fail always to have been agreeable from the primitive times, whether or not its agreeableness found expression or even became definitely conscious. The love of wild Nature is a love of scenery from which man is excluded, of scenery which seems, though perhaps mistakenly, without utility for man. In the strict sense, therefore, such feeling may be described as originally both unsociable and luxurious. It tended to draw men away from their fellows and away from the useful arts of life. . . .

There can be little doubt that the love of the wild in Nature received a powerful impetus from influences associated with the development of primitive Christianity. It was, indeed, a by-product of Christianity, for there is nothing in the doctrine of Christianity which implies direct approval or disapproval of any aspects of Nature. Christian doctrine may be said to encourage indifference towards Nature altogether, abstracting man's attention from the external world and concentrating it on the problems of the soul. The last book of the New Testament, the "Revelation" associated with the name of the Apostle John, is very significant from this point of view. The author of this book declares that he is writing in Patmos — a barren island of volcanic origin, but it can scarcely be said that his book either reflects any love of the natural conditions around him or represents any reaction against his environment leading to the recall of scenery the writer had known in the past. Imagery was essential to his purpose, but the imagery he selects is purely imaginary and, so far as possible, deliberately selected from the mineral world. His "New Jerusalem" is a gorgeous palace blazing with metal and jewels. There are no flowers there, no sunshine, no hills, and we are expressly told that there was no longer any sea, so that the natural objects which were most familiar to the writer's vision must have been peculiarly repulsive to him. The New Jerusalem might be a goldsmith's Paradise.

The first and most obvious way in which Christianity contributed to develop the love of the wild was by driving men out into the wilds. It was a necessary and inevitable result, among sensitive and receptive men not untouched by culture in many cases, that some should be found to respond to this new environment and find beauty there. That was, indeed, an extension of the fact recognised by Cicero that the least attractive places through familiarity often grow pleasing. It was not, it is true, an invariable fact, either among Christians or pagans. The seer of the New Jerusalem saw nothing in his island home, and a very different person, Ovid, was altogether blind to the beauty that surrounded him in exile on the Black Sea. But the new outburst of Christianity led to a prodigious exodus from the cities into the wildest and most desert spots of emotional, high-strung young people, who thus cut themselves off from the excitements of urban life, and often from the pleasures of social intercourse. They had not gone into the desert to find the beauty of the desert, but there can be little doubt that in many cases they found that beauty, probably for the first time. So far as can be seen, the Christian hermits who swarmed out of the Roman world into the solitudes of Egypt first discovered the beauty of the African desert. Jerome was perhaps the most distinguished of these, and it is highly improbable that any earlier or non-Christian writer had ever broken out into such an eulogy of the desert as we find again and again in Jerome's delightful Epistles. "O desert," he exclaims, when writing to the monk Heliodorus, "blooming with Christ's flowers! O Solitude, from which are brought the stones to build the Apocalyptic city of the Great King! O familiar retreat delighting in God! How long will you let the houses press you down? How long will you shut yourself up in the prison of smoky cities? Believe me, I know nothing more brilliant than the light here. Here one lays aside the burden of the body and flies up into the pure and splendid æther." There is here, it is true, no deliberate æsthetic attentiveness to the special quality of the desert's beauty, but it is clearly and accurately felt. Jerome and those who obeyed the same impulse had, at the very least, for the first time woven beautiful associations into their memories of the desert.

It was not alone through a new familiarity with wild Nature that Christianity enlarged the conception of beautiful scenery. There was another reason which has already been implied, but it is so significant in explaining not only the influence of Christianity in this respect, but of every movement which has since enlarged the love of the wild, that it needs emphasis. A sensitiveness to the attraction of the wild lay in the special temperament of many of those who were most strongly drawn into the fold of Christianity. That is the really decisive moment in generating the love of the wild. It is necessary to point this out clearly, because it seems to be entirely ignored alike by those who imagine that that love is simply a result of civilisation, a statement that is only very partially true, and those who fancy that it is a normal and general characteristic of humanity in all ages.

The people who are Christians to-day, being for the most part born into Christianity, are, as we know, average members of society. It was not so at the beginning of the Christian era. A new faith so profoundly subversive of the accepted religious creeds and the established social order, inevitably attracted a considerable proportion of abnormal people, of the highly emotional, the exalted, the romantic, the people who, in relation to the society of their time were, and in no necessarily bad sense, anti-social. Such people are often of the finest character and the highest intelligence; their mental state has of late been minutely analysed by Pierre Janet, who terms their psychic condition psychasthenia.[1] These people are instinctively repelled by the ordinary social environments in which they live; they cannot adjust themselves to the ordinary routine of life; its banalities crush and offend them; the "real world" of their average fellow-men seems to them unreal, and they are conscious of a painful sense of inadequacy in relation to it; they seek for new and stronger stimulants, for new and deeper narcotics, a new Heaven and a new earth. There were many of them, we are able to divine — though the precise evidence is usually obscure — who were powerfully attracted to Christianity, and found there all that they craved. It was among such that the love of the wild found its earliest Christian apostles; it has been among such that in later centuries the fuller and more complete forms of that love have been first of all proclaimed.

There can be little doubt, indeed, that the same tendency existed in earlier than Christian days among the Romans. A passage in Seneca's treatise, *De Tranquillitate*, is significant in this connection:

> "There are some things which please our bodies though accompanied with a
> certain painful feeling. . . . Let us visit uncultivated lands; let us roam over the
> Bruttian and Lucanian passes [of Southern Italy]; let something pleasant yet
> be sought amid these desert places where our eyes, accustomed to the luxuri-
> ous, may be rested by the wide desolation of rough places."

It is noteworthy also that in his tragedies Seneca insists on the horrors, indeed, but also on the fascination of forests and other fantastic and solitary
spots. Much the same may be said of Lucan. The spirit of Christianity was
beginning to make itself felt among people who knew nothing of Christianity. The men of hypersensitive and abnormal temperament, Seneca and Lucan and Cicero—who must also be named in this connection—were tortured by the evils and injustices of the later Roman world; they turned from
the wildness of man to the wildness of Nature with a sense of peace and joy
that had never before been known. Earlier than these men, the great and
sombre Lucretius, the Roman Dante,—pursuing an isolated course in literature and in life, and dying, as legend declared, insane,—reveals a love of the
solitary and wild which led him to symbolise his own path in poetry as that
of untrodden mountains and intact fountains and new flowers:

> "Avia Pieridum peragro loca, nullius ante
> Trita solo: juvat integros accedere fontes
> Atque haurire, juvatque novos decerpere flores."

In the third century treatise, "On the Public Shows," attributed to Cyp-
rian, Bishop of Carthage, there is a memorable passage contrasting the shows
of Nature with the shows of the theatre, which illustrates the way in which
the solitary and, one may say, anti-social temper of the early Christian turned
from the urban amusements of the day to find relief and delight in the most
varied natural phenomena: sunrise and sunset, the waxing and waning
moon, the course of the seasons, the troops of stars, the heavy mass of the
earth balanced by mountains, the rivers and their sources, the seas with their
waves and shores, the mere air, and in the air the birds, in the water the fishes,
on earth man.

"Let these, I say, and other divine works, be the exhibitions for faithful Christians. What theatre built by hands could be compared with such works as these? Though reared with immense piles of stones the mountain crests are loftier; though the roofs glitter with gold they will be surpassed by the brightness of the starry firmament."

St. Augustine, also, though in a less didactic spirit, towards the end of the *De Civitate Dei*, enumerates and expatiates on "the manifold and various loveliness of sky and earth and sea." He makes, indeed, no mention of mountains, which he had little familiarity with, but he is enthusiastic over the sea, which he had often crossed or gazed on as he paced the fantastic mosaic esplanade of the harbour at Carthage, the emblem of his own turbulent and passionate, yet massive, spirit—"so grand a spectacle when it arranges itself as it were in vestures of various colours, now running through every shade of green and again becoming purple or blue. Is it not delightful," he adds, "to look at it in storm?" We are clearly beginning to witness the development of that feeling for the beauty of the terrible which we found only the first hints of in the Pagan Roman world.

In the attractive chapter at the beginning of the second volume of his *Kosmos*, in which Alexander von Humboldt first outlined the subject which concerns us here, he called attention to the letter in which St. Basil the Great, writing in 360 to Gregory of Nazianzen, described the scenery around his hut on a mountain summit in Armenia, overlooking the plain through which the river Iris impetuously rushed. This passage Humboldt regarded as the most remarkable natural description in all ancient literature. Biese, indeed, is less enthusiastic about Basil's landscape picture, remarking that a similar tone may be found in the Greek anthology and in Pliny the Younger. Yet the passage has its significance, for it expresses the delight in his wild surroundings felt by a man, not writing as an artist or a tourist, who had really come to live amid the solitary magnificence of Nature, and enjoyed describing in detail the spectacle presented to him and the peace and solitude of his lofty home, only disturbed now and again by hunters seeking stags or goats or hares. To that extent it represents a new attitude resulting from the special circumstances of Christian life and the special types of men who were attracted to that life.

During many succeeding centuries we may trace a close association between the most solemn or the most ascetic moments of Christian life and scenery that was constantly beautiful and sometimes in the highest degree romantically wild. It by no means usually follows that the spot was in the first place sought out because it possessed these qualities. There were several circumstances which led to this association. In the first place, utility came in for consideration. The pious hermit, however rigid his life, could not dispense with wood and water and shelter, and these were most easily obtainable in a forest-clad mountain. Ordericus Vitalis, the twelfth century Anglo-Norman monk, writing of a chapel in Normandy—supposed to have been founded much earlier—in which he had himself lived, says: "The site is pleasant and well suited to a hermit's life. A little river flows through a wild valley; the summit of the hill is clothed with a forest, the thick foliage of which forms a screen from the blasts of the wind. The chapel stands on a slope between the road and the stream. A fountain bursts out before the door." [2] Nowadays, when the question of wild beasts has been practically eliminated, this picture seems as pleasant, even to a school-girl, as it seemed to the hardy monk, yet this was a scene from which Cicero, and perhaps even Lucretius, would have shrunk in horror. A good deal of ground had certainly been traversed in those first thousand years of Christianity.

It is remarkable how many of the most famous and sacred religious shrines of Christianity are situated in spots which, though not beautiful according to the ancient standards of landscape beauty, appeal strongly to those who were affected by the modern love of the wild. No doubt in many cases the Christians were carrying on the old pagan traditions which associated divine influence with rugged and terrible spots, and in not a few cases also they were simply conquering for the new religion shrines which had already been hallowed by an earlier religion. But this cannot always be demonstrated, and in any case it only pushes the problem further back; we simply have to admit that the religious men of the earlier faith were moved by the same feelings. The Spanish shrine of Montserrat, one of the most famous goals of mediæval pilgrimage, has been a place of Christian worship for more than a thousand years, and a pagan temple before that; this rocky shrine on the top of a mountain is the kind of sacred place which Seneca speaks of with horror, yet the modern love of natural beauty justifies the choice of the early men of religion, and finds it one of the most fascinating spots in Europe. Sainte-Baume, the cave in a rocky height, which legend made the picturesque and secluded scene of Mary Magdalene's repentance, was certainly the home of ascetics at a very early period. Rocamadour, again, in France, is another delightful and romantic spot fixed on by religious men to become a famous shrine, though it is only now beginning to be generally recognised as a shrine of natural beauty. The Benedictines found their first home in the peculiarly wild and picturesque Apennine height of Monte Cassino, which dominates all the country round. Wherever we go we constantly find that the most solemnly and beautifully wild spots have been dedicated to religion at remote periods, when, to the general eye, though it may not have been so to the religious men who discovered or invented their sanctity, they had no beauty at all.

There was another reason why, as Christian asceticism became organised on a large scale, it tended to be associated with what we now regard as beautiful spots: such spots were cheaper. Pious benefactors, more or less gladly, for the good of their souls or for other motives, made gifts of land for the erection of religious houses. But they preferred to give land that was too uncultivated, too wild, too remote or inaccessible to be of much use to themselves. And if the land had to be bought there was the same reason for selecting the same kind of spot. For the more practical and social religious orders, it is true, such spots were usually unsuitable. The Benedictines, for instance, with their manifold human activities, generally, though not always, preferred to live in towns, and, of course, the various orders of friars whose work was entirely among the people were compelled to dwell among the people, like the Salvation Army to-day. But the contemplative orders not only felt no such necessity, but they were obviously better able to carry out their own special mission of working for the world by prayer and meditation when living in secluded spots. The demands of ascetic religion thus coincided with the demands of the more modern æsthetic love of landscape. When Bruno, in the eleventh century, established his ardent and solitary monks at the Grande Chartreuse, the primary consideration was a spot hard of access suited to continuous worship and peace. But the love of wild nature would, on purely æsthetic grounds, have selected exactly such a spot. In England we are familiar with the fact that the Cistercians, a contemplative order, have left the beautiful ruins of their abbeys in what now seem to us the most exquisite and romantic spots in the land, as at Fountains, at Furness, at Llanthony. Yet the contemporaries of the monks who selected these beautiful sites were astonished at the courage of those who dared to penetrate such horrible wildernesses, infested by wild beasts and far from the haunts of men. This is, for instance, clearly brought out by the old chroniclers as regards Furness, and again as regards Clairvaux, a beautiful valley, open to the sun, furnishing a most admirable site, but described by a contemporary of St. Bernard as merely "a dreary spot enclosed by gloomy woods and rugged mountains."

It is certainly true that a large part of the beauty we now find in these spots was the actual creation of the monks who planted themselves there. They cultivated and humanised these wild and remote haunts of untamed Nature. But they could not alter the essential features of the natural sites they selected. To-day we have to recognise that, however hard the task they undertook, they exercised the soundest judgment from every point of view, and we can well believe they sometimes smiled in their cowls when they heard laymen marvel at their courage. The spots they secured or selected were not only cheap in hard cash because despised, and secluded because often situated among the hills, but they had the further advantage that they were well wooded and that a stream ran through their midst. Often, also, as at Furness, the buildings were admirably placed in a kind of natural amphitheatre, so as to receive at once both the maximum of sunshine and of shelter. In addition to all this, we may well believe that the men of the contemplative orders, who showed what it is difficult not to regard as a deliberate predilection for romantically beautiful and wild spots, had a conscious appreciation of the scenery they lived amongst.[3] They had themselves been bred in some similar scene, so that the spot at the outset had something of that quality of familiarity which, in Cicero's eye, could alone render any wooded and mountainous place pleasing.[4]

For fifteen centuries, it seems probable, the love of wild natural scenery was cherished by a long succession of Christian ascetics, whose cult of Nature was for the most part silent, perhaps, indeed, most often unconscious, since it was not their vocation, and scarcely perhaps their interest, to cultivate deliberately the æsthetic perception of landscape. With Francis of Assisi, indeed, and his Hymn to the Sun, the love of Nature grew more articulate. Francis had his mountain height of Verna, — "his Tabor and his Calvary," — a place of exquisite beauty which arouses the enthusiasm of all his biographers. The Franciscan feeling for natural things in the thirteenth century — though it cannot be quite disassociated from the ancient ascetic feeling — has something of the charm of a new revelation. Outside the cloister, however, there seems little genuine love of wild Nature.

The Renaissance changed this condition of things. But the change thus effected was by no means of a startling or revolutionary character. It was simply a revival of the late classical feeling for landscape, carried out by cultivated Italian ecclesiastics, and it served to reintroduce a deliberate and consciously æsthetic enjoyment of agreeable scenery such as had appealed to the Romans of the Empire. That ecclesiastics like Bembo, Ænis Sylvius (afterwards Pius II.), and Petrarch took a leading part in this movement is an added indication of the closeness of the religious life to natural scenery; while the fact that these ecclesiastics were Italians shows that we are in the presence of a genuine revival of ancient feeling. The Italians were the pioneers in the modern discovery of landscape, just as they were the natural and inevitable pioneers in the discovery of classic civilisation generally. The evidence has been clearly and concisely summarised by Burckhardt, who regards Petrarch — "one of the first completely modern men" — as the full and definite representative of the revived admiration for landscape, while Ænis Sylvius was the first who not only enjoyed landscape, but described it enthusiastically in detail, and Aretino was the first to describe sunset effects. We might expect to find Leonardo da Vinci among these pioneers, and his name is, indeed, sometimes mentioned in this connection. It is, however, difficult to find among his writings any passage that can be definitely quoted in evidence. He clearly possessed a minute and impartial knowledge of Nature; he was evidently familiar with mountains; he describes atmospheric effects elaborately; but he approaches Nature less in the æsthetic spirit than in the searching scientific spirit. It is true that in the background of some of his pictures he introduces fantastic rock scenery, and it is difficult not to believe that his profound study of Nature involved a real love for wild Nature. At an earlier date, in the backgrounds of Flemish painters, we seem to detect this love, and later, in the seventeenth century, Ruisdael and Gaspar Poussin showed an absorption in wild scenery apart from men which we find no traces of in literature, while Salvator Rosa pictorially expressed the romantic in its most extravagant forms long before the Romantic school arose. But at that time pictures other than religious were inaccessible to all but a few amateurs, and these pioneers in art had no influence on life.

II.

This Renaissance movement towards Nature was a revival, in a more elaborate and more intense form, of the classic enjoyment of landscape, continuing, we may say, the tradition of Pliny the Younger. It was not primarily an attraction towards wild Nature, such as we seem to discern in the earlier ascetic Christian movement. But it embraced elements of the love of the wild, and these were notably shown in a new and actively adventurous love of mountains. The Italians had themselves, as Burckhardt points out, prepared the way for this feeling by freeing Nature from sin and the influence of demons. Dante, at an earlier date, was a very notable pioneer in this field. Though he showed no appreciation for mountains at a distance, he was, as he clearly shows, familiar with mountain climbing. In his enjoyment of mountains Dante was, indeed, a unique figure. He experienced, in a more conscious way, the mediæval ascetic attraction to wild Nature combined with the Renaissance inquisitive adventurous taste for exploring it. Petrarch possessed, in a high degree, the normal Renaissance feeling for landscape, that is to say, the revived feeling of the late Romans, and in addition he had a certain taste for mountain climbing, which was no longer so rare and abnormal as in Dante's day; he climbed Mount Ventoux, near Avignon, and he described his delight in this little achievement. The Swiss, from Renaissance days onwards, showed from time to time an enthusiastic admiration for the Alps in the shadow of which they live. Conrad Gesner, man of letters and science, wrote an account of his *Ascent of Pilatus*, as at a much later date (1729) another eminent Swiss, who was a bad poet and a great physiologist, Haller, wrote his poem on the Alps. Marti, in 1558, and Simler, in 1574, (as Mr. Coolidge has shown in his monumental work), were full of admiration for the peaks, chasms, precipices and glaciers of their native mountains, "deliciae nostrae, nostrique amores," as Marti called them. It is not difficult to account for the enthusiasm of these Swiss writers; it was the result of familiarity heightened by patriotism. Much more remarkable and more genuinely novel is the attitude of the Spanish soldier and poet from Valencia, Cristobal de Virues, in face of the Alps, which he had to cross as one of the leaders of the Spanish army which marched from Milan across the St. Gothard to Flanders in 1604. A Southerner from the Mediterranean is not predisposed to sympathy with the Alps, and for the soldier they have always been not objects for admiration, but hostile barriers to be overcome. Virues, who wrote a letter to his brother full of enthusiastic description of the Alps, represents a new attitude. He feels, indeed, the horror of the scene, but with something almost like pleasure, and he expressed these feelings in a sonnet on the St. Gothard pass which is certainly one of the earliest poems inspired by the Alps.

Such opinions as these, however, must not be taken as representing the typical attitude towards the Alps of even the finest minds of Europe at that

period. For most travellers the Alps still remained what they had been for
Livy and for Ammianus, a scene of unmitigated horror which no one could
approach for the sake of pleasure. By the beginning of the eighteenth century
this feeling, far from diminishing, had gained in strength, and it affected even
those who were most sensitive to natural beauty. In 1621 Howell, who, as a
Welshman, might have been expected to be appreciative of mountains, and
who possessed an alert mind very receptive to new impressions, wrote of the
"high and hideous" Alps, "uncouth huge, monstrous excrescences of nature," unlike "our mountains in Wales, which bear always something useful
to man or beast, some grass at least." Howell is still in this matter, we see, at
the standpoint of the savage who can find no beauty where there is no use;
the fascination of the wild has no meaning to him. Pepys, half a century later
(in 1668), experienced something of the same feelings when merely going
across Salisbury Plain, where he encountered "some great hills, even to
fright us."

Addison, at the beginning of the eighteenth century, represents, it is probable, a slight but yet definite advance, so far as England is concerned, in the
love of wild landscape. He was predisposed to a sympathetic appreciation of
the natural beauties he met with during his "grand tour" through Italy and
Switzerland by the fact that he was by birth and heredity a Westmoreland
man, and already familiar with the hills, waterfalls and lakes of his own region, that region which was a century later the home of the Lake School,
though for most people in Addison's time it probably was, as to Roger North,
a land of "hideous mountains." Addison was abroad from 1701 to 1703, and
in 1705 he published his *Remarks on Several Parts of Italy, etc.* It can scarcely
be said that he really admired wild Nature, but he went beyond the taste for
cultivated Nature which ruled in his time, and was attracted by the beauty of
natural disorder. At Albano the scene seemed to him "the most agreeable
confusion imaginable." He admired the Lake of Geneva half a century before that lake became the birthplace of the feeling for romantic beauty, and
the Alps, as seen from the Savoy side of the lake, he wrote, "fill the Mind
with an agreeable kind of Horror, and form one of the most irregular mis-
hapen Scenes in the World." This attitude very accurately represents a state
of transition; natural wildness was beginning to arouse an agreeable tone of
emotion, and yet it was still felt to be intrinsically ugly and repellent.

With Gray, a little later in the eighteenth century (in 1739), we hear a
somewhat new voice, that of a man who was to some extent a pioneer in his

vision of Nature. Gray was a poet, a sensitive, solitary man of neurotic heredity, predisposed to this task. There is a note of enthusiasm in Gray's feeling
towards wild Nature which we scarcely hear in any other equally notable
writer of his time. He went up to the monastery of the Grande Chartreuse
and wrote: "Not a precipice, not a torrent, not a cliff, but is pregnant with
religion and poetry." If he had been born in St. Bruno's day, he declared, he
would himself have been among his disciples. It was, he said, "one of the
most solemn, the most romantic, and the most astonishing scenes I ever beheld." He still hesitated amid Alpine scenes on a large scale. "Mount Cenis,
I confess," he wrote, "carries the permission mountains have of being frightful rather too far, and its horrors were accompanied by too much danger to
give one time to reflect upon their beauties." Yet even the apologetic form
in which this sentence is thrown indicates a new attitude. We are here carried far beyond the usual eighteenth century tourist whose enthusiasm for
the picturesque generally reached its climax when he had climbed the few
feet which lead up to the ruined little temple at Tivoli.

In this movement towards the appreciation of wild Nature England was at
this period distinctly ahead of France. There the attitude towards mountains
remained one of unmitigated repulsion. Mission, in 1687, spoke of the Alps
as "ces affreuses montagnes," and compared the line of their summits, — for
the first time, as Remy de Gourmont believes, — to the foam-covered waves
of an extremely angry sea. In the "Voyage" of Chapelle and Bachaumont in
the same century, they have nothing to say about the Pyrenees; they scarcely
seem to have looked at them, for Nature only appealed to them on a small
scale, when dainty and pleasant. They visited Sainte-Baume, "an almost inaccessible spot," they said, "and which cannot be viewed without terror";
they hastened away as soon as possible. What pleased them best in their
whole tour was a place in the environs of Toulouse, "a little cultivated island,
kept as neat as a garden," and they were much impressed by a fountain they
found there which rose to a great height. It was the age of beautifully ordered
and symmetric gardens; the monstrous disorder of wild and sterile Nature
could inspire no emotion but antipathy. Its very existence, indeed, seemed
to call for explanation. Malebranche declared that the irregularities of the
earth's surface, like the uncertainty of its seasons, both so painful to philosophical geometricians, are due to the fact that God has intended that our
thoughts should be fixed on the world to come, and not on a world which is
the abode of sinners, a world which He has ordained to be given up to dis-

order, as indicated by the irregularities of its rocks and the cliffs of its coast. That was a view of the matter which Rousseau rendered for ever impossible.

There were at least two reasons why the men of the seventeenth and early eighteenth centuries, more especially in France, should adopt an attitude towards wild Nature so unlike that which subsequently prevailed. There was, in the first place, their high cultivation of the social instincts. They cultivated sociability, the art of fine human relationships, with an ardour that almost amounted to passion. It never occurred to them to turn from man to the silence and solemnity of wild Nature, for Nature in those aspects had no voice for them; Nature only spoke to them in the beautifully ordered alleys and fountains of Versailles. There was probably another and more subtle reason why it was peculiarly difficult for the men of that age to approach sympathetically the rugged wildness and confusion of Nature, and that was the sudden rise and popular expansion of geometrical and mathematical studies during the latter half of the seventeenth century. The interests and ideals of men in one field are apt to spread, unknown even to themselves, into other fields of thought and taste with which they seem to have nothing in common. As we look back at that period to-day it is difficult not to see that there was a real relationship between the geometrical studies then in the ascendant and the love of orderly and regular gardens, the horror of disorderly and confused Nature, which was expressed in so simple-minded a spirit by Malebranche, the geometrical philosopher.

By the middle of the eighteenth century this attitude towards Nature had become so completely dominant, at all events in France — for in England, as we have seen, a new movement had already begun to make itself felt — that scarcely a discordant voice could be heard. That was the opportunity of Rousseau. With his new vision and the magic of his impassioned eloquence, he created a new feeling for Nature, a new sensibility, almost a new sense. The attitude of men towards Nature was suddenly and lastingly changed.

In 1759 appeared *La Nouvelle Heloise* (described in the sub-title as *Lettres de Deux Amants Habitants d'une Petite Ville au Pied des Alpes*), Rousseau's most popular book, perhaps, indeed, the most influential novel that was ever written; and in Letter XXIII. of the first Part he describes an expedition in the Haut Valais, which well illustrates the qualities he had found in Nature and taught others to see. It can scarcely be said that Rousseau admired aspects of Nature which had never been admired before. In late classic days, in early Christian days, and at the Renaissance, there were certainly men who would have found beautiful most of the things that Rousseau found beautiful. But their admiration had remained inarticulate, or else received only tepid and conventional expression. Rousseau's immense motive power lay in the fact that he had found a reason for his love of Nature, and that he could express that love in the clearest, the most fervent, the most winning of ways. He preached Nature as a Gospel; and Nature in mountain and Nature in unsophisticated man were to him one. He had, as he described himself in the *Confessions*, an almost morbid passion for walking. It was only in walking that ideas came to him; he could not write before a table: "I write in my brain as I walk among rocks or in woods." He found locomotion the prime stimulant and sedative of his restless and tortured organism: "I need torrents, rocks, pines, dark forests, mountains, rough paths to climb, by precipices that fill me with fear." Solitude, motion, the spectacle of Nature unpolluted by the hand of man, the tonic resistance of steep climbs, the exhilaration of keen air — these were the things that more than anything else in the world brought joy and peace to Rousseau. In proclaiming them to mankind he knew of what he was speaking.

There was thus a double reason why Rousseau became to his generation the revealer of Nature. In the first place, he was Swiss, and thus belonged to a people traditionally and patriotically attached to those wild aspects of Nature with which they had grown familiar. It is true they had never given adequate expression to that attachment. It may well have been, indeed, that Rousseau also would not have become the apostle of a new vision of wild landscape if he had not in youth been transferred to the other side of the lake and learnt to know the slightly different landscape of Savoy, for over-familiarity dulls rather than heightens the perceptions. Apart from this predisposing factor of race and birthplace there was another and decisive factor: his abnormal and even morbid personal organisation. This was undoubtedly congenital, as his *Confessions* clearly show; Rousseau's psychic anomalies were not the result, but largely the cause, of the insane delusions which finally preyed upon him. Inapt for all the ordinary duties and relationships of life, awkward and unsociable, with a timidity that sometimes rebounded to the opposite extreme of insolence, and beneath this unpromising exterior seething with emotions and aspirations, young Rousseau, suffering, tormented, diseased — "the prince of psychastheniacs," as Janet has called him — was predestinate to the love of wild Nature. Here, amid the strong and beautiful impressions of a wildness untouched by man, his restless, exhausted nervous system was at once stimulated and soothed; he found the peace and joy which the world of civilised men could never give to one of his temperament. And the might of his genius—his exquisite sensibility, his acute analysis, his entrancing eloquence—enabled him to transfer his vision to the brains of his fellow-men, and to inoculate the world with his own emotion. Henceforth it was felt to be at least in bad taste to apply to mountains that epithet of "horrible" which had been the conventionally correct description for over a thousand years, while for some, as for Shelley at the sight of Mont Blanc, that feeling of horror was now replaced by "a sentiment of ecstatic wonder, not unallied to madness."

How instinctively the craving for wild Nature makes itself felt in men of Rousseau's temperament is witnessed by Rétif de la Bretonne, who has been accurately described as the gutter Rousseau ("le Rousseau du ruisseau"). Born some twenty years later than Rousseau, and with a like abnormal nervous organisation, and a like impulse to war with the civilised society of his time, it was Rétif's lot, unlike Rousseau's, to spend all his life, after childhood, in Paris. Yet we find in him the same spontaneous cry after the savagery of Nature. The environs of Paris, he declares,—writing of himself as a boy of fourteen in his extraordinary autobiography, *Monsieur Nicolas*,—charming as they were, satisfied no desire of his heart:

> "I would like to have lived in a wood, in some half savage spot, so long as the castle was far away. I have felt what few have experienced, but what a savage would have felt if brought to France, on seeing our beautiful things."

And then he speaks of English gardens, which, it must be remembered, for the men of his time represented the beginning of a new movement towards unfettered Nature in scenery.

> "Ah! if I had then seen an English garden! I should have fallen into ecstasy, I could not have left it! . . . I would have fled to America if I had had the means, not to make my fortune, but to become a savage. It was the only kind of life that suited me; to civilise me was to do violence to my nature."

Rousseau, like Rétif de la Bretonne, was not only anti-social in relation to the society of his own day; he was abnormal to a degree that may properly be termed morbid. That was why he was peculiarly fitted to be receptive to natural influences and to become the discoverer of new aspects of wild Nature. But all the pioneers of the approach to Nature, if we consider the matter, have been, so far as we are in a position to discover the facts, men of a more or less abnormal temperament placed in a position of hostility to the society of their time. Lucretius, Jerome and the other conspicuous early Christians, Dante, the extreme ascetics of the contemplative Orders, — these were not people of the *homme moyen sensuel* type, who instinctively accept the world as they find it. For the most part also they have had the temperament of genius which so often causes a man to view the world at a different angle from his fellows, to reverse the emotional values of life, *in tristitia hilaris, in hilaritate tristis.* The men who followed Rousseau to complete the movement to which he had given the chief impetus showed the same characteristics, notably the two great poets who in England finally completed it, Byron and Wordsworth. Byron was, after Goethe, undoubtedly the most brilliant and influential of the distinguished poets who came to the school of Rousseau on the shores of Lake Leman to learn his lesson and to proclaim it to the world. By the force of his temperament, and the immense prestige of his genius, he effectually acclimatised in England the new gospel of Nature. At the same time Wordsworth, a more subtle and a more profound revolutionary, quietly elaborated on the heights of his own lake-country the spiritual significance of that gospel of Nature, and left nothing further to be said.

The result was that the old habit and fashion of speaking of mountains and wild Nature as "hideous" was replaced by the new convention of speaking of them as "romantic." That, indeed, was an essential part of the great Romantic movement. It is sometimes said that Addison, on his foreign tour, was the first to apply the word "romantic" in a favourable sense to natural scenery. That is scarcely correct. The word was current at least nearly half a century before. I find that it occurs twice in Pepys's *Diary*. In 1666 Pepys visited Windsor and wrote enthusiastically that "It is the most romantique castle that is in the world." Next year he refers contemptuously to "romantic lies." The word was applied to something that seemed to belong to the region of romance, of fiction, and in its favourable sense it was for a long time most commonly applied to a landscape containing a castle in ruins, as being a scene suitable for a novel. It lost its stricter meaning as the interest in Nature grew wider, but in Addison it still indicates a scene for a story. His vessel put into Cassis, not far from Sainte-Baume, on the voyage to Genoa, and he writes: "We were here shown at a distance the Desarts that have been rendered so famous by the Presence of Mary Magdalene, who is said to have wept away the rest of her life among those solitary Rocks and Mountains. It is so Romantic a Scene that it has always probably given occasion to such Chimerical Relations." Goethe, in Friedländer's opinion, probably adopted the word from Tobler's translation of Thomson's *Seasons* (1765). As its use grew general and conventionalised, it became applicable to any scene of wild Nature which commended itself to the spectator, though it is probable that in the use of the epithet there was an underlying feeling that the scene described as "romantic" constituted a fitting background for a delightful story.

The movement which led to the consecration of wild Nature in mountains fully ran its course in Byron and Wordsworth. There was no further progress along that path. No poet eager to shun the ways of man, no pioneer in the love of wild Nature, would nowadays dream of finding inspiration on the shores of the lake of Geneva, or of writing a poem on the distant prospect of Mont Blanc. Comfortable and pleasant these regions have become to the average man, and Chamonix is almost a railway centre; Rousseau and Byron and Shelley would now certainly hasten away in horror. In the nineteenth century the pioneer in the love of wild Nature began to seek beauty not in the ruggedness of mountains, but, reverting to the early Christian feeling associated with Jerome, in the dreariness of plains and deserts. We already find a hint of this in Shelley's *Julian and Maddalo*, when, writing at Venice of the Lido, he says:

> "I love all waste
> And solitary places where we taste
> The pleasure of believing what we see
> Is boundless, as we wish our souls to be."

Shelley was impartial in his love of all aspects of wild and unfettered Nature, though for the most part of the school of Rousseau, whose genius seemed to him almost more than human. A more characteristic example of this modern form of the love of wild Nature is perhaps furnished by George Borrow, who, it has been said, "could draw more poetry from a widespreading marsh, with its straggling rushes, than from the most beautiful scenery, and would stand and look at it with rapture." In Thoreau this fascination became highly developed. Thoreau was in love with wildness: "Life consists with wildness," he declared. "The most alive is the wildest." And he found the wildness he sought by no means supremely, if, indeed, at all, in mountains, but in dreary wastes. "My spirits," he wrote in his journal, "infallibly rise in proportion to the outward dreariness. Give me the ocean, the desert or the wilderness!" Borrow and Thoreau had the abnormal temperament, the instinctive antagonism to the society of their time, which we find among the mountain men of the earlier love of wild Nature, but their passion for wild Nature sought a different outlet. The difference is well described in the interesting introductory chapter of Mr. Thomas Hardy's *Return of the Native*, concerning Egdon Heath. It is a question, remarks Mr. Hardy, who has always shown a minute and loving reverence for heathlands, whether the exclusive reign of the orthodoxly beautiful landscape is not approaching its last quarter. "The new Vale of Tempe may be a gaunt waste in Thule: human souls may find themselves in closer and closer harmony with external things wearing a sombreness distasteful to our race when it was young." The time is coming when the tourist will find the chastened sublimity of a moor most in keeping with his moods, and "Heidelburg and Baden be passed unheeded as he hastens from the Alps to the sand-dunes of Scheveningen." It is doubtless true that the marsh and the moor and the desert have not exerted the same potent fascination and poetic reverence as the scenes which stirred the lovers of wild Nature a century earlier. But there can be no doubt that it is in this direction rather than towards mountains that men's thoughts of wild Nature have tended to turn, and the growing attraction of North Africa cannot fail to strengthen that tendency.

When we glance back over the great field of human emotion we have here rapidly traversed, it becomes possible to see what amount of truth there is in the opposing views which have been maintained concerning the evolution of the love of wild Nature. While it is by no means true that the attraction to mountains is, as Mr. Freshfield supposes, "a healthy, primitive and almost universal human instinct," the more widely current view that that attraction dates from little more than a century back is still further opposed to the truth. A psychological interpretation of the facts shows us that while there have probably always and everywhere been a few persons who have ascended mountains or gone out into the desert, the pioneers in such movements have been temperamentally exceptional persons, and by their abnormal constitutions instinctively thrown into a state of more or less violent and indignant opposition to the moral and æsthetic ideals of their time. They have gone into the mountains to seek peace for themselves and a new inspiration for life, and they have returned with a new table of commandments.

"Thou hast a voice, great Mountain, to repeal
Large codes of fraud and woe; not understood
By all, but which the wise, and great, and good
Interpret, or make felt, or deeply feel."

For the men of this make the natural terrors of the wild become a source of joy and strength, and they return to mankind with the authority of law-givers. These ardent and passionate explorers pave the way for the mob that follow them, but the mob feel none of their emotion. "Nature is for them merely a spectacle," it has been truly said; "they go to the Righi as they go to the Opera." Even the mountain-climber is often, perhaps usually, untouched by the passion for wild Nature, and quite incapable of entering into the emotion of Rousseau of Wordsworth. Sir Leslie Stephen was a prominent and enthusiastic Alpinist. But he wrote: "Scenery, even the wildest that is really enjoyable, derives half its charm from the occult sense of the human life and social forms moulded upon it; the Alps would be unbearably stern but for the picturesque society preserved among their folds." Thereby Stephen betrayed the fact that he was in feeling a man of the early eighteenth century. The appeal of wild Nature can only be perfectly felt by men who are, by temperament and circumstance, rebels against the laws and conventions of their time. It is a passion that arises in ages of splendid individualism. The representative men of such a period experience what Nietzsche describes as that "sympathy for the horrible and questionable which arises when one is oneself horrible and questionable." That is why, in an age like the present, when the instincts of social and urban development are dominant over those of revolutionary individualism, the search for wild Nature sometimes seems to be a spiritual adventure which constitutes an almost closed chapter in the history of the human soul. We are drawn to-day to the more humanised and socialised forms of Nature, mixed with personal intercourse and deliberate art. We witness the revived love of beautiful gardens.

NOTES

1. Janet & Raymond, *Les Obsessions et la Psychasthénie*, 2 vols. 1903.

2. Ordericus Vitalis: *Ecclesiastical History*, Book iii, Chap. v.

3. This is suggested by the attractive names the Cistercians gave to their houses. Clair-vaux, Bonmont, etc. Ordericus Vitalis, who refers to this point, remarks that "the very

names invited the hearers to hasten to places whose names bespoke the blessedness to be found in them." It is noteworthy that St. Odo of Cluny, who often crossed the Alps, was accustomed (his friend and biographer remarks) to point out the natural beauties of the way.

4. The Cistercians settled in Llanthony and found themselves at home there. But when the Austin canons, who were accustomed to towns, were removed from Colchester to Llanthony they were unable to like it at all and were finally transferred to Gloucester. "We may believe," remarks Freeman, who records this episode, "that the very presence of the hills, which is to us the chief charm of the spot, was to them a matter of horror."

Dallas Lore Sharp on
Sincerity in Nature Writing
(1911)

Born in New Jersey in 1870, Dallas Lore Sharp graduated from the South Jersey Institute and then attended Brown University, where he supported himself by working in a campus biological laboratory and pastoring a nearby Methodist Episcopal Church. He later earned a degree in theology from Boston University, then worked as a pastor, a librarian, English instructor, and magazine editor. His first book, *Wild Life Near Home,* came out in 1901; he would go on to publish some twenty more books and hundreds of magazine articles. Two of his nature books, *A Watcher in the Woods* (1903) and *Beyond the Pasture Bars* (1914), reputedly sold more than 100,000 copies each — phenomenal numbers for the time.

In the essay below, excerpted from *The Face of the Fields* (1911), Sharp explores the question of "what nature-writing, pure and undefiled, may be, and the nature-writer, what manner of writer he ought to be." He gently satirizes the more fanciful animal romances of the "nature fakers" but by no means wishes to restrict nature writing to the mere recitation of scientific fact. He goes on to urge nature writers to concentrate on their home ground; sounding at times like an early Wendell Berry, he insists that the "best possible use for this earth is to make a home of it, and for this span of life, to live it like a human, earth-born being." The nature writer, especially, must heed this advice, for "[g]ood nature-literature, like all good literature, is more lived than written. Its immortal part hath elsewhere than the ink-pot its beginning."

Dwelling inland, far from those of us who go down to the sea in manuscripts, may be found the reader, no doubt, to whom the title of this essay is not anathema, to whom the word nature still means the real outdoors, as the word culture may still mean things other than "sweetness and light." It is different with us. We shy at the word nature. Good, honest term, it has suffered a sea-change with us; it has become literary. Piety suffers the same change when it becomes professional. There has grown up about nature as a literary term a vocabulary of cant, — nature-lover, nature-writer, nature- ———. Throw the stone for me, you who are clean! Inseparably now these three travel to-gether, arm in arm, like Tom, Dick, and Harry — the world, the flesh, and the devil. Name one, and the other two appear, which is sad enough for the nature-writer, because a word is known by the company it keeps.

The nature-writer deserves, maybe, his dubious reputation; he is more or less of a fraud, perhaps. And perhaps everybody else is, more or less. I am sure of it as regards preachers and plumbers and politicians and men who work by the day. Yet I have known a few honest men of each of these several sorts, although I can't recall just now the honest plumber. I have known hon-est nature-writers, too; there are a number of them, simple, single-minded, and purposefully poor. I have no mind, however, thus to pronounce upon them, dividing the sheep from the goats, lest haply I count myself in with the wrong fold. My desire, rather, is to see what nature-writing, pure and unde-filed, may be, and the nature-writer, what manner of writer he ought to be.

For it is plain that the nature-writer has now evolved into a distinct, al-though undescribed, literary species. His origins are not far to seek, the course of his development not hard to trace, but very unsatisfactory is the attempt, as yet, to classify him. We all know a nature-book at sight, no matter how we may doubt the nature in it; we all know that the writer of such a book must be a nature-writer; yet this is not describing him scientifically by any means.

Until recent years the nature-writer had been hardly more than a variant of some long-established species — of the philosopher in Aristotle; of the mor-alizer in Theobaldus; of the scholar and biographer in Walton; of the traveler in Josselyn; of the poet in Burns. But that was in the feudal past. Since then the land of letters has been redistributed; the literary field, like every other field, has been cut into intensified and highly specialized patches — the short story for you, the muck-rake essay for me, or magazine verse, or wild animal biography. The paragraph of outdoor description in Scott becomes the modern nature-sketch; the "Lines to a Limping Hare" in Burns run into a wild animal romance about the length of "The Last of the Mohicans"; the occasional letter of Gilbert White's grows into an annual nature-volume, this year's being entitled "Buzz-Buzz and Old Man Barberry; or, The Thrilling Young Ladyhood of a Better-Class Bluebottle Fly." The story that follows is how she never would have escaped the net of Old Man Barberry had she been a butterfly—a story which only the modern nature-writing specialist would be capable of handling. Nature-writing and the automobile business have developed vastly during the last few years.

It is Charles Kingsley, I think, who defines "a thoroughly good naturalist" as one "who knows his own parish thoroughly," a definition, all questions of style aside, that accurately describes the nature-writer. He has field enough for his pen in a parish; he can hardly know more and know it intimately enough to write about it. For the nature-writer, while he may be more or less of a scientist, is never mere scientist—zoölogist or botanist. Animals are not his theme; flowers are not his theme. Nothing less than the universe is his theme, as it pivots around him, around the distant boundaries of his immediate neighborhood.

His is an emotional, not an intellectual, point of view; a literary, not a scientific, approach; which means that he is the axis of his world, its great circumference, rather than any fact—any flower, or star, or tortoise. Now to the scientist the tortoise is the thing: the particular species Thalassochelys kempi; of the family Testudinidae; of the order Chelonia; of the class Reptilia; of the branch Vertebrata. But the nature-writer never pauses over this matter to capitalize it. His tortoise may or may not come tagged with this string of distinguishing titles. A tortoise is tortoise for a' that, particularly if it should happen to be an old Sussex tortoise which has been kept for thirty years in a yard by the nature-writer's friend, and which "On the 1st November began to dig the ground in order to the forming of its hybernaculum, which it had fixed on just beside a great tuft of hepaticas.

"P.S.—In about three days after I left Sussex, the tortoise retired into the ground under the hepatica."

This is a bit of nature-writing by Gilbert White, of Selborne, which sounds quite a little like science, but which you noticed was really spoiled as science by its "tuft of hepaticas." There is no buttonhole in science for the nosegay. And when, since the Vertebrates began, did a scientific tortoise ever retire?

One more quotation, I think, will make clear my point, namely, that the nature-writer is not detached from himself and alone with his fact, like the scientist, but is forever relating his tortoise to himself. The lines just quoted were from a letter dated April 12, 1772. Eight years afterwards, in another letter, dated Selborne, April 21, 1780, and addressed to "the Hon. Daines Barrington," the good rector writes:—

"DEAR SIR,—The old Sussex tortoise, that I have mentioned to you so often, is become my property. I dug it out of its winter dormitory in March last, when it was enough awakened to express its resentments by hissing, and, packing it in a box with earth, carried it eighty miles in post-chaises. The rattle and hurry of the journey so perfectly roused it that, when I turned it out on the border, it walked twice down to the bottom of my garden."

Not once, not three times, but twice down to the bottom of the garden! We do not question it for a moment; we simply think of the excellent thesis material wasted here in making a mere popular page of nature-writing. Gilbert White never got his Ph.D., if I remember, because, I suppose, he stopped counting after the tortoise made its second trip, and because he kept the creature among the hepaticas of the garden, instead of on a shelf in a bottle of alcohol. Still, let us admit, and let the college professors, who do research work upon everything except their students, admit, that walking twice to the bottom of a garden is not a very important discovery. But how profoundly interesting it was to Gilbert White! And how like a passage from the Pentateuch his record of it! Ten years he woos this tortoise (it was fourteen that Jacob did for Rachel) and wins it—with a serene and solemn joy. He digs it out of its winter dormitory (a hole in the ground), packs it carefully in a box, carries it hurriedly, anxiously, by post-chaises for eighty miles, rousing it perfectly by the end of the journey, when, liberating it in the rectory yard, he stands back to see what it will do; and, lo! it walks twice to the bottom of the garden!

By a thoroughly good naturalist Kingsley may have meant a thoroughly good nature-writer, for I think he had in mind Gilbert White, who certainly was a thoroughly good naturalist, and who certainly knew his own parish thoroughly. In the letters from which I have quoted the gentle rector was writing the natural history of Selborne, his parish. But how could he write the natural history of Selborne when his tortoise was away over in Sussex!

> A tortoise down by Sussex's brim
> A Sussex tortoise was to him,
> And it was nothing more—

nothing at all for the "Natural History of Selborne" until he had gone after it and brought it home.

Thus all nature-writers do with all their nature in some manner or other, not necessarily by post-chaise for eighty miles. It is characteristic of the nature-writer, however, to bring home his outdoors, to domesticate his nature, to relate it all to himself. His is a dooryard universe, his earth a flat little planet turning about a pop-hole in his garden — a planet mapped by fields, ponds, and cowpaths, and set in a circumfluent sea of neighbor townships, beyond whose shores he neither goes to church, nor works out his taxes on the road, nor votes appropriations for the schools.

He is limited to his parish because he writes about only so much of the world as he lives in, as touches him, as makes for him his home. He may wander away, like Thoreau, to the Maine woods, or down along the far-off shores of Cape Cod; but his best writing will be that about his hut at Walden.

It is a large love for the earth as a dwelling-place, a large faith in the entire reasonableness of its economy, a large joy in all its manifold life, that moves the nature-writer. He finds the earth most marvelously good to live in — himself its very dust; a place beautiful beyond his imagination, and interesting past his power to realize — a mystery every way he turns. He comes into it as a settler into a new land, to clear up so much of the wilderness as he shall need for a home.

Thoreau perhaps, of all our nature-writers, was the wildest wild man, the least domestic in his attitude. He went off far into the woods, a mile and a half from Concord village, to escape domestication, to seek the wild in nature and to free the wild in himself. And what was his idea of becoming a wild man but to build a cabin and clear up a piece of ground for a bean-patch! He was solid Concord beneath his war-paint — a thin coat of savagery smeared on to scare his friends whenever he went to the village — a walk which he took very often. He differed from Gilbert White as his cabin at Walden differed from the quaint old cottage at Selborne. But cabin and cottage alike were to dwell in; and the bachelor of the one was as much in need of a wife, and as much in love with the earth, as the bachelor in the other. Thoreau's "Walden" is as parochial and as domestic with its woodchuck and beans as White's "Natural History of Selborne" with its tame tortoise and garden.

In none of our nature-writers, however, is this love for the earth more manifest than in John Burroughs. It is constant and dominant in him, an expression of his religion. He can see the earth only as the best possible place to live in — to live with rather than in or on; for he is unlike the rector of Selborne and the wild-tame man of Walden in that he is married and a farmer — conditions, these, to deepen one's domesticity. Showing somewhere along every open field in Burroughs's books is a piece of fence, and among his trees there is always a patch of gray sloping roof. He grew up on a farm (a most excellent place to grow up on), became a clerk, but not for long, then got him a piece of land, built him a home out of unhewn stone, and set him out an eighteen-acre vineyard. And ever since he has lived in his vineyard, with the Hudson River flowing along one side of it, the Catskills standing along another side of it, with the horizon all around, and overhead the sky, and everywhere, through everything, the pulse of life, the song of life, the sense of home!

He loves the earth, for the earth is home.

"I would gladly chant a paean," he exclaims, "for the world as I find it. What a mighty interesting place to live in! If I had my life to live over again, and had my choice of celestial abodes, I am sure I should take this planet, and I should choose these men and women for my friends and companions. This great rolling sphere with its sky, its stars, its sunrises and sunsets, and with its outlook into infinity — what could be more desirable? What more satisfying? Garlanded by the seasons, embosomed in sidereal influences, thrilling with life, with a heart of fire and a garment of azure seas and fruitful continents — one might ransack the heavens in vain for a better or a more picturesque abode."

A full-throated hymn, this, to the life that is, in the earth that is, a hymn without taint of cant, without a single note of that fevered desire for a land that is fairer than this, whose gates are of pearl and whose streets are paved with gold. If there is another land, may it be as fair as this! And a pair of bars will be gate enough, and gravel, cinders, grass, even March mud, will do for paving; for all that one will need there, as all that one needs here — here in New England in March — is to have "arctics" for one's feet and an equator about one's heart. The desire for heaven is natural enough, for how could one help wanting more after getting through with this? But he sins and comes short of the glory of God who would be quit of this world for the sake of a better one. There isn't any better one. This one is divine. And as for those dreams of heaven in old books and monkish hymns, they cannot compare for glory and for downright domestic possibilities with the prospect of these snow-clad Hingham hills from my window this brilliant winter morning.

That "this world is not my resting-place" almost any family man can believe nowadays, but that "this world is not my home" I can't believe at all. However poor a resting-place we make of it, however certain of going hence upon a "longe journey," we may not find this earth anything else than home without confessing ourselves tenants here by preference, and liable, therefore, to pay rent throughout eternity. The best possible use for this earth is to make a home of it, and for this span of life, to live it like a human, earth-born being.

Such is the credo of the nature-writer. Not until it can be proved to him that eternal day is more to his liking than the sweet alternation of day and night, that unending rest is less monotonous than his round of labor until the evening, that streets of gold are softer for his feet than dirt roads with borders of grass and dandelions, that ceaseless hallelujahs about a throne exalt the excellency of God more than the quiet contemplation of the work of His fingers — the moon and the stars which He has ordained — not until, I say, it can be proved to him that God did not make this world, or, making it, spurned it, cursed it, that heaven might seem the more blessed — not until then will he forego his bean-patch at Walden, his vineyard at West Park, his garden at Selborne; will he deny to his body a houselot on this little planet, and the range of this timed and tidy universe to his soul.

As between himself and nature, then, the thoroughly good nature-writer is in love — a purely personal state; lyric, emotional, rather than scientific, wherein the writer is not so much concerned with the facts of nature as with his view of them, his feelings for them, as they environ and interpret him, or as he centres and interprets them.

Were this all, it would be a simple story of love. Unfortunately, nature-writing has become an art, which means some one looking on, and hence it means self-consciousness and adaptation, the writer forced to play the difficult part of loving his theme not less, but loving his reader more.

For the reader, then, his test of the nature-writer will be the extreme test of sincerity. The nature-writer (and the poet) more than many writers is limited by decree to his experiences — not to what he has seen and heard only, but as strictly to what he has truly felt. All writing must be sincere. Is it that nature-writing and poetry must be spontaneously sincere? Sincerity is the first and greatest of the literary commandments. The second is like unto the first. Still there is considerable difference between the inherent marketableness of a cold thought and a warm, purely personal emotion. One has a right to sell one's ideas, to barter one's literary inventions; one has a right, a duty it may be, to invent inventions for sale; but one may not, without sure damnation, make "copy" of one's emotions. In other words, one may not invent emotions, nor observations either, for the literary trade. The sad case with much of our nature-writing is that it has become professional, and so insincere, not answering to genuine observation nor to genuine emotion, but to the bid of the publisher.

You will know the sincere nature-writer by his fidelity to fact. But, alas! suppose I do not know the fact? To be sure. And the nature-writer thought of that, too, and penned his solemn, pious preface, wherein he declares that the following observations are exactly as he personally saw them; that they are true altogether; that he has the affidavits to prove it; and the Indians and the Eskimos to swear the affidavits prove it. Of course you are bound to believe after that; but you wish the preface did not make it so unnecessarily hard.

The sincere nature-writer, because he knows he cannot prove it, and that you cannot prove it, and that the scientists cannot prove it, knows that he must not be asked for proofs, that he must be above suspicion, and so he sticks to the truth as the wife of Caesar to her spouse.

Let the nature-writer only chronicle his observations as Dr. C. C. Abbott does in "A Naturalist's Rambles about Home," or let him dream a dream about his observations as Maeterlinck does in "The Life of the Bee," yet he is still confined to the truth as a hermit crab to his shell — a hard, inelastic, unchangeable, indestructible house that he cannot adapt, but must himself be adapted to, or else abandon. Chronicle and romance alike we want true to fact. But this particular romance about the Bee will not thus qualify. It was not written for beekeepers, even amateur beekeepers, for they all know more or less about bees, and hence they would not understand the book. It was written for those, the city-faring folk, like my market-man, who asked me how many pounds of honey a bee would gather up in a year, and whether I kept more than one bee in a hive. A great many persons must have read "The Life of the Bee," but only one of them, so far as I know, had ever kept bees, and she had just a single swarm in between the wall of her living room and the weather-boards outside. But she had listened to them through the wall, and she sent me her copy of "The Life," begging me to mark on the margins wherever the Bee of the book was unlike her bee in the wall. She had detected a difference in the buzz of the two bees.

Now the two bees ought to buzz alike—one buzz, distinct and always distinguishable from the buzz of the author. In the best nature-writing the author is more than his matter, but he is never identical with it; and not until we know which is which, and that the matter is true, have we faith in the author.

I knew a big boy once who had almost reached the footprint in "Robinson Crusoe" (the tragedy of almost reaching it!) when some one blunderingly told him that the book was all a story, made up, not true at all; no such island; no such Crusoe! The boy shut up the book and put it forever from him. He wanted it true. He had thought it true, because it had been so real. Robbed of its reality, he was unable to make it true again.

Most of us recover from this shock in regard to books, asking only that they seem real. But we are eternally childish, curious, credulous, in our thought of nature, she is so close and real to us, and yet so shadowy, hidden, mysterious, and remote! We are eager to listen to any tale, willing to believe anything, if only it be true. Nay, we are willing to believe it true—we were, I should say, until, like the boy with the book, we were rudely told that all this fine writing was made up, that we have no such kindred in the wilds, and no such wilds. Then we said in our haste, all men—who write nature-books— are liars.

"How much of this is real?" asked a keen and anxious reader, eyeing me narrowly, as she pointed a steady finger at an essay of mine in the "Atlantic." "Have you, sir, a farm and four real boys of your own, or are they faked?"

"Good heavens, madam!" I exclaimed. "Has it come to this? My boys faked!"

But it shows how the thoughtful and the fearful regard the literary naturalist, and how paramount is the demand for honesty in the matter of mere fact, to say nothing of the greater matter of expression.

Only yesterday, in a review in the "Nation" of an animal-man book, I read: "The best thing in the volume is the description of a fight between a mink and a raccoon—or so it seems. Can this be because the reader does not know the difference between a mink and a raccoon, and does know the difference between a human being and the story-teller's manikin?"

This is the wandering wood, this Errour's den,

is the feeling of the average reader—of even the "Nation's" book reviewer— nowadays, toward nature-writing, a state of mind due to the recent revelations of a propensity in wild-animal literature to stand up rather than go on all fours.

Whatever of the Urim and of the Thummim you put into your style, whatever of the literary lights and the perfections, see to it that you make the facts "after their pattern, which hath been shewed thee in the mount."

Thou shalt not bear false witness as to the facts.

Nor is this all. For the sad case with much nature-writing, as I have said, is that it not only fails to answer to genuine observation, but it also fails to answer to genuine emotion. Often as we detect the unsound natural history, we much oftener are aware of the unsound, the insincere, art of the author.

Now the facts of nature, as Mr. Burroughs says, are the material of nature literature — of one kind of such literature, let me add; for, while fabrications can be made only into lies, there may be another kind of good nature-literature compounded wholly of fancies. Facts, to quote Mr. Burroughs again, are the flora upon which the nature-writer lives. "I can do nothing without them." Of course he could not. But Chaucer could. Indeed, Chaucer could do nothing with the facts; he had to have fancies. The truth in his story of the Cock and the Fox is a different kind of truth from the truth about Burroughs's "Winter Neighbors," yet no less the truth. Good nature-writing is literature, not science, and the truth we demand first and last is a literary truth — the fidelity of the writer to himself. He may elect to use facts for his material; yet they are only material, and no better as material than fancies. For it is not matter that counts last in literature; it is manner. It is spirit that counts. It is the man. Only honest men make literature. Writers may differ in their purpose, as Burroughs in his purpose to guide you through the woods differs from Chaucer's purpose to entertain you by the fire; but they are one in their spirit of honesty.

Chaucer pulls a long face and begins his tale of the Cock and the Fox with a vivid and very realistic description of a widow's cottage,

> B'syde a grovë, standing in a dalë,

as a setting, not for the poor widow and her two daughters, not at all; but rather to stage the heroic comedy between Chauntecleer and his favorite wife, the scarlet-eyed Pertelote.

It is just before daybreak. They are not up yet, not off the roost, when they get into a discussion about the significance of dreams, Chauntecleer having had a very bad dream during the night. The dispute waxes as it spreads out over medicine, philosophy, theology, and psychology. Chauntecleer quotes the classics, cites famous stories, talks Latin to her:—

> For, also sicker as In principio
> Mulier est hominis confusio;

translating it for her thus:

> Madam, the sentence of this Latin is—
> Woman is mannës joy and all his blis,

while she tells him he needs a pill for his liver in spite of the fact that he wears a beard. It is fine scorn, but passing sad, following so close upon the old English love song that Chauntecleer was wont to wake up singing.

It is here, at this critical juncture of the nature-story, that Chaucer pauses to remark seriously:—

> For thilkë tyme, as I have understondë,
> Bestës and briddës couldë speke and singë.

Certainly they could; and "speking and singing in thilkë tyme" seems much more natural for "bestës and briddës" than many of the things they do nowadays.

Here, again, is Izaak Walton, as honest a man as Chaucer—a lover of nature, a writer on angling; who knew little about angling, and less about nature; whose facts are largely fancies; but—what of it? Walton quotes, as a probable fact, that pickerel hatch out of the seeds of the pickerel-weed; that toads are born of fallen leaves on the bottoms of ponds. He finds himself agreeing with Pliny "that many flies have their birth, or being, from a dew that in the spring falls upon the leaves of the trees"; and, quoting the divine du Bartas, he sings:—

> So slow Boötes underneath him sees
> In th' icy isles those goslings hatch'd of trees,
> Whose fruitful leaves, falling into the water,
> Are turn'd, they say, to living fowls soon after.

But the "Compleat Angler" is not a scientific work on fishes, nor a handbook on angling for anglers. It is a book for all that are lovers of literature; for "all that are lovers of virtue; and dare trust in his providence; and be quiet; and go a Angling."

This is somewhat unscientific, according to our present light; but, wonderful as it seemed to Walton, it was all perfectly natural according to his light. His facts are faulty, yet they are the best he had. So was his love the best he had; but that was without fault, warm, deep, intense, sincere.

Our knowledge of nature has so advanced since Walton's time, and our attitude has so changed, that the facts of nature are no longer enough for literature. We know all that our writer knows; we have seen all that he can see. He can no longer surprise us; he can no longer instruct us; he can no longer fool us. The day of the marvelous is past; the day of the cum laude cat and the magna cum laude pup is past, the day of the things that I alone have seen is past; and the day of the things that I, in common with you, have honestly felt, is come.

There should be no suggestion in a page of nature-writing that the author—penetrated to the heart of some howling summer camp for his raw material; that he ever sat on his roof or walked across his back yard in order to write a book about it. But nature-books, like other books, are gone for that way—always and solely for the pot. Such books are "copy" only—poor copy at that. There is nothing new in them; for the only thing you can get by going afar for it is a temptation to lie; and no matter from what distance you fetch a falsehood—even from the top of the world—you cannot disguise the true complexion of it. Take the writings of the morning and dwell in the uttermost parts of the sea, and you will find nothing new there; ascend into heaven or make your bed in hell for copy, as is the fashion nowadays.—But you had better look after your parish, and go faithfully about your chores; and if you have a garden with a tortoise in it, and you love them, and love to write about them, then write.

Nature-writing must grow more and more human, personal, interpretative. If I go into the wilderness and write a book about it, it must be plain to my reader that "the writing of the book was only a second and finer enjoyment of my holiday in the woods." If my chippy sings, it must sing a chippy's simple song, not some gloria that only "the careless angels know." It must not do any extraordinary thing for me; but it may lead me to do an extraordinary thing—to have an extraordinary thought, or suggestion, or emotion. It may mean extraordinary things to me; things that have no existence in nature, whose beginnings and ends are in me. I may never claim that I, because of exceptional opportunities, or exceptional insight, or exceptional powers of observation, have discovered these marvelous things here in the wilds of Hingham. My pages may be anthropomorphic, human; not, how-ever, because I humanize my bees and toads, but because I am human, and nature is meaningful ultimately only as it is related to me. I must not confuse myself with nature; nor yet "struggle against fact and law to develop and keep" my "own individuality." I must not anthropomorphize nature; never denature nature; never follow my own track through the woods, imagining that I am on the trail of a better-class wolf or a two-legged bear. I must never sentimentalize over nature again—write no more about "Buzz-Buzz and Old Man Barberry"; write no more about wailing winds and weeping skies; for mine is not "a poet's vision dim," but an open-eyed, scientific view of things as they actually are. Once I have seen them, gathered them, if then they turn to poetry, let them turn. For so does the squash turn to poetry when it is brought in from the field. It turns to pie; it turns to poetry; and it still remains squash.

Good nature-literature, like all good literature, is more lived than written. Its immortal part hath elsewhere than the ink-pot its beginning. The soul that rises with it, its life's star, first went down a horizon of real experience, then rose from a human heart, the source of all true feeling, of all sincere form. Good nature-writing particularly must have a pre-literary existence as lived reality; its writing must be only the necessary accident of its being lived again in thought. It will be something very human, very natural, warm, quick, irregular, imperfect, with the imperfections and irregularities of life. And the nature-writer will be very human, too, and so very faulty; but he will have no lack of love for nature, and no lack of love for the truth. Whatever else he does, he will never touch the flat, disquieting note of make-believe. He will never invent, never pretend, never pose, never shy. He will be hon-est—which is nothing unusual for birds and rocks and stars; but for human beings, and for nature writers very particularly, it is a state less common, perhaps, than it ought to be.

Norman Foerster on
Nature Cultists and American Literature
(1912 and 1923)

Norman Foerster (pronounced "Firster") was born in 1887 in Pittsburgh. He earned a bachelor's degree from Harvard in 1910 and a master's in 1912 from the University of Wisconsin; he would eventually receive honorary doctorates from the University of the South, Grinnell College, and the University of North Carolina. His teaching career took him to the University of Wisconsin, North Carolina, the University of Iowa, and finally to Duke. He is most remembered as an early champion of American writing and the author or editor of nearly two dozen books.

In his most influential book, *Nature in American Literature* (1923), Foerster argued that "the story of American culture" was essentially that of Europe, only "modified" by the absence of ancient traditions and by the presence "of physical circumstances destined to affect profoundly her mind and heart" — that is, by the encounter with wild nature. In no other national literature was the Wordsworthian sort of natural presence "more prominent than in the literature of America"; indeed, with "only two or three exceptions, all of our major writers have displayed . . . an ardent emotional devotion to nature because of her beauty or divinity."

In demonstrating these points, Foerster became one of the first academic critics to pay serious attention to John Muir, and in one of the excerpts below he performs some skillful readings of Muir's prose, revealing some of the technical qualities that elevate it above "mere description." He notes in addition how Muir managed to transform a rather orthodox Christianity into an early biocentrism, into the genuinely original blend of theology and deep ecology that informs so much of his writing. Another excerpt gives the same careful attention to the work of John Burroughs. Foerster clearly admires Burroughs but does not hesitate to point up that author's deeply conflicted attitude toward science, and the general naïveté of Burroughs's philosophy.

The excerpts below are reprinted from "The Nature Cult To-Day," which appeared originally in the *Nation* in 1912, and from *Nature in American Literature*.

౿౿ ౿౿ ౿౿

"The Nature Cult To-Day"

Talking with a sober farmer of Concord, one day, I asked him about the location of Thoreau's famous bean-field. "Bean-field?" — the man was honestly puzzled — "I didn't know he ever did anything. Thoreau was a loafer."

I was as much refreshed and pleased as I suspect Thoreau himself would have been had he returned incognito to twentieth century Concord. Every one else — save this honest farmer and his kind — would have told him that Thoreau was the great poet of Nature, the American Wordsworth, the famous hermit who communed with the god of the Open Air at Walden, the misanthrope who taught us how to fall at the feet of Nature worshipfully — to see the Compelling Vision and know the Great Secret — or, perchance, how to be accepted "nature-lovers." And if he turned away sadly, with the loneliness of the great spirit, it would have been to suffer the same sort of reception wherever he went. He would have heard of "the Godful woods," of "the forest-cathedral," of "tree-thoughts," of "Nature's old love-song" (I quote from one or two of the Nature Books of the past year); he would have been told that the meadowlark surpasses any opera, that the orchid of the fields is, like man, fashioned from the earth, but is "a fairer and lovelier product," that birds are the best of friends, for they bring no "misunderstandings and disappointments" and never grow old and they sometimes have "so much to express, so much temperament" — at least if you can assume "the viewpoint of the bird." The follower of the trail would have told him of "the splendid, untamed, savage West," where one may slip off one's perplexing personality as if it were a waistcoat and become admirably like the horse that bears one on to "broad vistas and silence." The wanderer returned from the Sierras would have told him of "the mountain-joy," of a "passionate ecstatic pleasure-glow not explainable," of fine views that make one shout and gesticulate "in a wild burst of ecstasy," and of dreaming by night that one is "rushing through the air above a glorious avalanche of water and rocks." Forgetting that Thoreau himself had fished in Walden Pond, they would have told him of terribly wicked people who actually fished in the Yosemite: "Sport they called it. Should church-goers try to pass the time fishing in baptismal fonts while dull sermons were being preached, the so-called sport might not have been so bad; but to play in the Yosemite temple, seeking pleasure in the pain of fishes struggling for their lives, while God himself is preaching his sublimest water and stone sermons!" "Ah, Henry," the female enthusiast would have added, "we are fallen upon evil times. Our wild flowers are fast disappearing. The few people who do go to the country always come back with huge wilted bouquets — if only *everybody* went to the country and cut a *few!*" Had Thoreau's acute sense of logic caused him to remark that the result would be pretty much the same, the good woman would doubtless not have heard him in her enthusiasm over "a lifetime to live in the forest, inexhaustible plates, indestructible cameras, wells of ink, and pens of magic." And after all this, and much more besides, Thoreau would have been driven, weary, stifled, and very melancholy, to seek the comfort of the hills — only to find that our scenery has been well-nigh destroyed as a result of the facilities for seeing it. In his note-book he would then have copied a sentence from his Journal (March 13, 1841): "I like better the surliness with which the woodchopper speaks of his woods, handling them as indifferently as his axe, than the mealy-mouthed enthusiasm of the lover of nature."

"Walden" is doubtless one of the great books of American literature. But between "Walden" and the "Nature Books" of the present day there is not so much a difference of degree as of kind, and this important difference of kind Thoreau would have observed instantly. Had he had an opportunity to watch the influence of his work until now, it is highly probable, I think, that he would have scornfully repudiated most of his readers and imitators on the ground that they almost totally misunderstood him. The emphasis in Thoreau is not on nature, not on men, but on man — on character. With his acceptation of the idea of natural goodness and of the idea that man and nature are akin, he combined the Puritan moral earnestness that lived its second life in the decades of American Transcendentalism. This Puritan strain predominated in Thoreau, and had two noteworthy results. In the first place, "the sober and solemn mystery of nature" evoked in him awe rather than the latter-day curiosity and somewhat cheap desire for intimacy. Today nature is commonly wooed as if she were a coquette or a mistress, prettily or with shallow "mealy-mouthed" abandon; nature is a creature whose blandishments cause her lovers to be at once very silly and very garrulous — and if books result, as they ordinarily do, they prove very remunerative. Thoreau, on the other hand, found that his "truest, serenest moments are too still for emotion; they have woollen feet"; and it is unfair to assert that he was posing when he said that he wrote his books "to purchase silence with." In the second place, the Puritan earnestness of Thoreau manifested itself in an esteem for character and will. "Only character can command our reverent love. It is all mysteries in itself." It may be that "All's right with the world," as most of our nature-lovers are echoing every day; but it certainly was not so in Thoreau's world. A thousand nameless sins hovered over him wherever he went, and made him yearn more eagerly every day for an erectness and innocence, towards which he must strive unceasingly, but which in the end could come only if he were one of the elect — "no man knoweth in what hour his life may come." His life was thus an endless quest for character. He yearned to attain serene purity and wisdom; he did not yearn for indestructible cameras and wells of ink.

The difference in kind, then, between Thoreau and the nature-lover of to-day seems to me to lie in the fact that Thoreau's view of life was genuinely imaginative, sincerely idealistic, whereas the view of life that one finds in the typical nature-writing of the twentieth century is absurdly shallow and sentimental. "This hypethral temple," I read in one of the recent books, " . . . is the only temple on earth where there is no cant, no twaddle, no hypocrisy, and no croaking about our sins." What is this if it is not cant and twaddle? Few will deny that religion has ceased to be fashionable, and that cant is to be found well-nigh everywhere; but the worshippers of nature have not yet convinced us that they are themselves free from the ills that beset the more orthodox sects. As for "No croaking about our sins," this is palpably not good Thoreau doctrine, either in phrasing or meaning; it is, rather, a pale and sickly reflection from the brightly-shining optimism of Browning and Whitman. If we croak at all, they tell us to-day, let it be as the frogs croak, carelessly, jubilantly, with an appreciative eye on the opal sunset. Let us be as frogs, or if frogs are not lovely enough, let us "assume all that is shy and birdlike" or any other-like that is not manlike.

Of course all this is beside the question. What the nature-lover really desires is not to be a part of nature, but to be a part of himself. He would cast away "worldly cares" and city life with its difficulties, as well as farm life with *its* difficulties, so that he may be, like the inhabitants of the Garden of Eden, "free to roam and to reminisce under the pines." In other words, he would abandon his right to be a rational animal, together with his right to have what life in any human community demands — character; and having given over these unpleasant rights of thinking and being a moral creature, he would find freedom and happiness in a community of song sparrows and fern fronds. That is, after all, what one of the most estimable of our nature writers means when he remarks, "Only spread a fern frond over a man's head and worldly cares are cast out, and freedom and beauty and peace come in." One is tempted to amend: "Only spread a fern frond over a man's head and he ceases to be a man."

In practice, the hypethral temple of nature, where one may find diviner company than the town affords, becomes the scene either of placid lotos-eating — loafing and inviting the soul in vain — or of an intoxicated sensuousness. If the worshipper of nature is of a dreamy disposition that leads him to the kindly hills of Massachusetts, he is prone to dream — and usually dreams prone. If he has the "dynamic" temper that leads him to the higher Sierras, he experiences the exuberant sensuous joys of the eagle and the mountain goat. One of our dreamy women nature-lovers tells us soberly that she "worships" certain moths. One of our vibrant men nature-lovers explains a part of his Bacchanal ritual as follows: "I drink the blue of gentians and the red of cardinal lobelias and scarlet buglers; I plunge into the golden fields of baeria and bathe in the yellow flood of poppies." But whether the nature-lover is dreamy or "dynamic," his joys are dominantly sensuous without being spiritually sensuous. In the manner of the sentimentalist, he would place himself in a position that will yield sensation in variety and abundance. He seeks the delights of shimmering water, of olive-green velvety shadows, of the resinous incense in pine groves, of insect murmur and ethereal bird-song, of bracing wine-like air; delights, indeed, that are not to be spurned. White of Selborne enjoyed the grace of the *hirundines* and of English beeches with gentlemanly candor; Wordsworth, with the poet's vision, derived spiritual manna from the grandeur of Helvellyn; Thoreau, who also had the poet's vision, profited by the goodly fellowship of the Concord River and the chill, leaden November days that fanned into flame his "deep, inward fires." The senses may indeed be inlets of spirituality. But in the typical nature-lover of the present day one observes a great deal sensuousness and a negligible degree of spirituality. He is akin, not to the Thoreaus and Wordsworths that he apes, but rather to the "week-ender," and the amateur naturalist who lives in the city. What to these is recreation is to him a mode of life.

From *Nature in American Literature*

A land of promise, America is virtually without a past. Her children need not look far back to the founders of her civilization, a civilization not yet freed, and doubtless never to be freed, from its European prototype. The story of her culture — of her art, her philosophy, her education — remains to this day an account of the transfer to a new world of the culture of modern Europe, modified, it is true, by the omission of an intimate sense of that august tradition which reaches back to the primitive Northern folks and the ancient Greeks and Hebrews, and by the addition of physical circumstances destined to affect profoundly her mind and heart. Elizabethan and Puritan in lineage, America has approached maturity, has lived through her most impressionable years, in that confused period of romanticism, democracy, and science from which the modern world has not yet emerged to clearness and faith.

In the age in which the American nation was adolescent, the distinguishing feature of men's thoughts and feelings — and consequently of their literature — was apparently a new gospel of nature. From Jean Jacques Rousseau to Walt Whitman and his disciples, whatever the cross-currents and back-eddies in the intellectual and emotional stream of the time, the prevailing current seems to have been a fresh enthusiasm for nature — for the natural man's impulses, for "natural rights," for natural science. The classical and Christian emphasis on human and internal standards and ideals, dominant up to the nineteenth century, has given place to an emphasis on standards and ideals sought in the external universe, in nature, and in nature within man. Science has applied itself to the understanding and mastery of nature with astonishing results; philosophy has undertaken to determine in what sense inner and outer are one, until, within our own time, it has been well-nigh absorbed by natural science; and literature, faithfully mirroring the passions of the era, has either become realistic in its representation of natural and human life, or has turned to the outer world for an answer to its emotional cravings — or, often, it has done both simultaneously. Thus, Wordsworth, for instance, the high-priest of nature, would not only picture "the infinite variety of natural appearances which had been unnoticed by the poets of any age or country," but also express something of the ecstatic illumination that he felt flow in upon him from a spirit or presence in nature —

> . . . a sense sublime
> Of something far more deeply interfused,
> Whose dwelling is the light of setting suns,
> And the round ocean and the living air,
> And the blue sky, and in the mind of man.

A new sight, a new insight — these are sought in all the literature from the time of Wordsworth to the present moment.

Nowhere are they more prominent than in the literature of America. With only two or three exceptions, all of our major writers have displayed both a striking curiosity as to the facts of the external world — an intellectual conscience in seeking to know them with exactness — and an ardent emotional devotion to nature because of her beauty or divinity; and this curiosity and this devotion have become so pervasive that, especially in our time, even writers outside the main intellectual and emotional currents of the age — such as contributors to rural newspapers and to college magazines in the most remote sections of the country — reveal the new absorption in nature quite as clearly as the typical poets and essayists of the day, and perhaps more clearly than the great writers of the nineteenth century. It is the purpose of the studies that follow to trace the development of this naturalistic movement in American literature from Bryant to Whitman and the typical essayists of the present century, determining more fully and precisely than has yet been done how much of nature our authors were acquainted with and what place she held in their hearts and thoughts. . . .

No doubt there are various reasons why John Muir, author, inventor, botanist, geologist, explorer, mountaineer, rancher, conservationist, wrote his first book when he was nearing sixty. The fundamental reason, however, is simply that he was too busy enjoying life to say much about it. Experience was to him not merely stuff for artistic essays or scientific monographs, still less material for carving an imposing career, but a thing to be sought for its own sake. He thought only — and how fervidly! — of beauty and knowledge; he was intoxicated with the various beauty of the world and with the perfection of its natural law. Like his contemporary Fabre, "the insect's Homer," he had the ecstasy of both the poet and the scientist. His prevailing attitude is one of wonder — not that of the undisciplined romanticist dissolved in a Byronic emotion "too deep for thought," but that of a true poet-naturalist, eager to analyze as well as enjoy nature's beauty and perfection. He was a poet well schooled in the discipline of facts. . . .

But nature, to John Muir, was vastly more than matter permeated with law. Had he looked upon it so, he might have been a more productive scientist; but he regarded it, instead, as the unspeakably beautiful work of a loving creator, and consequently produced books that are only secondarily scientific, and primarily literary. More and more, as time goes on, and as later botanists, geographers, physiographers, and geologists supplement Muir's studies till they are covered over with accretions, as if they belonged to an earlier geological age, we shall go to such books as *The Mountains of California, Our National Parks,* and *My First Summer in the Sierra* for a living and accurate picture of the Great West such as no one else is likely soon to duplicate.

Muir emphasized several causes that make it impossible for most men to look upon nature, with him, as the unspeakably beautiful work of a loving creator, the temple of God in which man may worship. One cause is fear. Men are afraid of nature. They will sometimes venture into the wilderness when they can lean on each other, but to entrust their precious selves to cruel nature alone is too much. Yet, as Muir points out, all the "dangers" of the wilderness — all the colds, fevers, Indians, bears, snakes, "bugs," impassable rivers, jungles of brush, and quick and sure starvation — are either imaginary or grossly exaggerated, and even if they are not, amount to nothing in comparison with the dangers of living indoors in crowded cities. If a man is in good health to begin with, there is nowhere such physical well being as in the kindly wilderness. A wise man will perceive that frightful canyons and glacier crevasses are part of an orderly whole; that a great storm is "a cordial outpouring of Nature's love"; that all, indeed, "that we in our unbelief call terrible" is really an expression of the divine love.

Another cause for the blindness of men is the mistaken conception of nature as existing for man's use. Blandly asserting that nature was made for man's material needs — sheep for his clothing, oil for lighting his dark ways, lead for his bullets — most men cherish a curious view of the importance of man. Man is only one of many creatures, and the Lord loves them all. "The creation of all for the happiness of one" seems to this fellow-countryman of Adam Smith an inequitable arrangement of the universe: instead he proposes as the probable object "the happiness of each one of them," and goes on to confute his opponents by pointing out that this earth-ship on which we proudly sail had made many a successful journey round the heavens before *Homo sapiens* was created, and that things may be conducted very satisfactorily after man has disappeared from the world. Why, then, he asks, should man value himself as more than one small part of the great whole? Man is not distinct from, not above nature, but a part of it with his brother winds and rocks, all alike "fashioned with loving care" and all equally admirable.

Still another cause is the meanness of man. Man has desecrated not only nature but himself. More and more men live in cities, dirty, ugly, and morally impure cities. If they live in the country it is perhaps only to seek wealth in sheep, and the shepherd type is produced, living in many-voiced nature but hearing only "baa"! "Even the howls and ki-yis of coyotes might be blessings if well heard, but he hears them only through a blur of mutton and wool, and they do him no good." Or they become gold miners, hardy, adventurous, blazing a trail to nature's utmost fastnesses in disregard of dangers innumerable, as bold as Muir himself tracing his glaciers to their lairs in the mountains — but always blind to the beauty they desecrate, utterly deaf in their immorality, to the celestial love-music of nature. Beholding what God has made of nature, we may indeed deplore what man has made of man. One of the noblest of men, Emerson, Muir terms the sequoia of the human race, yet makes us feel that compelled to choose between the two, he would have discarded the man and kept the tree. The same choice he made more broadly in constantly quoting, as his ministerial friend Young tells us he did, Wordsworth's famous stanza:

> One impulse from a vernal wood
> May teach you more of man,
> Of moral evil and of good,
> Than all the sages can.

Beauty and love in nature, then, we shall see only if emancipated from fear, utilitarianism, and meanness of soul. That Muir was never threatened by any one of the three is manifest from his books and the story of his life. Others have responded to nature more profoundly, but none with more rampant enthusiasm. The wealth of one mountain day was enough to make him run home in the moonlight happy beyond words, and he recorded such days in his journal with a lover's abandon. According to Young, his constant exclamation on beholding a fine landscape was, "Praise God from whom all blessings flow!" It was a never-failing cause of surprise and gratitude to him "to think that He should plan to bring us feckless creatures here at the right moment, and then flash such glories at us." In his first summer in the Sierra, upon seeing a certain view he shouted and gesticulated so extravagantly that the sheep-dog Carlo came up to him with the most ludicrous puzzled expression in his eyes, and a brown bear in the thicket ran away in a panic, tumbling over the manzanita bushes in his haste. He was so enamoured of the Sierras that he asserted that he would be content among them forever if tethered to a stake; and with more literal truth, he said that, if it were not for the need of bread, civilization would never see him again. In his enthusiasm for all of God's handiwork he refused to kill animals for food, and even spared the rattlesnakes that he encountered — after all, they were not *his* snakes.

Rapt away by his enthusiasm, Muir enjoyed many hours when his scientific pursuits were laid aside, together with the whole of his rational impedimenta, and his personality was freely immersed in the landscape. Like the bees and butterflies, he would "lave in the vital sunshine, too richly and homogeneously joy-filled to be capable of partial thought," till he became "all eye, sifted through and through with light and beauty." Intoxicated with the champagne water, distilled air, and his own glad animal movements, it seemed to him that beauty entered, not through the eyes alone, but through all his flesh, like heat radiating from a camp-fire, "making a passionate, ecstatic pleasure-glow not explainable," as if his flesh-and-bone tabernacle were transparent as glass to the beauty surrounding it, "truly an inseparable part of it, thrilling with the air and trees, streams and rocks, in the waves of the sun — a part of all nature, neither old nor young, sick nor well, but immortal" — immortal because life now seemed neither long nor short, and time meant no more to him than to the trees and stars. In such hours Muir was impressed with the familiarity of natural objects, their human warmth; "no wonder," he says, "when we consider that we have the same Father and Mother." Yet he never went so far as to maintain that, in such hours, he was laid asleep in body and became, with Wordsworth, a living soul privileged to "see into the life of things." It was not spiritual insight that he enjoyed, but a pleasure-glow, a pure sensation, not a sensation exalted by thought; his body, deliciously alive, pulsed with nature. What we might call the human ele-

ment in man had not been transcended but simply omitted. Muir was inclined to think that man is at his best, not when he is most human, but when
he is most natural.

But one does not go to John Muir for a criticism of life. He understood
neither the heights and depths of his own nature, which he avoided as most
of us avoid the dizzy heights and depths of the material world, nor the complexities of social life — the boundless results of man's being a gregarious animal. When Emerson said of him that he was greater than Thoreau, he must
have been thinking, not of Thoreau the moralist, but of Thoreau the naturalist. It is as a literary naturalist that Muir is perhaps greater than Thoreau
and certainly equal to Burroughs. Knowing his facts perfectly, he had the
capacity to present them not only with truth but also with charm. His description of nature — and most of his writing is merely description — has a
degree of vividness that reminds one of those ocularly-minded masters of his
day, Carlyle and Ruskin.

His sensuous perception, like Thoreau's, was unspoiled by tobacco and
liquor — he drank only tea and mountain water. Then, he had a good plastic
sense, saw the compositions of nature with an artist's eye, throwing up his
arms for a frame, and often sketching in order to commemorate a scene or
to bolster up his geological notes. But far more important than his sensuous
alertness and aesthetic appreciation was his enthusiasm — his passionate absorption in nature's law and nature's beauty. He had, as we began by saying,
the ecstasy of both the scientist and the poet, and it is this ecstasy, more than
anything else, that gives power to his account of natural appearances.

Everywhere his enthusiasm revealed to him the principle of life. His landscape is ever "filled with warm God"; it is a living, breathing, moving landscape, rather than so much expressionless matter outstaring the beholder. His
clouds, his very rocks, are instinct with life. A primrose by the river's brim
was to him far more than a primrose. An ordinary drop of rain was no less
than this: "a silvery newborn star with lake and river, garden and grove, valley
and mountain, all that the landscape holds reflected in its crystal depths,
God's messenger, angel of love sent on its way with majesty and pomp and
display of power that make man's greatest shows ridiculous." In imagination
he followed each drop, some penetrating to the roots of meadow plants, some
shivered to dust through the pine needles, some drumming the broad leaves
of veratrum or saxifrage, some plunging straight into fragrant corollas, or into
the lake, dimpling it daintily, some flinging themselves into the wild heart of

falls or cascades eager to take part in the dance and the song. He remembered without an effort that everything called "destruction" in nature is really creation, a passage from one use to another, one form of beauty to another. The immobile and changeless face of nature, which appalls the unimaginative visitor, was to him replete with fascinating alteration.

Partly for this reason his descriptions of moving water, and storms, and the aurora borealis are usually his best work. The rain-storms of Alaska and the thunder-storms of the Sierras he described with power again and again; perhaps the best of his storm descriptions, however, is the wonderful chapter on "A Wind-Storm in the Forests," which bathes the reader with thrilling light, intoxicates him with piny fragrance, and exhilarates him with pure air and swaying, straining motion. . . .

Where there is action, where there is a narrative element in description, as in Muir's account of moving water, roving storms, and evanescent Northern lights, the picture is held together by the cohesive quality of the subject itself. But, as Lessing demonstrated long ago, where this chronological thread is wanting, the picture easily falls apart, one group of details canceling another group, so that the total impression is a blur or a blank. Sheer description in literature is indeed dangerous, now as in the eighteenth century, and yet the suffusion of modern descriptive passages with imagination — not a conspicuous commodity in the age of prose and reason — has gone far to justify "pen portraits" and literary landscape-painting. In Muir's writing, thanks to his kindling imagination, one rarely feels that he is going beyond the boundaries of literature and foolishly competing with the painter; a principle of life animates all his work — life in the thing seen, life in the seer.

Nowhere does this principle of life manifest itself more strikingly than in the fresh, free-ranging figures of speech that are nearly certain to illuminate his scenes wherever they are in danger of being darkened with words. The muddy floods that rush down the gorges and gulches during a shower roar "like lions rudely awakened, each of the tawny brood actually kicking up a dust at the first onset." The mountain tarns in early summer "begin to blink and thaw out like sleepy eyes." The hairs of the squirrel's tail quiver in the breeze "like pine-needles." In the dry weather of midsummer in the lower part of the Sierra "the withered hills and valleys seem to lie as empty and expressionless as dead shells on a shore." Muir's metaphors and similes are abundant, new, and apt; they reveal because they proceed from the poet in him.

Life, too, results from his frequent use of onomatopoeia. His very words become sentient and mimic the mood of the moment. There are obvious instances everywhere, and also subtle ones that easily escape notice. This is obvious (the topic is icebergs on the Pacific coast):

> "Nearly all of them are swashed and drifted by wind and tide back and forth in the fiords until finally melted by the ocean water. . . ."

In the following, the contrast between two types of motion is emphasized by the word sounds:

> "Butterflies, too, and moths . . . ; some wide-winged like bats, flapping slowly and sailing in easy curves; others like small flying violets shaking about loosely in short zigzag flights."

One more, in which the style reflects perfectly the quiet grace of the deer:

> "Deer give beautiful animation to the forests, harmonizing finely in their color and movements with the gray and brown shafts of the trees and the swaying of the branches as they stand in groups at rest, or move gracefully and noiselessly over the mossy ground about the edges of beaver-meadows and flowery glades, daintily culling the leaves and tips of the mints and aromatic bushes on which they feed."

This means of adding to verisimilitude is not rare in Muir's style, but is, rather, a normal method. In all his description he seems to have felt, more than most writers do, that the sound of his phrases and sentences must carry a large part of the sense, and this is clearly one reason why his description is impressive.

Finally, he attained life through speed. His language does not emerge soberly, but flings itself out and hastens on as if word pursued word, sentence pursued sentence, like the pouring notes of a musical composition that rush over every obstacle to their triumph. This is not to say that he wrote with facility, since we know that he did not. "Very irksome" he pronounced "this literary business"; he worked laboriously, rewriting many of his most poetical chapters repeatedly. Hard writing often makes easy reading, and indeed no style could be much simpler than Muir's. It is perhaps too simple, too unvaried, too coordinated, too breathless in its persistent predication, so that one longs to stop, now and then, to rest and muse. At times his style has the melody and the imaginative magnificence of Ruskin, but the melody is rarely swelling, the magnificence rarely deep and reserved. Both Muir and Ruskin were nourished on the Bible and knew most of it by heart, and both became ardent admirers of nature and described her beauties with a lover's eye for detail; but whereas Muir became a scientist, Ruskin became a critic of life in several distinct fields; his work is therefore reflective. It is Muir's lack of reflection, betrayed by his restless, hurried style, that prevented his attaining a high position in our literature. Accurate and enthusiastic description of nature will go far, but no matter how remarkably accurate and enthusiastic, it cannot reach preeminence without the deeper elements infused by the mind and the spirit. . . .

Since the death of Thoreau in 1862, the outstanding American prose writers on nature, among an ever-gathering host, have been John Muir and John Burroughs. Set apart by their union of scientific accuracy with power of expression, these two writers have established a virtually new type of literature, the nature essay. As a naturalist, Muir was superior to Burroughs, by virtue of his more systematic studies and more important additions to our knowledge; as a writer, however, he was less certainly superior, since both of them display not only an admirable capacity for penetrating description but also a prevailing negligence of both the architectonics and the detail of literary form. Of the two, Burroughs published far more abundantly and steadily, so that he has perhaps impressed the American public as Muir, with all his personal charm, never did, though Burroughs's preeminence may be attributed in no small measure to his having become, like Thoreau, a *genius loci*. While Muir was wandering alone in the wilderness, or rather a dozen wildernesses, Burroughs, happily secluded in one of his successive hermitages, attracted pilgrims without number — nature lovers true and false, Burroughs clubs, Vassar girls, cyclists, artists, authors, reporters, children, old men — all of whom found him accessible and picturesque, and many of whom subsequently celebrated the object of their pilgrimage in a magazine or newspaper article. They came seeking not so much a poet-naturalist, whom they might better have found in Muir, as a natural philosopher, one of the sages of this latter day whose wisdom was authenticated by his equability and his closeness to the soil. While Muir, with his buoyant vitality, reminded his acquaintances of the Douglas squirrel that won his heart, Burroughs seems rather akin to the phlegmatic woodchuck. . . .

We have seen that Thoreau, who began like Burroughs as a poetic observer of nature, remained essentially a poetic observer all his days, despite his matter-of-fact journalizing. Burroughs did not; in him the poetic observer was early dominated by the scientific observer, by a lively curiosity with regard to the fact, like that of Gilbert White, whom he rightly set down as a type of the born observer, "the man with the detective eye." White was, indeed, one of the first of the true field naturalists; the time had gone by when a Goldsmith could be found inspecting "curious scraps of descriptions of animals scrawled upon the wall with a black lead pencil," and the time was come when a Gilbert White could be seen rambling through the beech woods and over the rolling downs with eye and ear alert to every unwonted phenomenon. Yet it was not so much the detective eye of the gentleman-naturalist of Selborne that made his book a classic, as the winning spirit of the man himself and the measured charm of his eighteenth-century style. And likewise Thoreau, who lacked "the detective eye of the great naturalist," as Burroughs remarked in an early essay, who never really perceived the goings on in the world about him, whose most unusual observation that Burroughs could recall was his discovery that the wild apple-tree outwits the browsing cattle by protecting itself with dense, thorny branchlets and sending a favored shoot up beyond their reach, who bragged that he would not go round the corner even to see the world blow up (to which Burroughs responds that *his* curiosity would certainly bring him there) — Thoreau likewise owes his place to temperamental and spiritual qualities, and not to his skill in observation. As a creator of literature, Burroughs, too, must owe what measure of success he has achieved to his literary qualities, which his detective aptitude serves while remaining distinct.

It must be remembered, however, that Burroughs did not regard himself as primarily a literary writer, but rather as a student of nature. If he has sacrificed the literary values, he has sacrificed them to an end that, through most of his life, seemed more important than they: understanding of the ways of nature. Similarly, it may be said that what represents a loss to him who reads Burroughs in the literary spirit represents a gain to him who reads him in the scientific spirit — who seeks in his pages fresh knowledge of the natural order and stimulation toward the independent pursuit of such knowledge. Most men are indeed blind to the little dramas of nature, as Burroughs never tired of pointing out; do not read the sudden signals and gestures, penetrate the screens, untangle the skeins, distinguish between the commonplace and the significant. In the book of nature, "there is coarse print and fine print; there are obscure signs and hieroglyphics. We all read the large type more or less appreciatively, but only the students and lovers of nature read the fine line and the footnotes. . . . For my part, my delight is to linger long over each page of this marvelous record, and to dwell fondly upon its most obscure text." In this study, the first thing needful is a sharp eye. I think I have seen sharply, until I am challenged, as when, says Burroughs, a lady asks me to draw an outline of the tulip-tree leaf and I realize how blurred my sight has been. Here, again, is a chickadee nest, from which the birds are absent, with apparently some hair of a small animal at the edges of the cavity in the tree — their nest has been rifled. But a microscopic examination of the hair proves it to be not hair but a vegetable fiber, which had caught at the entrance to the nest while the chickadees were drawing it in. A sharp eye first, then; and secondly, patience. It is not enough to see clearly; you must also see steadily and carefully. The error in this matter of the chickadee nest sprang not only from defective observation but also from hasty inference, as it did in the following incident. A lawyer once sent John Burroughs an egg-shell of the quail to testify that the mother bird, not the young, had broken the shells, since the edges were bent *in*. But the observer was hasty, had not considered the effect of the shrinking of the skin lining the shell; he had failed to sift all the evidence, had not cross-questioned the facts, had not applied legal methods. Legal methods, medical methods, scholarly methods — they are all alike the critical or scientific method, always a rare possession, which John Burroughs has in high degree. As he saunters across the open fields and through the woods, stopping here and there to listen more acutely or see more accurately, there is little in the drama of nature that escapes his perspicuous perception. Drama in a sense it is, and he the audience; yet, as he points out in an essay on "Hasty Observation," it is not the drama as we humanly produce it:

> "It is not like the play at the theatre, where everything is made conspicuous and aims to catch the eye, and where the story clearly and fully unfolds itself. On nature's stage many dramas are being played at once, and without any reference to the lookers-on, unless it be to escape their notice. The actors rush or strut across the stage, the curtain rises or falls, the significant thing happens, and we heed it not."

To the observer of the natural drama, to the reader in the book of nature, there is ever a new act, a new page. Now it is a yellowish-white moth mimicking the droppings of birds, or a shrike impaling a mouse on a thorn, or a vireo harassing an intruding cowbird, or a pair of eagles celebrating their nuptials in mid-air, or a chipmunk preparing his winter quarters in July, or a salamander revealing himself after years as the source of a mysterious plaintive piping in the woods of summer and autumn, or a genuine English lark showering melody over a Hudson valley meadow, or a skunk—here is the skunk story:

> "I did something the other day with a wild animal that I had never done before or seen done, though I had heard of it: I carried a live skunk by the tail, and there was "nothing doing," as the boys say. I did not have to bury my clothes. I knew from observation that the skunk could not use its battery with effect without throwing its tail over its back; therefore, for once at least, I had the courage of my convictions and verified the fact."

If in one season, says Burroughs, he picks up two or three facts in natural history that are new to him, he considers himself lucky; as well he might, in comparison with Thoreau's findings in twenty years of daily excursions in the country. With time, Burroughs naturally became more keen of eye and ear, more patient in drawing his conclusions. More and more, after his poetic period, his scientific observation dictated the substance and spirit of his books, from, let us say, the *Locusts and Wild Honey* of 1879 to the *Leaf and the Tendril* of 1908. Repeatedly he wrote essays on "The Art of Seeing Things," "Straight Seeing and Straight Thinking," "Intensive Observation," "Hasty Observation," and "Sharp Eyes," and repeatedly exemplified his own superiority in these matters by essays made up of incidents afield, offhand experiments, rambling speculation regarding the habits of natural life and geologic phenomena. Of course, the "nature fakers" of our time disturbed him greatly, and called forth his authoritative condemnation. Of course, the great French naturalist Fabre, whose translated works appeared in Burroughs's later years, won his hearty admiration. In a chapter on "The Insect Mind" he has properly remarked that Maeterlinck's praise of Fabre as "the insects' Homer," widely quoted to-day, is aside of the mark. Fabre, says Burroughs, is not the insects' Homer but rather the insects' Sherlock Holmes. For in Fabre we find the same detective eye that Gilbert White and John Burroughs have, but concentrated to a single study, directed firmly to one definite purpose after another, and supplemented by the laboratory experimentation of his *harmas*. He was both a more systematic and a greater detective than Burroughs.

From this period of detective observation Burroughs passed without sharp transition into a period of scientific study and speculation. The detective eye and the detective mind were not put aside — far from it; they interplay with an increasingly conscious application of scientific standards to nature and human life, and with deliberate acquisitions of knowledge in various sciences. "Study" is perhaps not the word to designate the new attitude, since Burroughs speaks of "playing the geologist and the naturalist, or half-playing them," and elsewhere of extremely offhand inquiries in astronomy, geology, botany, zoology, physics, chemistry, and natural history. "I do little more than graze in these fields. I select what tastes good to me. I want only the vital nourishing truths; for the hard, mechanical facts, the minute details, the thistles of technical knowledge I have little appetite. I join inquiry with meditation. I loiter about the rocks, but I carry no geologist's hammer. I observe the birds, but I take no notes. I admire the flowers, but I leave them on their stems; I have no herbarium to fill. I am curious about the insects, I consider their ways, but I make no collection."

There is nothing conciliatory in his attitude toward the scientists. "With what desperate thoroughness," he exclaims, "the new men study the birds" — and what does it all lead to? Though in his earlier years he himself employed a gun in naming the birds, he now has no use even for the notebook and the field glass. When he goes into a natural history museum, he says, he feels as if he were attending a funeral. No museums; and no laboratory: "The other day I saw a lot of college girls dissecting cats and making diagrams of the circulation and muscle-attachments," and he was shocked. "I myself," he says a little complacently, "have got along very well without" the discipline of biology. What is the use of all this dull work, destructive of love and life; what does it produce? "I fear the experimenters unduly exalt their office. The open-air naturalist arrives at most of their results, and by a much more enjoyable and picturesque route. Without all their pother and appliances and tiresome calculations," he reaches essentially the same conclusions. In a word, the exact science of our day is little more than a vast humbug: a verdict not altogether pleasing to the scientists themselves, who, by no means impressed with the results of the informal research of John Burroughs, shrug their shoulders and quietly smile. It is not a pretty spectacle. No doubt our scientists are very fussy, but their fussiness, after all, is only the pedantry that must impregnate the great mass of workers in any thriving science, and the part of wisdom is to deplore their excesses rather than reject their labors altogether. This attitude of Burroughs is the more unfortunate when one remembers that his preoccupation through many years and books was to praise the achievements of modern science.

Burroughs the scientist manifested himself at least as early as Burroughs the poetic observer. According to Clara Barrus, the first of all his published writings was an article in the Bloomfield *Mirror* of May 13, 1856, on "Vagaries vs. Spiritualism," written when he was only nineteen, in his Johnsonian style, but otherwise not unlike numerous later essays, as the opening sentence will serve to indicate:

> "MR. MIRROR,—Notwithstanding the general diffusion of knowledge in the nineteenth century, it is a lamentable fact that some minds are so obscured by ignorance, or so blinded by superstition, as to rely with implicit confidence upon the validity of opinions which have no foundation in nature, or no support by the deductions of reason."

This is clearly not the wood of *Wake-Robin, Winter Sunshine, Birds and Poets,* and the other early volumes, though even in *Birds and Poets* there are pages prophetic of the later books in praise of science. But it is precisely the mood of *The Light of Day,* published many years later, with the incoming twentieth century, by which time the scientific temper of the age had completely won him. In *Pepacton* he had contrasted the protean subjectivity of the poet of nature with the exact meanings and laws achieved by the man of science, asserting that "the scientific reading or interpretation of nature is the only real one"; and in *Indoor Studies* he had mused over the austerities forced upon us by the revelations of modern science, turning us out into the cold to face "the eternities and the infinities of geologic time and sidereal space. We are no longer cozily housed in pretty little anthropomorphic views of things. . . . We feel the cosmic chill"—a passage repeated almost word for word a quarter of a century later in *Time and Change.* He himself, bravely relinquishing anthropomorphic religion and immersing himself in the cosmic chill, became "toughened and indifferent," "content to let the unseen powers go their own way with me and mine without question or distrust."

The Light of Day is the celebration of this victory. A Thoreau in *Wake-Robin*, in *The Light of Day* he is substantially another Huxley.

The object of the book is to demonstrate that the mysteries of religion vanish before the light of day, that is, the test of reason, and that the natural order revealed by reason is universal and sufficient. On its negative side the book is so belated that the writer is really knocking down a man of straw — the authority of revealed religion had already been destroyed when Burroughs entered the lists. His success is to be attributed more to the weakness of the enemy than to his own strength, since in chapter after chapter he relies upon manifold suggestion and repeated assertion rather than upon coherent argument. Religion itself, as distinguished from orthodox religion, he permits as a vague sentiment; but he clearly does not value it in comparison with science. For in the end both religion and science reach the same goal, God; and science by the surer path. "Think you the man of science does not also find God? that Huxley and Darwin and Tyndall do not find God, though they may hesitate to use that name? Whoever finds truth finds God, does he not? whoever loves truth loves God?" It is well that this somewhat naive assertion is put interrogatively, for it has now become abundantly certain that the spiritual dilemma of the modern world will not be settled by an identification of religion and science. The paean for science has but a rudely festive air. The dirge for literature and religion that also runs through the book like a motif is premature. Literature and religion are on the wane, but science is young, is "now probably only in the heat of its forenoon work." The future belongs to science. Yet, somewhat oddly, he goes on to assert that four fifths of life lies quite outside the domain of science; "four fifths of life is sentiment." The great ages of civilization, the great literatures, he reminds us, belong to sentiment, to patriotism, love, benevolence, admiration, worship. Although there is nothing in the Sermon on the Mount, he remarks, that appeals to our reasoning faculties, we must value it highly. Is there not a lurking paradox here, in this celebration of science as the lord of the future and its relegation to a realm covering only one fifth of life? Would not John Burroughs have done better to devote himself more often, in his writings and in his mode of life, to the realities of the preponderating "sentiment," instead of regarding himself as the champion of the scientific spirit, which is the "only" real interpreter of nature?

Aldo Leopold on
Forestry and the Hebrew Bible

(1920)

Aldo Leopold, one of the moving forces behind the preservation of National
Forest wilderness, was born in 1886 in Burlington, Iowa. He received bachelor's
and master's degrees from Yale University, where he was one of the first to graduate from the new school of forestry. From 1909 until 1924 he worked for the Forest
Service; later he taught wildlife management at the University of Wisconsin. In
1934, President Franklin Roosevelt appointed him to the Special Committee on
Wildlife Restoration in 1934, and in 1948 he served as a conservation adviser to
the United Nations. He served also as a president of the American Wildlife Society and the Ecological Society of America.

Leopold's experiences as a field ranger in New Mexico's national forests convinced him that conservation must ultimately be rooted in ecology rather than
the human-centered concept of "natural resources." He was instrumental in setting aside the Gila Primitive Area and was one of the founding members of the
Wilderness Society. He is best known as the author of *A Sand County Almanac*
(1949), in which he enunciates his famous "land ethic," eloquently arguing that
conservation involves not just science but ethics as well. Humans have moral
obligations not only to each other, Leopold insists, but to all life on the planet:
human action "is right when it tends to preserve the integrity, stability, and
beauty of the biotic community. It is wrong when it tends otherwise."

Leopold was a rhetorically skilled writer, having honed his craft through years
of presenting complex scientific ideas in language that his often skeptical audi-
ences of ranchers, farmers, and hunters would find accessible and convincing.
In his "Forestry and the Prophets," first published in the *Journal of Forestry* in
1920 and reprinted below, we see his reader-friendly approach in action; he keeps

the tone light and makes frequent comparisons of the biblical prophets to well-known figures like Theodore Roosevelt and John Muir. Leopold's examination of the ecological awareness of the ancient Israelites is, as he admits, amateurish. It is nonetheless an interesting and suggestive example of what today would be termed "ecotheology."

Toward the end of this essay, Leopold indicates a desire to write future essays on biblical ecology, but apparently he never did so.

🦜 🦜 🦜

Who discovered forestry? The heretofore accepted claims of the European nations have of late been hotly disputed by the Piutes. I now beg leave to present a prior claim for the children of Israel. I can hardly state that they practiced forestry, but I believe it can be shown that they knew a lot about forests. (Also, if any of them set fires, they knew better than to admit it.) The following notes, gleaned from a purely amateur study of the Books of the Prophets of the Old Testament,[1] may be of interest to other foresters, and may possibly suggest profitable fields of research for competent Hebraists and physiographers.

The most interesting side of forestry was then, as it is now, the human side. There is wide difference in the woodcraft of the individual prophets — the familiarity with which they speak of forests, and especially the frequency with which they use similes based on forest phenomena. It appears that in Judaea, as in Montana, there were woodsmen and dudes.

Isaiah was the Roosevelt of the Holy Land. He knew a whole lot about everything, including forests, and told what he knew in no uncertain terms. He constantly uses the forest to illustrate his teachings, and in doing so calls the trees by their first names. Contrast with him the sophisticated Solomon, who spoke much wisdom, but whose lore was city lore — the nearest he comes to the forest is the fig tree and the cedar of Lebanon, and I think he saw more of the cedars in the ceiling of his palace than he did in the hills. Joel knew more about forests than even Isaiah — he is the preacher of conservation of watersheds, and in a sense the real inventor of "prevent forest fires." David speaks constantly and familiarly about forests and his forest similes are especially accurate and beautiful. Ezekiel was not only a woodsman and an artist, but he knew a good deal about the lumber business, domestic and foreign. Jeremiah had a smattering of woods lore, and so did Hosea, but neither shows much leaning toward the subject. Daniel shows no interest in forests. Neither does Jesus the son of Sirach, who was a keen business man, a philosopher, and a master of epigram, but his tastes did not run to the hills. Strange to say the writer of the Book of Job, the John Muir of Judah, author of the immortal eulogy of the horse and one of the most magnificent essays on the wonders of nature so far produced by the human race, is strangely silent on forests. Probably forests were his background, not his picture, and he took for granted that his audience had a knowledge of them.

Forest Fires in the Holy Land

Every forester who reads the Prophets carefully will, I think, be surprised to see how much they knew about fires. The forest fire appealed strongly to their imagination and is used as the basis for many a simile of striking literary beauty. They understood not only the immediate destructive effects of fires, but possibly also the more far reaching effects on watersheds. Strangely enough, nothing is said about causes of fires or whether any efforts were ever made toward fire suppression.

The book of Joel opens with an allegory in which the judgment of God takes the form of a fire.[2] This is perhaps the most convincing description of fire in the whole Bible. "Alas for the day!" says Joel. "The herds of cattle are perplexed, because they have no pasture; Yea, the flocks of sheep are made desolate. O Lord, to thee do I cry, for a fire hath devoured the pastures of the wilderness, and a flame hath burned all the trees of the field. Yea, the beasts of the field pant unto thee, for the water brooks are dried up. Blow ye the trumpet in Zion, and sound an alarm in my holy mountain; let all the inhabitants in the land tremble! For . . . a fire devoureth before them; and behind them a flame burneth: the land is a garden of Eden before them, and behind them a desolate wilderness!"

Joel's story of the flames is to my mind one of the most graphic descriptions of fire ever written. It is "a day of clouds and thick darkness," and the fire is "like the dawn spread upon the mountains." The flames are "as a great people, set in battle array," and the "appearance of them is as horses, and as horsemen, so do they run. Like the noise of chariots on the tops of the mountains do they leap, . . . they run like mighty men; they climb the wall like men of war; and they march every one on his way. They break not their ranks: neither doth one thrust another; they march every one on his path. . . . They leap upon the city; they run upon the wall; they climb up into the houses; they enter in at the windows like a thief. The earth quaketh before them: the heavens tremble: the sun and the moon are darkened, and the stars withdraw their shining."

Joel is evidently describing a top fire or brush fire of considerable intensity. Is there at present any forest cover in Palestine of sufficient density to support such a fire? I do not know, but I doubt it. If not, it is interesting to speculate whether the reduced forest cover is a cause or an effect of the apparent change in climate.[3] Isaiah (64:1) adds some intensely interesting evidence as to the density of forest cover in Biblical times when he says: "when fire kindleth the brushwood. . . . the fire causeth the waters to boil." Have there been any fires in this country, even in the Northwest or the Lake States which caused the waters to boil? One writer, who had to take refuge in a creek during one of the big fires in the Northwest in 1918, states that falling brands caused the temperature of the creek to rise "several degrees," which sounds very tame in comparison with Isaiah's statement. In fact, Isaiah's statement seems almost incredible. Was he telling fish stories? Or is there some special explanation, such as a resinous brushwood producing great heat, or drainage from a sudden rain on a hot fire, or a water hole containing bitumen or oil from a mineral seep? I will leave this question for some one personally familiar with the country.

That top fires actually occurred in the Holy Land is abundantly proven by many writers in addition to Joel. Isaiah says (10:19) that a fire "shall consume the glory of his forest, and of his fruitful field . . . and the remnant of the trees in his forest shall be few, that a child may write them." "It kindleth in the thickets of the forest, and they roll upward in thick clouds of smoke." The individual tree at the moment of combustion he likens most effectively to a "standard-bearer that fainteth." Those who have actually seen the "puff" of the dying tree, as the fire rushes up through the foliage, will not miss the force of this simile. Ezekiel says (20:46): "A fire . . . shall devour every green tree . . . and every dry tree: the flaming flame shall not be quenched."

Surprisingly little is said about how fires started. Man-caused fires were no doubt frequent, as were to be expected in a pastoral community. Tobacco fires were of course still unknown. (Samuel Butler says the Lord postponed the discovery of tobacco, being afraid that St. Paul would forbid smoking. This, says Butler, was a little hard on Paul.) Lightning was no doubt the principal natural cause of fire. Very heavy lightning seems to have occurred in the mountains. David, in the "Song of the Thunderstorm" (Psalm, 29), says: "The God of glory thundereth, . . . the voice of the Lord breaketh the cedars; Yea, the Lord breaketh in pieces the cedars of Lebanon." His voice "cleaveth the flames of fire . . . and strippeth the forest bare." It is not entirely clear whether this refers to lightning only, or possibly also to subsequent fire.

How much did the prophets really know about the effects of fires? Joel has already been quoted as to the effects on streamflow, but there is a possibility that he meant that his "water-brooks" dried up, not as the ultimate effect of fires, but as the immediate effect of a drouth prevailing at the time of the particular fire which he describes. David (Psalm, 107) plainly states that changes in climate occur, but no forest influences or other cause are mentioned. I think it is quite possible that the effect of forests on streamflow was known empirically to a few advanced thinkers like Joel, but it is quite certain that their knowledge went no further or deeper. The habit of thinking of natural phenomena as acts of God instead of as cause and effect prevails to this day with a majority of people, and no doubt prevailed at that time in the minds of all. But even if the prophets were ignorant of science, they were wise in the ways of men. "Seemeth it a small thing unto you to have fed upon the good pasture, but ye must tread down with your feet the residue of your pasture? And to have drunk of the clear waters, but ye must foul the residue with your feet?" (Ezekiel 24:18). Here is the doctrine of conservation, from its subjective side, as aptly put as by any forester of this generation.

Forest Utilization in the Holy Land

The old Hebrew used both saws and axes in cutting timber. Isaiah (10:15) says: "Shall the axe boast itself against him that heweth therewith? Shall the saw magnify itself against him that shaketh it?" "Shaking" the saw is a new bit of woods vernacular that leads one to wonder what the instrument looked like. Here is more woods vernacular: ". . . he shall cut down the thickets of the forest with iron, and Lebanon shall fall by a mighty one." While I am not competent to go behind the translation, the word "iron" seems to be used here in much the same way as our modern engineers used the word "steel," that is, to indicate certain manufactured tools or articles made of steel.

Very close utilization of felled timber seems to have been practiced. Solomon (Wisdom, 13:11) tells how a woodcutter sawed down a tree, stripped off the bark, carved the good wood into useful vessels, cooked his dinner with the chips, and used the crooked and knotty remainder to fashion a graven image. Expertness in whittling then, as now, seems to have been a trait of the idle, for Solomon says the woodcutter shaped the image "by the diligence of his idleness, and . . . by the skill of his indolence." Isaiah (44:14) also tells how a man plants a fir tree, and after the rain has nourished it, he cuts it down and uses a part to warm himself, a part to bake bread, a part to make utensils, and a part to fashion a graven image. Graven images, if one is to believe the prophets, must have been an important product of the wood using industries of that day.

Here is an unsolved mystery in woods practice: "The carpenter . . . heweth him down cedars, and taketh the holm tree and the oak, and *strengtheneth for himself* one among the trees of the forest" (Isaiah, 44:14). What is meant by "strengtheneth for himself"? Some process of seasoning? Some custom of individual branding such as is practiced on bee trees? Some process of lamination in wood-working to give strength and lightness?

Ezekiel (27:4) records some interesting data on the sources and uses of timber in his satire on the glories of Tyre. "They have made all thy planks of fir trees from Senir: they have taken cedars from Lebanon to make a mast for thee. Of the oaks of Bashan have they made thine oars; they have made thy benches of ivory inlaid in boxwood, from the isles of Kittim." Isaiah (2:18) also mentions "the oaks of Bashan." Oak would seem to be a bit heavy for the long oars used in those days.

Who made the first cedar chest? Ezekiel (27:24) says that "chests of rich apparel, bound with cord, and made of cedar" were an article of commerce in the maritime trade of Tyre. The use of cedar chests for fine clothing seems to be nearly as old as the hills. Solomon's palanquin was also made of cedar. Here is his own description of it, as taken from the Song of Songs (3:9): "King Solomon made himself a palanquin of wood of Lebanon. He made the pillars thereof of silver, the bottom thereof of gold, the seat of it of purple, the midst thereof being inlaid with love from the daughters of Jerusalem."

(I doubt whether Solomon "made himself" this palanquin. He does not give the impression of a man handy with tools. No doubt he had it made by the most cunning artificers of his kingdom.)

Cedar construction in Biblical days seems to have been a kind of mark of social distinction, as mahogany is today. (Witness also the marble-topped walnut of our Victorian forbears!) Solomon's bride boasts (Song of Songs, 1:16): "Our couch is green. The beams of our house are cedars, and our rafters are firs." Jeremiah (22:14) accuses Jehoiakim of building with ill-gotten gains "a wide house . . . with windows . . . ceiled with cedar, and painted with vermillion." "Shalt thou reign," exclaims Jeremiah, "because thou strivest to *excel in cedar?*"

The cedar seems to have grown to large size. Ezekiel, in a parable (31), says of one tree: "The cedars in the garden of God could not hide him; the fir trees were not like his boughs, and the plane trees were not as his branches." This cedar was Pharaoh, and the Lord "made the nations to shake at the sound of his fall."

The close utilization which seems to have been practiced at least in some localities, the apparently well developed timber trade of the coast cities, and the great number of references to the use and commerce in cedar, would lead to the surmise that the pinch of local timber famine might have been felt in the cedar woods. That this was actually the case is indicated by Isaiah (14:7). After prophesying the fall of Babylon, he tells how all things will rejoice over her demise. "Yea, the fir trees rejoice at thee, and the cedars of Lebanon: 'Since thou art laid down, no feller is come up against us.'" This impersonization of trees is characteristic of the Biblical writers; David (Psalm, 96) says, "Then shall all the trees of the wood sing for joy."

The relative durability of woods was of course fairly well known. Isaiah (9:10) says: "The bricks are fallen, but we will build with hewn stone; the sycamores are cut down, but we will change them into cedars." Ecclesiasticus (12:13) likens the permanency and strength of wisdom to "a cedar in Libanus, and . . . a cypress tree on the mountains of Hermon."

Fuel wood was evidently obtained not only from cull material, as already indicated, but by cutting green timber. Ezekiel (39:9) predicts that after the rout of the invading army of Gog, "they that dwell in the cities of Israel shall go forth, and make fires of the weapons and burn them, . . . and they shall make fires of them seven years; so that they shall take no wood out of the field, neither cut down any out of the forests." It would seem that Biblical fuel bills were either pretty light, or else Gog left behind an extraordinary number of weapons.

Hebrew Silviculture

There are many passages in the books of the prophets showing that some of the rudimentary principles of silviculture were understood, and that artificial planting was practiced to some extent. Solomon (in Ecclesiastes 2:4) says that he planted great vineyards, orchards, gardens, and parks, and also "made me pools of water, to water therefrom the forest where trees were reared." Isaiah (44:14) speaks of a carpenter who planted a fir tree, and later used it for fuel and lumber. The context gives the impression that such instances of planting for wood production were common, but probably on a very small scale. Isaiah (41:9) seems to have had some knowledge of forest types and the ecological relations of species. He quotes Jehovah in this manner: "I will plant in the wilderness the cedar, the acacia tree, and the myrtle, and the oil tree; I will set in the desert the fir tree, the pine, and the box tree together." He also makes the following interesting statement (55:13) which possibly refers to the succession of forest types: "Instead of the thorn shall come up the fir tree, and instead of the briar shall come up the myrtle tree."

Some of the peculiarities of various species in their manner of reproduction are mentioned. Isaiah (44:4) says: "They shall spring up among the grass as willows by the watercourses." He also speaks of the oak and the terebinth reproducing by coppice (6:12). Job (14:7) also mentions coppice, but does not give the species. Ezekiel (17) in his parable of the Eagles and the Cedar, tells about an eagle that cropped off the leader of a big cedar and planted it high on another mountain, and it brought forth boughs, and bore fruit, and was a goodly tree. I do not know the cedar of Lebanon but it sounds highly improbable that any conifer should grow from cuttings. I think this is a case of "poetic license."

Isaiah (65:22) realized the longevity of some species in the following simile: "They shall not build, and another inhabit; they shall not plant, and another eat; for as the day of a tree shall be the day of my people, and my chosen shall long enjoy the work of their hands." Isaiah disappoints us here in not telling the species. Unlike Solomon and Daniel and Ecclesiasticus, he is not given to calling a tree just "a tree."

Miscellaneous

Barnes has written a very interesting article on grazing in the Holy Land, and there is much additional material on this subject which would be of interest to foresters.[4] One matter which some entomologist should look up occurs in Isaiah (7:18). Isaiah says: "And it shall come to pass in that day, that the Lord shall hiss for the fly that is in the uttermost part of the rivers of Egypt, and for the bee that is in the land of Assyria. And they shall come, and shall rest all of them in the desolate valleys, and in the holes of the rocks, and upon all thorns, and upon all pastures." What fly is referred to? The Tetse fly, or the Rinderpest?

There is also considerable material on game and fish in the Old Testament, and additional material on forests in the historical books, both of which I hope to cover in future articles.

In closing, it may not be improper to add a word on the intensely interesting reading on a multitude of subjects to be found in the Old Testament. As Stevenson said about one of Hazlitt's essays, "It is so good that there should be a tax levied on all who have not read it."

NOTES

1. Quotations are from Moulton's Reader's Bible, which is based on the Revised English Version.

2. Parts of Joel 1 and 2 have been used in printed matter issued by the Southwestern District as fire prevention propaganda.

3. Prof. Ellsworth Huntington's book, *The Pulse of Asia*, contains some very readable and convincing material on climatic cycles in Asia Minor.

4. *National Wool Grower*, February, 1915.

D. H. Lawrence on
Hector St. Jean de Crèvecoeur
(1923)

The famed novelist, poet, playwright, and critic David Herbert Lawrence was born in 1885 in Eastwood, Nottinghamshire. His first published poems appeared in Ford Madox Ford's *English Review,* and his first novel, *The White Peacock,* was published in 1911. He would go on to write prolifically; in addition to his poetry, he would produce such novels as *Sons and Lovers, Women in Love,* and *The Plumed Serpent,* and such critical works as *Psychoanalysis of the Unconscious* and *Studies in Classic American Literature.* In the fall of 1922, at the invitation of Mabel Dodge Luhan, he moved to Taos, New Mexico, where he hoped to find a healthier climate (he suffered from tuberculosis) and a more pristine intellectual environment, far removed from polluted air and social hypocrisy. He spent the warmer months of the year in Taos until leaving for Italy late in 1925; he died five years later.

Much of Lawrence's writing explores the possibility of living fully and authentically in a mechanized, repressive civilization, which helps explain his interest in New Mexico in particular and America in general. As a young nation, closer to its soil and still in contact with what Lawrence considered its "savage" forebears — that is, with Native Americans such as New Mexico's Pueblo peoples — America seemed to him to be in touch with energies long exhausted in Europe. Such romanticized primitivism may strike us today as racist and naive, but Lawrence was nonetheless a brilliant critic of American literature. As several of his biographers have pointed out, he could analyze American culture perceptively because he admired it yet was decidedly not of it. It helped, too, that he was not an academic; free of the constraints of the scholarly research ethos, he could practice a hermeneutics of suspicion that seems ahead of its time. He was free to peer beneath the surface of the text, searching for deeper meanings of which even the original author was unaware — a procedure motivated partly by his reading of Freud, and partly by his belief that Americans "refuse everything explicit and always put up a sort of double meaning."

The essay below is excerpted from Lawrence's *Studies in Classic American Literature*, first published in 1923. The book's introduction makes clear the author's belief in environmental determinism:

> Every continent has its own great spirit of place. Every people is polarized in some particular locality, which is home, the homeland. Different places on the face of the earth have different vital effluence, different vibration, different chemical exhalation, different polarity with different stars: call it what you like. The Nile Valley produced not only the corn, but the terrific religions of Egypt.

This "spirit of place" can work its magic, however, only on the native inhabitants of the soil. Lawrence stresses that newcomers remain at odds with this spirit as long as they play the role of usurper. Eventually, however, when the work of conquest is complete, they will face a moment of environmental reckoning:

> A curious thing about the Spirit of Place is the fact that no place exerts its full influence upon a new-comer until the old inhabitant is dead or absorbed. So America. While the Red Indian existed in fairly large numbers, the new colonials were in a great measure immune from the daimon, or demon, of America. The moment the last nuclei of Red life break up in America, then the white men will have to reckon with the full force of the demon of the continent. . . . Up till now, the unexpressed spirit of America has worked covertly in the American, the white American soul. But within the present generation the surviving Red Indians are due to merge in the great white swamp. Then the Daimon of America will work overtly, and we shall see real changes.

Before that time, only the most exceptional writers will betray any trace of the "covert" influence of this spirit of place. In the essay below, Lawrence argues that Hector St. Jean de Crèvecoeur was such a writer.

Crèvecoeur was born in France, at Caen, in the year 1735. As a boy he was sent over to England and received part of his education there. He went to Canada as a young man, served for a time with Montcalm in the war against the English, and later passed over into the United States, to become an exuberant American. He married a New England girl, and settled on the frontier. During the period of his "cultivating the earth" he wrote the *Letters from an American Farmer*, which enjoyed great vogue in their day, in England especially, among the new reformers like Godwin and Tom Paine.

But Crèvecoeur was not a mere cultivator of the earth. That was his best stunt, shall we say. He himself was more concerned with a perfect society and his own manipulation thereof, than with growing carrots. Behold him, then, trotting off importantly and idealistically to France, leaving his farm in the wilds to be burnt by the Indians, and his wife to shift as best she might. This was during the American War of Independence, when the Noble Red Man took to behaving like his own old self. On his return to America, the American Farmer entered into public affairs and into commerce. Again tripping to France, he enjoyed himself as a littérateur Child-of-Nature-sweet-and-pure, was a friend of old Benjamin Franklin in Paris, and quite a favourite with Jean Jacques Rousseau's Madame d'Houdetot, that literary soul.

Hazlitt, Godwin, Shelley, Coleridge, the English romanticists, were, of course, thrilled by the *Letters from an American Farmer*. A new world, a world of the Noble Savage and Pristine Nature and Paradisal Simplicity and all that gorgeousness that flows out of the unsullied fount of the ink-bottle. Lucky Coleridge, who got no farther than Bristol. Some of us have gone all the way.

I think this wild and noble America is the thing that I have pined for most ever since I read Fenimore Cooper, as a boy. Now I've got it.

Franklin is the real *practical* prototype of the American. Crèvecoeur is the emotional. To the European, the American is first and foremost a dollar-fiend. We tend to forget the emotional heritage of Hector St. John de Crèvecoeur. We tend to disbelieve, for example, in Woodrow Wilson's wrung heart and wet hanky. Yet surely these are real enough. Aren't they?

It wasn't to be expected that the dry little snuff-coloured Doctor should have it all his own way. The new Americans might use venery for health or offspring, and their time for cultivating potatoes and Chicagoes, but they had got *some* sap in their veins after all. They had got to get a bit of luscious emotion somewhere.

NATURE.

I wish I could write it larger than that.

NATURE.

Benjamin overlooked NATURE. But the French Crèvecoeur spotted it long before Thoreau and Emerson worked it up. Absolutely the safest thing to get your emotional reactions over is NATURE.

Crèvecoeur's *Letters* are written in a spirit of touching simplicity, almost better than Chateaubriand. You'd think neither of them would ever know how many beans make five. This American Farmer tells of the joys of creating a home in the wilderness, and of cultivating the virgin soil. Poor virgin, prostituted from the very start.

The Farmer had an Amiable Spouse and an Infant Son, his progeny. He took the Infant Son —who enjoys no other name than this —

> "What is thy name?
> I have no name.
> I am the Infant Son —"

to the fields with him, and seated the same I. S. on the shafts of the plow whilst he, the American Farmer, ploughed the potato patch. He also, the A. F., helped his Neighbours, whom no doubt he loved as himself, to build a barn, and they laboured together in the Innocent Simplicity of one of Nature's Communities. Meanwhile the Amiable Spouse, who likewise in Blakean simplicity has No Name, cooked the dough-nuts or the pie, though these are not mentioned. No doubt she was a deep-breasted daughter of America, though she may equally well have been a flat-bosomed Methodist. She would have been an Amiable Spouse in either case, and the American Farmer asked no more. I don't know whether her name was Lizzie or Ahoolibah, and probably Crèvecoeur didn't. Spouse was enough for him. "Spouse, hand me the carving knife."

The Infant Son developed into Healthy Offspring as more appeared: no doubt Crèvecoeur had used venery as directed. And so these Children of Nature toiled in the wilds at Simple Toil with a little Honest Sweat now and then. You have the complete picture, dear reader. The American Farmer made his own Family Picture, and it is still on view. Of course the Amiable Spouse put on her best apron to be *Im Bild*, for all the world to see and admire.

I used to admire my head off: before I tiptoed into the Wilds and saw the shacks of the Homesteaders. Particularly the Amiable Spouse, poor thing. No wonder she never sang the song of Simple Toil in the Innocent Wilds. Poor haggard drudge, like a ghost wailing in the wilderness, nine times out of ten.

Hector St. John, you have lied to me. You lied even more scurrilously to yourself. Hector St. John, you are an emotional liar.

Jean Jacques, Bernardin de St. Pierre, Chateaubriand, exquisite François Le Vaillant, you lying little lot, with your Nature-Sweet-and-Pure! Marie Antoinette got her head off for playing dairy-maid, and nobody even dusted the seats of your pants, till now, for all the lies you put over us.

But Crèvecoeur was an artist as well as a liar, otherwise we would not have bothered with him. He wanted to put NATURE in his pocket, as Benjamin put the Human Being. Between them, they wanted the whole scheme of things in their pockets, and the things themselves as well. Once you've got the scheme of things in your pocket, you can do as you like with it, even make money out of it, if you can't find in your heart to destroy it, as was your first intention. So H. St. J. de C. tried to put Nature-Sweet-and-Pure in his pocket. But Nature wasn't having any, she poked her head out and baa-ed.

This Nature-sweet-and-pure business is only another effort at intellectualizing. Just an attempt to make all nature succumb to a few laws of the human mind. The sweet-and-pure sort of laws. Nature seemed to be behaving quite nicely, for a while. She has left off. That's why you get the purest intellectuals in a Garden Suburb or a Brook Farm experiment. You bet, Robinson Crusoe was a high-brow of high-brows.

You can idealize or intellectualize. Or, on the contrary, you can let the dark soul in you see for itself. An artist usually intellectualizes on top, and his dark under-consciousness goes on contradicting him beneath. This is almost laughably the case with most American artists. Crèvecoeur is the first example. He is something of an artist, Franklin isn't anything.

Crèvecoeur the idealist puts over us a lot of stuff about nature and the noble savage and the innocence of toil, etc., etc. Blarney! But Crèvecoeur the artist gives us glimpses of actual nature, not writ large.

Curious that his vision sees only the lowest forms of natural life. Insects, snakes and birds he glimpses in their own mystery, their own pristine being. And straightway gives the lie to Innocent Nature.

"I am astonished to see," he writes quite early in the *Letters*, "that nothing exists but what has its enemy, one species pursue and live upon the other:

unfortunately our kingbirds are the destroyers of those industrious insects [the bees]; but on the other hand, these birds preserve our fields from the depredation of crows, which they pursue on the wing with great vigilance and astonishing dexterity."

This is a sad blow to the sweet-and-pureness of Nature. But it is the voice of the artist in contrast to the voice of the ideal turtle. It is the rudimentary American vision. The glimpsing of the king-birds in winged hostility and pride is no doubt the aboriginal Indian vision carrying over. The Eagle symbol in human consciousness. Dark, swinging wings of hawk-beaked destiny, that one cannot help but feel, beating here above the wild centre of America. You look round in vain for the "One being Who made all things, and governs the world by His Providence."

"One species pursue and live upon another."

Reconcile the two statements if you like. But, in America, act on Crève-coeur's observation.

The horse, however, says Hector, is the friend of man, and man is the friend of the horse. But then we leave the horse no choice. And I don't see much friend, exactly, in my sly old Indian pony, though he is quite a decent old bird.

Man, too, says Hector, is the friend of man. Whereupon the Indians burnt his farm; so he refrains from mentioning it in the Letters, for fear of invalidating his premises.

Some great hornets have fixed their nest on the ceiling of the living-room of the American Farmer, and these tiger-striped animals fly round the heads of the Healthy Offspring and the Amiable Spouse, to the gratification of the American Farmer. He liked their buzz and their tiger waspishness. Also, on the utilitarian plane, they kept the house free of flies. So Hector says. Therefore Benjamin would have approved. But of the feelings of the Amiable S., on this matter, we are not told, and after all, it was she who had to make the jam.

Another anecdote. Swallows built their nest on the veranda of the American Farm. Wrens took a fancy to the nest of the swallows. They pugnaciously (I like the word pugnaciously, it is so American) attacked the harbingers of spring, and drove them away from their nice adobe nest. The swallows returned upon opportunity. But the wrens, coming home, violently drove them forth again. Which continued until the gentle swallows patiently set about to build another nest, while the wrens sat in triumph in the usurped home. The

American Farmer watched this contest with delight, and no doubt loudly applauded those little rascals of wrens. For in the Land of the Free, the greatest
delight of every man is in getting the better of the other man.

Crèvecoeur says he shot a king-bird that had been devouring his bees. He
opened the craw and took out a vast number of bees, which little democrats,
after they had lain a minute or two stunned, in the sun roused, revived,
preened their wings and walked off debonair, like Jonah up the seashore; or
like true Yanks escaped from the craw of the king-bird of Europe.

I don't care whether it's true or not. I like the picture, and see in it a parable
of the American resurrection.

The humming-bird.

"Its bill is as long and as sharp as a coarse sewing-needle; like the bee,
nature has taught it to find out in the calyx of flowers and blossoms those
mellifluous particles that can serve it for sufficient food; and yet it seems to
leave them untouched, undeprived of anything our eyes can possibly distinguish. Where it feeds it appears as if immovable, though continually on the
wing: and sometimes, from what motives I know not, it will tear and lacerate
flowers into a hundred pieces; for, strange to tell, they are the most irascible
of the feathered tribe. Where do passions find room in so diminutive a body?
They often fight with the fury of lions, until one of the combatants falls a
sacrifice and dies. When fatigued, it has often perched within a few feet of
me, and on such favourable opportunities I have surveyed it with the most
minute attention. Its little eyes appear like diamonds, reflecting light on every side; most elegantly finished in all parts, it is a miniature work of our
great parent, who seems to have formed it smallest, and at the same time the
most beautiful, of the winged species."

A regular little Tartar, too. Lions no bigger than inkspots! I have read about
humming-birds elsewhere, in Bates and W. H. Hudson, for example. But it
is left to the American Farmer to show me the real little raging lion. Birds
are evidently no angels in America, or to the true American. He sees how
they start and flash their wings like little devils, and stab each other with
egoistic sharp bills. But he sees also the reserved, tender shyness of the wild
creature, upon occasion. Quails in winter, for instance.

"Often, in the angles of the fences, where the motion of the wind prevents
the snow from settling, I carry them both chaff and grain; the one to feed
them, the other to prevent their tender feet from freezing fast to the earth, as
I have frequently observed them to do."

This is beautiful, and blood-knowledge. Crèvecoeur knows the touch of birds' feet, as if they had stood with their vibrating, sharp, cold-cleaving balance, naked-footed on his naked hand. It is a beautiful, barbaric tenderness of the blood. He doesn't after all turn them into "little sisters of the air," like St. Francis, or start preaching to them. He knows them as strange, shy, hot-blooded concentrations of bird-presence.

The *Letter* about snakes and humming-birds is a fine essay, in its primal, dark veracity. The description of the fight between two snakes, a great water-snake and a large black serpent, follows the description of the humming-bird: "Strange was this to behold; two great snakes strongly adhering to the ground, mutually fastened together by means of the writhings which lashed them to each other, and stretched at their full length, they pulled, but pulled in vain; and in the moments of greatest exertions that part of their bodies which was entwined seemed extremely small, while the rest appeared inflated, and now and then convulsed with strong undulations, rapidly following each other. Their eyes seemed on fire, and ready to start out of their heads; at one time the conflict seemed decided; the water-snake bent itself into two great folds, and by that operation rendered the other more than commonly outstretched. The next minute the new struggles of the black one gained an unexpected superiority; it acquired two great folds likewise, which necessarily extended the body of its adversary in proportion as it had contracted its own."

This fight, which Crèvecoeur describes to a finish, he calls a sight "uncommon and beautiful." He forgets the sweet-and-pureness of Nature, and is for the time a sheer ophiolater, and his chapter is as handsome a piece of ophiolatry, perhaps, as that coiled Aztec rattlesnake carved in stone.

And yet the real Crèvecoeur is, in the issue, neither farmer, nor child of Nature, nor ophiolater. He goes back to France, and figures in the literary salons, and is a friend of Rousseau's Madame d'Houdetot. Also he is a good business man, and arranges a line of shipping between France and America. It all ends in materialism, really. But the *Letters* tell us nothing about this.

We are left to imagine him retiring in grief to dwell with his Red Brothers under the wigwams. For the War of Independence has broken out, and the Indians are armed by the adversaries; they do dreadful work on the frontiers. While Crèvecoeur is away in France his farm is destroyed, his family rendered homeless. So that the last letter laments bitterly over the war, and man's folly and inhumanity to man.

But Crèvecoeur ends his lament on a note of resolution. With his amiable spouse, and his healthy offspring, now rising in stature, he will leave the civilized coasts, where man is sophisticated, and therefore inclined to be vile, and he will go to live with the Children of Nature, the Red Men, under the wigwam. No doubt, in actual life, Crèvecoeur made some distinction between the Indians who drank rum à la Franklin, and who burnt homesteads and massacred families, and those Indians, the noble Children of Nature, who peopled his own predetermined fancy. Whatever he did in actual life, in his innermost self he would not give up this self-made world, where the natural man was an object of undefiled brotherliness. Touchingly and vividly he describes his tented home near the Indian village, how he breaks the aboriginal earth to produce a little maize, while his wife weaves within the wigwam. And his imaginary efforts to save his tender offspring from the brutishness of unchristian darkness are touching and puzzling, for how can Nature, so sweet and pure under the greenwood tree, how can it have any contaminating effect?

But it is all a swindle. Crèvecoeur was off to France in high-heeled shoes and embroidered waistcoat, to pose as a literary man, and to prosper in the world. We, however, must perforce follow him into the backwoods, where the simple natural life shall be perfected, near the tented village of the Red Man.

He wanted, of course, to imagine the dark, savage way of life, to get it all off pat in his head. He wanted to know as the Indians and savages know, darkly, and in terms of otherness. He was simply crazy, as the Americans say, for this. Crazy enough! For at the same time he was absolutely determined that Nature is sweet and pure, that all men are brothers, and equal, and that they love one another like so many cooing doves. He was determined to have life according to his own prescription. Therefore, he wisely kept away from any too close contact with Nature, and took refuge in commerce and the material world. But yet, he was determined to know the savage way of life, to his own *mind's* satisfaction. So he just faked us the last *Letters*. A sort of wish-fulfilment.

For the animals and savages are isolate, each one in its own pristine self. The animal lifts its head, sniffs, and knows within the dark, passionate belly. It knows at once, in dark mindlessness. And at once it flees in immediate recoil; or it crouches predatory, in the mysterious storm of exultant anticipation of seizing a victim; or it lowers its head in blank indifference again; or it advances in the insatiable wild curiosity, insatiable passion to approach that which is unspeakably strange and incalculable; or it draws near in the slow trust of wild, sensual love.

Crèvecoeur wanted this kind of knowledge. But comfortably, in his head, along with his other ideas and ideals. He didn't go too near the wigwam. Because he must have suspected that the moment he saw as the savages saw, all his fraternity and equality would go up in smoke, and his ideal world of pure sweet goodness along with it. And still worse than this, he would have to give up his own will, which insists that the world is so, because it would be nicest if it were so. Therefore he trotted back to France in high-heeled shoes, and imagined America in Paris.

He wanted his ideal state. At the same time he wanted to know the other state, the dark, savage mind. He wanted both.

Can't be done, Hector. The one is the death of the other.

Best turn to commerce, where you may get things your own way.

He hates the dark, pre-mental life, really. He hates the true sensual mystery. But he wants to "know." To KNOW. Oh, insatiable American curiosity!

He's a liar.

But if he won't risk knowing in flesh and blood, he'll risk all the imagination you like.

It is amusing to see him staying away and calculating the dangers of the step which he takes so luxuriously, in his fancy, alone. He tickles his palate with a taste of true wildness, as men are so fond nowadays of tickling their palates with a taste of imaginary wickedness — just self-provoked.

"I must tell you," he says, "that there is something in the proximity of the woods which is very singular. It is with men as it is with the plants and animals that grow and live in the forests; they are entirely different from those that live in the plains. I will candidly tell you all my thoughts, but you are not to expect that I shall advance any reasons. By living in or near the woods, their actions are regulated by the wildness of the neighbourhood. The deer often come to eat their grain, the wolves to destroy their sheep, the bears to kill their hogs, the foxes to catch their poultry. This surrounding hostility immediately puts the gun into their hands; they watch these animals, they kill some; and thus by defending their property they soon become professed hunters; this is the progress; once hunters, farewell to the plough. The chase renders them ferocious, gloomy, and unsociable; a hunter wants no neighbour, he rather hates them, because he dreads the competition. . . . Eating of wild meant, whatever you may think, tends to alter their temper. . . ."

Crèvecoeur, of course, had never intended to return as a *hunter* to the bosom of Nature, only as a husbandman. The hunter is a killer. The husbandman, on the other hand, brings about the birth and increase. But even the husbandman strains in dark mastery over the unwilling earth and beast; he struggles to win forth substance, he must master the soil and the strong cattle, he must have the heavy blood-knowledge, and the slow, but deep, mastery. There is no equality or selfless humility. The toiling blood swamps the idea, inevitably. For this reason the most idealist nations invent most machines. America simply teems with mechanical inventions, because nobody in America ever wants to *do* anything. They are idealists. Let a machine do the doing.

Again, Crèvecoeur dwells on "the apprehension lest my younger children should be caught by that singular charm, so dangerous at their tender years"—meaning the charm of savage life. So he goes on: "By what power does it come to pass that children who have been adopted when young among these people [the Indians] can never be prevailed upon to readopt European manners? Many an anxious parent I have seen last war who, at the return of the peace, went to the Indian villages where they knew their children had been carried in captivity, when to their inexpressible sorrow they found them so perfectly Indianized that many knew them no longer, and those whose more advanced ages permitted them to recollect their fathers and mothers, absolutely refused to follow them, and ran to their adopted parents to protect them against the effusions of love their unhappy real parents lavished on them! Incredible as this may appear, I have heard it asserted in a thousand instances, among persons of credit.

"Their must be in their (the Indians') social bond something singularly captivating, and far superior to anything to be boasted of among us; for thousands of Europeans are Indians, and we have no examples of even one of those Aborigines having from choice become Europeans. . . ."

Our cat and another, Hector.

I like the picture of thousands of obdurate offspring, with faces averted from their natural white father and mother, turning resolutely to the Indians of their adoption.

I have seen some Indians whom you really couldn't tell from white men. And I have never seen a white man who looked really like an Indian. So Hector is again a liar.

But Crèvecoeur wanted to be an *intellectual* savage, like a great many more we have met. Sweet children of Nature. Savage and bloodthirsty children of Nature.

White Americans do try hard to intellectualize themselves. Especially white women Americans. And the latest stunt is this "savage" stunt again.

White savages, with motor-cars, telephones, incomes and ideals! Savages fast inside the machine; yet savages enough, ye gods!

Lewis Mumford on
Thoreau, Nature, and Society
(1926)

The acclaimed architectural and literary critic, social philosopher, city planner, and author Lewis Mumford was born in 1895 in New York City. He never completed a college degree, though he studied at City College of New York, Columbia, the New School for Social Research, and Stanford. After serving briefly as a radio engineer in the U.S. Navy, he began a writing and teaching career that would produce more than thirty books — on topics ranging from Herman Melville to technology to architecture to urban expansion — and take him from MIT to Berkeley and several campuses in between. Perhaps his most influential book was *The City in History*, which won a National Book Award in 1961.

Mumford's topic frequently was the increasing subordination of humane values to industrial technology. He always insisted that "in a mature society, man himself, not his machines or his organizations, is the chief work of art," and he was among the first to predict the destructive environmental and cultural consequences of the nation's increasing reliance on freeways. These themes echo through "The Dawn," Mumford's critique of Thoreau's writing and values. He notes Thoreau's early perception of a pernicious American consumerism, quoting the observation that the American "clutches everything, he holds nothing fast, but soon loosens his grasp to pursue fresh gratifications." He praises Thoreau for recognizing that science is not "objective" in its view of nature but itself embodies preconceptions that prevent one from observing natural phenomena "totally unprejudiced"; instead "[y]ou must be aware that nothing is what you take it to be." Finally, Mumford insists that Thoreau was not the misanthrope he is often taken to be. Quite the contrary: Thoreau valued nature primarily for its ability to improve people and society. "Just as Thoreau sought Nature," Mum-

ford writes, "in order to arrive at a higher stage of culture, so he practiced individualism, in order to create a better order of society."

"The Dawn" is excerpted from *The Golden Day* (1926).

చ్చి చ్చి చ్చి

The pioneer who broke the trail westward left scarcely a trace of his adventure in the mind: what remains are the tags of pioneer customs, and mere
souvenirs of the past, like the Pittsburg stogy, which is our living connection
to-day with the Conestoga wagon, whose drivers used to roll cigars as the first
covered wagons plodded over the Alleghenies.

What the pioneer felt, if he felt anything, in the midst of these new solitudes; what he dreamt, if he dreamt anything; all these things we must surmise from a few snatches of song, from the commonplace reports issued as
the trail was nearing its end, by the generation of Mark Twain and Hamlin
Garland, or by the reflections of their sons and daughters, romantically eager,
like John G. Neihardt's, critically reflective, like Susan Glaspell's, or wistfully
sordid, like Edgar Lee Masters' *Anthology*. Those who really faced the wilderness, and sought to make something out of it, remained in the East; in
their reflection, one sees the reality that might have been. Henry David Thoreau was perhaps the only man who paused to give a report of the full experience. In a period when men were on the move, he remained still; when
men were on the make, he remained poor; when civil disobedience broke
out in the lawlessness of the cattle thief and the mining town rowdy, by sheer
neglect, Thoreau practiced civil disobedience as a principle, in protest
against the Mexican War, the Fugitive Slave Law, and slavery itself. Thoreau
in his life and letters shows what the pioneer movement might have come to
if this great migration had sought culture rather than material conquest, and
an intensity of life, rather than mere extension over the continent.

Born in Concord about half a generation after Emerson, Thoreau found
himself without the preliminary searchings and reachings of the young clergyman. He started from the point that his fellow-townsman, Emerson, had
reached; and where he first cleared out of his mind every idea that made no
direct connections with his personal experience, Thoreau cleared out of his
life itself every custom or physical apparatus, to boot, which could not stand
up and justify its existence. "A native of the United States," De Tocqueville

had observed, "clings to the world's goods as if he were certain never to die; and he is so hasty at grasping at all within his reach, that one would suppose he was constantly afraid of not living long enough to enjoy them. He clutches everything, he holds nothing fast, but soon loosens his grasp to pursue fresh gratifications." Thoreau completely reversed this process: it was because he wanted to live fully that he turned away from everything that did not serve towards this end. He prized the minutes for what they brought, and would not exercise his citizenship at the town meeting, if a spring day by Walden Pond had greater promise; nor would he fill his hours with gainful practices, as a maker of pencils or a surveyor, beyond what was needed for the bare business of keeping his bodily self warm and active.

Thoreau seized the opportunity to consider what in its essentials a truly human life was; he sought, in Walden, to find out what degree of food, clothing, shelter, labor was necessary to sustain it. It was not animal hardihood or a merely tough physical regimen he was after; nor did he fancy, for all that he wrote in contempt of current civilization, that the condition of the woodcutter, the hunter, or the American Indian was in itself to be preferred. What he discovered was that people are so eager to get the ostentatious "necessaries" of a civil life that they lose the opportunity to profit by civilization itself: while their physical wants are complicated, their lives, culturally, are not enriched in proportion, but are rather pauperized and bleached.

Thoreau was completely oblivious to the dominant myths that had been bequeathed by the Seventh Century. Indifferent to the illusion of magnitude, he felt that Walden Pond, rightly viewed, was as vast as the ocean, and the woods and fields and swamps of Concord were as inexhaustible as the Dark Continent. In his study of Nature, he had recourse on occasion to the scientific botanists and zoölogists; but he himself had possession of a method that they were slow to arrive at; and it is easier for us to-day to understand the metaphysical distinction of Thoreau's kind of nature study than it would have been for Gray or Agassiz. Like Wordsworth before him, like Bergson after him, he realized that in current science "we murder to dissect," and he passed beyond the artful dismemberments of contemporary science to the flower and the bird and the habitat themselves. "Not a single scientific term or distinction," he wrote once in his notebook, "is the least to the purpose. You would fain perceive something and you must approach the object totally unprejudiced. You must be aware that nothing is what you take it to be. . . . Your greatest success will be simply to perceive that such things are, and you will have no communication to make to the Royal Society." In other words, Thoreau sought in nature all the manifold qualities of being; he was not merely in search of those likenesses or distinctions which help to create classified indexes and build up a system. The aesthetic qualities of a fern were as important for his mode of apprehension as the number of spores on a frond; it was not that he disdained science, but that, like the old herbalists and naturalists he admired, he would not let the practical offices of science, its classification, its measurements, its numerations, take precedence over other forms of understanding. Science, practiced in this fashion, is truly part of a humane life, and a Darwin dancing for joy over a slide in his microscope, or a Pupin, finding the path to physics through his contemplation of the stars he watched as a herdboy through the night, are not poorer scientists but richer ones for these joys and delights: they merely bow to the bias of utilitarianism when they leave these things out of their reports. In his attitude toward scientific truth Thoreau was perhaps a prophetic figure; and a new age may do honor to his metaphysics as well as to his humanity.

The resolute acceptance of his immediate milieu as equal to the utmost that the earth could offer stood by Thoreau in his other activities, too. He captained huckleberry parties as he might have led a battle, and was just as much the leader in one as he would have been in the other. His courage he reserved for better occasions than the battlefield, for he was ready to go to jail for his principles, and to mock Emerson for remaining outside. As for his country, he loved the land too well to confuse it with the shifting territorial boundaries of the National State. In this, he had that vital regional consciousness which every New Englander shared: Hawthorne himself had said that New England was as large a piece of territory as could claim his allegiance. Thoreau was not deceived by the rascality of politicians, who were ready to wage war for a coveted patch of Mexico's land; nor did he side with those who, for the sake of the Union, were ready to give up the principles that alone had made the Union valuable. What he loved was the landscape, his friends, and his companions in the spirit: when the Political State presumed to exercise a brass counter-claim on these loyalties it might go to the devil.

Thoreau's attitude toward the State, one must note, was just the opposite to that of the progressive pioneer. The latter did not care what sort of landscape he "located" in, so long as he could salute the flag of his country and cast his vote: Thoreau, on the contrary, was far too religious a man to commit the idolatry of saluting a symbol of secular power; and he realized that the

affairs controlled by the vote represented only a small fraction of an interesting life, while so far from being indifferent to the land itself, he absorbed it,
as men have absorbed legends, and guarded it, as men preserve ceremonies.
The things which his contemporaries took for the supreme realities of life,
matter, money, and political rights, had only an instrumental use for Thoreau: they might contribute a little to the arrangement of a good life, but the
good life itself was not contained, was not even implied in them. One might
spend one's life pursuing them without having lived. "There is not one of my
readers," he exclaimed, "who has yet lived a whole human life."

In Thoreau's time, industrialism had begun to puff itself up over its mul-
tiplication of goods and the increase of wants that it fostered, in order to
provide the machine with an outlet for its ever-too-plentiful supply. Thoreau
simply asked: "Shall we always study to obtain more of these things, and not
sometimes be content with less?" "If we do not get our sleepers and forge
rails and devote long days and nights to work," he observed ironically, "but
go tinkering with our lives to improve *them*, who will build the railroads?"
Thoreau was not a penurious fanatic, who sought to practice bare living
merely as a moral exercise: he wanted to obey Emerson's dictum to save on
the low levels and spend on the high ones. It is this that distinguishes him
from the tedious people whose whole existence is absorbed in the practice of
living on beans, or breathing deeply, or wearing clothes of a vegetable origin:
simplification did not lead in Thoreau to the cult of simplicity: it led to a
higher civilization.

What drove Thoreau to the solitude of the woods was no cynical contempt
for the things beyond his reach. "Before we can adorn our houses with beautiful objects, the walls must be stripped, and our lives must be stripped, and
beautiful house-keeping and beautiful living be laid for a foundation: now, a
taste for the beautiful is most cultivated out of doors, where there is no house,
and no housekeeper." The primeval woods were a favorable beginning for
the search; but Thoreau did not think they could be the end of it. The land
itself, however, did stir his imagination; he wrote:

> All things invite this earth's inhabitants
> To rear their lives to an unheard of height,
> And meet the expectation of the land.

"The expectation of the land!" One comes upon that phrase, or its equivalent, in almost every valid piece of early American thought. One thinks of

moorland pastures by the sea, dark with bayberries and sweet fern, breaking out among the lichened rocks; and the tidal rivers bringing their weedy tang to the low meadows, wide and open in the sun; the purple pine groves, where the needles, bedded deep, hum to the wind, or the knotted New England hills, where the mountain laurel in June seems like upland snow, left over, or where the marble breaks through into clusters of perpetual laurel and everlasting; one sees mountain lakes, giant aquamarines, sapphires, topazes, and upland pastures where the blue, purple, lavender and green of the huckleberry bushes give way in autumn to the fringe of sumach by the road-side, volcanoes of reds and crimsons; the yellow of September cornfields, with intenser pumpkins lying between the shocks, or the naked breasts and flanks of the autumn landscape, quivering in uneasy sleep before the white blanket puts it to rest. To smell this, taste this, and feel and climb and walk over this landscape, once untouched, like an unopened letter or a lover unkissed—who would not rise to meet the expectation of the land? Partly, it was the challenge of babyhood: how will it grow up and what will become of it? Partly, it was the charm of innocence; or again, it was the sense of the mighty variety that the whole continent gives, as if between the two oceans every possible human habitat might be built, and every conceivable variety of experience fathomed.

What the aboriginal Indian had absorbed from the young earth, Thoreau absorbed; what the new settlers had given her, the combing of the plow, the cincture of the stone fence or the row of planted elms, these things he absorbed too; for Thoreau, having tasted the settled life of Concord, knew that the wilderness was not a permanent home for man: one might go there for fortification, for a quickening of the senses, for a tightening of all the muscles; but that, like any retreat, is a special exercise and wants a special occasion: one returned to Nature in order to become, in a deeper sense, more cultivated and civilized, not in order to return to crudities that men had already discarded. Looking ahead, Thoreau saw what was needed to preserve the valuable heritage of the American wilderness. He wrote:

> The kings of England formerly had their forests to hold the king's game, for sport or food, sometimes destroying villages to create and extend them; and I think that they were impelled by a true instinct. Why should not we, who have renounced the king's authority, have our national preserves, where no villages need be destroyed, in which the bear and panther, and some even of the

hunter race, may still exist, and not be "civilized off the face of the earth,"—
our own forests, not to hold the king's game merely, but to hold and preserve
the king himself also, the lord of creation,—and not in idle sport of food, but
for inspiration and our own true recreation? or shall we, like the villains, grub
them all up, poaching on our own national domain?

These pregnant suggestions of Thoreau, which were to be embodied only
after two generations in our National and State Parks, and in projects like
Mr. Benton MacKaye's great conception of the Appalachian Trail, make the
comments of those who see in him only an arch-individualist, half-Diogenes,
half-Rousseau, seem a little beside the point. The individualism of an Emerson or a Thoreau was the necessary complement of the thoroughly social-
ized existence of the New England town; it was what prevented these towns
from becoming collections of yes men, with never an opinion or an emotion
that differed from their neighbors. He wrote for his fellow-townsmen; and his
notion of the good life was one that should carry to a higher pitch the existing
polity and culture of Concord itself.

> As the nobleman of cultivated taste surrounds himself with whatever conduces
> to his culture—genius—learning—wit—books—paintings—statuary—mu-
> sic—philosophical instruments, and the like; so let the village do—not stop
> short at a pedagogue, a parson, a sexton, a parish library, and three selectmen,
> because our pilgrim forefathers got through a cold winter once on a bleak rock
> with these. To act collectively is according to the spirit of our institutions; and
> I am confident that our circumstances are more flourishing, our means are
> greater than the nobleman's.

Do not these sentences alter a little our stereotype of home-spun New England, of Individualistic America?

Just as Thoreau sought Nature, in order to arrive at a higher state of culture, so he practiced individualism, in order to create a better order of society.
Taking America as it was, Thoreau conceived a form, a habitat, which would
retain what was unique in the American contact with the virgin forest, the
cultivated soil, and the renewed institutions of the New England town. He
understood the precise thing that the pioneer lacked. The pioneer had exhausted himself in a senseless external activity, which answered no inner
demands except those for oblivion. In his experiment at Walden Pond, Thoreau "learned this, at least . . . that if one advances confidently in the direc-

tion of his dreams, and endeavors to live the life which he has imagined, he will meet with success unexpected in the common hours. . . . In proportion as he simplifies his life, the laws of the universe will appear less complex, and solitude will not be solitude, nor poverty poverty, nor weakness weakness. If you have built castles in the air, your work need not be lost; that is where they should be. Now put the foundations under them."

In short, Thoreau lived in his desires; in rational and beautiful things that he imagined worth doing, and did. The pioneer lived only in extraneous necessities; and he vanished with their satisfaction: filling all the conditions of his environment, he never fulfilled himself. With the same common ground between them in their feeling towards Nature, Thoreau and the pioneer stood at opposite corners of the field. What Thoreau left behind is still precious; men may still go out and make over America in the image of Thoreau. What the pioneer left behind, alas! was only the burden of a vacant life.

Henry Chester Tracy on
Women Nature Writers
(1930)

Born in 1876 in Athens, Pennsylvania, Henry Chester Tracy spent much of his childhood living in Turkey. After returning to the United States he majored in the natural sciences at Oberlin; after graduating he taught biology for two years at nearby Oberlin Academy, then worked on a trail crew in Montana's Glacier National Park. In the ensuing years he worked at a variety of jobs and earned a master's degree in biology at the University of California, Berkeley. After several years of teaching at Hollywood High School—"drowning his literary aspirations in laboratory and field routine," as one biographer put it—he finally published his first book, *An Island in Time*, in 1924. Several others would follow, including *Towards the Open* (1927), *The Shadow Eros* (1927), *English as Experience* (1928), and *American Naturists* (1930). In 1942 he was picked to direct the literary program of the Common Council for American Unity, a group devoted to improving American race relations.

In the essay below, excerpted from *American Naturists*, Tracy notes that men have dominated the field of nature writing but argues that the roots of such dominance are social rather than intrinsic, the product of "natural accidents and social causes." In a remark that seems particularly prescient, given the appearance three decades later of Rachel Carson's *Silent Spring*, Tracy claims that "the most potent influence in the future may be that of a woman."

Many of those who read these sketches and interpretations will be women. Those of them who are acquainted with the author will know that he has not the slightest bias in favor of men as nature-writers, and that he has taken the leading figures as they come, selecting those who seem to have made the most distinctive contributions and the most lasting impression on our feeling for out-of-door things. Yet his list contains twenty-one major contributors, of whom only two are women. Why is this?

The question was first put to the author by a brilliant woman who agrees, in the main, with the selections, and was passed on at once to another, in a drawing-room from which sham was long ago banished. Her answer was swift and short: "Because men are more sentimental." This amplifies into a statement that men at heart are impractical, inclined to the pursuit of useless things, while women, although they may be equally impressionable, align their efforts with useful ends, a view not to be idly dismissed. If we take as types of nature-seer the two greatest that English-speaking countries have produced we find in Henry Thoreau and W. H. Hudson two men whose influence is entirely against utilitarianism — "impractical" men, careless of personal advantage and establishment, completely for a mode of perception and participation in the nature-life. There is no nest-feathering instinct in Thoreau, no urge toward economic security in Hudson. Neither one would have valued an estate or servants, houses, dogs, horses, and social magnificence. Both wished for leisure to be in contact with the things they liked best, and these things were: roughly, birds, fishes; a stridulating insect; wood-shade, and water; the drip of rain-drops; snow; leaf-mold, and the flora of a bog; fox, hornet, heron — every sort of wild creature irrespective of its use to them or to any man. If our word "naturist" has any meaning, these men are the type. If our word "sentiment" does not connote the quality of their interest that is a fault of language, and we have no proper word. It has not been coined.

But whatever the quality of their interest and of that inner drive which propels them toward nature it cannot be construed as distinctively feminine. By long inheritance and habit a woman's interest is personal and indoor. It does not go out instinctively to an impersonal and a useless outdoor world. When she has become further emancipated, perhaps it will. As she has already rid herself to a great extent of masculine domination, she may one day be freed of the compelling necessity to possess all kinds of convenient and useful things. And if that should occur it will mean a very real emancipation

from those economic slaveries which, while they release her from social para-
sitism, make her a creature of business hours and exacting professional work.
Therefore a study of the nature movement is a forward-looking subject and
not an academic appraisal of deeds accomplished by men. No masculine
bias enters into it. Due to natural accidents and social causes men have pio-
neered along this path, hitherto. They have not come to the end of it. The
issue hangs very much in the balance and the most potent influence in the
future may be that of a woman. Indeed it is hard to see how there can be any
check to the growing artificiality of our American living until women,
around whose interests it centers, reinterpret the nature world from their own
point of view. When they do this, their contribution will not be imitative but
original, as it is in the two cases described in this book.

A modern woman when she drinks, smokes and adopts the "single standard" is not doing anything original. She is merely taking over some of the
pastimes of the male. There is no form of amusement or of behavior which
she will not copy, and none that men will not tolerate. But when she goes to
the field and the wood, or to the river and the lake, not to shoot or fish but
merely to be there, and for the sake of an awareness that she does not find in
town, she is no mimic. This awareness which comes so thinly to park or
common, and is quite deleted in a many-storied city apartment, is no masculine perquisite. Considered crudely as recreation it is not now, it never was
the pleasure or predilection of men. From the beginning, they hunted and
fished, but what they saw in the world around them—whether of sights,
scents or activities, and the whisper of inanimate things—depended wholly
on the qualities of their mind and spirit; depended on something more than
their keenness in pursuit of game. It was neither masculine nor feminine. It
was human, in the highest sense. When the sportsman's impulse dropped
out and one went out solely to perceive and to feel, to enjoy and perhaps
record his impressions, we had something new. The age of the naturists had
begun. There was no reason why woman should not share the experience
equally with man. In any case she could not copy, for there is no copying in
the thing we are describing. It is original or else it is spurious. You cannot,
by cramming your mind with nature-lore in book form, have a single valid
impression. From Bartram to Beebe the books act as stimuli and as lures. By
reading them you clarify your own seeing and quicken your senses. If as an
effect of one such volume you hear more in a cricket's chirp than you had
heard before, your time has not been wasted. It is not a matter of information.

A naturist does not tell you about nature. He drives you to it or he remains a naturalist, and nothing more. Our common-school education has become a cult of the second-hand, therefore the originals are few, and none are expected. But in this field right perception is original perception. Nothing else counts.

Mary Austin has given us original perception. She is pre-eminent among living nature writers who are women because she has done this with force, with feeling and with a prophetic quality in the writing which is a mark of naturists of the first rank. She has not merely seen the flowers, shrubs, storms, mesas of the desert but she has swept all of these and their impalpable nuances into a vision which is not fanciful but real — real as only intuitive and poetic perceptions can be. Through her close and colorful interpretations the lives of Mesa folk, of whatever race, but especially that of the Pueblo Indians, become moving realities within an intelligible nature scheme. They can never again be wholly misunderstood. No naturist has done finer work from a human point of view, and the work is not yet complete. It will not be finished until every person who lives has the chance to know, if only for a child's glimpse, the world out of which he was made, and the moods of it. Let us hope for more naturists who are women. After all, is not nature our "mother"? Inexorable law, grim and exacting to the end — that's a masculine conception. In the cosmos itself, and not merely in the Church, we need a Madonna, and let who can, be her spokesman.

Mary Hunter Austin on
Literature and the Regional Environment
(1932)

Mary Hunter Austin was born in Carlinville, Illinois, in 1868. She studied the
physical sciences at Blackburn College, graduating in 1888. Shortly afterward her
father died, and her mother moved the family to an isolated ranch in California's
San Joaquin Valley—where, her biographers say, Austin learned to love the austere landscapes of the arid West. In 1891 she moved to Lone Pine, in the even
drier and more remote Owens Valley east of the Sierra Nevada. Her writing career began in earnest in 1900, when she began publishing in the *Atlantic
Monthly*; three years later she published *Land of Little Rain*, her elegant tribute
to the Owens Valley and the book for which she is perhaps best known today.
She would go on to publish some thirty books and more than two hundred magazine articles on topics ranging from Native American culture to contemporary
feminism. In 1900, along with such writers as George Sterling and Jack London,
she helped found the famous literary colony in Carmel. Austin's real home,
however, was Santa Fe, New Mexico, where she lived the last two decades of her
life and became something of an institution to her many admiring guests. (It
was in Austin's Santa Fe home that Willa Cather wrote *Death Comes for the
Archbishop*.)

In the essay below, published in 1932 in the *English Journal*, Austin outlines
her deeply held belief that the "regional environment . . . orders and determines"
practical life and thus permeates "that field of consciousness from which all invention and creative effort of every sort proceed." With D. H. Lawrence, that is,
she shared an environmental determinism; unlike Lawrence, she felt that the
native environmental influence had already deeply influenced American culture. "The really astonishing thing," she wrote, "would have been to find the

American people as a whole resisting the influence of the natural environment in favor of the lesser influences of a shared language and a common political arrangement."

Such a thoroughgoing determinism is now discredited; few critics would argue today that Nature trumps Culture as thoroughly as Austin appeared to believe. But this belief prompted some of Austin's most astute criticism of American literature, much of which she faulted for attempting to depict only "one vast, pale figure of America," when in reality there exist "several Americas, in many subtle and significant characterizations." She blamed this state of affairs in part on William Dean Howells, who flattened out regional distinctions by his "deliberate choice," as both author and editor, "of the most usual, the most widely distributed of American story incidents, rather than the most intensively experienced." It is also to this universalizing impulse that Austin attributes "our long disappointed expectation of the 'great American novel.'" She argues instead for a sort of "multiregionalism"—for a regionally grounded version of today's multiculturalist vision.

At its best, Austin insists, American literature is not only *about* the country but *of* the country, "flower of its stalk and root, in the way that *Huckleberry Finn* is of the great river, taking its movement and rhythm, its structure and intention, or lack of it, from the scene."

🪷 🪷 🪷

"Regionalism in literature," says Dorothy Canfield in a recent review of what she considers an excellent example of it, "is the answer to the problem of getting any literature at all out of so vast and sprawling a country as ours." She might as truthfully have said it of any art and any country which is large enough to cover more than one type of natural environment. Art, considered as the expression of any people as a whole, is the response they make in various mediums to the impact that the totality of their experience makes upon them, and there is no sort of experience that works so constantly and subtly upon man as his regional environment. It orders and determines all the direct, practical ways of his getting up and lying down, of staying in and going out, of housing and clothing and food-getting; it arranges by its progressions of seed times and harvest, its rain and wind and burning suns, the rhythms of his work and amusements. It is the thing always before his eye, always at his ear, always underfoot. Slowly or sharply it forces upon him behavior patterns such as earliest become the habit of his blood, the unconscious factor of adjustment in all his mechanisms. Of all the responses of his psyche, none pass so soon and surely as these into that field of consciousness from which all invention and creative effort of every sort proceed. Musical experts say that they can trace a racial influence in composition many generations back, and what is a race but a pattern of response common to a group of people who have lived together under a given environment long enough to take a recognizable pattern?

Everybody has known this a long time. We have known it about classic Greek and ancient Egypt. We know that the distinctions between Scotch and Irish and British literature have not been erased, have scarcely been touched by their long association of all three under one political identity; we know in fact that at last the pattern of Irish regionalism has prevailed over polity, and it is still a problem of the Irish Free State to withstand the separative influences of regionalism on their own green island. We recognize Moorish and Iberian elements in Spanish art, at the same time that we fully realize something distinctive that comes to this mixed people out of the various regional backgrounds within the Spanish peninsula. Knowing all this, it is rather surprising to find critics in the United States speaking of regionalism as something new and unprecedented in a territory so immensely varied as ours. The really astonishing thing would have been to find the American people as a whole resisting the influence of natural environment in favor of the lesser influences of a shared language and a common political arrangement.

Actually this notion, that the American people should differ from all the rest of the world in refusing to be influenced by the particular region called home, is a late by-product of the Civil War and goes with another ill-defined notion that there is a kind of disloyalty in such a differentiation and an implied criticism in one section of all the others from which it is distinguished. It would be easy to trace out the growth of such an idea, helped as it is and augmented in its turn by the general American inability to realize the source of all art as deeper than political posture, arising, as people truly and rudely say, in our "guts," the seat of life and breath and heartbeats, of loving and hating and fearing. It is not in the nature of mankind to be all of one pattern in these things any more than it is in the nature of the earth to be all plain, all seashore, or all mountains. Regionalism, since it is of the very nature and constitution of the planet, becomes at last part of the nature and constitution of the men who live on it.

Since already a sense of the truth of these things, as applicable to our own country, has worked through to the common consciousness, our real concern is not to argue the case, but to fortify ourselves against the possibility of our missing the way again by failing to discriminate between a genuine regionalism and mistaken presentiments of it. We need to be prompt about it, before somebody discovers that our resistance so far has been largely owed to intellectual laziness which flinches from the task of competently knowing, not one vast, pale figure of America, but several Americas, in many subtle and significant characterizations.

As a matter of fact, our long disappointed expectation of the "great American novel," for which every critic was once obliged to keep an eye out, probably originated in the genuine inability of the various regions to see greatness in novels that dealt with fine and subtle distinctions in respect to some other region. But we have only to transfer this wishful thinking for a single book, or a single author, who would be able to overcome our inextinguishable ignorance of each other, to Europe to become aware of its absurdity. To Europeans our American regional differentiations, all comprised under one language and one government, are very puzzling. That is one reason why they have seized so promptly on *Main Street* and especially on *Babbitt* as just the broad, thin, generalized surface reflection of the American community and American character which the casual observer receives. Babbitt is an American type, the generalized, "footless" type which has arisen out of a rather widespread resistance to regional interests and influences, out of a determined fixation on the most widely shared, instead of the deepest rooted, types of American activity. That Babbitt is exactly that sort of person and that he is unhappy in being it, is probably exactly what Mr. Lewis meant to show. But that millions of Americans rise up to reject him as representing "our part of the country" only goes to show that, deep down and probably unconsciously, all the time that one set of influences has been shaping the shallow Babbitt citizen, another set has been at work to produce half a dozen other regionally discriminated types for whom there is, naturally, no common literary instance.

Perhaps the country does not fully realize that in rejecting Babbitt as our family name, it has declared for the regional types such as the best American fictionists have already furnished us. Probably the American reading public never has understood that its insistence on fiction shallow enough to be common to all regions, so that no special knowledge of other environments than one's own is necessary to appreciation of it, has pulled down the whole level of American fiction. It is more than likely that even the critics, who can be discovered surrendering to the idea of strongly marked regional fiction, have no notion of the work they are cutting out for themselves under the necessity of knowing good regional books when they see them. But there it is, the recognition and the demand. People of the South aren't satisfied to go on forever reading novels about New York and Gopher Prairie, people of the Pacific Coast want occasionally to read "something more like us." They are willing to be tolerant and even interested in other regions on consideration that they get an occasional fair showing for themselves.

Fortunately, if we go back far enough, we have plenty of regional fiction to furnish a prototype and a criterion of criticism. It is, in fact, the only sort of fiction that will bear reading from generation to generation. Any confirmed novel reader of more than a generation's experience, or any teacher of English, should be able to name a score of them offhand. I begin my own list with *Queechy* as the best novel of rural life in New England ever written. I should begin with one of Herman Melville's, except that I am trying to omit for the moment regionalism which has also a narrow time limit; the environment of the whaler's sea that Melville knew has already been eaten up in time. I would name Hawthorne's *The House of the Seven Gables* rather than *The Scarlet Letter*, the latter being less of the land and more of the temper of Puritanism, more England than New England. To these I would add something of that gifted author of *The Country of the Pointed Firs*, Sarah Orne Jewett. Of Henry James, *Washington Square* most definitely fulfils the regional test of not being possible to have happened elsewhere. Out of New York I would choose *The House of Mirth*; but we have Hergesheimer's *Three Black Pennys* and *Balisand* and James Branch Cabell's least known, and to my thinking, best, *The Rivet in Grandfather's Neck*. When Mr. Cabell tells us the true story of why he never wrote another like it, but invented the region of Poictesme in old France against which to display his literary gifts, we shall know many revealing things about the influences shaping literature in the United States.

In the Mississippi Valley, one thinks at once of *Tom Sawyer* and *Huckle-*

berry Finn. Along the Middle Border there are Hamlin Garland's earlier tales, such as *Main Travelled Roads*; and on the edge of the Plains are Ed Howe's neglected masterpiece, *The Story of a Country Town,* and Willa Cather's *My Antonia.* Of the Southwest, unless you will accept the present writer's *Starry Adventure,* there is as yet very little genuinely representative — not that there are not stories of that country which are well worth the reading, and at least one immortal short story, Stephen Crane's *The Bride Comes to Yellow Sky.* Our Southwest, though actually the longest-lived-in section of the country, has not yet achieved its authentic literary expression in English. On the California coast there are a number of entirely characteristic short stories. Chester Bailey Fernald's *The Cat and the Cherub* comes instantly to mind, and at least two of Frank Norris' novels.

This is to name only those titles which occur irresistibly in this connection — fiction which has come up through the land, shaped by the author's own adjustments to it — and leave out many excellent and illuminating works which are colored, not only by the land, but by the essence of a period, a phase of its social development, a racial bias, a time element too short to develop essential characteristics. Such as these are the stories of George W. Cable, and Grace Medard King of Old Louisiana, Bret Harte's tales of "Forty-Nine," and such delicate but inerasable sketches as F. Hopkinson Smith's *Colonel Carter of Cartersville.* I should think, indeed, that an importantly readable anthology of tales dealing with these local rather than regional shorter phases of American life could be easily gathered; but I am concerned chiefly to establish a criterion of what is first class regional fiction than to name every item that could possibly be included in that category. Lovers of W. D. Howells will wonder why his name does not appear here. If it belongs here, it is largely on account of *Silas Lapham.* Many sections of America could have produced Silas, but the things that happened to him in Howells' story could have happened only in Boston, and in that sense it is a true regional expression, and very likely will be estimated as Howells' best piece, chiefly because it has that deep-rooted motivation which is the essential quality of regionalism. But it has always seemed to me that Howells was the first, and the most eminent, of the American novelists responsible for the thinning out of American fiction by a deliberate choice of the most usual, the most widely distributed of American story incidents, rather than the most intensively experienced. Between Howells and Sinclair Lewis we have the whole history of that excursion of the American novelist away from the soil, undertaken on the part of Howells in a devout pilgrim spirit, bent on the exploration of the social expression of democracy, and on the part of Lewis with a fine scorn and a hurt indignation for the poor simp who, having filled his belly with husks, does not yet know enough to say, "I will arise and go to my father."

In all this instancing of archetypes, we must by no means leave out the books for children which belong in this list, and more than any other sort of literature overlap in the lists. We begin chronologically with Cooper's tales, of which half a dozen are absolute types, and then think at once of *Tom Sawyer* and *Huckleberry Finn*. It is only because the Alcott books are less picaresque that we fail to realize them as not the less regional, possible only to a long settled culture, so much longer settled than most American cultures at the time they were written, that much of their charm for the country at large lay in the note of nostalgia for the richer and more spiritual life which they aroused. This writer, who read them as they came fresh from the pen of the Boston spinster, knows well how intimately they presented the social and moral aspirations of the still crude Middle West of that time. It is their profound fidelity to what was the general American feeling for the best in family life that makes the Alcott stories still moving and popular. It is the greatest mistake in the world not to recognize that children are affected by these things, being at heart the most confirmed regionalists. What they like as background for a story is an explicit, well mapped strip of country, as intensively lived into as any healthy child lives into his own neighborhood.

Two other writers of my youth, who might well be kept on the children's list, were Eggleston and Trowbridge, along with half a dozen of the stories of Mayme Reid. If I name nothing modern it is because my acquaintance with modern literature for children is too scanty for me to feel sure of naming the best. When I was young the best of everything appeared in *St. Nicholas*; and the best was always explicitly localized, dealt with particular birds and beasts, trees and growing things, incidents that had their source in the four great causatives: climate, housing, transportation, and employment.

There is, for children, another region, often completely closed to their elders, for which the same rules hold. I mean the world of fairy adventure. Grown up people often make the oddest, most lamentable mistakes in attempting to deal with this world; the most unforgivable is to treat it as though there were no rules, no such thing as fairy logic. The fact is that this fairy world is precisely the grownup world as it presented itself to the childhood of the race. To be wholly satisfying, stories of this world must be made to hang together as it hung together for our ancestors of the Stone Age. Fortunately the very greatest geniuses among fairy-world realists, like Lewis Carroll, Hans Christian Anderson, and Rudyard Kipling, are perfectly aware of the regional rules and never violate them in the least particular. In the *Jungle Book*, tigers are always true to their tigerishness and wolves to the imaginary lore of the pack. Mr. Kipling's jungle may not be the verifiable jungle of India, nor even of little Hindu girls and boys, but it is the complete jungle of the childhood of the race. Mowgli is as full of forest guile as any other young animal, and as completely innocent of heart, so that the young reader shares with him every thrill of the daily hunt and kill, without ever once realizing that what Mowgli eats is hot raw meat which he tears apart with his teeth and hands. A writer less able to understand innocence of heart than Mr. Kipling would have conscientiously tried to make a complete vegetarian of him.

In the same way the countries down the rabbit hole and behind the looking glass never depart for an instant from fidelity to the topsy-turviness of the land of dreams. No item except such as a perfectly normal little girl like Alice might take with her into dreamland is ever allowed to intrude incongruously into the story. These two regions of our Ancestral European past and topsy-turvy-dream are by this time so well mapped that it is sheer stupidity for a writer to go astray in them. But there is another story-region to which every American child has right of access, all the laws which have been so violated by well-meaning and ill-informed writers, that it ought to be a penal offense to keep on doing so — I mean the world of American Indian lore. This world begins in the dooryard of every American child; it can be fully entered at the edge of every American town, it can be looked out upon from every train window and crossed by every automobile. But so ignorant of this region are most grown up Americans, that there are but three guides to whom I could unhesitatingly recommend the exploring child to trust: Joel Chandler Harris, James Willard Schultz, and Arthur Parker. There are, of course, individual works, such as Frank Hamilton Cushing's *Zuni Folk Tales*, which are absolute in their transcription of Indian regionalism.

But the trouble with ninety-nine out of every hundred Indian books offered to American children is that their authors fail to know that everything an Indian does or thinks is patterned by the particular parcel of land which is his tribal home. Thus at its very source the processes of regional culture, from which the only sound patriotism springs, are corrupted by the same inchoate jumble of environmental elements which so irritates us when pointed out by distinguished foreigners.

Until within the last twenty years the literary expectation of the United States could be quite simply allocated to New England; New York City; a "misty midregion" known as the Middlewest, as weird as Weir and not any more explicitly mapped; to which append the fringing Old South and the Far West. At the present, the last two have completely receded into the dimension of time past. The Old South has given rise to the New South; the Far West has split into the Southwest, the Northwest, the California Coast, and the Movie West. Cleavages begin to appear in the Middlewest, outlining *The Great Meadow*, the title of the best book about the section just south of Ohio. Farther north lies the Middle Border and Chicago. Within New York City we are aware of the East Side and Harlem which is the capital of the new Negro world, each producing its own interpreters. Even in the Indian region there is faint indication of splitting off from the children's Indian country of a meagerly explored adult interest.

To the average citizen, notice of these recent annexations to the literary world comes in the form of a new book which everybody is talking about, dealing with life as it is lived there, as it unmistakably couldn't be lived anywhere else. And immediately the average citizen who, however much he wishes to read what everybody else is reading, secretly hankers to be able to discriminate for himself, begins to cast about for a criterion of what acceptable regionalism in literature should be. For to be able to speak of the credibility of reports of the various countries contained within our country requires a nimble wit and a considerable capacity for traveling in one's mind. How, the reader inquires inwardly, without having lived it myself, shall I feel certain that this book does give in human terms the meaning of that country in which the action of the story takes place? One might answer shortly, by the same means that it has become a proverb in the country where I live that "a wool grower knows a wool buyer." Whoever has lived deeply and experientially into his own environment, is by so much the better prepared to recognize the same experience in another. But there are criteria not to be ignored for recognizing regionalism in literature.

The first of the indispensable conditions is that the region must enter constructively into the story, as another character, as the instigator of plot. A natural scene can never be safely assumed to be the region of the story when it is used merely as a back drop—not that the scenic backdrop cannot be used effectively by way of contrast, or to add a richer harmonization to a story shaped by alien scenes. Henry James is master of this trick, as when in *The Golden Bowl* he uses aristocratic England as a setting for a group of rich Americans and one Italian Prince; or, as in *The Ambassadors,* he unfolds a New England complication against smart Paris. Edith Wharton does it less handsomely in *The Children,* and Sinclair Lewis less importantly in *Dodsworth.* Willa Cather does it most appealingly in *Death Comes for the Archbishop.* I am often asked if this last is not what I mean by a "regional" book of the Southwest. Not in the least. The hero is a missionary arriving here at an age when the major patterns of his life are already set; a Frenchman by birth, a Catholic by conviction and practice, a priest by vocation, there is little that New Mexico can do for him besides providing him an interesting backdrop against which to play out his missionary part. Miss Cather selects her backgrounds with care, draws them with consummate artistry, in this case perverting the scene from historical accuracy, and omitting—probably, herself, in complete ignorance of it—the tragic implications of its most significant item and so makes it convincing for her audience. I am not saying that this is not a legitimate literary device. That Archbishop Lamy, who was the historic prototype of Miss Cather's leading character, also missed the calamity to Spanish New Mexican culture, of the coming of the French priests, is the one profoundly human touch that so competent a literary artist as Miss Cather should not have overlooked. It makes her story, with all its true seeming, profoundly untrue to the New Mexican event, which removes it from the category of regional literature.

One of the likeliest mistakes the inexperienced reader will make in allocating books to their proper regional source, is to select stories about the region rather than of it. Such a reader would for example class *Uncle Tom's Cabin* as a southern book, when, in fact, its approach, its moral and intellectual outlook is New England from the ground up, and so are its most telling characters. The South never saw itself in Harriet Beecher Stowe's light, never looked on slavery as she displayed it. Southerners would not deny the book's regional character, but they are still protesting after nearly three-quarters of a century that it is not of their region. In the same manner, old Californians, forty years ago, could be heard denying the regional authenticity of *Ramona.* They recognized neither themselves nor their Indians in Helen Hunt Jackson's presentation. The regionally interpretive book must not only be about the country, it must be of it, flower of its stalk and root, in the way that *Huckleberry Finn* is of the great river, taking its movement and rhythm, its structure and intention, or lack of it, from the scene. In the way that Edna Ferber's *Cimarron* isn't of the land but pleasingly and reasonably about it.

With these two indispensable conditions of the environment entering constructively into the story, and the story reflecting in some fashion the essential qualities of the land, it is not easy to put one's finger on representative regional fiction. *Slow Smoke* by Charles Malam is the novel Dorothy Canfield mentions. A book I have in mind as fulfilling all the conditions completely is Frank Applegate's *Indian Stories from the Pueblos*. These are native tales which he tells in the manner in which the natives would tell them. Work of this kind comes on slowly. Time is the essence of the undertaking, time to live into the land and absorb it; still more time to cure the reading public of its preference for something less than the proverbial bird's-eye view of the American scene, what you might call an automobile eye view, something slithering and blurred, nothing so sharply discriminated that it arrests the speed-numbed mind to understand, characters like garish gas stations picked out with electric lights. The one chance of persuading the young reader to make these distinctions for himself would be to whet his appreciation on the best regional literature of our past so that he may not miss the emerging instance of his own times.

Mark Van Doren on
Donald Culross Peattie
(1937)

Born in 1894 in Hope, Illinois, Mark Van Doren received a bachelor's degree from the University of Illinois and a Ph.D. from Columbia, where for nearly forty years he taught literature to the likes of Louis Zukovsky, Lionel Trilling, and Thomas Merton. From 1924 to 1928, he was literary editor for the *Nation;* in 1940 he received a Pulitzer Prize for his *Collected Poems.* His other published works include nearly two dozen more books of poetry, several plays, numerous collections of short stories, and several critical studies of American and British authors.

As both poet and critic, Van Doren was regarded as competent but cautious. Alfred Kazin called him "the Great Neutral," noting that he had "an ardent mind" but "also a tidy one . . . often piercing in its intuitions, but very careful never to overreach." In the following essay on Donald Culross Peattie, excerpted from "A New Naturalist," Van Doren credits Peattie with tending toward what today would be termed "biocentrism": "It is as if his center were removed from most of ours," he writes. "His center is the center of life, not the hopes and fears of man; whom nevertheless he loves and respects." Peattie is thus concerned less with such human constructs as "landscape" or "natural beauty" than with "the incessant hum of existence" itself, and "his achievement as a writer consists in having learned how to place his reader likewise in a large world—large, and at the same time swarming with detail, dense with more life than we shall ever know how to catalogue."

"A New Naturalist" first appeared in 1937 in the *North American Review.*

It is perhaps not strange that the literary naturalists have been extraordinarily good writers. Their subject matter is the most interesting we have in these latter centuries when man's view has become more and more limited to the thing we call "life." I have heard it argued that human energy was greater in the days before vitality began to be worshipped as an end in itself—when it was assumed, and the search went on for peace and truth. The proposition is interesting, but it is irrelevant to the peculiar fascination exercised by certain nineteenth and twentieth century literary figures for whom men, animals, plants, clouds, stones, and stars were everything; and certainly it is irrelevant to the literary power of Mr. Peattie, which has a magnitude of its own beyond any help or hindrance from history. It is conceivable that Zoroaster, Confucius, and Thomas Aquinas would not know what he is talking about if they were to return and take up one of his books. But we know, not only without difficulty, but with positive gratitude and pleasure; and that is enough for the present.

To call Mr. Peattie a worshipper of life without further explanation would be unjust to him, since many a fatuous person kneels at that familiar altar today, and since to do so is frequently a sign of some mortal weakness in the suppliant. It is rather that Mr. Peattie is consumed by an interest in life which will not let him alone, and that he seems constantly to be aware of it on a scale hitherto unknown among his tribe. It is this awareness that distinguishes him, this almost abnormal sensitiveness to the little and the great things that are growing and dying every split second of the earth's time—by day and by night, on this hemisphere and on that, under his feet and under yours; and to the immeasurable spaces surrounding us in which nothing grows or dies.

> If there are planets outside the solar system, it is probable he [man] will never see them. If there is life beneath the clouds of Venus, he will not know it. No, it seems to him that the play of man will be enacted only on these boards, this warped and dusty and glamorous stage, set with the changing backdrop of the geologic ages. Haltingly and impromptu he reads his lines. He has no audience but himself. So he lives, our common man, our every man—because he can do no otherwise—as if the stars were after all only configurations of fanciful meaning. As if he had a great destiny, in time and space. All life is with him, aboard this curious Ark of earth. It breathes and runs and flings out its spores in the night and with feathered antennae senses significant odors through the

dark miles, precisely as if it were not limited in its rounds to a zone as fine
as a circlet of thread. It denies death, by every birth, and by every existence
builds as if it were possible for anything to be built to last. Like an aristocracy,
the organisms have arrogance to match their frailty; though they came up
from the clods, their every gesture proclaims the pride of race, the beauty
of form, the rapture of living.

This, from the concluding pages of *A Book of Hours*, only seals the statement which all of Mr. Peattie's books have made, and which is comparable
to the statement the poems of Walt Whitman were always trying to make.
Whitman likewise carried in him a constant sense of the multitude of things
existing outside himself. Hence his "catalogues," his lists of things — rivers,
occupations, place names. It was as if he felt the need of living everywhere
at once; not only in his Brooklyn boarding house on a hot July night, with
the buses going by and the young people laughing along the dark street, but
simultaneously in every street on earth, and down every country road as well,
and off the roads, in the rice fields, the live oak thickets, the spruce forests,
and the grains of desert sand. The difference between the two writers is of
course greater than the resemblance. Mr. Peattie thinks of a thousand things
which Whitman could never have imagined. He has looked through micro-
scopes at the smallest forms of movement; he has followed the life cycles of
grubs and flies; he knows his chemistry, his geology, his astronomy, his elec-
tricity. His sense of existence is therefore infinitely more refined, at least from
the laboratory point of view, than Whitman's was. And he is not nearly so
moral; never, indeed, is he hortatory. Yet there is the resemblance, and it may
help anyone to state for himself the precise quality of the excitement which
Mr. Peattie's books may have started going in his mind.

His heroes among the great naturalists are those who have gone out and
seen for themselves, as he likes to do, the many lives of earth, and who have
felt, even when they could only imperfectly express it, the incessant hum of
existence. He loves Audubon because Audubon's hunger for more and more
knowledge of American birds and forests led him so long a chase — his eyes
glowing, his hair streaming behind him, his mind always fresh and green
with desire. But Mr. Peattie's first hero, and doubtless his last, is Linnaeus.
For Linnaeus was the pioneer of botanical travelers. With him "the green
world opens." When he set off on his Lapland voyage it was as if a million

ferns began to wave their fronds after millenniums of stiff silence in the pages of books. He it was who started the scouring of earth which still goes on: for specimens, for knowledge of how things grow in their secret places.

Any reader of *An Almanac for Moderns* must have taken particular delight in the seventy-first page, commemorating Linnaeus's departure from the University.

In May, 1732, there rode out of the gates of gray old Upsala a thin young man in a light coat of West Gothland linsey without folds, lined with red shalloon, having small cuffs and a collar of shag; he wore leather breeches, and a round wig topped by a green leather cap, his feet in a pair of half-boots. On his saddle he carried a small leather bag containing two pairs of false sleeves, two half-shirts and one whole one, an inkstand, pencase, microscope, a gauze cap to protect him from gnats, a comb, drying papers for plants, and a few books. A fowling-piece hung at his side, and a graduated stick for measuring. In his pocket was a passport for Lapland from the governor of Upsala. Linnaeus was going into the field. In a sense that journey was the first of its kind ever made. It was the morning, the springtime of science, after the dark winter of the bookridden Middle Ages, when men wrangled over Aristotle and quoted Pliny's authority. Linnaeus was the first man to whom it occurred to take a great trip to Nature itself. No wonder that as he rode north, the very larks burst into song.

Those who like may compare these sentences with the sentences Linnaeus himself wrote about his first day out of Upsala, and about the things he wore. Mr. Peattie has quoted them in *Green Laurels*, and it is easy to see there with what loving skill he has condensed and brightened what was already, to be sure, good writing. But the writing is not the point, except in so far as its nervous, enthusiastic quickness at the start and all the way through is an index to the ardor Mr. Peattie feels for the man who opened the world he now can write about in the certainty that two centuries have made it a property of man's imagination. The point is that in Linnaeus, perhaps because he is a long way off in time, Mr. Peattie has found a shining symbol of the thing he admires most in any man — the need and the capacity to acquaint himself with the living universe.

So, as I have said, with Audubon, whom Mr. Peattie can ask us to envy

because he lived through America's "Homeric age," and lived through it intimately, with his feet on all of it he could touch, and with his fine large eyes
on everything. Not merely on birds, though birds were his passion. On
people, too, whether along the lower Mississippi or in the woods of western
Pennsylvania, or in the cane brakes south of the Ohio. Audubon had a vast
curiosity about life, and delighted in it just as he found it. So, within the
narrower realm of botany proper, had John and William Bartram, the Phila-
delphians, whose intimacy with the American wilderness was even earlier,
and whose chapter in *Green Laurels* begins with a rushing description of the
American continent before men came to it. Mr. Peattie needs always to look
at things that way, against their broadest backgrounds, in order to see them
with the clearness he desires. And his achievement as a writer consists in
having learned how to place his reader likewise in a large world—large, and
at the same time swarming with detail, dense with more life than we shall
ever know how to catalogue. . . .

. . . Mr. Peattie gives me the impression of knowing how to talk about
anything, and I am confident that he does, for I cannot imagine a subject in
which he has not been interested. This again is because his imagination
cannot rest while birds fly, insects crawl, darkness and light pursue each other
a thousand miles an hour about the earth, and men lie down to sleep like
falling dominoes as the sun sets from county to county, from continent to
continent. And there is no subject which does not interest him intensely. I
assume that most readers of the *Almanac* remember best the several pages
in which the noise of seventeen-year cicadas shrills without a pause while
Mr. Peattie reflects upon all that portion of earthly life which is not made for
man either to understand or to enjoy, and which some day he will be unable
to survive. But all of the book is equally interested, and therefore equally
interesting.

The terribleness of all that life which we shall not survive is a theme to
which Mr. Peattie often returns in his books. Yet his interest in the theme is
not morbid. The chances that something microscopic will wipe us out, that
another flying body will crash into the earth and demolish it, that the sun
will cease, that the temperature will change, these chances are everpresent
in his mind without decreasing the zest with which he contemplates existence. The theme has been the inspiration of much gloomy writing in our
time, but not so with Mr. Peattie, whose energies seem not to be sapped by
the prospect of annihilation. It is as if his center were removed from most of

ours — off the earth a little, shall we say, though not too far off for visibility. His center is the center of life, not the hopes and fears of man; whom nevertheless he loves and respects. The combination is rare if not unique, betokening as it does a man without illusions yet without the impotence which normally accompanies their loss.

Donald Culross Peattie on
Thoreau, Science, and Nature
(1938)

Donald Culross Peattie was born in Chicago in 1898 into a decidedly writerly family: his mother, Elia Amanda Wilkinson, was a novelist and critic, and his father, Robert Burns Peattie, wrote for the *Chicago Tribune*. Donald studied at the University of Chicago and later at Harvard, where he completed a bachelor's degree in 1922. That same year he won the Witter Bynner Poetry Prize, but he did not immediately pursue a literary career; instead he took a job as a botanist for the Department of Agriculture's Office of Foreign Seed and Plant Introduction. Within a few years, however, he was putting his growing botanical expertise to literary use — first as a nature columnist for the *Washington Star* and eventually as a full-time writer who would produce some three dozen novels, children's books, and works of natural history.

Though he was not a radical innovator, Peattie tinkered occasionally with the formal boundaries of the genres in which he wrote. *A Prairie Grove* (1938), for example, was an experimental "ecological novel" that blended biography and history with graceful and perceptive descriptions of the changing midwestern environment. (It should be noted here that several of his books are not exclusively "his" but rather were written in close collaboration with his wife, Louise Redfield Peattie, who was herself a talented and prolific novelist. Some of the works they wrote together appeared under both names, but some appeared under Donald's name only.)

The excerpt below first appeared in 1938 in the *North American Review* as a review of Henry Seidel Canby's anthology, *Thoreau*. Peattie uses the review as an occasion to explore the sometimes profound gap between transcendentalism and nineteenth-century science. He faults Thoreau in particular for neglecting nineteenth-century scientific discoveries concerning protoplasm and chlorophyll. As "the very seat of life," these ought to have been of particular interest to the transcendentalist, if only as facts that might have been expected to "flower into truths." Thoreau's indifference to his day's best and most suggestive science disqualifies him as a "modern" writer—though Peattie adds that, from the literary perspective, Thoreau's anachronistic biology is as inconsequential as Homer's dated understanding of warfare.

🪷 🪷 🪷

Mr. Canby . . . claims that Thoreau is modern where most of his contemporaries are dated. And the proposition is worth examining. With this republication of Thoreau, especially if it does become the best-seller it deserves to be, the man and his thoughts are shorn of the limp-leather immunity accorded to unread classics, to Scripture, to saintly lives of the past. He is bruited; his pages are flung wide open. They will be read, I hope with Mr. Lewis, by those who acknowledge no fealty to the grace of things past, but judge every writer by today's standards. By high-school boys who think of chemistry as the touchstone of Cosmos, by students in New York City College who look at the world sociologically. By persons not less fanatically conscientious than Thoreau, who believe it their first duty to picket for the garment-workers' strike, and by others whose conscience dictates that they shall bash the heads of such picketers. And by countless more whose persuasions, trainings, emergencies were undreamed of in Concord in 1838. What will they find in Thoreau?

First let us take a swallow-flight over the table of contents, representing Mr. Canby's preferences among the works of his master. We open with some selections from the great poetic and philosophic quarry of the *Journals*. They are selections rather carefully dissected out of Thoreau's natural tissue of sheer nature writing. For Mr. Canby believes that "much damage has been done to his [Thoreau's] reputation as a writer to be read, by the still current belief that he was only a nature writer." (And of course he wasn't only a nature writer.) And "while he was a nature writer *a outrance* as he was a protestant *a outrance*, and paid the penalty of all those whose ambition is infinitely to know, that is not the way to begin to read him."

Mr. Canby does give us some of the nature essays, not the immediate,

Thoreau-afoot of the diaries, but for the most part the reworked and highly
finished products which he either sent to the printer or must have been
nearly ready so to do. The one called *Wild Apples* is especially Thoreauvian,
and for myself I could wish that it led off the book. . . .

[Thoreau's] self-exploration was accomplished well nigh to perfection. It
is clearer than Whitman's, and to my taste more decent than Tolstoi's. To be
what he wished, even in the face of social opposition and ridicule, was his
right and his great triumph. When we ask whether his splendid disobedience
and his affirmations and doubts are widely applicable to moderns, we are
asking his biographers to tell us what befell him. Mr. Canby answers that
question when he says that the solutions worked out in *Walden* are not for
family men. He might have added that, on the whole, they are not for
women. Or children. Thoreau chose to have no personal ardors, and underwent no great personal griefs. He was sheltered from most hard-bought human knowledge, so that he can say, "I have heard no bad news." Thank God
that it was so.

But he knew Nature. By Nature he means of course Cosmos. He means
the nature of Nature, the fundamental structure of the Universe that shall
manifest itself in the revolution of the moons of Jupiter, and the six-sided
crystals of a snowflake, and the hiving of bees and the curious ways of
women. When he speaks of the surface of Nature, of a terrestrial, a New
England view of it, he writes as a poet and a lover. But to be a Transcendentalist, particularly Thoreau's especial brand, is to seek through all Nature for
some higher law, some reality transcending that which the senses proclaim.

This idea is inherent in Greek philosophy of which Greek science is but
a department. It reached Christian theology early, and came to New England, no doubt, in the sermons to which Thoreau listened, as a child under
compulsion, and, as a man tramping past the meeting house, with horror.
Platonic realism or Scholastic Aristotelianism in Thoreau's youth, enjoyed a
recrudescence in the sciences. Beginning in Germany as romantic Natural
Philosophy, it had spread to other nations briefly. Coleridge brought it to the
Lake poets, Wordsworth brought it to the world. Alcott and, if I am not mistaken, Emerson brought it to Concord. Thoreau, the only naturalist among
them, made it peculiarly his own:

> *Jan. 21, 1853.* A fine still warm moonlight evening. . . . I am somewhat op-
> pressed and saddened by the sameness and apparent poverty of the heavens,

that these irregular and few geometrical figures which the constellations make
are no other than those seen by the Chaldaean shepherds. I pine for a new
world in the heavens as well as on the earth, and though it is some consolation
to hear of the wilderness of stars and systems invisible to the naked eye yet the
sky does not make that impression of variety and wildness that even the forest
does. . . . It makes an impression rather of simplicity and unchangeableness, as
of eternal laws. . . . I seem to see it pierced with visual rays from a thousand
observatories. It is more the domain of science than of poetry. It is the stars as
not known to science that I would know, the stars which the lonely traveler
knows. . . . The classification of the stars is old and musty. . . . A few good
anecdotes is our science, with a few opposing statements respecting distance
and size, and little or nothing about the stars as they concern man. It teaches
how he may survey a country or sail a ship, and not how he may steer his life.
Astrology contained the germ of a higher truth than this . . . the sun is ninety-
five millions of miles distant . . . a statement which never made any impression
on me because I never walked it, and which I cannot be said to believe. . . .
Though observatories are multiplied, the heavens receive very little attention.
The naked eye may easily see farther than the armed. Man's eye is the true star-
finder, the comet-seeker. No superior telescope to this has been invented. . . .
The astronomer's eye . . . does not see far beyond the dome of the observatory.

Transcendentalism is here very clearly and consistently expressed; one
might even say, nobly. But it declares its profound difference from modern
science, or even indeed from the best science of Thoreau's time, which he
took many occasions to deride and belittle. Out of love for Thoreau, I do not
quote them; they are, I think, best passed over.

Nor are we to blame Thoreau for not being a scientist. Any educated man,
however, can understand some science if he will, and Thoreau understood
it quite enough to utilize it. But he distrusts it; he claims that its findings are
less important than those which Transcendentalism will presently divine.

And even in his own times the sciences were discovering the structure,
behavior, and nature of protoplasm, which is the very seat of life and ought
to have interested a Transcendentalist transcendingly. There was already current a body of knowledge about chlorophyll, perhaps the most significant
single substance in the world, the very link between cosmic energy and terrestrial life. But I can find no reference in Thoreau to these facts. While the
Transcendentalists were proclaiming the mystery of life, science has rather

beat them to a solution of many of those mysteries at the despised gait of the tortoise. Nor has this been accomplished at any great monetary advantage to the scientist, nor in a scramble for fame, but in an incorruptible search for the truth. As for the Transcendental truths, they have never been advanced since Thoreau did what was just possibly all that could be done for them.

Is Thoreau then a modern? It seems hard to prove it; the gap between his century and ours is one of the greatest in the history of the human structure, greater perhaps than the change from classic civilization to barbarian romanticism. It asks too much of him to bridge it.

But were it any great compliment to say that he is modern? Would he himself be pleased to hear it? Would he not prefer to be "dated?" So, he might say, is the *Iliad* dated, so far as siege tactics, or the picture of the human soul in war-time are concerned. But the poetry of the *Iliad* is timeless. And so is the poetry of *Walden*. As Nature's lover, Henry David Thoreau is the greatest in the English language.

And it is as a Nature writer that I hope he will be read forever.

F. O. Matthiessen on the Organic Style of Emerson and Thoreau

(1941)

Born in Pasadena, California, in 1902, Francis Otto Matthiessen earned a bachelor's degree from Yale and a doctorate from Harvard, where he would teach for most of his career. His experience of the Great Depression and his admiration for Van Wyck Brooks convinced him to ground his criticism in what he saw as the scholar's "social responsibilities," and at Harvard he would become a charter member of the Teacher's Union and one of the earliest explicitly political academic critics. His books include *Sarah Orne Jewett* (1929), *Translation: An Elizabethan Art* (1931), and *The Achievement of T. S. Eliot* (1935). The work upon which his reputation rests, however, is *American Renaissance: Art and Expression in the Age of Emerson and Whitman* (1941).

With *American Renaissance*, Matthiessen successfully applied a New Critical approach to the long-standing problem of establishing and validating an American literary tradition. (The New Critics, with their Eurocentric bias and low opinion of romanticism, had previously paid scant attention to nineteenth-century American literature.) By establishing a firm critical basis for the now-familiar canon of American literature — centered on the period 1850–55 and the writers Emerson, Hawthorne, Thoreau, Melville, and Whitman — Matthiessen probably did more than anyone else to legitimate American literature as an academic field.

Crucial to that effort was the link between American nature and what Matthiessen argued was the organicism of nineteenth-century American literature. In the essay below, excerpted from *American Renaissance*, he analyzes the work of Emerson and Thoreau. He is concerned not so much with the verisimilitude of their representations of wild nature as with how their handling of it produces the sort of structural unity valued by the New Criticism. He admits that both writers tend to idealize nature, so that their treatment of landscape lacks the concreteness and immediacy that will later be found in D. H. Lawrence and Ernest Hemingway. Thus neither Emerson nor Thoreau was truly "wild"; for Emerson "the realm of nature remained strictly subordinate to the ideal," while Matthiessen notes wryly of Thoreau that "his more characteristic mood is that of the Sunday morning worshipper of Pan," so that few readers today sense in his work "more than a whiff of wildness." Nonetheless their work is "natural" in the Coleridgean sense that it synthesizes natural object and intellectual ideal into an "appropriate form"; it is *organic* in a uniquely American way that helps to justify Matthiessen's use of the phrase "American Renaissance."

ॐ ॐ ॐ

"Concord woods were more to me than my library, or Emerson even.
They were more to him than they were to me, and still more to Thoreau than
either of us. Take the forest and skies from their pages, and they, E. and T.,
have faded and fallen clean out of their pictures."
—Alcott's *Journal* (1851)

One reason why both Emerson and Thoreau thought instinctively of art as "a natural fruit," was that they had chosen visible nature for so much of their subject matter. To be sure, they both insisted that their interest in this was subordinate to their concern with man. Nevertheless, what drew man out in Concord, what constituted a major resource unknown to cities, was the beauty of his surroundings. One way, therefore, of distinguishing between Emerson's and Thoreau's handling of the organic style is by appraising the differing qualities of their landscapes.[1]

William James, who also loved New England landscapes, singled out as among Emerson's best things the opening of his second essay on "Nature": "There are days which occur in this climate, at almost any season of the year, wherein the world reaches its perfection." These halcyons may be looked for with most assurance in that pure October weather called Indian summer, for then "the day, immeasurably long, sleeps over the broad hills and warm wide fields," then "everything that has life gives signs of satisfaction, and the cattle that lie on the ground seem to have great and tranquil thoughts." This buoyant tone bears out the fact that if "the two most obvious characteristics of Nature are loveliness and power," as Whitehead has suggested, the former was all that Emerson generally saw. This is curious, in view of his environment, for even though he was not hemmed in by the savage energies of the jungle, "red in tooth and claw," nevertheless two centuries of New England had provided enough lessons of the hardihood essential to wrest a living from the bare recalcitrant elements. However, by Emerson's time the struggle had relaxed in the self-subsisting villages that "whitened the land." His own assurance could lead him into such blind generalizations as this in "Prudence," which Melville marked: "The terrors of the storm are chiefly confined to the parlor and the cabin. The drover, the sailor, buffets it all day, and his health renews itself at as vigorous a pulse under the sleet, as under the sun of June." "To one who has weathered Cape Horn as a common sailor," said Melville, "what stuff all this is." His experience had taught him that primitive brutality was not gone out of the world — not out of nature, and not out of man, as he knew man in America: a conviction that actuated his bitter attack on transcendentalism in *Pierre*.

That Emerson was not wholly negligent of nature's power can be seen in his early (1838) detailed analysis of the task confronting any American who would record her. Notwithstanding his joy in the English poets, he felt that they had conversed with the mere surface and show, that whenever he went into the forest he would find all as new and undescribed as "the honking of the wild geese flying by night." Debating, three years later, whether he ought not call his first collection *Forest Essays*, he seized upon what was still the significant feature of the American landscape. For Harriet Martineau had recently reported that in her travels throughout the country she was never out of sight of the woods except when on the prairies of Illinois. Emerson had tried to describe his mixed sensation at seeing the day break in Concord — of pain at feeling himself in "an alien world," a world not yet subdued by thought, and of exultation as his soul broke down its narrow walls and ranged out to the very horizon. He came to the source of his sensation when he wrote:

> The noonday darkness of the American forest, the deep, echoing, aboriginal woods, where the living columns of the oak and fir tower up from the ruins of the trees of the last millennium; where, from year to year, the eagle and the crow see no intruder; the pines, bearded with savage moss, yet touched with grace by the violets at their feet . . . where the traveller, amid the repulsive plants that are native in the swamp, thinks with pleasing terror of the distant

town; this beauty, — haggard and desert beauty, which the sun and the moon, the snow and the rain, repaint and vary, has never been recorded by art . . .

In view of this desire to catch nature's very features, we are surprised at Emerson's early hostility towards Wordsworth. At his first discussion of him (1826), Emerson was bothered by his "being too much a *poet*," and could not read his "mystic and unmeaning verses without feeling that if he had cultivated poetry less, and learning and society more, he would have gained more favor at the hands of the Muses" — an objection that you could readily imagine to have been written against the later Emerson by a survivor from the eighteenth century. Two years later he was still put off by Wordsworth's "trying to distil the essence of poetry from poetic things . . . He mauls the moon and the waters and the bulrushes, as his main business." He had a low opinion of *The Excursion* since it was wanting in fact, in coarse and tangible details, and was merely "metaphysical and evanescent." Such strictures are the sharpest reminder of how much inherited rationalism Emerson had to throw away before he could begin to feel (1831) that Wordsworth had written lines "that are like outward nature, so fresh, so simple, so durable," or could come to his final recognition (1840) that, in spite of the poet's many glaring lapses in talent, his genius was "the exceptional fact of the period," since he had done "as much as any living man to restore sanity to cultivated society."

Even then he would still have felt that no Englishman could speak to him adequately of the different nature he knew, not trim hedgerows but a great sloven continent, "nature sleeping, overgrowing, almost conscious, too much by half for man in the picture, and so giving a certain *tristesse*, like the rank vegetation of swamps and forests seen at night" — for such remained one of his dominant images. But its sadness was only infrequently uppermost. In some lines that he wrote soon after his arrival in Naples (1833), he said that

> Not many men see beauty in the fogs
> Of close, low pinewoods in a river town.

But for him, as he looked back across the ocean, there was no happier vision than that of a morning walk by a moist roadside where

> Peep the blue violets out of the black loam.

Ten years earlier the stiff abstractness of his poem, "Good-bye, proud world! I'm going home," had been relieved by the details that drew him to the country—the blackbird, the pines and the evening star. He liked to call himself "the bantling of a country Muse," and when he came to write "Self-Reliance" he was still certain that "My book should smell of pines and resound with the hum of insects." The year before writing *Nature* he had played with the idea of composing a book of the seasons, which "should contain the natural history of the woods around my shifting camp for every month in the year"—a partial description of what was fulfilled by *Walden*. In 1837, only a few months before the first mention in his journal of Thoreau, he said that "the American artist who would carve a wood-god, and who was familiar with the forest in Maine where . . . huge mosses depending from the trees and the mass of timber give a savage and haggard [again those adjectives] strength to the grove, would produce a very different statue from the sculptor who only knew a European woodland—the tasteful Greek, for example."

Yet when Emerson came to carve his own, even Alcott had to say that his Nature, "caught, it is true, from our own woods," was "never American, nor New English, which were better, but some fancied realm, some Atlantides of this Columbia, very clearly discernible to him but not by us." As Alcott conceived it, Emerson "was forbidden pure companionship with Nature" because "he dwelt rather in an intellectual grove." Emerson himself declared (1849) that the characteristic of the Greek age was that "men deified Nature"; of the Christian, that Nature was looked upon as evil and that the soul craved a heaven above it; of the modern age, that men have returned again to Nature, "but now the tendency is to marry mind to Nature, and to put Nature under the mind." The conclusion of scholarship, in J. W. Beach's *The Concept of Nature in Nineteenth-Century English Poetry* (1936), reinforces Alcott's perception by finding that "Emerson almost invariably views nature all too blandly through the eyes of the 'mind' . . . Almost never does it occur to him that the mind may have something to learn from nature, from the world which it finds given to it from without." Emerson phrased the relationship in two lines in "Woodnotes":

> So waved the pine-tree through my thought
> And fanned the dreams it never brought.

The nature to which he gave utterance is far more etherealized than Wordsworth's since it has so little of the freshening that was produced by Wordsworth's delicate but full trust in the knowledge that came from his senses.

Emerson approached nearest to such trust when he confessed that, although the realm of nature remained strictly subordinate to the ideal, he had no hostility towards it, but rather a child's love for its "gypsy attraction." In such moments of shy fondness he achieved the lyric grace of his "Gardener," who,

> True Brahmin, in the morning meadows wet,
> Expound[s] the Vedas of the violet.

The single blossom against the soil is again the apt symbol for his kind of beauty, as were the petals of the rhodora in the black waters of the pool. From these fragile details his eye always moved off to the horizon, since he believed that in its distant line "man beholds somewhat as beautiful as his own nature."

It is no wonder then that many of his landscapes were composed not out of tangible materials but from the evanescent light of reflections. He liked to recount his excursions with Henry, how "with one stroke of the paddle I leave the village politics and personalities, yes, and the world of villages and personalities, behind, and pass into a delicate realm of sunset and moonlight, too bright almost for spotted man to enter without novitiate and probation. We penetrate bodily this incredible beauty; we dip our hands in this painted element; our eyes are bathed in these lights and forms." Or, again, with Ellery: "My eye rested on the charming play of light on the water which he was striking with his paddle. I fancied I had never seen such color, such transparency, such eddies; it was the hue of Rhine wines, it was jasper and verd-antique, topaz and chalcedony, it was gold and green and chestnut and hazel in bewitching succession . . ." [2]

When Thoreau came to describe the course of his boat on the river, the impression is quite different, as a passage near the outset of the *Week*, a sample of his level style, can show:

> Late in the afternoon we passed a man on the shore fishing with a long birch pole, its silvery bark left on, and a dog at his side, rowing so near as to agitate his cork with our oars, and drive away luck for a season; and when we had rowed a mile as straight as an arrow, with our faces turned towards him, and the bubbles in our wake still visible on the tranquil surface, there stood the fisher still with his dog, like statues under the other side of the heavens, the only objects to relieve the eye in the extended meadow; and there would he stand abiding his luck, till he took his way home through the fields at evening with his fish. Thus, by one bait or another, Nature allures inhabitants into all her recesses.

Unlike Emerson's series of ejaculations, the aim of Thoreau's passage is not just to suggest the diffused radiance that stimulated him, but to present by minute notations the record of a whole scene. Although the perceived details are the slightest—the silvery bark on the pole, the bubbles on the tranquil surface—their exactness carries you down that particular unswerving mile, and gives you the illusion of sharing in the lapse of space and time during which the fisherman was still standing still on the bank with his dog. The quality of Thoreau's landscapes depends on his belief that "man identifies himself with earth or the material." Yet he also remained clear that "we are not wholly involved in Nature," and, in the awareness of his partial detachment, felt that he associated with it as a soul with its body. Although he often contrasted nature's innocence and serenity with perturbable man, in *The Maine Woods*, at least, he declared that "we have not seen pure Nature, unless we have seen her thus vast and drear and inhuman, though in the midst of cities. Nature was here something savage and awful, though beautiful." It was "Matter, vast, terrific," not man's familiar Mother Earth but the realm "of Necessity and Fate."

Here Thoreau was most akin to the tradition of the pioneer settlers, who had regarded the lonely wilderness with awe that could mount to terror. But it was not in his temperament to dwell on the diabolic power of the unsubdued dark wastes; his more characteristic mood is that of the Sunday morning worshipper of Pan. He repeatedly asserted that "in literature it is only the wild that attracts us." On that ground he felt that the English poets had "not seen the west side of any mountain," that they had missed the sterner primeval aspects, that Wordsworth was "too tame for the Chippeway." And despite his pleasure in Gilpin's *Forest Scenery*, Thoreau decided that the limitations of its mild picturesqueness came from looking too much at nature with the eye of the artist instead of in the more normal way of the hunter or woodchopper. In saying, "as Cowley loved a garden, so I a forest," he implied just the relation that he wanted and that he developed in *Walden*: "I found in myself, and still find, an instinct toward a higher, or, as it is named, spiritual life, as do most men, and another toward a primitive rank and savage one, and I reverence them both." He could describe this second instinct with a dash of humor when he said he might learn some wisdom from the woodchuck, since "his ancestors have lived here longer than mine"; or when he delivered the jeremiad of the huckleberry picker over the fact that "the wild fruits of the earth" disappear before the encroachments of civilization; or when he veered for a moment into thinking of Concord as an effete and emasculated region with its nobler animals exterminated, and thanked God for New Hampshire "everlasting and unfallen." He spoke from his heart when he said that he had no greater satisfaction in America than when he reflected that what William Bradford saw he still could see, since "aboriginal Nature" had not changed one iota. And one night at Chesuncook, listening to his guide talk to the other Indians, he felt that he had come as near to primitive man as any of the discoverers ever did.

He left at his death eleven manuscript notebooks, running to over half a million words, in which he had recorded what he had learned of the Indians, their customs and lore, and their enduring struggle with the elements. He believed it the duty of the poet to report the residual effects that this race had made on the life of his own white generation. He felt an untold debt to the example of their discipline as he trained himself to comparable alertness of eye and ear. When Emerson said that his friend had "turned a face of bronze to expectations," he symbolized the fact that the stoic strain in his behavior was owing far more to his veneration of the red man than to any study of Zeno. Certainly the lessons he had learned from them contributed to the firm reality that distinguishes his portrayal of nature. And they had helped him discover that beneath the bright surfaces of the civilized mind, "the savage in man is never quite eradicated."[3]

In contrasting Thoreau with Emerson, Alcott felt that the former revealed secrets of nature "older than fields and gardens," that "he seems alone, of all the men I have known, to be a native New Englander." Yet he could not help regretting at times that Thoreau was so earthbound, and wished that he might come out of the woods to the orchards, and so be pastoral instead of wild. It is doubtful whether most readers now sense in Thoreau more than a whiff of wildness. He wanted to bring into his writing "muck from the meadows"; but what he really managed to bring finds an apter image in the delicate fragrance of the ferns or perhaps the ranker odor of the pines. His instinct towards the higher life was so inordinately encouraged by his contemporaries that it was only by the sturdiest action that he held fast to the soil. He described his most fertile process while saying why he went to the woods: "Let us settle ourselves, and work and wedge our feet downward through the mud and slush of opinion, and prejudice, and tradition, and delusion, and appearance, that alluvion which covers the globe, through Paris and London, through New York and Boston and Concord, through Church and State, through poetry and philosophy and religion, till we come to a hard bottom and rocks in place, which we can call *reality*, and say, This is, and no mistake."

This positive dredging beat reminds us again of his awareness of the physical basis of rhythm. It can remind us also of what Lawrence felt, that "the promised land, if it be anywhere, lies away beneath our feet. No more prancing upwards. No more uplift." Lawrence's discovery was quickened by watching and almost identifying himself with the downward thrust into the earth of the feet of Indian dancers. But Thoreau's knowledge was owing less directly to the Indians than to his re-creation for himself of the conditions of primitive life. He approximated Lawrence's words when he said that in good writing, "the poem is drawn out from under the feet of the poet, his whole weight has rested on this ground." Emerson, by contrast, wanted to "walk upon the ground, but not to sink." What Thoreau's language gained from his closer contact can be read in his evocation of a river walk, where every phrase is expressive of acute sensation: "Now your feet expand on a smooth sandy bottom, now contract timidly on pebbles, now slump in genial fatty mud, amid the pads."

But as you think again of the prolonged sensuous and rhythmical experience that Lawrence was able to make out of his response to the New Mexican corn dance, or of Hemingway's account of fishing on Big Two-Hearted River, you realize that Thoreau's product was ordinarily somewhat less full-bodied. When he said, "Heaven is under our feet as well as over our heads," he was speaking of the luminous clarity of the pond. A characteristic example to put beside Emerson's "Snow-Storm" is the poem "Smoke":

> Light-winged Smoke, Icarian bird,
> Melting thy pinions in thy upward flight,
> Lark without song, and messenger of dawn,
> Circling above the hamlets as thy nest;
> Or else, departing dream, and shadowy form
> Of midnight vision, gathering up thy skirts;
> By night star-veiling, and by day
> Darkening the light and blotting out the sun;
> Go thou my incense upward from this hearth,
> And ask the gods to pardon this clear flame.

The delicacy of the wraith-like movement finds its articulation in the succession of predominantly high-pitched vowels in the opening two lines. The

"Icarian bird," a neat image for the melting away of the smoke in the bright morning sky, may then lead into too many fanciful conceits, but any tendency to vagueness is checked by the accurate epithet, "star-veiling." With that the contrast between the "shadowy form" and the rays of light, latent from the start, flowers exquisitely and prepares the way for the final statement, which makes the poem no mere descriptive exercise but Thoreau's declaration of his ever fresh renewal of purpose with the kindling of his fire in the morning. The "clear flame" of his spirit is so distinct and firm that it needs his plea for pardon to keep him from verging on *hubris* as he confidently contrasts his life with a world which is obscure and desperate in its confusion. That full contrast, to be sure, emerges only through the poem's context in *Walden*, but enough of the human situation is implied in the verses themselves to let them serve as a rounded, if minute, instance of Coleridge's distinction between imitation and mere copying. Coleridge held that the artist must not try to make a surface reproduction of nature's details, but "must imitate that which is within the thing . . . for so only can he hope to produce any work truly natural in the object and truly human in the effect." That combination has been created in this poem, since the reader's pleasure does not spring from the specific recordings, however accurate, but from the imperceptible interfusion with these of the author's own knowledge and feeling, and of his skill in evolving an appropriate form.

NOTES

1. Both Emerson and Thoreau were treated in great detail by Norman Foerster, *Nature in American Literature* (1923).

2. It seems worth notice in passing that Hawthorne also described such an excursion with Channing. Although his language is more stiffly Latinate and unable to register Emerson's vibrancy, he arrives at a conception of beauty to which Emerson could have subscribed: "The river sleeps along its course and dreams of the sky and of the clustering foliage, amid which fall showers of broken sunlight, imparting specks of vivid cheerfulness, in contrast with the quiet depth of the prevailing tint. Of all this scene, the slumbering river has a dream picture in its bosom. Which, after all, was the most real—the picture, or the original?—the objects palpable to our grosser senses, or their apotheosis in the stream beneath? Surely the disembodied images stand in closer relation to the soul." Notwithstanding such a transcendent flight, Hawthorne proceeds to a conclusion very different from the thoughts of liberation that Emerson rejoiced in: "And yet how sweet, as we floated homeward adown the golden river at sunset,—how sweet was it to return within

the system of human society, not as to a dungeon and a chain, but as to a stately edifice, whence we could go forth at will into statelier simplicity!" As he saw the Old Manse from the river, he thought "how gently did its gray homely aspect rebuke the speculative extravagances of the day! It had grown sacred in connection with the artificial life against which we inveighed; it had been a home for many years in spite of all." And reflecting that it was his home too, he "prayed that the upper influences might long protect the institutions that had grown out of the heart of mankind."

3. Although repelled by transcendentalism and by what he considered Thoreau's eccentricities, Parkman made a kindred response to the forest as the great feature of the American landscape. He said that at sixteen he had become "enamored of the woods." "Before the end of the sophomore year my various schemes had crystallized into a plan of writing the story of what was then known as the "Old French War," that is, the war that ended in the conquest of Canada, for here, as it seemed to me, the forest drama was more stirring and the forest stage more thronged with appropriate actors than in any other passage of our history. It was not until many years later that I enlarged the plan to include the whole course of the American conflict between France and England, or, in other words, the history of the American forest; for this was the light in which I regarded it. My theme fascinated me, and I was haunted with wilderness images day and night." Out of his lifelong devotion to that theme sprang the most imaginative work of history that we have yet had in America.

D. S. Savage on
Nature and Immediacy in Poetry
(1942)

Derek Stanley Savage, pacifist and environmentalist, poet, playwright, and critic, was born in 1917 in Harlow, England. His many books include several collections of poetry and three critical works: *The Personal Principle* (1944), *The Withered Branch* (1950), and *Hamlet and the Pirates* (1950). In the essay below, which appeared in 1942 in *Poetry: A Magazine of Verse*, he relates T. S. Eliot's concept of the "dissociation of sensibility" to contemporary environmental degradation. Medieval Christianity, Savage argues, can be seen "as a struggle for the liberation of the human image from submergence in the inner life of nature." In the process of this struggle, "the human consciousness was forced to objectify nature," with the result that natural objects lost "their original sensuous density and vitality." Language itself, he suggests further, is not completely abstract but rather an outgrowth "of the corporate organism, the body-mind," a phenomenon that ultimately "bears the impression of the sensitive and muscular hands which thumbed it manually into shape and correspondence with an environment of earth, mud, straw, and stone, rain and wind, the blood of men and beasts." Literary history since the time of Shakespeare is thus to be understood as a gradual impoverishment, "intimately connected with man's alienation from his natural sources." The situation is not hopeless, however. Among the many more practical benefits of environmentalism — of the English-speaking world's belated reaction to its denaturalized environment — Savage hopes for the "discovery of a new earthiness and sane natural dignity" that can reinvigorate poetry.

One way, and not the least suggestive, of looking at the development of modern history is to regard it from the aspect of man's changing relationship with the natural world. Modern history begins with the Renaissance, a period of an unparalleled accession of individuality and individual creativeness, leaving its mark upon Elizabethan England in the amazing outburst of poetry of which the drama of Shakespeare is the purest flower. But the Renaissance had its roots in the Middle Ages. Nicolas Berdyaev, in *The Meaning of History*, has some illuminating remarks to make upon the subject of medieval Christian asceticism, which he sees as a struggle for the liberation of the human image from submergence in the inner life of nature. In its struggle for liberation from its elemental bonds, the human consciousness was forced to objectify nature and thus to prepare the way for its eventual mechanization. Modern history is a record of this process of separation and mechanization, with all its concomitants, a process which has left an unmistakable impression upon culture. It does, however, appear that for a brief time before the rise of Baconian science there was a period in which conditions conspired to make possible a free play of creative power within the human personality which had discovered itself as superior to, without as yet being positively estranged from, its natural elements. But from sixteenth century humanism, through seventeenth century puritan individualism and eighteenth century rationalism, the process of estrangement is at work.

This process manifests itself collectively in man's increasing control over the secrets of the organic world and the increasing de-naturalization of the individual's environment. Thus, while Elizabethan civilization is still rudimentary and personal, succeeding centuries see a progressive subordination of nature to the world of man, of countryside to the city, of particularity to standardization, until in our own time the structure of civilization has virtually severed itself from its organic foundations.

A parallel indication of man's alienation from natural sources is given in his attitude towards the natural element in his own composition. From the sixteenth century to the twentieth there has in fact been a peculiar accentuation of puritanism and sexual prudery. We are accustomed to contrast the lewdness of Restoration Comedy with the straight-laced Victorian attitude towards sexual matters, but are inclined to overlook that it is distinguishable in its turn from the open, gusty coarseness we find in Elizabethan drama—which was later to call into operation the surgical pen of Bowdler—by a certain titillating depravity which depends for its very effectiveness upon the violation of semi-puritan standards which it entails.

Graphs could be drawn from various points to illustrate the effects upon society and culture of this progressive estrangement, and whether traced through philosophy, science, painting, drama or the novel they would follow a similar curve. Here I want to relate the process to the history of poetry, and for this purpose my thesis is the following: that since Shakespeare the history of English poetry is one of a gradual impoverishment of the medium of verse, and that this impoverishment is intimately connected with man's alienation from his natural sources.

To assert that there has been such an impoverishment of the medium of verse is not at all the same thing, of course, as to say that every individual poet since the time of Shakespeare has written a little worse than his predecessors. Certain results have been achieved within the impoverished, or refined, medium which we might never have seen had both the human poetic consciousness and the idiom of verse retained their original sensuous density and vitality. What has in fact occurred is that each succeeding poet has been forced involuntarily and unconsciously into a position where complete poetic creativeness becomes increasingly circumscribed—where the possibility of bringing into play the forces of his entire being becomes increasingly more difficult, both by virtue of the pressure exerted upon the poet as a craftsman through the limitations of the idiom which he receives from his predecessors and contemporaries, and the commensurate influence which his total situation exerts directly upon the formation of his personality. So that while Tennyson and Swinburne have to work within a more abstract and attenuated poetic idiom than Milton or Donne, it is obvious that they themselves perpetuate and help to formulate the idiom from the necessities of their human situation, and that the commerce between man and medium is reciprocal.

Granted then that this attenuation of the idiom of poetry is a fact, it is interesting to trace out its lineage and its roots in the cultural situation, although nothing more than the briefest consideration of the matter is possible here. We have glanced at the situation of the Elizabethan poet, a situation which permitted in poetry that combination of physical immediacy with a high degree of cerebral articulation which causes Mr. Eliot to describe the directly following period of the Metaphysical poets as one in which the intellect was "immediately at the tips of the senses." Certainly, behind the word-structures of Marlowe, Shakespeare, Webster, Donne, one feels the active presence, not only of a brain, but of a physique. To this quality of *immediacy* in poetry I shall return. But with time, as perception became increasingly intellectualized and abstract, idiom and diction were canalized and passed through a filter which eliminated what seemed gross and impure into a stream of increasing limpidity. The "elevation" of poetic diction which Milton instigated reached its apotheosis in the flowery poetic jargon current among second-rate versifiers towards the close of the eighteenth century.

With Marvell, following the Metaphysical poets with their sensuous fusion of conceit and imagery, begins the subordination of the sensuous element in poetry to the play of wit. There is nothing turbulent in Marvell, who deploys a neat, clever line in which passion is well controlled by intellect. In his poetry, exquisite as it is, there is a planing-down of surface, a diminution of physical impact by the tendency to smooth the cragginess of individual words over into neatly scissored phrases. In Marvell, too, the natural world is appropriately enough an Arcadia of hayfields and neatly planned gardens:

> See how the archëd earth does here
> Rise in a perfect hemisphere!
> The stiffest compass could not strike
> A line more circular and like,
> Nor softest pencil draw a brow
> So equal as this hill does bow;
> It seems as for a model laid,
> And that the world by it was made.

The fact that English verse-satire virtually began with Marvell (for the practice of satire predicates a conventionalized, urban, polite society) points out his affinities with the later age of Dryden, Pope and Swift, who also subjugated the more rugged elements of verse to the play of wit, smoothing down the surface texture of the verse to the admired, "correct" polish. It is instructive to compare Donne's *Satyres* in their original form with the versions made by Pope. Donne's idiosyncrasy is an organic quality, Pope's regularity is both abstract and mechanical. Thus Donne writes (in *Satyre II*):

> But hee is worst, who (beggarly) doth chaw
> Other wits fruits, and in his ravenous maw
> Rankly digested, doth those things out-spue,

> As his own things; and they are his owne, 'tis true,
> For if one eate my meate, though it be knowne
> The meate was mine, th' excrement is his owne.

But when Pope "versifies" it (with breathtaking aplomb), it is smoothed down to this:

> Wretched indeed! But far more wretched yet
> Is he who makes his meal on others' wit:
> 'Tis changed, no doubt, from what it was before;
> His rank digestion makes it wit no more:
> Sense, pass'd through him, no longer is the same;
> For food digested takes another name.

Pope's version reveals how too squeamish a refinement results in a sensuous impoverishment of the actual verse-texture. In Donne, the words seem to have been chewed over physically. In Pope, the verse has been refined of its physical grossness in its passage through the versifier's more civilized mentality, and concreteness of epithet is readily sacrificed for a conceit and an epigram.

But this brings us to an important point. Superficially, we can consider the evolution of the relationship between human consciousness and the world of nature as it affects poetry in two ways — the measure in which such relationship determines the subject-matter of verse and the way in which it affects its form and texture. Actually it is not much easier to separate the two aspects than it is to disentangle the two interfused elements within the poem itself.

Poetry is made with words. But what are words? Certainly they are more than abstract ciphers, an algebra of analytical communication. Words are very mysterious entities which seem to have an organic connection with the human psyche. The English language was not constructed theoretically by a corpus of learned grammarians, hallmarked and passed out for public circulation by a royal proclamation. It was brought elementally to labored birth out of man's profound need for articulation and communion — a dual communion, both between man and man and (to simplify the rather complex psychical exchange) between man and the external world. It seems to be a primary need of the human psyche to find through language a series of mind-gestures which exactly and satisfactorily correspond to the disequilibrium caused through the impact of the "objective" world upon the subjective consciousness, and which, at need, will actually evoke it. This is not strictly a mental, cerebral relationship, but rather one of the corporate organism, the body-mind. Language perpetually passes through the slow mill of the common mind. At its roots our tongue bears the impression of the sensitive and muscular hands which thumbed it manually into shape and correspondence with an environment of earth, mud, straw and stone, rain and wind, the blood of men and beasts. This sense of physical immediacy is the most notable thing in very early English verse, and it is found too in Chaucer and Skelton. It is essentially a folk-quality, born of the common experience of feudal humanity, at one with the particular, idiosyncratic environment of the natural world.

A poem, somebody has said, is a complex word. Similarly, a word is an elementary poem. And if we separate the apparent constituents of aesthetic experience, we shall find that its physical quality, what I have called the quality of *immediacy*, is one of its most important elements. As A. E. Housman pointed out in his well-known lecture, the completely satisfying poem affects us with a palpable physical impact, although it may modify our awareness in other ways as well. It is this physical, or physiological, quality which is so characteristic a feature of Elizabethan poetry. With the Metaphysical poets it becomes somewhat cerebrized, and later still the cerebral element comes to predominate over the physiological, although, it is hardly necessary to say, this latter element can never be eliminated completely, and even in the age when trousers were referred to as "unmentionables," there was actually a man, etc., beneath the trousers.

It may appear somewhat fanciful to associate the gradual refinement and abstraction of the medium of verse with man's altering relationship to nature. But nature, which provides us with the material basis of our being, in which to some extent we are incorporated, is precisely the realm of the tangible, the concrete and the particular, and the further we move both in our individual consciousness and in the extension of our civilization from this concrete source, the more simplified and abstract becomes our mode of perception, and the more mechanical. The human product of a perfectly de-naturalized environment, say the hypothetical result of some kind of Huxleyan parthenogenesis conditioned altogether within a laboratory civilization of electrical energy and glass tiles, would be lacking almost completely in what we call aesthetic apprehension, because the features necessary for the education of the senses would be absent. By opposition, the richly sentient culture of certain primitive tribes has a real connection with their intimate responsiveness to natural rhythms and their participation within "the inner life of nature."

As it happens, a study of the history of poetry in England shows us clearly that when consciousness was showing signs of too prolonged and exhausting an intellectualization, individual poets have felt a strong inward urge towards a reinvigoration of both medium and consciousness through a communion with the organic world. Is it not significant that Wordsworth, in endeavoring to break through the sterile conventions of an outworn mode — to accomplish a specifically poetic revolution — should have found it necessary in so doing deliberately to seek nourishment and inspiration for his purpose in a personal communion with nature? Indeed, the whole movement of Romanticism was bound up with a new organic conception of nature, but the Romantic impulse, vigorous at its source, petered out into a sometimes hysterical flamboyance because it failed to connect with and influence society at large, remaining a literary peculiarity. Even Keats's new-found richness — or, compared with the Elizabethans, lushness — of vocabulary sprang from a vital romanticism of sex. When a late Victorian poet arises with an equally luscious and passionate awareness of the organic world, allied to a keen and masculine intellect, he feels himself so alien to the poetic currents of the time that he is forced to forge for himself in isolation an entirely personal idiom and prosody, which is yet much closer to the folk-tongue than the literary idiom which he rejected. And after Hopkins, the desperate attempt of D. H. Lawrence to center himself experientially within the depths of the living cosmos, driven by the need to recover not merely an invigoration of language but primarily of being, is full of meaning both for poetry and for civilization.

Some kind of homogeneity of society is essential for a vital flourishing of art, a free interchange between the folk-consciousness in which language is born and nourished, and the more sophisticated consciousness of the educated. Now that literature has become completely unofficial, and even subversive, and there is no longer any but a vestigial folk-life, the poet is more free to penetrate into an organic relationship with reality, and perhaps to foreshadow a new wholeness of human living.

None but the exceedingly naive speak any longer with optimism of a creative synthesis of art and society within the framework of the "machine age." On the subject of the intractability of the de-naturalized modern environment as poetic material it is hardly necessary to speak here. While the poet himself is implicated in urban-industrial experience there is an evident necessity for him to bring that experience within the radius of his poetic powers, but there is no obligation upon the poet to meet industrialism halfway. That the poet is unhappy in a de-naturalized environment is abundantly illustrated by the circumlocutions of modern poets in their attempts to skirt round the tract which T. S. Eliot explored in *The Waste Land*; in Yeats's aristocratism and romanticism of swords, tapestries and towers; in Robert Graves's time-traveling which makes him write, as well as historical novels, historical poems with their imagery drawn from pre-industrial sources; in Harold Monro's *poésie des brefs départs*. And Mr. Eliot, the acknowledged poet *par excellence* of the "modern experience," illustrates himself the progress of the poetic mind through the waste land of the modern consciousness, dying of drouth and suffering from febrile hallucinations, through a deliberate medievalism into what promises to be a discovery of a new earthiness and sane natural dignity.

Joseph Wood Krutch on the
Intellectual History of Nature Writing
(1950)

Joseph Wood Krutch (pronounced "Krootch") was born in 1893 in Nashville, Tennessee. He was educated at the University of Tennessee and then Columbia, where he received his Ph.D. in 1923. After teaching at Brooklyn Polytechnic Institute, Vassar College, and the New School for Social Research, he returned finally to Columbia. He was a prolific literary critic, a nature writer, and a drama critic for the *Nation* (for which he also covered the Scopes Trial in 1925). His many critical works include a 1948 study of Thoreau; his nature books include *The Twelve Seasons* (1949), *The Desert Year* (1951), and *The Voice of the Desert* (1955). Most of his books were still in print when he died in 1970.

In the essay below, which appeared in 1950 under the title "A Kind of Pantheism," Krutch notes that by his day there had already been a good deal of criticism concerning "'the appreciation of nature' as a literary phenomenon," yet little critical attention had yet been paid to nature writing "as an emergent literary form struggling for its own independence." In order to account for the appearance of the form itself, he felt we must appeal to intellectual history, because the fundamental questions concern not just originality and individual genius but also historical conditions of possibility. Krutch demonstrates below that even such an apparently idiosyncratic nature writer as Henry David Thoreau was in fact "less fundamentally original than he himself supposed." If Thoreau *was* in some degree original, "the originality consisted in the extent to which he succeeded in giving highly personal expression to an attitude which history had made possible."

After its initial publication in the *Saturday Review of Literature*, "A Kind of Pantheism" appeared again as part of the introduction to Krutch's anthology, *Great American Nature Writing*.

☙ ☙ ☙

Stephen Leacock once remarked that our ancestors were too busy clearing forests to find the time to take exercise. In a somewhat similar sense it may be assumed that primitive man was not interested in nature. But it would also appear that he had hardly got himself urbanized before he began, in imagination at least, to return to it.

No doubt there is some truth in the oft-repeated assertions that Petrarch was the first man to climb a mountain for the view, that the dweller in the medieval city obviously preferred what we should call intolerable over-crowding, and that, as Macaulay pointed out, men do not admire wild mountains until danger ceases to press upon them in their daily life. But it is equally true that the legend of a golden age when man lived in harmony with nature seems to be almost as old as civilization itself. Moscus and Bion were already idealizing the shepherd's life. Virgil wrote about the delights of the country less like a farmer than like some city man who retires to a week-end estate. And in imperial Rome the literary cult of the simple life had reached a point where Juvenal could satirize it in the lines which Dryden magnificently translated:

> In Saturn's reign, at Nature's early birth,
> There was that thing called chastity on earth;
> When in a narrow cave, their common shade,
> The sheep, the shepherds, and their gods were laid;
> When reeds and leaves, and hides of beasts were spread
> By mountain huswives for their homely bed.
> And mossy pillow, raised, for the rude husbands' head.
> Unlike the niceness of our modern dames,
> (Affected nymphs with new affected names:)
> The Cynthias and the Lesbias of our years,
> Who, for a sparrow's death dissolve in tears.
> Those first unpolished matrons, big and bold,

Gave suck to infants of gigantic mold;
Rough as their savage lords who ranged the wood,
And fat with acorns belched their windy food.

Obviously then, much "nature writing" of today springs from impulses almost as old as Western culture. To claim for it absolute originality of either feeling or expression would be foolish. The fact remains, nevertheless, that there is a recognizable genre of belles-lettres whose remoter history seems hardly to go back beyond the end of the seventeenth century and much of that writing does define certain attitudes to some extent novel — in their emphases at least. There is in it some "feeling for nature" which is not quite that of the ancients or that of the romantics.

There is, to be sure, a vast body of scholarly writings devoted to the analysis of what is loosely called "the appreciation of nature" as a literary phenomenon. But such writing concerns itself largely with poetry and other traditional forms of belles-lettres, especially during the romantic revival. It generally pays but scant attention to "nature writing" as an emergent literary form struggling for its own independence.

Histories of English literature frequently mention *The Compleat Angler* and *The Natural History of Selborne* as somehow sufficiently novel in form and spirit to make them almost unique in their time. Similar histories of American literature generally devote considerably more space to Thoreau, in whom they recognize another uniqueness. Sometimes, indeed, they acknowledge him as the immediate begetter of the whole subsequent school. But there does not seem to have been before the present day any group of writers closely comparable to that which includes, for example, William Beebe, Gustav Eckstein, Donald Culross Peattie, Julian Huxley, and scores of others who produce a flood of widely read books neither purely scientific nor easily placeable in any of the traditional departments of belles-lettres.

What is new in them is certainly not the impulse to escape the complexities of civilization nor the desire to celebrate the soothing or inspirational effects of natural scenery. Neither is it an interest in natural history as such, for natural history was already a science in Aristotle's time. Yet there is some element of novelty. Either something new has been added, some new point of view introduced, or some new synthesis made. Thoreau was not merely following in the footsteps of Aristotle and Gilbert White any more than he was merely following in those of Wordsworth. And if it is true not only that Thoreau was the most original of the modern nature writers, but also that nearly everyone who has come after has learned something from him, then it ought to be possible to put one's finger upon some aspect of his uniqueness.

Perhaps no man before him had ever taken quite so literally the term "fellow creatures" and perhaps that is one of the most significant things about him. When he spoke of having "a little fishy friend in the pond," when he held interviews with a woodchuck or hoped that one of his games had taught the fox something, he was expressing in his own special humorous way a sense of intimacy and of fellowship to some degree novel. In so far as it was simply an outpouring of love, the banal analogy would be, of course, St. Francis. But there is an intellectual difference which is of some importance. Thoreau could feel as he did, not so much because he was tender toward inferior creatures as because he did not think of them as inferior: because he had none of that sense of superiority or even separateness which is the inevitable result of any philosophy or any religion which attributes to a man a qualitative uniqueness and therefore, inevitably, suggests that all other living things exist for him. St. Francis preached to the birds; many moderns have hoped, on the contrary, that the birds would preach to them.

Many writers later than Thoreau — some of them far more scientific than he in training and temperament — have expressed his attitude in terms less humorous as well as less emotional when they have insisted upon looking at nature from some point of view common to all of its creatures rather than from that of man's own special desires and purposes. And it may be that one distinguishing characteristic of the nature writings of our time, one common to Thoreau and the whole school, is the result of just this sense of oneness, this conviction that we are all, as it were, in the same boat.

It would be absurd, of course, to suggest that no one before Thoreau's time had ever to some extent anticipated this attitude or to some extent given expression to it. A Christian work sometimes attributed to St. Augustine supplied one volume of the austere Cambridge *Natural History* with a very appropriate motto, which may be translated thus:

> He created in heaven the angels and in the earth worms; nor was He superior in the one case or inferior in the other. If no other hands but His could create the angels, neither could any other create the worms.

And it can hardly be said that whoever wrote that sentence failed to share the conviction that the wonder of man is no greater than the wonder of all living things.

But the seed of such an idea does not find its most congenial soil in a mind which continues to insist, as the orthodox Christians did, upon at least some absolute uniqueness in man and refuses to admit that he is really continuous with the rest of nature. Even Thoreau could not have written as he did had he not been the inheritor of the whole intellectual revolution which had been in progress since the Renaissance and which was finally, just after his own time, to convince Westerners that they were the grandsons of the ape at least as truly as they were the sons of God.

Long before the romantic poets had made the appreciation of nature a touchstone of sensibility, the eighteenth-century gentleman of an older school was familiar, at least through his Pope, with the assumption that man's place is *in* nature rather than apart from it. He probably knew by heart many of the crucial passages of the "Essay on Man," in the course of which Pope hammers home in epigrammatic couplets the fundamental premise that the universe is not to be understood unless it can be seen from the point of view of the whole rather than from that of man's own particular needs or desires:

> Has God, thou fool! work'd solely for thy good,
> Thy joy, thy pastime, thy attire, thy food?
> Who for thy table feeds the wanton fawn,
> For him as kindly spreads the flowery lawn.
> Is it for thee the lark ascends and sings?
>
> Joy tunes his voice, joy elevates his wings.
> Is it for thee the linnet pours his throat?
> Loves of his own and raptures swell the note.
> The bounding steed you pompously bestride
> Shares with his lord the pleasure and the pride.
>
> Know Nature's children all divide her care;
> The fur that warms a monarch warm'd a bear.
> While Man exclaims, "See all things for my use!"
> "See man for mine!" replies a pamper'd goose:
> And just as short of Reason he must fall,
> Who thinks all made for one, not one for all.

The feeling of this passage is obviously far closer to that of a paragraph in Thoreau or William Beebe than it is to that of either the Cartesian or the pure laboratory scientist of the early eighteenth century or of any other time. Pope was, of course, merely formulating for his contemporaries something which they were ready to accept and he is quoted here only to illustrate what by his time could be felt. But how had the possibility of such an attitude come about? What had generated this conviction which is at the opposite extreme from any which Cartesianism could have produced? It has been reiterated countless times since by innumerable writers down to those of our own day, many of whom seem to be rediscovering it for themselves. Thus John Muir can devote several pages of *The Story of My Youth* to expounding what is in effect a prose version of Pope's couplets and Ezra Pound can translate the same thought into the idiom of his controversial "Pisan Cantos":

> The ant's a centaur in his dragon world.
> Pull down thy vanity, it is not man
> Made courage, or made order, or made grace,
> Pull down thy vanity, I say pull down.
> Learn of the green world what can be thy place
> In scaled invention or true artistry,
> Pull down thy vanity,
> Paquin pull down!
> The green casque has outdone your elegance.

But there was a time when the attitude really was new.

No doubt Thoreau was less fundamentally original than he himself supposed. In so far as he was original in any absolute sense the originality consisted in the extent to which he succeeded in giving highly personal expression to an attitude which history had made possible. But he is well enough known to be immediately used in raising a central question: by what series of steps had it become possible for a man to write as he wrote and to be read as sympathetically as he has been read? There is involved a question of what he knew, a question of the emotional attitudes he took towards that knowledge, and finally the question of the literary form which he employed in setting all these things forth.

In the light of these questions let us consider him first in contrast to those writers about plants and animals whom he least resembles — namely some popular authors of the Middle Ages. So far as the pure science of natural history was concerned, it had been carried little beyond the point at which Aristotle and Pliny had left it and if even they did not always successfully distinguish between fact and fable their remote followers added many fables but few facts. Nevertheless what interfered most decisively with the development of the feeling for nature as such was less the paucity of facts than the strength of certain theological notions which served to discourage certain kinds of wonder by supplying ready answers to every question concerning the why of the universe outside man. The sun was put in the heavens to give light by day and the moon to give light by night. Sun or moon may also declare the glory of God and so, for that matter, may the lamb. But the most obvious reason for the existence of them all is the meat which the last supplies for man's consumption and the light which the other two supply him to eat it by.

Both histories of science and histories of literature have frequently emphasized the resulting fact that most medieval writing about nature seems to us remote and merely quaint. This is less because of how little, comparatively speaking, its authors knew than because of their attitude toward the nature of evidence on the one hand and toward the purpose of knowledge on the other. The more learned among them might revere Aristotle and later learn something from the Orient. But what at least the general public found most to its taste was contained in the various versions of *Physiologus*, the popular compilations of unnatural history drawn from an accumulated stock of misinformation but offering both an abundance of wonders and an almost inexhaustible store of morals to be drawn from them. Such writings seem to us absurd not primarily because their compilers knew so much that was not true and so little that was but because the whole tendency of their thinking was homocentric and teleological.

They never for a moment doubted that the right question to ask was the question "what practical use or what moral instruction did God intend to provide for me when He created this creature or that?" And they were so sure of the rightness of the question that once they had heard a satisfactory answer they seldom doubted its correctness or felt the impulse to investigate it. If few ever troubled to see whether or not the toad, "ugly and venomous, bears yet a precious jewel in his head" that was simply because it seemed to them so inherently probable that he did. What reason other than the desire to teach man a useful lesson could God possibly have had for cluttering his beautiful earth with creatures so repulsive?

Here is a bit about the whale, translated from an Anglo-Saxon version of

Physiologus and therefore one of the very first writings in English about natural history:

> His appearance is like that of a rough boulder so that seamen imagine they are going upon an island, and moor their high-prowed ship with cables to that false land, make fast the ocean courses at the seas' end and boldly climb up on that island; the vessels stand by the beach, enringed by the flood. The wear-hearted sailors then encamp, dreading not of peril. . . . On the island they start a fire, kindle a mounting flame. Now when the cunning plotter feels that the seamen are firmly established upon him, and have settled down to enjoy the weather, the great ocean beast sinks without warning. . . .
>
> Such is the way of demons, the worst of devils; they spend their lives outwitting men by their secret power.

Those who read with delight this tale of a whale were obviously not deficient in that sense of wonder which has sometimes been cited as one of the distinguishing characteristics of Thoreau as well as of many subsequent writers. In that respect they were perhaps closer than some later anatomists and taxonomists to the spirit of Thoreau as well as to that of a Julian Huxley or Gustav Eckstein. But they obviously had neither a sense of fact nor, above all, a sense of the wonder of fact, no suspicion that the study of nature might do more than supply confirmation and illustration. The whale is important because he illustrates the ways of demons. The natural world could teach nothing radically new. It was merely a collection of metaphors and fables ingeniously repeating in figurative language the truths already known from authority. On occasion, to be sure, it might propound riddles to tempt the ingenuity of man, as in the case of the toad and his jewel. But the answer, when found, would always be one consonant with what was already known. Nothing really new would ever be discovered. The meaning of the universe, the proper place of man in it, was already known, completely and finally.

This does not mean that the medieval writer had lost the power of observation. It means at most that he had relatively little respect for it, that it seemed to him a crude instrument, and that when he used it he was at best indulging in a mere whim. Consider, for example, the case of Bartholomew Anglecanus, the monk whose encyclopedia *De Proprieteribus Rerum* was compiled in the thirteenth century and translated into wonderful English in the fourteenth. In its own time it was held in the highest respect and today it is regarded as a monument of medieval literature. A great many of its entries are devoted to animals, real or fabulous, concerning which, for the most part, the author recounts what he has read of them in other equally ill-informed books. It tells us, for example, about the crocodile who weeps after he has killed a man and about the elephant who is captured by cutting down the tree against which he has leaned to sleep. But the modern reader who turns his pages may have the good luck to fall upon a few items, one, for instance, on the dog and another on the cat, which leap up from the page because they are so obviously the product of original observation and because the author's real delight in what he has seen for himself still shines through:

> Of the Cat: He is a full lecherous beast in youth, swift, pliant, and merry, and leapeth and rusheth on everything that is to fore him: and is led by a straw, and playeth therewith: and is a right heavy beast in age and full sleepy, and lieth slyly in wait for mice: and is aware where they be more by smell than by sight, and hunteth and rusheth on them in privy places: and when he taketh a mouse, he playeth therewith, and eateth him after the play. In time of love is hard fighting for wives, and one scratcheth and rendeth the other grievously with biting and with claws. And he maketh a ruthful noise and ghastful when one proffereth to fight with another: and unneth is hurt when he is thrown down off an high place. And when he hath a fair skin, he is as it were proud thereof, and goeth fast about: and when his skin is burnt, then he bideth at home, and is oft for his fair skin taken of the skinner, and slain and flayed.

Obviously Bartholomew knew cats. He drew of them a generic portrait which in some respects suggests the famous animal portraits of Buffon and in some respects is superior to them. But it is not only knowledge which shines through his lines. Wonder may be largely absent for Bartholomew had, perhaps, no sense that a cat is as wonderful as the dragon — to which he devoted a fuller account — would be if the dragon had ever existed. He is, nevertheless, capable of feeling and capable of communicating an emotion in which Buffon was notably deficient but which every good modern writer about nature must to some extent exhibit — namely, love.

Bartholomew may or may not have "liked cats" in the vulgar meaning of that phrase. He may or he may not have kept pets or fed the birds. But in one of the truest senses of the word he must have loved the cat, since only love could so sharpen the observation, so wing the words which he chose in order to recreate the cat's whole being. For once he was describing something whose most important meaning was itself, which existed and which ought to exist in its own right, which was not useful to man, either directly or as an allegory, but was quite simply its own excuse for being.

From that passage it is hardly a step to the finest of Chaucer's little pictures of barnyard life or of the cat which had to be lifted from the best chair before the monk sat down. Yet in all the *De Proprieteribus Rerum* there are only one or two other examples of anything so genuine or so telling. The man who wrote them might obviously have left an account of the sights and sounds and smells of the medieval world, the like of which nowhere exists. He might have drawn to the life both the men and the beasts among whom he lived. But no doubt he would have regarded the task as unworthy and perhaps when he permitted himself to describe the dog and the cat he did so with a certain sense of being truant. They lacked dignity; they lacked importance. The dragon and the fabulous whale were far more profitable and instructive.

Obviously Bartholomew is in some sense of the term a "nature writer." The animal kingdom is one of his principal subjects and he writes about it with an enthusiasm which suggests a general interest in that subject itself. He is not incapable of observation and not incapable of love. But observation remains a method only occasionally employed, and love an emotion perhaps hardly recognized for what it is. He differs from the modern nature writer not only because he has fewer facts at his disposal but because he seems less aware of what a fact is or why it is important. He differs also in a perhaps even more significant way because he cannot rationalize or perhaps even respect the love which went out from him toward the dog and the cat. If he had read Thomas Aquinas he was, indeed, probably ready to accept the Thomistic doctrine that although cruelty to animals is a sin it is so, not because it results in pain to the animals (which have no souls), but because it may lead to similar cruelty toward men.

Charles Darwin published *The Origin of Species* in 1859 (some three years before Thoreau's death) and then crossed his t's with *The Descent of Man* twelve years later. This was science's official recognition of the fact that man is literally a part of nature. But there is a sense in which it might be truly said that Darwin's formulation was no more than one way of stating a conviction which had been growing during the two preceding centuries. In all probability his theory would never have occurred to him at all had he not been prepared to believe as a matter of inherent probability that man is merely the most highly organized of the animals. Certainly that theory would not have been so readily accepted if the public had not been similarly prepared. Thus there is a sense in which one may say that Darwinism is the effect rather than the cause of the convictions which it states.

Darwin's grandfather Erasmus Darwin had implied everything except a theory of the mechanism of evolution when he wrote in 1796 that the snout of the pig and the trunk of the elephant had "been gradually produced during the many generations by the perpetual endeavor of the creatures to supply the want of food and have been delivered to their posterity with constant improvement of them for the purposes required." But none of the tentative approaches to a theory of evolution from that of the eccentric Lord Monboddo—who was convinced that sooner or later explorers would discover a missing link in the form of an aborigine with a tail—down through that of Darwin's most important predecessor, Lamarck, is as important as the atmosphere generated by the common-sense conviction that man is a part of nature and by the emotional willingness to accept that fact.

Shortly before Thoreau died he heard of *The Origin of Species* and expressed some mild interest in its theories though it is not clear to what extent he really understood them. The matter is, however, of little importance because Thoreau's intuitions had already convinced him of the only fact which he could use in the development of his philosophy—the fact, that is to say, that man is somehow a part of nature and that, therefore, only the emotional as well as the intellectual recognition of that fact can bring him spiritual or mental health. For him the observation of nature and the learning *from* her had become not merely a way but almost the only way of learning anything about either man or the universe in which he lives. Authority was gone; transcendental intuition was, so far as he was concerned, going. Nothing remained except the possibility of looking about him and of drawing what conclusions one could.

In so far as the "feeling for nature" has undergone any important development since Thoreau's time that development has come about through the influence of a science which was in its infancy when Thoreau came to his early death. The evolutionists had stressed the gross mechanical parallels between the human body and the animal. Since then the biochemists have investigated the fundamental stuff of those bodies and discovered in protoplasm the chemical basis for the unity of all living things. They have pushed their search into the secrets of life until they have discovered its ultimate material embodiment in the colloid jelly which is in itself the same, whether it be organized into an amoeba or a man. And that fact would, I suspect, have interested Thoreau more than the theory of evolution, partly because it makes all living things not merely related by remote descent but still essentially one. Here, if you like, is the physical manifestation of the bond which he felt between himself and all other creatures, the physical aspect of that sense of kinship which made it possible to have "little fishy friends" in Walden pond. The fellowship he felt was the fellowship defined by protoplasm itself, which is the chemical embodiment of the world soul or, if one prefers, that aspect of the Great God Pan which can be perceived in a test tube.

Much "nature writing" today reflects more or less definitely this sense of identity, material as well as spiritual, with the fellow creatures which it studies and describes. It implies if it does not state a kind of pantheism in which the symbol of the unity of all living things is not an elusive spirit but a definable material thing. Yet this definable material thing is also a symbol and being such does not necessarily imply any thoroughgoing materialistic philosophy. It implies merely that Life itself rather than something still more mysterious called the "cause of life" is the bond between fellow creatures.

Perry Miller on
Nature and American Nationalism
(1955)

Perry Miller, born in 1905 in Chicago, earned his bachelor's and doctoral degrees from the University of Chicago, then taught at Harvard until his death in 1963. He wrote extensively on early American literature and is an important early figure in the field of American Studies; his books include *The New England Mind* (1939) and *Consciousness in Concord* (1958). He is perhaps best known for analyzing the evolution of New England's early Puritan theologies and tracing their effects on later generations of writers. In the essay below, "Nature and the National Ego," Miller explores the implications of "the fact that America came to its first essay in self-analysis and self-expression in the period we call romantic," a fact that may be "only fortuitous" but nonetheless has had important consequences—among them, it might be said without too much exaggeration, the birth of modern environmentalism.

As nineteenth-century America tried to define itself, Miller argues below, it had to wrestle with two related questions. Was the nation primarily a product of a lofty Puritan spirituality, or of a decidedly more worldly Enlightenment materialism? Was America fundamentally different from Europe, as it desperately wished to believe—and if so, how? The concept of "nature" helped the New England intelligentsia to finesse its answer to these questions. True, it was argued, the nation might *appear* to be crassly materialistic, but the presence of its wilderness—which increasingly came to be associated with God—kept its citizens morally uncorrupted and distinguished it from Europe. But how, asks Miller, "could we at one and the same time establish our superiority to artificial Europe upon our proximity to Nature, and then view with complacency the rapidity of our despoiling her?" As he points out, "almost as soon as the identification of virtue

with Nature had become axiomatic, the awful suspicion dawned that America
was assiduously erecting the barriers of artificiality between its citizens and the
precious landscape. If God speaks to us in the sublimity of Nature, then was not
the flood of pioneers a devilish stratagem for drowning the voice of God?"

The ideological use of nature thus raised as many questions as it answered.
The response was an intensified romantic fetishizing of wilderness that increasingly belied the reality of the nation's urban and industrial development. "The
more rapidly, the more voraciously, the primordial forest was felled," Miller
writes, "the more desperately painters and poets — and also preachers — strove to
identify the unique personality of this republic with the virtues of pristine and
untarnished, of 'romantic,' Nature." Such an argument certainly suggests that
nineteenth-century environmentalism was less about preserving American wilderness than about safeguarding the nation's identity.

"Nature and the National Ego" was delivered as a speech at Yale University in
1953 and published in the *Harvard Theological Review* in 1955.

🪷 🪷 🪷

On May 8, 1847, *The Literary World* — the newly founded vehicle in New
York City for the program of "nativist" literature — reviewed an exhibition at
the National Academy. The magazine had just undergone an editorial revolution and the new management was endeavoring to tone down the strident
nationalism of the first few issues; still, the exuberant patriotism of the reviewer could not be restrained, for he had just beheld two exciting landscapes of Staten Island painted by J. F. Cropsey.

This artist, said the reviewer, must be ranked along with the acknowledged
masters, Thomas Cole and Asher Durand — and this was high praise in 1847.
And as do these masters, young Cropsey illustrates and vindicates the high
and sacred mission of the American painter:

> The axe of civilization is busy with our old forests, and artisan ingenuity is fast
> sweeping away the relics of our national infancy. What were once the wild and
> picturesque haunts of the Red Man, and where the wild deer roamed in free-
> dom, are becoming the abodes of commerce and the seats of manufactures.
> Our inland lakes, once sheltered and secluded in the midst of noble forests,
> are now laid bare and covered with busy craft; and even the primordial hills,

once bristling with shaggy pine and hemlock, like old Titans as they were, are being shorn of their locks, and left to blister in cold nakedness in the sun. "The aged hemlocks, through whose branches have whistled the winds of a hundred winters," are losing their identity, and made to figure in the shape of deal boards and rafters for unsightly structures on bare commons, ornamented with a few peaked poplars, pointing like fingerposts to the sky. Yankee enterprise has little sympathy with the picturesque, and it behooves our artists to rescue from its grasp the little that is left, before it is for ever too late.

Students of the history of art recognize in this passage a doctrine that had, by 1847, become conventional among landscape painters in Europe, England, and America: that of a fundamental opposition of Nature to civilization, with the assumption that all virtue, repose, dignity are on the side of "Nature"—spelled with a capital and referred to as feminine—against the ugliness, squalor, and confusion of civilization, for which the pronoun was simply "it." However, though this passage proceeds from a premise as familiar in Dusseldorf as in New York, still it takes the form of an exhortation that is seldom, if ever, encountered in the criticism of Europe. In America the artist has a calling above and beyond an accurate reporting of scenery: he must work fast, for in America Nature is going down in swift and inexorable defeat. She is being defaced, conquered—actually ravished. Civilization is leading us into a horrible future, filled with unsightly structures, resounding with the din of enterprise. All too soon we shall become like Europe. In the old world artists may indeed paint only such "garden landscapes" as are dotted here and there in a setting that man has mastered; but our noble Hudson and "the wild witchery of our unpolluted inland lakes and streams," this Nature is not man's but "GOD's." American artists return from Europe, "their hands cramped with mannerism, and their minds belittled and debauched by the artificial stimulants of second-hand and second-rate creations." This was what America must resist, debauching artificiality. Yet if history is so irresistibly carrying the defiling axe of civilization into our sublime wilderness, will it not be merely a matter of time—no matter how furiously our Coles, Durands, and Cropseys, our poets and novelists, strive to fix the fleeting moment of primitive grandeur—before we too shall be cramped into mannerism, before our minds shall be debauched by artificial stimuli?

The reader may object that I am talking nonsense. This was the expanding, prospering, booming America of the 1840's; here, if ever in the annals of

man, was an era of optimism, with a vision of limitless possibilities, with faith
in a boundless futu-e. There was indeed some fear that the strife of North
and South might wreck the chariot of progress, but the more that threat
loomed the more enthusiastically the nation shouted the prospects of wealth
and prosperity, if only in order to show the folly of allowing politics to spoil
the golden opportunity. Dickens and other foreign visitors report a republic
constantly flinging into their faces preposterous vaunts about what it would
shortly become, and then steadily making good its wildest boasts. Surely this
society was not wracked by a secret, hidden horror that its gigantic exertion
would end only in some nightmare of debauchery called "civilization"?

The most cursory survey of the period does indeed display a seemingly
untroubled assurance about the great civilization America was hewing out
of the wilderness. This faith, with its corollaries of belief in progress and
republican institutions, might be called the "official" faith of the United
States. It was primarily an inheritance from the eighteenth century: back in
1758, the almanac-maker, Nathaniel Ames, writing from Dedham, Massachusetts, dreamed that within two hundred years arts and sciences would
transform nature "in their Tour from Hence over the Appalacian Mountains
to the Western Ocean," and that vast quarries of rocks would be piled into
cities. On the whole, despite the Jeffersonians' distrust of cities, I think it fair
to say that the founders had no qualms about doing harm to nature by thrust-
ing civilization upon it. They reasoned in terms of wealth, comfort, ame-
nities, power, in terms which we may conveniently call, though they had not
been derived from Bentham, "utilitarian."

Now in 1840, in 1850, the mighty tread of American civilization was heard
throughout the Ohio Valley, across the Mississippi, and the advanced guard
was rushing into California. But the astonishing fact about this gigantic material thrust of the early nineteenth century is how few Americans would any
longer venture, aside from their boasts, to explain, let alone to justify, the
expansion of civilization in any language that could remotely be called that
of utility. The most utilitarian conquest known to history had somehow to
be viewed not as inspired by a calculus of rising land values and investments
but (despite the orgies of speculation) as an immense exertion of the spirit.
Those who made articulate the meaning of this drama found their frames of
reference not in political economy but in Scott and Byron, in visions of "sublimity." The more rapidly, the more voraciously, the primordial forest was
felled, the more desperately poets and painters — and also preachers — strove

to identify the unique personality of this republic with the virtues of pristine and untarnished, of "romantic," Nature.

We need little ingenuity to perceive that behind this virtually universal American hostility to the ethic of utilitarian calculation lies a religious mood — one that seventeenth-century Puritanism would not have understood, and which was as foreign, let us say, to the evangelicalism of Whitefield as to the common sense of Franklin. We note, first of all, that this aversion to the pleasure-pain philosophy became most pronounced in those countries or circles in which a vigorous Christian spirit was alive. In the long run, the emotions excited in the era we call romantic were mobilized into a *cri du coeur* against Gradgrind. A host of nameless magazine writers uttered it on the plane of dripping sentiment, of patriotic or lachrymose verse, but on higher levels the poet Bryant, the novelists Cooper and Simms, the painters Durand and Cole — and on still more rarefied heights the philosopher Emerson — denounced or lamented the march of civilization. In various ways — not often agreeing among themselves — they identified the health, the very personality, of America with Nature, and therefore set it in opposition to the concepts of the city, the railroad, the steamboat. This definition of the fundamental issue of life in America became that around which Thoreau, Melville, and Whitman organized their peculiar expression. They (along with the more superficial) present us with the problem of American self-recognition as being essentially an irreconcilable opposition between Nature and civilization — which is to say, between forest and town, spontaneity and calculation, heart and head, the unconscious and the self-conscious, the innocent and the debauched. We are all heirs of Natty Bumppo, and cannot escape our heritage. William Faulkner, notably in "The Bear," is only the most dramatic of recent reminders.

Now, in this epoch, American Protestants were especially hostile to utilitarianism, even to the conciliatory form promulgated by John Stuart Mill. In England there were elements in the general situation which supported him, which could rally to his side a few sensitive and intelligent Christians. Sensitive and intelligent Christians in America were so constantly distressed by the charge that America was utterly given over to the most brutal utilitarianism that they in effect conspired to prevent the appearance of an American Mill. The more their consciences accused them of surrendering historic Christian concerns to the rush of material prosperity, the more they insisted that inwardly this busy people lived entirely by sentiment. A review of the

gift-books and annuals of the 1830's and 1840's — if one can bring himself to
it — will tell how, at that pitch of vulgarity, the image of America as tender,
tearful, dreaming noble thoughts, luxuriating in moonlit vistas, was constructed. These works were produced in huge numbers for the predominant
middle class — if the term be admissible; they reposed on the parlor tables of
wives whose husbands spent all day at the office pushing the nation on its
colossal course of empire. But the more sophisticated or learned disclaimers
of utility said, in this regard, about the same thing. An organ of Episcopalian
scholarship, *The New York Review*, declared for instance in 1837 that utilitarianism is a "sordid philosophy." And why? Because it teaches that virtue is the
creature of the brain, whereas true righteousness is "the prompt impulse of
the heart." Yet this review, with no awareness of inconsistency, was at the
same time rigorously preaching that because of the fall of Adam the impulses
of the natural heart are suspect!

There is one truism about the early nineteenth century which cannot too
often be repeated: in one fashion or another, various religious interests,
aroused against the Enlightenment, allied themselves with forces we lump
together as "romantic." In England the Established Church was surprised,
and momentarily bewildered, to discover that Scott, Wordsworth, and Coleridge started new blood pulsating through its veins, expelling the noxious
humors of indifference, deism, and skepticism. At Oxford, romantic religi-
osity indeed swung so far to the other extreme that it carried Newman all the
way to Rome. (His conversion so shattered the ranks of Episcopalian naturalists in America that *The New York Review*, finding itself unable to speak for
a united body, had to discontinue.) On the Continent there appeared a romantic Catholicism which could afford not to answer but to disregard the
philosophes as being no longer relevant. However, this ecstasy of romantic
piety did not always require institutions; it could amount simply to a passionate assertion against the Age of Reason. Carlyle and Chateaubriand might
have little love for each other, but they could embrace on one piece of
ground: they could dance together on the grave of Voltaire.

Everywhere this resurgence of the romantic heart against the enlightened
head flowered in a veneration of Nature. Wordsworth did speak for his era
when he announced that he had learned to look on her not as in the hour
of thoughtless — that is, eighteenth-century — youth, but as one who heard
through her the still, sad music of humanity. This was not the nature of
traditional theology: neither the law of nature of the Scholastics, nor the

simple plan of Newtonian apologists. It was Nature, feminine and dynamic, propelling all things. Wordsworth had no such vogue in America as had Scott or Byron, but he helped enthusiasts for both of them to find more precise, more philosophical, formulations for their enthusiasm. As early as 1840, Emerson could say, "The fame of Wordsworth is a leading fact in modern literature," because Wordsworth expressed the "idea" he shared with his coevals. Evert Duyckinck was a thorough New Yorker and thus despised Emerson's metaphysics; still, on reading *The Prelude,* Duyckinck hailed Wordsworth as one entitled to join the band of immortals "whose voices go up to Heaven in jubilant thanksgiving and acknowledgment of the Great High Priest, in whose temple they perpetually worship." And Wordsworth had taught both transcendentalist Emerson and Episcopalian Duyckinck that

> One impulse from a vernal wood
> May teach you more of man,
> Of mortal evil and of good
> Than all the sages can.

With so many Americans severally convinced that this had become ultimate truth, was not a further reflection bound to occur to a nation that was, above all other nations, embedded in Nature: if from vernal woods (along with Niagara Falls, the Mississippi, and the prairies) it can learn more of good and evil than from learned sages, could it not also learn from that source more conveniently than from divine revelation? Not that the nation would formally reject the Bible. On the contrary, it could even more energetically proclaim itself Christian and cherish the churches; but it could derive its inspiration from the mountains, the lakes, the forests. There was nothing mean or niggling about these, nothing utilitarian. Thus, superficial appearances to the contrary, America is not crass, materialistic: it is Nature's nation, possessing a heart that watches and receives.

In American literature of the early nineteenth century, this theme is ubiquitous. Social historians do not pay much attention to it; they are preoccupied with the massive expansion and the sectional tensions. Probably John Jacob Astor and the builders of railroads gave little thought to the healing virtues of the forests and swamps they were defiling. The issue I am raising — or rather that the writers themselves raised — may have little to do with how the populace actually behaved; nevertheless, it has everything to do with how the people apprehended their conduct. If there be such a thing as an American character, it took shape under the molding influence of these conceptions as much as under the physical impositions of geography and the means of transport.

So, let me insist upon the highly representative quality of an essay by one James Brooks, published in *The Knickerbocker* in 1835, which so phrased the theme that it was reprinted over the whole country. Manifestly, Brooks conceded, this country *seems* more dedicated to matter than to mind; there is indeed a vast scramble for property, and no encouragement is given the arts. But, though foreigners may sneer, we need not despair; we do not have to reconcile ourselves to being forever a rude, Philistine order. In the future we shall vindicate our culture, if only we can preserve our union. For this confidence, we have the highest authority:

> God has promised us a renowned existence, if we will but deserve it. He speaks this promise in the sublimity of Nature. It resounds all along the crags of the Alleghanies. It is uttered in the thunder of Niagara. It is heard in the roar of two oceans, from the great Pacific to the rocky ramparts of the Bay of Fundy. His finger has written it in the broad expanse of our Inland Seas, and traced it out by the mighty Father of Waters! The august TEMPLE in which we dwell was built for lofty purposes. Oh! that we may consecrate it to LIBERTY and CONCORD, and be found fit worshippers within its holy wall!

Walt Whitman had for years been drugging himself upon such prose; in him the conception comes to its most comprehensive utterance, so self-contained that it could finally dismiss the alliance with Christian doctrine which romantic Christians had striven to establish. However, he was so intoxicated with the magniloquent idea that he had to devise what to contemporaries seemed a repulsive form, and they would have none of it. Nevertheless, Whitman's roots reach deep into the soil of this naturalistic (and Christianized) naturalism. Today a thousand James Brookses are forgotten; Whitman speaks for a mood which did sustain a mass of Americans through a crucial half-century of Titanic exertion—which sustained them along with, and as much as, their Christian profession.

That is what is really astounding: most of the ardent celebrators of natural America serenely continued to be professing Christians. Or rather, the amazing fact is that they so seldom—hardly ever—had any intimation that the bases of their patriotism and those of their creed stood, in the slightest degree, in contradiction. Magnificent hymns to American Nature are to be found among Evangelicals and Revivalists as well as among scholarly Episcopalians. If here and there some still hard-bitten Calvinist reminded his people of ancient distinctions between nature and grace, his people still bought and swooned over pseudo-Byronic invocations to Nature. It was a problem, even for the clearest thinkers, to keep the orders separate. For example, *The New York Review* in January 1840, devoted an essay to foreign travelers, saying that their defect was an inability to behold in America not the nonexistent temples and statues but the "Future":

> A railroad, a penitentiary, a log house beyond the Mississippi, the last hotly-contested elections — things rather heterogeneous to be sure, and none of them at first glance, so attractive as the wonders of the old world — are in reality, and to him who regards them philosophically, quite as important, and as they connect themselves with the unknown future, quite as romantic.

For some pages the *Review* keeps up this standard chant, and then abruptly recollects its theology. Confidence in the American future, it remembers barely in the nick of time, must not betray us into the heresy of supposing man perfectible: "Tell a people that they are perfectible, and it will not be long before they tell you they are perfect, and that he is a traitor who presumes to doubt, not their wisdom simply, but their infallibility." Assuredly, the American Christian would at this point find himself in an intolerable dilemma, with his piety and his patriotism at loggerheads, did not the triumphant ethos seem to give him a providential way out: America can progress indefinitely into an expanding future without acquiring sinful delusions of grandeur simply because it is nestled in Nature, is instructed and guided by mountains, is chastened by cataracts.

> It is here that errors are rebuked, and excesses discountenanced. Nature preserves the identity and the individuality of its various races and tribes, and by the relation in which each stands to her, and the use which each makes of her, she becomes both a teacher and an historian.

So then — because America, beyond all nations, is in perpetual touch with Nature, it need not fear the debauchery of the artificial, the urban, the civilized. Nature somehow, by a legerdemain that even so highly literate Christians as the editors of *The New York Review* could not quite admit to themselves, had effectually taken the place of the Bible: by her unremitting influence, she, like Bryant's waterfowl, would guide aright the faltering steps of a young republic.

Here we encounter again the crucial difference between the American appeal to romantic Nature and the European. In America, it served not so much for individual or artistic salvation as for an assuaging of national anxiety. The sublimity of our natural backdrop not only relieved us of having to apologize for a deficiency of picturesque ruins and hoary legends: it demonstrated how the vast reservoirs of our august temple furnish the guarantee that we shall never be contaminated by artificiality. On the prairies of Illinois, Bryant asked the breezes of the South if anywhere in their progress from the equator they have fanned a nobler scene than this.

> Man hath no part in all this glorious work:
> The hand that built the firmament hath heaved
> And smoothed these verdant swells, and sown their slopes
> With herbage, planted them with island-groves,
> And hedged them round with forests.

Goethe might insist in ancient Germany that he devoted his life to Nature, but in Europe this meant that he became an elegant genius domesticated in the highly artificial court of Weimar. What could Europe show for all of Rousseau's tirades against civilization but a band of Bohemians, congregated amid the brick and mortar of Paris, trying to keep alive a yearning for such naturalness and spontaneity as any child of the Ohio Valley indubitably flaunted without, like them, becoming outcast from society? America, amid its forests, could not, even if it tried, lose its simplicity. Therefore let Christianity bless it.

But—could America keep its virtue? As *The Literary World*'s exhortation to the artists reveals, almost as soon as the identification of virtue with Nature had become axiomatic, the awful suspicion dawned that America was assiduously erecting the barriers of artifice between its citizenry and the precious landscape. If God speaks to us in the sublimity of Nature, then was not the flood of pioneers a devilish stratagem for drowning the voice of God? In the same issue that printed Brooks's "Our Country," *The Knickerbocker* also carried an oration on the Mississippi River, declaring that no words can convey what an American feels as he looks upon this moving ocean, because he sees not only the present majesty but the not distant period when the interminable stretch of vacantness shall become bright with towns, vocal with the sounds of industry: "When the light of civilization and religion shall extend over forests and savannahs." Or, as the same magazine vaunted in 1838, "Nature has been penetrated in her wildest recesses, and made to yield her hidden stores." But how could we at one and the same time establish our superiority to artificial Europe upon our proximity to Nature, and then view with complacency the rapidity of our despoiling her? And furthermore — most embarrassing of questions — on which side does religion stand, on Nature's or on civilization's? Once the dichotomy had become absolute, as in American sentiment it had become, then piety could no longer compromise by pretending to dwell in both embattled camps.

Once more, in Europe the problem was personal, a matter of the individual's coming to terms with himself, absorbing a taste for Nature into his private culture. Here it was a problem for the society—and so for the churches. Goethe had put it for Europe: the young revel in those aspirations of the sublime which in fact only primitive and barbaric peoples can experience; vigorous youth pardonably strives to satisfy this noble necessity, but soon learns circumspection:

> As the sublime is easily produced by twilight and night, when forms are blended, so, on the other hand, it is scared away by the day which separates and divides everything, and so must it also be destroyed by every increase of cultivation, if it is not fortunate enough to take refuge with the beautiful and closely unite itself with it, by which these both become immortal and indestructible.

By recognizing that the sublime is ephemeral, for a nation as for a person, Goethe inculcated the necessity of a mature reconciliation to the merely beautiful, in order to preserve a fugitive glory, one which might, by adroit cultivation, survive into a weary civilization as a memory out of the natural sublimity of youth. But the beautiful is only ornament, amenity, decoration. A nation cannot live by it, neither can a faith. It is far removed from the voice of God thundering out of lofty ridges and roaring waterfalls. Even the painter Cole in 1841 published "The Lament of the Forest," by which, he seemed to say, he found at the end of his self-appointed task only a tragic prospect. The forest stood for centuries, sublime and unsullied, until there came man the destroyer. For a few centuries thereafter, America was the sanctuary; now, even into it comes artificial destruction:

> And thus come rushing on
> This human hurricane, boundless as swift.
> Our sanctuary, this secluded spot,
> Which the stern rocks have guarded until now,
> Our enemy has marked.

It was this same Thomas Cole, this master interpreter of the American landscape whose death in 1848 was, according to *The New York Evening Mirror*, "a national loss," who most impressed his generation by five gigantic canvases entitled "The Course of Empire." The first shows the rude, barbaric state of man; the second is a perfect symbolization of that pastoral conception with which America strove to identify itself. Presiding over each scene is a lofty and rocky peak, which patently represents Nature, but in the pastoral panel, and only in this one, the point of view is shifted so that there can be seen looming behind and above the peak of Nature a still more lofty one, which even more patently is the sublime. In the third cartoon the perspective returns to that of the first, but the entire scene is covered with a luxurious civilization, only the tip of mountain Nature peering over the fabulous expanse of marble. In the fourth, barbarians are sacking the city, and the picture is a riot of rape, fire, pillage; in the fifth, all human life is extinguished, the temples and towers are in ruin, but the unaltered mountain serenely presides over a panorama of total destruction.

The orator who in *The Knickerbocker* anticipated the civilization to arise along the Mississippi was obliged to warn the young empire to learn from the history of the past, from the follies of the old world: it must so improve the condition of the *whole* people as to "establish on this continent an imperishable empire, destined to confer innumerable blessings on the remotest ages." Yet like so many vaunters of American confidence in this ostensible age of confidence, by admitting the adjective into his exhortation he indirectly confesses the lurking possibility of the perishable. Cole's "Course of Empire" was exhibited over and over again to fascinated throngs of the democracy; the series ought, said George Templeton Strong in 1838, "to immortalize him." Cole made explicit what the society instinctively strove to repress: the inescapable logic of a nationalism based upon the premises of Nature. (Many, even while forced into admiration, noted that the drama as Cole painted it, he being both a pious Christian and a devout Words-worthian, left out any hint of Christianity; the "Empire" is wholly material, and there is no salvation except for the mountain itself.) The moral clearly was that a culture committed to Nature, to the inspiration of Nature and of the sublime, might for a moment overcome its barbarous origins, take its place with the splendor of Rome, but it was thereby committed to an ineluc-table cycle of rise and fall. The American empire was still ascending, rising from Cole's second to his third phase. But if this rationale explained America, then was not the fourth stage, and after it the fifth, inescapable?

The creator of Natty Bumppo and of Harvey Birch (who was a vestryman and a close friend of Cole) grew worried. As Cooper reissued *The Spy* in 1849, he could only marvel at the immense change in the nation since 1821, when the book had first appeared. America had now passed from gristle into the bone, had indeed become a civilization, and had no enemy to fear — "but the one that resides within." In his mingling of anxieties and exultations, Cooper is indeed the principal interpreter of his period; even while glorify-ing the forest-born virtue of America, he had also portrayed the brutal Skin-ners in *The Spy* and the settlers in *The Pioneers* who wantonly slaughter Nature's pigeons.

It would not be difficult to show how widespread, even though covert, was this apprehension of doom in the America of Jackson and Polk. Of course it was so elaborately masked, so concertedly disguised, that one may study the epoch for a long time without detecting it. Yet it is there, at the heart — at what may be called the secret heart — of the best thought and expression the country could produce. So much so, indeed, that some patriots sought es-cape from the haunting course of empire by arguing that America was no more peculiarly the nation of Nature than any other, that it had been civi-lized from the start. For instance, in 1847 *The Literary World* noticed a work on the prairies by Mrs. Eliza Farnham which once more appealed to the piled cliffs, the forest aisles, the chant of rushing winds and waters in the West against the decadence of eastern civilization. The New York journal, conscious of the city's daily growth, had to ask if this tedious declamation was not becoming trite. After all, the *World* demanded, when men go deeper and deeper into wild and sublime scenes, do they in fact put off false and artificial ways? Do they become spontaneously religious? Unfortunately, we must ad-mit that some of the fairest portions of the earth are occupied by the most degraded of mankind; even sublimity works no effect on the rude and thoughtless, and so, instead of following a fatal course from the primordial to the metropolitan, perhaps we should try to stabilize this society at the merely decent and sane. "Moral and aesthetic culture require something more than the freest and most balmy air and mellow sunshine."

The *World* did not quote Goethe to justify this escape from the cycle of naturalism, but Emerson, who did know his Goethe, could never successfully resolve within himself the debate between Nature and civilization, solitude and society, rusticity and manners. In fact, something of the same debate went on through most of the fiction and poetry, and markedly among the architects and landscape gardeners, of the time. Very few of those who found themselves impelled in both directions consciously tried to find their way into civilization because, thanks to Cole, they had peered into the frightful prospect of Nature. Still, I think it can be demonstrated that some vague sense of doom was at work in all of them, as it surely was in both Cooper and Simms. As the implications of the philosophy of natural destiny forced themselves upon the more sentient, these were obliged to seek methods for living in civilization, all the more because civilization was so spectacularly triumphing over the continent. A growing awareness of the dilemma informed the thinking of Horace Bushnell, for instance, and he strove to turn American Protestantism from the revival, associated with the lurid scenery of Nature, to the cultivation of "nurture" which could be achieved only in a civilized context.

Of course, there was also the possibility of escape from the cycle of empire in another direction, opposite to that chosen by Bushnell. The nation could resolutely declare that it is invincibly barbaric, that it intends to remain so, and that it refuses to take even the first step towards civilization. Or at least, if the nation as a whole shrank from such audacity, if Christians fled for protection to older sobrieties they had come near to forgetting, a few brave spirits might seek the other spiritual solution, though they had to defy the palpable evidence of economic life and to renounce a Christianity that was proving itself incapable of mediating between forest and city. They would refuse to be content with the beautiful, they would defiantly wear their hats indoors as well as out, and would sound a barbaric (and American) yawp over the roof of the world. Possibly there were, in sum, no more than three Americans who chose this violent resort, and in their time they were largely ignored by their countrymen. Yet Whitman, Thoreau, and Melville speak for this society, and to it, in part because, by making their choice, they thrust upon it a challenge it cannot honestly evade. In 1855 Melville pictured John Paul Jones in Paris as a jaunty barbarian in the center of the very citadel of civilization; exclaiming over his incorruptibility amid corruption, Melville apostrophized: "Intrepid, unprincipled, reckless, predatory, with boundless ambition, civilized in externals but a savage at heart, America is, or may yet be, the Paul Jones of nations."

Possibly the fact that America came to its first essay in self-analysis and self-expression in the period we call romantic is only fortuitous. But perhaps there is a deeper conjunction. The suspicion that we are being carried along on some massive conveyor belt such as Cole's "Course of Empire" is hard to down. It is more nagging today than it was around the year 1900, when for the moment America could give up the dream of Nature and settle for a permanently prosperous civilization. It more pesters the religious conscience in our time, when a leading theologian expounds the "irony" of American history, than it did when the most conscientious were absorbed in "the social gospel." So, it is no longer enough to dismiss the period of romantic America as one in which too many Christians temporized their Christianity by merging it with a misguided cult of Nature. No scorn of the refined, no condescension of sophisticated critics toward the vagaries of romance, can keep us from feeling the pull: the American, or at least the American artist, cherishes in his innermost being the impulse to reject completely the gospel of civilization, in order to guard with resolution the savagery of his heart.

In that case, the savage artist poses for the Christianity of the country a still more disturbing challenge, as Thoreau, Melville, and Whitman posed it: if he must, to protect his savage integrity, reject organized religion along with organized civilization, then has not American religion, or at any rate Protestantism, the awful task of reexamining, with the severest self-criticism, the course on which it so blithely embarked a century ago, when it dallied with the sublime and failed to comprehend the sinister dynamic of Nature?

Sherman Paul on
Thoreau, *The Maine Woods,*
and the Problem of Ktaadn
(1958)

Sherman Paul was born in 1920 in Cleveland, Ohio. After earning his bachelor's degree from Iowa State University and his Ph.D. from Harvard, he taught at the University of Illinois and wrote widely on American literature. His books include *Emerson's Angle of Vision: Man and Nature in the American Experience* (1952) and *The Shores of America: Thoreau's Inward Exploration* (1958). In the essay below, Paul examines Thoreau's shifting attitudes toward the wilderness, relating them to the development of the early environmental consciousness that led Thoreau to call for the creation of a national park and wilderness preserve. He pays particular attention to what he terms the "unresolved problem of 'Ktaadn'—if primitive nature and civilization are contemporary in America, how should one use nature?" Like many of his contemporaries, Thoreau "was stirred by the heady national consciousness that had awakened a sense of the need for an American past," and he came to feel that the highest use to which nature could be put was the creation of such a past.

This was the sense in which Thoreau conceived of wilderness as the "raw material" of civilization—not merely as lumber and soil but as the opening chapter in a uniquely American history. Paul notes how Thoreau treated his ascent toward the "unhandseled nature" of Ktaadn as if "he retraced in reverse order the process of civilization"—structuring a narrative that deftly transformed Nature into History, and thus incidentally helped justify nature's preservation. Yet this movement was complicated by Thoreau's recognition that wilderness, at least as he experienced it high on Ktaadn, was too wholly Other to be so easily assimilated into a national narrative. "The Creator of Ktaadn was obviously not the Artist of the railroad cut," as Paul puts it, "for matter here was not fluid and obedient to idea, and even his body, Thoreau felt, had become matter which was strange to him. Overcome and unmoored by this experience, he wrote the most frenzied passage he was ever to write."

The selection below is excerpted from *The Shores of America*.

૮ૐ ૮ૐ ૮ૐ

Of all of Thoreau's travel books, *The Maine Woods* best reveals his development, simply because each excursion was complete in itself. Like *Cape Cod*, it covered three trips extending over a period of years. Though the development is also apparent in *Cape Cod*, especially in the last chapter on the discovery of America, the later excursions were worked into the narrative of the first, and *Cape Cod*, therefore, was a more unified work. In all of his travel writing, however, Thoreau followed his actual itinerary, and thus the material of the narrative itself determined his treatment. Although all of his trips to Maine were confined to the same area — that extending north of Bangor to Eagle Lake and the headwaters of Canadian rivers, with Moosehead Lake to the west and the east branch of the Penobscot and the Penobscot to the east, and with Ktaadn roughly in the center — each had a different itinerary; and since his trips to Maine were farther apart in time, having been taken in 1846, 1853, and 1857, each had a different goal and a different quality.

The first trip, for example, was taken during the Walden years, when he was in good health and eager to compare his "sylvan" experiment with an experience of the primitive wilderness. This trip was perhaps his greatest adventure, the equivalent in his career of Mark Twain's *Roughing It* or perhaps of Parkman's trip in the same year along the Oregon Trail; nothing he ever wrote was so irrepressibly adventurous, so full of delight in frontier hardship and skill and masculinity, so full of Thoreau's sense of release and expectancy. The second trip does not convey this excitement because Thoreau had become more of an observer than participant, a poet-naturalist who was unwilling to hunt the moose and a more seasoned traveler for whom the wilderness was a less ecstatic experience. One recognizes a change in style: it has less of the direct matter-of-fact seriousness of the first, is more jocose and satirical because he is not so completely one, as he formerly was, with what he sees. The last trip cannot be judged so readily by its style because the narrative had not been prepared for the reader, having been taken from the *Journal*. Nevertheless, Thoreau shares his enjoyment here and is more relaxed; his learning is lighter and his humor is easier — all perhaps because at last he had found an Indian (as he did not on the second trip) who was worthy of study. Over a period of eleven years, then, his interest in the wilderness, upon which he staked so much, did not diminish but took instead a less absolute place in his thought; he began to place it in the context of civilization much in the same way that his comparative botanizing helped him place Concord; his private experience became less important to him than what he saw, and he became an observer who extended his range to the study of men — not only to the Indian whose life in the woods brought him close to the aboriginal condition the first explorers saw, but to the hunter, logger, and pioneer who, in the mid-nineteenth century, were re-enacting all the stages in the founding and settlement of America.

"Ktaadn" was the first of Thoreau's travel articles — that is, if we make the distinction which should be made between his travels and his more poetically rendered excursions such as "A Walk to Wachusett." It was probably solicited by Horace Greeley, a busy editor who took the trouble to act as Thoreau's literary agent and who sold it to *The Union Magazine*. In this way he did as much to further Thoreau's career as Emerson did; for if Emerson helped Thoreau by suggesting the field of nature writing, Greeley, with his check for fifty dollars, opened the door to the kind of writing that would pay and for which Thoreau had equally substantial gifts. Thereafter, for the next ten years in fact, Thoreau published his travels in *Putnam's Monthly Magazine* and *The Atlantic Monthly* until the editorial mishandling of his manuscripts aroused his anger and forced him to close the door. When Greeley received "Ktaadn" he had told Thoreau that his article "on Maine scenery" was "too fine for the million," yet nothing that Thoreau wrote was better suited to a popular audience; and while he was arduously gathering the materials for his Kalendar, the only fruits of which were "Autumnal Tints" and "Wild Apples," his travel writings kept him before the public. There was indeed something too fine for the million — a never fully developed but deep and abiding concern for the renewal of America — but there was always the immediate appeal of the scenery: there were always the rivers, lakes, and primitive forests, the sea and the desert, or the Great River of Canada, as if Thoreau had gone in search of the elemental facts of nature; and certainly, one of his gifts was his ability to restore these facts by means of his own historically sharpened sensibility to their original grandeur. Maine and Cape Cod, even eastern Canada, moreover, were out-of-the-way places whose appeal, if not to the extent of Typee or Tahiti, lay in the possibility of strange and exotic adventure.

Now "Ktaadn" was an adventure up the Penobscot into the wilderness above Nicketow, an adventure culminating in the ascent of Mt. Ktaadn, a mountain first ascended by white men in 1804, and again only as recently as 1836, 1837, and 1845. For Thoreau, who took the stance of a civilized man (which indeed he was), it was his first experience with "the grim, untrodden wilderness" where the river was the only highway and where, as in the days of the Canadian *voyageurs*, one still had to travel by batteau. The batteau, in fact, had a prominent place in his narrative comparable to the canoe in the later excursions — and as he shot the rapids he was more exhilarated than he had ever been before while boating. This dangerous mode of traveling gave "new emphasis" to the Canadian boat song that he had known from his youth, for, as he remarked, it described "precisely our own adventure and was inspired by the experience of a similar kind of life. . . ." His aim on all his travels was always to come into the conditions that would provide the experience of a similar kind of life; and as he went from the civilization of Bangor, the port through which the white pine forest passed into lumber, to Oldtown, where the once-powerful Penobscots reminded him of rum and the fur trade and the history of their extinction, to the burning clearings of settlers and to the loggers' camps still deeper in the woods, he retraced in reverse order the process of civilization until he came at last to unhandseled nature, to the naked, inviolable rocks of Ktaadn.

The wilderness and Ktaadn were what he had come to see, but as he passed in rapid review of civilization and saw the beginnings of trade and the divestment of the forest, he was distressed by the waste and the inevitable doom of the wilderness — first made aware perhaps of the need to preserve the wild, a theme which, with increasing insistence, he developed in his later years. Although he admired the sturdy self-reliance and worldliness of settlers like George McCauslin and Tom Fowler, who served as his guides, and was so much involved in his own Walden experiment that he advised the poverty-stricken and the emigrant to "begin life as Adam did" in the woods; although he approved of the utilitarian functionalism of the loggers' camp and the skill and heroism of loggers and drivers, he did not see in these signs, as he did later, the warrant of progress but rather of destruction. His heart was set on the wilderness, on a pure nature uninhabited by man, where the moose and the Indian had "never been dispossessed, nor nature disforested." On his other trips to Maine he was always aware of the presence of man, but when he ascended Ktaadn the wilderness of his dream was realized, and he was reminded that, even though America had leaped to the Pacific, there were "many a lesser Oregon and California unexplored behind us," that civilization had only a slight tenure in America, that within a day or two from Concord "there still waves the virgin forest of the New World."

The nature he discovered in the wilderness, however, was not entirely what he had expected. The uninterrupted forest was "even more grim and wild" than he had anticipated, "a damp and intricate wilderness, in the spring everywhere wet and miry," and its aspect was "universally stern and savage" save for the lakes, which he felt were "mild and civilizing in a degree." Here, he found, "one could no longer accuse institutions and society, but must front the true source of evil." For here, as he made his way to Ktaadn, he found the primordial world of "gray, silent rocks," a dreary and desolate scenery with ancient trees as "old as the flood," and pathless places that reminded him of Satan's difficulties through Chaos. He had ascended mountains before, and in his last years was to return to them as if compelled to try once more their inspirational powers; but the ascent of Ktaadn did not work that miracle, no more than did the sea at Cape Cod, because he was overcome by a vast, titanic, and inhuman nature. He was reminded, he said, "of Atlas, Vulcan, the Cyclops, and Prometheus. Such was Caucasus and the rock where Prometheus was bound. Aeschylus had no doubt visited such scenery as this. It was vast, Titanic, and such as man never inhabits." Describing his own impressions, he said that

some part of the beholder, even some vital part, seems to escape through the loose grating of his ribs as he ascends. He is more lone than you can imagine. There is less of substantial thought and fair understanding in him than in the plains where men inhabit. His reason is dispersed and shadowy, more thin and subtile, like the air. Vast, Titanic, inhuman Nature has got him at disadvantage, caught him alone, and pilfers him of some of his divine faculty. She does not smile on him as in the plains. She seems to say sternly, Why came ye here before your time. This ground is not prepared for you. Is it not enough that I smile in the valleys? . . . I cannot pity not fondle thee here, but forever relentlessly drive thee hence to where I *am* kind.

One wonders how much this experience, coming earlier in Thoreau's development, would have altered his conception of nature; if, say like Melville, he had known the sea in his youth instead of the pastoral nature of Concord. For now he realized as never before "the presence of a force not bound to be kind to man," an otherness which was not conditional — a phase of his inspirational process — but absolute. On Ktaadn he had a presentiment of the alien, cold, indifferent nature of naturalism: here was "*Nature,*" "primeval, untamed, and forever untamable," a savage and awful Earth "made out of Chaos and Old Night" with which man was not to be associated. Instead of "Mother Earth" here was "Matter" — "the home, this, of Necessity and Fate." Here, he found, "was no man's garden, but the unhandseled globe. . . . a specimen of what God saw fit to make this world. . . . some star's surface, some hard matter in its home!" The Creator of Ktaadn was obviously not the Artist of the railroad cut; for matter here was not fluid and obedient to idea, and even his body, Thoreau felt, had become matter which was strange to him. Overcome and unmoored by this experience, he wrote the most frenzied passage he was ever to write, a passage that could not be passed off as extravagance: "What is this Titan that has possession of me? Talk of mysteries! Think of our life in nature, — daily to be shown matter, to come in contact with it, — rocks, trees, wind on our cheeks! The *solid* earth! The *actual* world! The *common sense!* Contact! Contact! Who are we? where are we?" This passage is difficult and perhaps ambiguous, for in one sense Thoreau felt the sublimity of this otherness, the elemental purity and awful grandeur of it. But "contact" was a word he never used when describing his sympathy with nature, not even in *Walden* where he spoke of his desire to reach "hard bottom and rocks in place," and here it seems to suggest the recognition of otherness rather than the overcoming of it. To be reminded by *contact* of this otherness would indeed have changed his life in nature, would, as the "*Who* are we? *where* are we?" indicates, have destroyed the possibility of communion.

When he looked back on this first excursion, therefore, he resolved his difficulties by moralizing his experience in terms of the forest rather than the mountain, and thus the newness of the New World lost some of its terrors.

The wilderness of the Indian was primitive enough, and he could even contemplate his Walden life there—"a flute to play at evening here, while his strains echo to the stars, amid the howling of wolves; [to] live, as it were, in the primitive age of the world, a primitive man." The life of the Indian (who, incidentally, did not pry into the secrets of the gods, who respected the sacred and mysterious mountaintop) was as far back into history as he wanted to go. And though the life of the Indian reminded him that "America is still unsettled and unexplored," and made it possible for him to maintain his belief in the virtue of the wild, when he went to the Maine woods thereafter, visions of a more genial and humanized nature invaded his mind.

If "Ktaadn" introduced Thoreau to the primitive life, like Melville's *Typee*, it also took him as far back into time as he could go, to rocks as primordial as those of the ancient religious structures Melville mused over, and, if not to savage physicality, to matter equally unredeemed by mind. "It was a place," Thoreau wrote, "for heathenism and superstitious rites,—to be inhabited by men nearer of kin to the rocks and to wild animals than we." Undoubtedly this experience was reflected in the chastened primitivism of *Walden*, as it was in his second trip in 1853 which dramatized the conflict between the hunter and the poet-naturalist and the unresolved problem of "Ktaadn"—if primitive nature and civilization are contemporary in America, how should one use nature? Were it not for these problems, "Chesuncook," with its account of the hunting of the moose, would have an attraction comparable to that of *The Green Hills of Africa*. But even though Thoreau did his best to make the hunt exciting—measuring the moose, as Melville did the whale, to suggest its great size, citing "the quaint John Josselyn" on the moose's "'transcendentia,'" and retelling Governor Neptune's Indian fable in which the moose was once a whale left stranded when the sea withdrew—he no longer had the "strange thrill of savage delight" he spoke of in *Walden*, he no longer had the temptation to devour a woodchuck raw. In "Higher Laws," where this conflict was thoroughly explained, he said that he was only hungry for that "wildness which he [the woodchuck] represented." Such was his hunger for the moose in "Chesuncook," and by creating a mythical beast as much a symbol of the wilderness as Faulkner's bear he was incapable of sharing in the abandon of the hunt. "I had not come a-hunting," he said, "and felt some compunctions about accompanying the hunters, [but] I wished to see a moose near at hand, and was not sorry to learn how the Indian managed to kill one. I went as reporter or chaplain to the hunters. . . ." His compunctions, not his inability to hunt, stood between him and his narrative, and the excitement of the hunt was dissipated by the judgment he passed on it: in the death of the moose he saw the doom of the wilderness.

Reflecting on the killing of the moose, he said that "the afternoon's tragedy, and my share in it, as it affected the innocence, destroyed the pleasure of my adventure." Though he preferred to live like a philosopher on the fruits he had raised, he thought that he might with satisfaction spend a year in the woods hunting and fishing, not for sport, but merely for subsistence. For what appalled him, as it had Natty Bumppo, was the wanton waste, the base and coarse motives of the "hirelings" and even the Indians who did not come to the forest out of love for the wild but "to slay as many moose and other wild animals as possible." And what was true of the moose was also true of the white pine which was almost as scarce. While his companions continued the hunt, therefore, Thoreau went naturalizing, enacting that love of nature which distinguished the poet from the hunter and the lumberman, and which provided the framework for his remarks, made famous by Lowell's deletion, on the immortality of the pine. The lumberman, he said, was not the lover of the pine, but the poet—"it is the living spirit of the tree, not its spirit of turpentine with which I sympathize, and which heals my cuts. It is as immortal as I am, and perchance will go to as high a heaven, there to tower above me still."

Even if the poet made a higher use of the wilderness, it was ultimately in the interest of poetry, in the humanization of nature, that the poet should turn to a nature something less than wild. As a "resource and a background, the raw material of our civilization," the wilderness, however, continued to be necessary for Thoreau. For strength and beauty, for inspiration and true recreation, "the poet," he wrote, "must, from time to time, travel the logger's path and the Indian's trail, to drink at some new and more bracing fountain of the Muses, far in the recesses of the wilderness." This was the reason why, in these later years, he became a champion of natural preserves and advised his neighbors to keep their woods and fields for a "common"—why he glorified the Boxboro woods and the Easterbrooks country, places still as wild and shaggy and swampy as the Maine woods. Here, at least, one would not have "to gnaw the very crust of the earth for nutriment." And yet for "a permanent residence" he felt that "our smooth, but still varied landscape" was better. Where he had once believed that the revitalization of poetry required the wild and had belittled the English nature poets, he now returned to that tradition: "The partially cultivated country it is which chiefly has inspired, and will continue to inspire, the strains of poets. . . ." For he now realized that the poet's path was not the logger's but the woodman's, that the "logger and pioneer have preceded him . . . banished decaying wood and the spongy mosses which feed on it, and built hearths and humanized Nature for him." In the dreamy state from which the call of the moose aroused him, he had seemed to be "floating through ornamental grounds," he had seen "an endless succession of porticoes and columns, cornices and facades, verandas and churches," and he had lost himself in the thought of "that architecture and the nobility that dwelt behind and might issue from it." In the midst of the wilderness had he been dreaming of Concord? Of the higher society?

Perhaps it was Thoreau's growing awareness of his inability to master the wild that turned him from his youthful exaltation of the Indian to those exacting studies of Indian life of his last years. This interest, of course, increased along with his researches in the discovery of America; for like the poets of American "epics" who had gone before him, he saw in the Indian the first chapter of American history. This chapter, however, was almost always forgotten, though the "antiquities" of "our predecessors" could be easily found, as Thoreau often found arrowheads, by turning the soil. "Why, then," he asked, "make so great ado about the Roman and the Greek, and neglect the Indian?" He studied the Indian because, as he said, "New earths, new themes expect us. Celebrate not the Garden of Eden, but your own"—he was stirred by the heady national consciousness that had awakened a sense of the need for an American past. But he also studied the Indian because he was "the indigenous man of America" who had mastered the aboriginal environment of America. "If wild men, so much more like ourselves than they are unlike, have inhabited these shores before us," he wrote, "we wish to know particularly what manner of men they were, how they lived here, their relation to nature, their arts and their customs, their fancies and superstitions. They paddled over these waters, they wandered in these woods, and they had their fancies and beliefs connected with the sea and the forest, which concern us quite as much as the fables of Oriental nations do."

To this end Thoreau hired Indian guides on his last two trips to Maine. Joe Aitteon accompanied him in "Chesuncook," but in spite of his skill, with his popular airs (he whistled "O Susanna") and his confession that he could not live in the woods as his ancestors had, he was not enough of an Indian to kindle Thoreau's imagination. The Indian did not have the prominent part in "Chesuncook" that he did in "The Allegash and East Branch"; and only the episode at the Indian camp was given over to him in "Chesuncook." There, sharing the Indians' dwelling (though the dirt bothered him), amidst the moose hides stretched and curing on poles and the carcasses left on the ground, Thoreau, who knew their history better than the Indians did, was "carried back at once three hundred years." The method of smoking moose meat reminded him of what he had seen in de Bry's *Collectio Peregrinationum* (1588) and his experience of the campfire recalled the sufferings of the Jesuit missionaries. What he had learned of the Abenaki language in Father Rasles' *Dictionary* was confirmed, and listening to their talk, he felt that he "stood, or rather lay, as near to the primitive man of America . . . as any of its discoverers ever did." "These Abenakis gossiped, laughed, and jested, in the language in which Eliot's Indian Bible is written," he said, "the language which has been spoken in New England who shall say how long? These were the sounds that issued from the wigwams of this country before Columbus was born; they have not yet died away. . . ."

When Thoreau went to Maine for the last time he was fortunate to find a guide whose forest ways as well as the sounds of whose language had not yet died away. Although he had represented his tribe at Augusta and Washington, had felt the attraction of great cities like New York, had called on Webster; although he had a neat frame house at Oldtown, was worth six thousand dollars, sent his boy to school with the whites, and kept the Sabbath even in the wilderness, Joe Polis, unlike most Indians, had made good use of civilization without losing any of his woodcraft. Not only could he handle the canoe expertly, he could build one; he knew how to make spruce thread, skillfully splitting roots with his knife while he used his teeth as "a third hand," and he could make pitch (the secret of which he kept from Thoreau) in order to repair his canoe on the spot. He was completely at home in the wilderness, having those finer senses, the "Indian wisdom," that Thoreau praised in the "Natural History." His familiarity with nature had sharpened and educated his senses and had made him self-reliant. "His Indian instinct," Thoreau wrote, "may tell him still as much as the most confident white man knows. He does not carry things in his head, nor remember the route exactly like a white man, but relies on himself at the moment." He could call a muskrat, make a new kind of herb tea every night or a lily-bulb soup, tell the medicinal use of every plant, and find his way through the woods so easily that it seemed uncanny even to Thoreau. Indeed, he had good reason to lament, as Thoreau recorded, "that the present generation of Indians 'had lost a great deal.'" He taught Thoreau his language, as he had agreed to—a language always specific and so full of the geography of the place that Thoreau was reminded that he was not one of the earlier discoverers of the Maine woods, that "it was thus well known and suitably named by Indian hunters perhaps a thousand years ago." His religious chant, finally, carried Thoreau back "to the period of the discovery of America, to San Salvador and the Incas, when Europeans first encountered the simple faith of the Indian."

Carried back beyond the dispossession and degeneration of the Indian, Thoreau realized anew their natural faith: "There was, indeed, a beautiful simplicity about it; nothing of the dark and savage, only the mild and infantile. The sentiments of humility and reverence chiefly were expressed." And when almost immediately afterward he discovered phosphorescent wood— his great find on this excursion—the wild lost some of its terror for him. "I little thought," he wrote, making a symbol of this discovery, "that there was such a light shining in the darkness of the wilderness for me." Unable to humanize the wilderness sufficiently, he now strengthened his faith in nature by recognizing that the Indians had found spirit there: "Nature must have made a thousand revelations to them which are still secrets to us." "I exulted," he wrote, "like 'a pagan suckled in a creed' that had never been worn at all, but was bran new. . . . I let science slide. . . . I believed that the woods were not tenantless, but chokeful of honest spirits as good as myself any day. . . ." His humor here guarded a faith that had been worn and that was only partially restored; for it was no longer the confident Thoreau of the *Week* who wrote, "I have much to learn of the Indian, nothing of the missionary."

Indeed, in spite of all that Joe Polis taught him of the possibility of a sympathetic communion with the wild, and in spite of his feeling that "here was travelling of the old heroic kind over the unaltered face of nature," the wilderness still had its terrors. The swamp at Mud Pond carry, where he took the wrong path, was the genuine wilderness "ready to echo the growl of a bear, the howl of a wolf, or the scream of a panther," and only in retrospect could he treat it humorously: "a howling wilderness does not howl: it is the imagination of the traveller that does the howling." The "denseness of the forest, the fallen trees and rocks, the windings of the river, the streams emptying in, and the frequent swamps to be crossed" made him "shudder." When his companion was lost in a desolation of burnt-over trees, jutting rocks, rapids and falls—a landscape that in the telling at least Thoreau transformed into a Gothic setting worthy of Brockden Brown—he was overcome not only by anxiety for his hapless friend but by the sudden awareness of his own impotence in the wilderness. And once the initial feeling of release wore off, even the impenetrable forests that enclosed and darkened the rivers depressed him, until he looked forward to the "liberating and civilizing" expanse of the lakes. The lakes were openings in the sky, they let in light, and the "influx of light merely," Thoreau said, making light and dark carry spiritual meaning, "is civilizing." Lakes, he wrote, "give ample scope and range to our thought." He sympathized, therefore, with the settlers who clustered around lakes for the sake of neighborhood and who, he thought, were establishing "great centres of light." And cleared land now excited him: "Such, seen far or near, you know at once to be man's work, for Nature never does it. In order to let in the light to the earth as on a lake, he clears off the forest on the hillsides and plains, and sprinkles fine grass-seed, like an enchanter, and so carpets the earth with a firm sward." The advance of civilization to Nicketow, an outpost eleven years before, did not elicit the jeremiad of his first excursion. Instead in one image he condensed the entire course of civilization: "not long since similar beds [of fir twigs] were spread along the Connecticut, the Hudson, and the Delaware, and longer still ago, by the Thames and Seine, and they now help to make the soil where private and public gardens, mansions and palaces are." Rivers were the paths of discovery and the highways of civilization; the wilderness was the soil of civilization. If he disapproved of the misuse of nature they inevitably introduced, he no longer wholeheartedly despaired, for having known the darkness of the wilderness, he knew the value of light.

Leo Marx on the
Pastoral in American Literature
(1964)

Born in 1919 in New York City, Leo Marx received his Ph.D. from Harvard in 1950. He taught at the University of Minnesota and at Amherst before taking a position at Massachusetts Institute of Technology, where he was named Kenan Professor of American Cultural History in 1977. During the 1950s he was instrumental in establishing the field of American Studies, which brought new concepts of culture — developed in such varied disciplines as anthropology, history, and literary studies — to bear on the study of American life. He served as president of the American Studies Association from 1976 to 1978.

Like Foerster's *Nature in American Literature* and Matthiessen's *American Renaissance*, Marx's *The Machine in the Garden* helped elevate the status of American literature, in no small part by focusing on that literature's treatment of nature. His analysis of American authors' handling of the pastoral mode implicitly validated those writers by making them part of an ancient and highly regarded tradition. At the same time, by arguing that American pastoral was particularly concerned with the intrusion of industrialism into the wilderness — with the recurring presence of the "machine in the garden" — he deepened the distinction between American letters and their European counterparts.

Marx treats pastoralism in general as an attempt to resolve the conflict between civilization and nature. In the essay below, excerpted from *The Machine in the Garden*, he stresses the pervasiveness of "the image of the machine's sudden appearance" in the seemingly natural setting, terming it "a metaphoric design which recurs everywhere in our literature." Analyzing a passage from Nathaniel Hawthorne's journals, Marx argues that it is a mistake to consider this "basic design . . . as a product of modern romanticism." Its underlying pattern, rather, is that of the ancient pastoral, whose topic has always been not so much romantic nature as the "incursion of history" into Edenic myth. In a rapidly industrializing America on the verge of developing an environmental sensibility, such a pattern provided a timely, if painful, reminder of "the existence of a reality alien to the pastoral dream."

෯ ෯ ෯

On the morning of July 27, 1844, Nathaniel Hawthorne sat down in the woods near Concord, Massachusetts, to await (as he put it) "such little events as may happen." His purpose, so far as we can tell, was chiefly literary. Though he had no reason to believe that anything memorable would happen, he sat there in solitude and silence and tried to record his every impression as precisely as possible. The whole enterprise is reminiscent of the painstaking literary exercises of his neighbor, Henry Thoreau. Hawthorne filled eight pages of his notebook on this occasion. What he wrote is not a finished piece of work and yet, surprisingly enough, neither is it a haphazard series of jottings. One incident dominates the rest of his impressions. Around this "little event" a certain formal—one might almost say dramatic—pattern takes shape. It is to this pattern that I want to call attention.[1]

To begin, Hawthorne describes the setting, known in the neighborhood as "Sleepy Hollow":

> . . . a shallow space scooped out among the woods, which surround it on all sides, it being pretty nearly circular, or oval, and two or three hundred yards— perhaps four or five hundred—in diameter. The present season, a thriving field of Indian corn, now in its most perfect growth, and tasselled out, occupies nearly half of the hollow; and it is like the lap of bounteous Nature, filled with bread stuff.

Then, in minute detail, he records what he sees and hears close by. "Observe the pathway," he writes, "it is strewn over with little bits of dry twigs and decayed branches, and the sear and brown oak leaves of last year that have been moistened by snow and rain, and whirled about by harsh and gentle winds, since their departed verdure . . ." And so on. What counts here, needless to say, is not the matter so much as the feeling behind it. Hawthorne is using natural facts metaphorically to convey something about a human situation. From several pages in this vein we get an impression of a man in almost perfect repose, idly brooding upon the minutiae of nature, and now and then permitting his imagination a brief flight. Along the path, for example, he notices that "sunshine glimmers through shadow, and shadow effaces sunshine, imaging that pleasant mood of mind where gaiety and pensiveness intermingle." For the most part, however, Hawthorne is satisfied to set down unadorned sense impressions, and especially sounds — sounds made by birds, squirrels, insects, and moving leaves.

But then, after a time, the scope of his observations widens. Another kind of sound comes through. He hears the village clock strike, a cowbell tinkle, and mowers whetting their scythes.

Without any perceptible change of mood or tone, he shifts from images of nature to images of man and society. He insists that "these sounds of labor" do not "disturb the repose of the scene" or "break our sabbath; for like a sabbath seems this place, and the more so on account of the cornfield rustling at our feet." He is describing a state of being in which there is no tension either within the self or between the self and its environment. Much of this harmonious effect is evoked by the delicate interlacing of sounds that seem to unify society, landscape, and mind. What lends most interest, however, to this sense of all-encompassing harmony and peace is a vivid contrast:

> But, hark! there is the whistle of the locomotive — the long shriek, harsh, above all other harshness, for the space of a mile cannot mollify it into harmony. It tells a story of busy men, citizens, from the hot street, who have come to spend a day in a country village, men of business; in short of all unquietness; and no wonder that it gives such a startling shriek, since it brings the noisy world into the midst of our slumbrous peace. As our thoughts repose again, after this interruption, we find ourselves gazing up at the leaves, and comparing their different aspect, the beautiful diversity of green. . . .

With the train out of earshot and quiet restored, Hawthorne continues his observations. An ant colony catches his eye. Possibly, he muses, it is the very model of the community which the Fourierites and others are pursuing in their stumbling way. Then, "like a malevolent genius," he drops a few grains of sand into the entrance of an ant hole and obliterates it. The result is consternation among the inhabitants, their frantic movements displaying their "confusion of mind." How inexplicable, he writes, must be the agency which has effected this mischief. But now it is time for him to leave. Rising, he notices a cloud moving across the sun; many clouds now are scattered about the sky "like the shattered ruins of a dreamer's Utopia. . . ." Then, in a characteristic tone of self-deprecation, he remarks upon the "narrow, scanty and meagre" record of observation he has compiled during his morning in the woods. What troubles him is the discrepancy between the shallow stream of recorded thought ("distinct and expressed thought") and the broad tide of dim emotions, ideas, and associations that had been flowing all the while somewhere at the back of his mind. "When we see how little we can express," he concludes, "it is a wonder that any man ever takes up a pen a second time."

Yet the fact is that Hawthorne has succeeded in expressing a great deal. True, there are no memorable revelations to be got from these notes, no surprises, nothing of immediate interest from a biographical, historical, or critical standpoint. And yet there is something arresting about the episode: the writer sitting in his green retreat dutifully attaching words to natural facts, trying to tap the subterranean flow of thought and feeling and then, suddenly, the startling shriek of the train whistle bearing in upon him, forcing him to acknowledge the existence of a reality alien to the pastoral dream. What begins as a conventional tribute to the pleasures of withdrawal from the world—a simple pleasure fantasy—is transformed by the interruption of the machine into a far more complex state of mind.

Our sense of its evocative power is borne out by the fact that variants of the Sleepy Hollow episode have appeared everywhere in American writing since the 1840's. We recall the scene in *Walden* where Thoreau is sitting rapt in a revery and then, penetrating his woods like the scream of a hawk, the whistle of the locomotive is heard; or the eerie passage in *Moby-Dick* where Ishmael is exploring the innermost recesses of a beached whale and suddenly the image shifts and the leviathan's skeleton is a New England textile mill; or the dramatic moment in *Huckleberry Finn* when Huck and Jim are floating along peacefully and a monstrous steamboat suddenly bulges out of the night and smashes straight through their raft. More often than not in these episodes, the machine is made to appear with startling suddenness. Sometimes it abruptly enters a Happy Valley, at others a traveler suddenly comes upon it. In one of Melville's tales ("The Tartarus of Maids"), the narrator is trying to find a paper mill in the mountains; he drives his sleigh into a deep hollow between hills that rise like steep walls, and he still cannot see the place when, as he says, "suddenly a whirring, humming sound broke upon my ear. I looked, and there, like an arrested avalanche, lay the large whitewashed factory." The ominous sounds of machines, like the sound of the steamboat bearing down on the raft or of the train breaking in upon the idyll at Walden, reverberate endlessly in our literature. We hear such a sound, or see the sight which accompanies it, in *The Octopus, The Education of Henry Adams, The Great Gatsby, The Grapes of Wrath,* "The Bear" — and one could go on. Anyone familiar with American writing will recall other examples from the work of Walt Whitman, Sarah Orne Jewett, Henry James, Sherwood Anderson, Willa Cather, Eugene O'Neill, Robert Frost, Hart Crane, T. S. Eliot, John Dos Passos, Ernest Hemingway — indeed it is difficult to think of a major American writer upon whom the image of the machine's sudden appearance in the landscape has not exercised its fascination.[2]

What I am saying, in other words, is that Hawthorne's notes mark the shaping (on a microscopic scale to be sure) of a metaphoric design which recurs everywhere in our literature. . . . By looking closely at the way these notes are composed we can begin to account for the symbolic power of the "little event" in Sleepy Hollow.

Considered simply as a composition, as a way of ordering language to convey ideas and emotions, the first thing to notice about these casual notes is the decisive part played by the machine image. Taken by itself, what comes before we hear the train whistle scarcely arouses our interest. Descriptions of contentment seldom do. But the disturbing shriek of the locomotive changes the texture of the entire passage. Now tension replaces repose: the noise arouses a sense of dislocation, conflict, and anxiety. It is remarkable how evocative the simple device is, especially when we consider that at bottom it consists of nothing more complicated than noise clashing through harmony. This is the sensory core of the larger design, its inherent power to be revealed by its receptivity to the connotations that Hawthorne gathers about it. Like the focal point of a complicated visual pattern, this elemental, irreducible dissonance contains the whole in small.

These observations suggest the conventional character of Hawthorne's composition. For all the apparent spontaneity of his response to the event, and in spite of the novelty of the railroad in 1844 — a recent and in many ways revolutionary invention — it is striking to see how little there is here that can be called "original." One suspects indeed that if we had access to all the notebooks kept by aspiring American writers of the 1840's we would find this "little event" recorded again and again. Two years earlier, for example, one of Hawthorne's literary neighbors, Ralph Waldo Emerson, had made this entry in his journal:

> I hear the whistle of the locomotive in the woods. Wherever that music comes it has its sequel. It is the voice of the civility of the Nineteenth Century saying, "Here I am." It is interrogative: it is prophetic: and this Cassandra is believed: "Whew! Whew! Whew! How is real estate here in the swamp and wilderness? Ho for Boston! Whew! Whew! . . . I will plant a dozen houses on this pasture next moon, and a village anon. . . ."

So far from being unusual, in fact, the "little event" doubtless belongs among the literary commonplaces of the age. Critics with a sociological bent often slight such a derivative aspect of the writer's response. Eager to fix his relations to his age, they look to a writer's work for direct, which is to say, spontaneous, original, unmediated reactions — as if inherited attitudes, forms, and conventions had had little or no part in shaping them. In this case, however, we have only to notice the name of the place in the woods to realize that Art, as usual, has been on the scene first. Not only has it named Sleepy Hollow, but in effect it has designed the symbolic landscape in which the industrial technology makes its appearance.[3]

The ground of Hawthorne's reaction, in other words, had been prepared by Washington Irving and Wordsworth and the "nature poets" of the previous century. In 1844, as it happens, Wordsworth wrote a sonnet protesting against the building of a railroad through the lake country. It begins: "Is then no nook of English ground secure / From rash assault? . . ." and it ends with a plea to "thou beautiful romance / Of nature" to "protest against the wrong." By placing the machine in opposition to the tranquility and order located in the landscape, he makes it an emblem of the artificial, of the unfeeling utilitarian spirit, and of the fragmented, industrial style of life that allegedly follows from the premises of the empirical philosophy. To Wordsworth the new technology is a token of what he likes to call the "fever of the world."[4]

The pattern, moreover, can be traced back to the beginnings of industrialization. In England, as early as the 1780's, writers had been repelled by the ugliness, squalor, and suffering associated with the new factory system, and their revulsion had sharpened the taste, already strong, for images of rural felicity. We think of Blake:

And did those feet in ancient time
  Walk upon England's mountains green?
And was the holy Lamb of God
  On England's pleasant pastures seen?
And did the Countenance Divine
  Shine forth upon our clouded hills?
And was Jerusalem builded here
  Among these dark Satanic Mills?

It is evident that attitudes of this kind played an important part in quickening the massive shift in point of view which was to be called the romantic movement. Just how important they were it is difficult to say. If we regard the movement (to use Whitehead's acute phrase) as "a protest on behalf of the organic view of nature," then the contrast between the machine and the landscape would seem to embody its very essence.[5]

And yet it is misleading to think of the basic design of Hawthorne's notes as a product of modern romanticism. When we strip away the topical surface, particularly the imagery of industrialism and certain special attitudes toward visible nature, it becomes apparent that the underlying pattern is much older and more universal. Then the Sleepy Hollow motif, like a number of other conventions used by romantic writers, proves to be a modern version of an ancient literary device. It is a variation upon the contrast between two worlds, one identified with rural peace and simplicity, the other with urban power and sophistication, which has been used by writers working in the pastoral mode since the time of Virgil.

Although Theocritus is regarded as the first pastoral poet, Virgil's *Eclogues* are the true fountainhead of the pastoral strain in our literature. For one thing, in these poems Virgil (as one classical scholar puts it) "discovered" Arcadia. It is here that he created the symbolic landscape, a delicate blend of myth and reality, that was to be particularly relevant to American experience. For another, it is in the *Eclogues* that the political overtones of the pastoral situation become evident. In the background of the first eclogue, sometimes called "The Dispossessed," there was a specific action of the Roman government: the expropriation of a number of small landholders (including the poet himself) so that military veterans might be rewarded with the seized land. This display of political power no doubt intensified Virgil's feeling for the land as a symbolic repository of value; at the same time it

compelled him to acknowledge the implacable character of the forces threat-
ening the established order. Both responses are accommodated by the thematic structure of Virgil's poem; let us consider it in greater detail.[6]

The poem takes the form of a dialogue between two shepherds. Tityrus,
like Virgil, has successfully petitioned for the return of his land. At the outset he is happily playing upon his pipe when Meliboeus, who has been
evicted, comes by with his herd. Here are the opening lines as translated by
E. V. Rieu:

> Tityrus, while you lie there at ease under the awning of a spreading beech and
> practise country songs on a light shepherd's pipe, I have to bid good-bye to the
> home fields and the ploughlands that I love. Exile for me, Tityrus — and you
> lie sprawling in the shade, teaching the woods to echo back the charms of
> Amaryllis.

Tityrus answers with praise of the patron in Rome to whom he owes his
liberty and his "happy leisure." The man gave his word, says Tityrus, "and
my cattle browse at large, while I myself can play the tunes I fancy on my
rustic flute." In reply, Meliboeus disclaims any feeling of jealousy. "My only
feeling is amazement — with every farm in the whole countryside in such a
state of chaos. Look at myself, unfit for the road, yet forced to drive my goats
on this unending trek." He points to one animal he can "hardly drag" along.
"Just now," he explains, " . . . she bore two kids — I had been counting on
them — and had to leave the poor things on the naked flints." He berates
himself for not anticipating "this disaster."

The first eclogue certainly represents more than a simple wish-image of
bucolic pleasure. No sooner does Virgil sketch in the ideal landscape than
he discloses an alien world encroaching from without. Meliboeus represents
this other world. Through his lines we are made aware that the immediate
setting, with its tender feeling and contentment, is an oasis. Beyond the green
hollow the countryside is in a state of chaos. The very principle of natural
fecundity is threatened (he has been forced to abandon his newborn kids).
What is out there, from the reader's point of view, is a world like the one he
inhabits; it contains great cities like Rome, organized power, authority, restraint, suffering, and disorder. We are made to feel that the rural myth is
threatened by an incursion of history. The state of mind of Meliboeus — we
should call it alienation nowadays — brings a countervailing force to bear

upon the pastoral ideal. Divested of his land, he faces the prospect of unending anxiety, deprivation, and struggle:

> . . . the rest of us are off; some to foregather with the Africans and share their
> thirst; others to Scythia, and out to where the Oxus rolls the chalk along; others
> to join the Britons, cut off as they are by the whole width of the world. Ah, will
> the day come, after many years, when I shall see a place that I can call my
> home . . . ?

The whole thrust of the poem is toward a restoration of the harmony established in the opening lines. Lying at ease under the beech, playing his
pipe, Tityrus embodies the pastoral ideal. Here, incidentally, the distinction
between the pastoral and primitive ideals may be clarified. Both seem to
originate in a recoil from the pain and responsibility of life in a complex
civilization—the familiar impulse to withdraw from the city, locus of power
and politics, into nature. The difference is that the primitivist hero keeps
going, as it were, so that eventually he locates value as far as possible, in space
or time or both, from organized society; the shepherd, on the other hand,
seeks a resolution of the conflict between the opposed worlds of nature and
art. Since he often is the poet in disguise—Tityrus represents Virgil himself—he has a stake in both worlds. In the first eclogue nothing makes the
mediating character of the pastoral ideal so clear as the spatial symbolism in
which it is expressed. The good place is a lovely green hollow. To arrive at
this haven it is necessary to move away from Rome in the direction of nature.
But the centrifugal motion stops far short of unimproved, raw nature.
"Happy old man!" the unfortunate Meliboeus says to his friend: "So your
land will still be yours. And it's enough for you, even though the bare rock
and marshland with its mud and reeds encroach on all your pastures. Your
pregnant ewes will never be upset by unaccustomed fodder; no harm will
come to them. . . ."
     This ideal pasture has two vulnerable borders: one separates it from Rome,
the other from the encroaching marshland. It is a place where Tityrus is
spared the deprivations and anxieties associated with both the city and the
wilderness. Although he is free of the repressions entailed by a complex civilization, he is not prey to the violent uncertainties of nature. His mind is
cultivated and his instincts are gratified. Living in an oasis of rural pleasure,
he enjoys the best of both worlds—the sophisticated order of art and the

simple spontaneity of nature. In a few lines Virgil quickly itemizes the solid satisfactions of the pastoral retreat: peace, leisure, and economic sufficiency. The key to all these felicities is the harmonious relation between Tityrus and the natural environment. It is a serene partnership. In the pastoral economy nature supplies most of the herdsman's needs and, even better, nature does virtually all of the work. A similar accommodation with the idealized landscape is the basis for the herdsman's less tangible satisfactions: the woods "echo back" the notes of his pipe. It is as if the consciousness of the musician shared a principle of order with the landscape and, indeed, the external universe. The echo, a recurrent device in pastoral, is another metaphor of reciprocity. It evokes that sense of relatedness between man and not-man which lends a metaphysical aspect to the mode; it is a hint of the quasi-religious experience to be developed in the romantic pastoralism of Wordsworth, Emerson, and Thoreau. Hence the pastoral ideal is an embodiment of what Lovejoy calls "semi-primitivism"; it is located in a middle ground somewhere "between," yet in a transcendent relation to, the opposing forces of civilization and nature.[7]

What is most impressive, when we read the first eclogue with Hawthorne's notes in mind, is the similarity of the root conflict and of the over-all pattern of thought and emotion. By his presence alone Meliboeus reveals the inadequacy of the Arcadian situation as an image of human experience. His lines convey the intervention of reality; they are a check against our susceptibility to idyllic fantasies. In 1844 Hawthorne assigns a similar function to the machine. Like Virgil's unfortunate herdsman, the sound of the locomotive "brings the noisy world into the midst of . . . slumbrous peace." Although the railroad is a recent invention (the first American railroad had begun operations in 1829), many of the associations it is made to carry are more or less timeless features of *the* world, that is to say, the great world as it traditionally had been conceived in literature from the Old Testament to the poetry of Wordsworth. The train stands for a more sophisticated, complex style of life than the one represented by Sleepy Hollow; the passengers are "busy men, citizens, from the hot street. . . ." The harsh noise evokes an image of intense, overheated, restless striving—a life of "all unquietness" like that associated with great cities as far back as the story of the tower of Babel. The central device of Hawthorne's notes is to expose the pastoral ideal to the pressure of change—to an encroaching world of power and complexity or, in a word, to history.

NOTES

1. *The American Notebooks*, ed. Randall Stewart, New Haven, 1932, pp. 102–5.

2. *The Complete Stories of Herman Melville*, ed. Jay Leyda, New York, 1949, p. 198.

3. *Journals of Ralph Waldo Emerson*, ed. E. W. Emerson and W. E. Forbes, Boston, 1909–14, VI, 322; for the concept of convention used here, see Harry Levin, "Notes on Convention," *Perspectives of Criticism*, Harvard Studies in Comparative Literature, Cambridge, 1950.

4. "On the Projected Kendall and Windermere Railway," *The Poetical Works of Wordsworth*, ed. Thomas Hutchinson, London, 1904, pp. 282–3.

5. *The Poetical Works of William Blake*, ed. John Sampson, London, 1913, p. 370; Alfred North Whitehead, *Science and the Modern World*, New York, 1947, p. 138.

6. Bruno Snell, "Arcadia: The Discovery of a Spiritual Landscape," *The Discovery of the Mind: The Greek Origins of European Thought*, trans. T. G. Rosenmeyer, Cambridge, Mass., 1953; *Virgil, The Pastoral Poems*, trans. E. V. Rieu, Penguin Books, Harmondsworth, England, 1949. Quoted by permission of the publisher.

7. Arthur O. Lovejoy, et al., *A Documentary History of Primitivism and Related Ideas*, Baltimore, 1935, p. 369; Lovejoy saw the roots of cultural primitivism as "various and incongruous." "Common to them all, indeed, is the conviction that the time—whatever time may, for a given writer, be in question—is out of joint; that what is wrong with it is due to an abnormal complexity and sophistication in the life of civilized man, to the pathological multiplicity and emulativeness of his desires and the oppressive overabundance of his belongings, and to the factitiousness and want of inner spontaneity of his emotions; that 'art,' the work of man, has corrupted 'nature,' that is, man's own nature; and that the model of the normal individual life and the normal social order, or at least a nearer approximation to it, is to be found among contemporary 'savage' peoples, whether or not it be supposed to have been realized also in the life of primeval man. Civilized man has been almost continuously subject to moods of revolt against civilization, which in some sense is, indeed, profoundly contrary to his nature; and in the serious preachers of primitivism this revolt has been chronic and intense. But the belief in the superiority of the simple life of 'nature' has been the manifestation sometimes of a hedonistic, sometimes of a rigoristic and even ascetic, conception of the nature of the good, and sometimes a mixture of both." Foreword to Lois Whitney, *Primitivism and the Idea of Progress in English Popular Literature of the Eighteenth Century*, Baltimore, 1934, pp. xiv–xv.

Sources of Selections

Abbott, Lyman. "The Roosevelt-Long Controversy." *Outlook* 86 (8 June 1907): 263.

———. "Imagination in Natural History." *Outlook* 86 (8 June 1907): 263–64.

Austin, Alfred. "The Poetic Interpretation of Nature." *Contemporary Review* 30 (1877): 961–80.

Austin, Mary Hunter. "Regionalism in American Fiction." *English Journal* 21 (Feb. 1932): 97–107.

Burroughs, John. "A Critical Glance into Thoreau." *Atlantic Monthly* 123 (June 1919): 777–86.

———. "Imagination in Natural History." *Outlook* 86 (29 June 1907): 457–59.

———. "The Literary Treatment of Nature." *Atlantic Monthly* 94 (July 1904): 38–43.

———. *Literary Values and Other Papers*. Boston: Houghton Mifflin, 1902.

———. *Notes on Walt Whitman, as Poet and Person*. New York: J. S. Redfield, 1867. Repr. New York: Haskell House, 1971.

———. "Real and Sham Natural History." *Nation* 91 (Mar. 1903): 298–309.

Carpenter, William Benjamin. "Man as the Interpreter of Nature." *Popular Science Monthly* 1 (Oct. 1872): 684–701.

Daniels, Charles Prescott. "Discord in the Forest: John Burroughs vs. William J. Long." *Boston Evening Transcript* (7 Mar. 1903): 23.

Deming, Harold S. "Mr. John Burroughs on Fake Natural History." *Outing Magazine* 50 (Apr. 1907): 124–27.

Eckstorm, Fannie. "Thoreau's 'Maine Woods.'" *Atlantic Monthly* 102 (1908): 242–50.

Ellis, Havelock. "The Love of Wild Nature." *Contemporary Review* 95 (1909): 180–99.

Foerster, Norman. "The Nature Cult To-Day." *Nation* 94 (11 Apr. 1912): 358.

———. *Nature in American Literature: Studies in the Modern View of Nature*. New York: Macmillan, 1923.

Hudson, W. H. "Truth Plain and Coloured." *Speaker* (9 Dec. 1905): 248–49.

Jefferies, Richard. "Nature and Books." *Fortnightly Review* 47 (1887): 646–56.

Krutch, Joseph Wood. "A Kind of Pantheism." *Saturday Review of Literature* 33 (10 June 1950): 7–8, 30–34.

Lawrence, D. H. *Studies in Classic American Literature*. New York: T. Seltzer, 1923. Repr. New York: Viking, 1964.

Leopold, Aldo. "The Forestry of the Prophets." *Journal of Forestry* 18 (Apr. 1920): 412–19.

Repr. *The River of the Mother of God and Other Essays by Aldo Leopold.* Ed. Susan L. Flader and J. Baird Callicott. Madison: University of Wisconsin Press, 1991. 71–77.

Long, William J. "The Modern School of Nature-Study and Its Critics." *North American Review* 176 (May 1903): 694.

———. "Science, Nature and Criticism." *Science* 19 (13 May 1904): 760–67.

Lowell, James Russell. "Thoreau." In *Literary Essays: Among My Books, My Study Windows, Fireside Travels.* 1865. Boston: Houghton Mifflin, 1890. 360–81.

Mabie, Hamilton Wright. "John Burroughs." *Century Magazine* 54 (Aug. 1897): 560–68.

———. *Nature and Culture.* 1896. Toronto: Morang & Co., 1904.

———. *Short Studies in Literature.* 1891. New York: Dodd, Mead, 1916.

Marx, Leo. *The Machine in the Garden: Technology and the Pastoral Ideal in America.* 1964. New York: Oxford University Press, 1967.

Matthiessen, F. O. *American Renaissance: Art and Expression in the Age of Emerson and Whitman.* 1941. New York: Oxford University Press, 1968.

Miller, Perry. "Nature and the National Ego." *Harvard Theological Review* 48 (Oct. 1955): 239–53. Repr. *Errand into the Wilderness* (Cambridge: Harvard University Press, 1993): 204–16.

Mumford, Lewis. *The Golden Day.* New York: Boni and Liveright, 1926.

Paul, Sherman. *The Shores of America: Thoreau's Inward Exploration.* Urbana: University of Illinois Press, 1958.

Peattie, Donald Culross. "Is Thoreau a Modern?" *North American Review* 245 (Mar. 1938): 159–69.

Roberts, Charles G. D. *The Kindred of the Wild: A Book of Animal Life.* Boston: L. C. Page & Co., 1902.

Roosevelt, Theodore. "Nature Fakers." *Everybody's Magazine* 17 (1907): 427–30.

Savage, D. S. "Poetry and Nature." *Poetry: A Magazine of Verse* 61 (Dec. 1942): 496–504.

Sharp, Dallas Lore. *The Face of the Fields.* 1911. Freeport, N.Y.: Books for Libraries, 1967.

Tracy, Henry Chester. *American Naturists.* New York: E. P. Dutton, 1930.

Tuckerman, Henry T. *America and Her Commentators. With a Critical Sketch of Travel in the United States.* New York: Scribner, 1864.

Van Doren, Mark. "A New Naturalist." *North American Review* 244 (1937): 162–71.

Whitcomb, Selden L. "Nature in Early American Literature." *Sewanee Review* 2 (1893): 159–79.

Woolley, Mary E. "The Development of the Love of Romantic Scenery in America." *American Historical Review* 3 (1897–98): 56–66.

Wright, Mabel Osgood. "Life Outdoors and Its Effect Upon Literature." *Critic* 42 (Apr. 1903): 308–11.

———. "Nature as a Field for Fiction." *New York Times Review of Books,* 9 Dec. 1905, 872.

Annotated Bibliography
of Early Ecocriticism

"The Animal Story." *Edinburgh Review* 214 (July 1911): 94–118. Largely sympathetic review of animal books by Charles G. D. Roberts, Ernest Seton-Thompson, Jack London, and William J. Long.

Backman, Melvin. "The Wilderness and the Negro in Faulkner's 'The Bear.'" *PMLA* 76 (Dec. 1961): 595–600. Discusses the role of wilderness as a symbol for Isaac McCaslin's "primitivistic communism."

Beebe, William. *The Book of Naturalists*. New York: Knopf, 1945. Beebe's introduction to part 2 of this anthology (pages 87–93) briefly discusses his criteria for good natural history writing.

Beers, Henry A. "The Modern Feeling for Nature." *Lippincott's Magazine* 32 (Dec. 1883): 604–15. Examines a variety of causes, including the "increasing tameness of human life" and the "rapid progress of the natural sciences," for the predominance of natural description in nineteenth-century literature.

Binkley, C. A. "Poetic Interpretation of Nature." *Poet-Lore* 13: 53–79. A lengthy, rambling discussion of the "objective" and "subjective" modes of the poetic treatment of nature.

Boynton, H. W. "Nature and Human Nature." *Atlantic Monthly* 89 (Jan. 1902): 134–41. Essay review of several nature books by authors including Gilbert White, John Muir, Ernest Seton-Thompson, Agnes Replier, Dallas Lore Sharp, and John C. Van Dyke.

Burroughs, John. *Accepting the Universe: Essays in Naturalism*. Boston: Houghton Mifflin, 1920. Includes lengthy philosophical musings on nature's relations to humankind, as expressed through religion and literature.

———. *Birds and Poets, with Other Papers*. New York: Hurd and Houghton, 1878. The chapter "Birds and Poets" discusses the treatment of birds as "a symbol and a suggestion" by poets ranging from the classical to the contemporary.

———. "Fake Natural History: Gold Bricks for the Editors." *Outing Magazine* 49 (Feb. 1907): 665–68. One of Burroughs's many sallies in the "nature faker" debate.

———. *Field and Study*. Boston: Houghton Mifflin, 1919. Includes a chapter, "Literature," that discusses Whitman at some length and also mentions Wordsworth, Burns, Thaxter, Bryant, and Shakespeare.

————. "Nature in Literature." In *Essays from "The Critic."* John Burroughs, Edmund Stedman, et al. Boston: James R. Osgood, 1882. 103–6. Brief note on the use of nature by poets from Virgil to Whitman.

————. "On Humanizing the Animals." *Century Magazine* 67 (Mar. 1904): 773–80. Comments on "nature faking."

————. "Sham Natural History." *Outing Magazine* (Apr. 1905): 118–19. More on the "nature fakers."

————. "Thoreau's Wildness." In *Essays from "The Critic."* John Burroughs, Edmund Stedman, et al. Boston: James R. Osgood, 1882. 9–18. Argues that Thoreau was less a naturalist than a "white Indian."

————. "The True Test of Good Nature Literature: An Introduction to the New Edition of the 'Nature Library.'" *Country Life in America* 6: 51–53. Stresses the limits of scientific objectivity in nature writing.

————. *Whitman: A Study.* Boston: Houghton Mifflin, 1896. Includes a discussion of Whitman's preference for the "wild" in nature as opposed to traditional "beauty."

Chawner, Mary Grove. "Nature in Emerson's Essays." *New England Magazine* 32: 215–19. Stresses the debt owed by Emerson's philosophy as a whole to his conception of "the correlation of nature and Spirit" (219).

Clark, Edward B. "Real Naturalists on Nature Faking." *Everybody's Magazine* 17 (1907): 423–27. Several professional naturalists defend Theodore Roosevelt's criticism of the "nature faker" William J. Long.

Clough, Wilson O. *The Necessary Earth: Nature and Solitude in American Literature.* Austin: University of Texas Press, 1964. Focuses on the use of the frontier environment to develop a distinctively American literary complex of language, metaphor, and theme.

Cook, May Estelle. "A Group of Holiday Nature-Books." *Dial* 39 (1 Dec. 1905): 372–75. Review of books by authors including Ernest Thompson Seton, William J. Long, Charles G. D. Roberts, William Beebe, and John Burroughs.

————. "Recent Nature Chronicles." *Dial* 35 (16 Dec. 1903): 467–70. Review of books by authors including Bradford Torrey, William J. Long, Ruth A. Cook, and Alice Jean Patterson.

Coulter, John M. "Nature Study and Intellectual Culture." *Science* n.s. 4 (20 Nov. 1896): 740–44. This speech, delivered before the National Education Association's Department of Natural Sciences Teaching, argues for the pedagogical efficacy of nature study.

Cutright, Paul. *Theodore Roosevelt the Naturalist.* New York: Harper, 1956. Includes occasional analyses of Roosevelt's natural history writings.

Dowden, Edward. "The Poetical Feeling for External Nature." *The Contemporary Review* 2 (1868): 535–56. Discussion of the growth of nature appreciation that ranges widely through literature and philosophy.

Fagin, Nathan Bryllion. *William Bartram, Interpreter of the American Landscape.* Baltimore: Johns Hopkins University Press, 1933. Includes lengthy discussions of Bartram's philosophy of nature and the relationship between his literary style and the "luxurious, indolent landscape" he described: "Had he described New England or Canada, it is doubtful whether his style would be so luscious and his book so fascinating" (71).

Fitzgerald, Margaret M. *First Follow Nature: Primitivism in English Poetry, 1725–1750.* New York: Columbia University Press, 1947. Detailed study of neoclassical British poets' use of nature as a source of social authority and as a philosophic, aesthetic, and ethical standard.

Foerster, Norman. "Burroughs as Bergsonist." *North American Review* 212 (Nov. 1920): 670–77. Argues that the philosophy of Henri-Louis Bergson helped Burroughs acknowledge "the immanence of spirit in nature" (673) while facilitating his conception of the unity of philosophy, science, and literature.

———. "The Humanism of Thoreau." *Nation* 105 (5 July 1917): 9–12. Argues against the popular notion of Thoreau as "fervidly worshipping Nature 'for her own sake' . . . and spurning everything that is distinctively human." Instead Thoreau lived primarily "in the spirit" of a universal humanity, albeit "without ceasing to live in the concrete" realm of nature (12).

———. "Lowell as a Poet of Nature." *Sewanee Review* 25 (Oct. 1917): 422–42. Faults James Russell Lowell for an "[u]nconscious insincerity" and "lack of artistic instinct" (437).

———. "Thoreau and the Wild." *Dial* 63 (28 June 1917): 8–11. Argues that what distinguishes Thoreau from other American writers is his attachment to "the wild," which Foerster characterizes as "living Nature, the inscrutable personality that animates the flux" (8).

———. "Whitman as a Poet of Nature." *Publications of the Modern Language Association of America* 31 (1916): 736–58. Lengthy discussion of Whitman's "sensuous receptivity" (746) to all aspects of nature, which unfortunately renders him "inebriate" where the "true poet is serene" (758).

Hale, Edward Everett, Jr. "American Scenery in Cooper's Novels." *Sewanee Review* 18 (July 1910): 317–32. Treats "scenery" as "something between Nature and Landscape" (317) and highlights the conservationist ethic represented by Judge Temple in *The Pioneers.*

Hall, James Norman. "The Spirit of Place." *Atlantic Monthly* 152 (Oct. 1933): 478–83. Argues that lyric poetry languishes in the United States because, unlike England, the nation has neglected the "spirit of place."

Halsey, Francis W. "The Rise of the Nature Writers." *American Monthly Review of Reviews* 26 (1902): 567–71. Attributes the phenomenal popularity of turn-of-the-century nature books to the rapid increase in urbanization.

Hicks, Phillip Marshall. *The Development of the Natural History Essay in American Literature.* Philadelphia: University of Pennsylvania, 1924. A wide-ranging literary-historical treatment of several writers, including Bartram, Thoreau, and Burroughs.

Homans, Margaret. "Repression and Sublimation of Nature in *Wuthering Heights*." *PMLA* 93 (Jan. 1978): 9–19. Draws on Sigmund Freud, Harold Bloom, and Jacques Derrida to argue that *Wuthering Heights*, however superficially saturated with the presence of nature, in fact "averts its eyes from nature" in a way that is highly symptomatic. For Cathy, literal nature is so closely associated with her forbidden love for Heathcliff that it must be sublimated into the figurative nature "which thrives on the textual surface of the novel."

Huth, Hans. *Nature and the American: Three Centuries of Changing Attitudes*. 1957. Lincoln: University of Nebraska Press, 1990. Ambitious intellectual history that pays considerable attention to nature writing.

"John Burroughs's Supremacy as a Nature Writer." *Current Literature* 49 (Dec. 1910): 680–81. Ranks Burroughs above such other nature writers as Gilbert White and Henry Thoreau on the basis of his "honesty, directness, [and] euphony" (681).

Johnson, Wingate M. "An Away-from-Nature Movement." *Atlantic Monthly* 150 (July 1932): 127–28. Takes issue with the more effusive expressions of the American "cult of nature," particularly as articulated in John Powys's *The Meaning of Culture*.

Judson, Alexander C. "Henry Vaughan as a Nature Poet." *Publications of the Modern Language Association of America* 42 (1927): 146–56. Literary-historical essay on the "precursor of the eighteenth-century romantic poets." Argues that in Vaughan's poetry nature serves three purposes: "(1) to furnish material for a Homeric simile or brief incidental comparison; (2) to provide a point of departure for a didactic poem; (3) to serve as a direct inspiration to man in his attitude toward his fellow men and toward God."

Knowlton, E. C. "Nature in Older Irish." *Publications of the Modern Language Association of America* 44 (1929): 92–122. Detailed study of the use of nature similes and other figures in Older Irish literature.

Kroeber, Karl. "'Home at Grasmere': Ecological Holiness." *PMLA* 89 (Jan. 1974): 132–41. Kroeber, the author of *Ecological Literary Criticism: Romantic Imagining and the Biology of Mind* (New York: Columbia University Press, 1994), was one of the first of the contemporary ecocritics. In this *PMLA* essay he argues for the relevance of modern ecological awareness to our appreciation of Wordsworth: "recent changes in our thinking about man, nature, and human life make it possible to recognize a special originality in Wordsworth's prosaic celebrations of serene egoism amidst remote mountain valleys" (132).

Krutch, Joseph Wood. "Communion with Her Visible Forms." *Nation* 144 (24 Apr. 1937): 469–71. Review of the work of Donald Culross Peattie, whose view of the oneness of nature Krutch praises for being "unmistakably modern . . . protoplasmic rather than spiritual" (469).

———. *Great American Nature Writing*. New York: Sloane, 1950. The *Saturday Review* article "A Kind of Pantheism" is excerpted from the foreword to this anthology.

———. *Henry David Thoreau*. New York: Sloane, 1948. Perceptive analysis of the many and often conflicting facets of Thoreau's understanding of nature. Krutch notes that on January 24, 1841, Thoreau wrote in his *Journal* that "[i]t is more proper for a spiritual fact to have suggested an analogous natural one than for the natural fact to have preceded the spiritual in our minds." Krutch comments that "no statements would seem to commit a man more absolutely to the intuitional as opposed to the scientific point of view. Yet it was later in the same year that he was proclaiming, 'The moral aspect of nature is a jaundice reflected from man'" (175–76).

Laurence, David. "William Bradford's American Sublime." *PMLA* 102 (Jan. 1987): 55–65. Argues that, while "Bradford is no romantic," the famous passage from *Of Plymouth Plantation*—the one which intones of the Pilgrims, "what could they see but a hideous and desolate wilderness"—constitutes a very early "prototype of the . . . romantic sublime" (55).

Long, William J. "Nature and Books." *Dial* 34 (1 June 1903): 357–60. For outdoor reading, Long dismisses Bryant and Wordsworth. Long recommends Ruskin, Emerson, Faust, and Shakespeare, but insists they all pale beside the *Book of Nature*.

Lutts, Ralph H. *The Nature Fakers: Wildlife, Science, and Sentiment*. Golden, Colo.: Fulcrum, 1990. Well researched and well written treatment of the nature faker controversy—the best single source on the topic.

Mabie, Hamilton Wright. "A Springtime Literary Talk: Nature in Poetry and Prose." *Ladies' Home Journal* 20 (Apr. 1903): 14. Brief synopsis of the genesis of nature writing.

Marsh, George Perkins. *Man and Nature; Or, Physical Geography as Modified by Human Action*. Cambridge: Harvard University Press, 1965. In order to buttress his groundbreaking arguments about looming environmental catastrophe, Perkins analyzes a wide variety of texts for evidence of historical ecological change.

Meyer, Gerard Previn. "Nature's Various Vitality." *Saturday Review of Literature* 37 (9 Oct. 1954): 18–19. Review of nature poetry by W. S. Merwin, Daniel G. Hoffman, and Padraic Colum.

Miller, Perry. "Thoreau in the Context of International Romanticism." *New England Quarterly* 34 (June 1961): 147–59. Repr. *Nature's Nation* (Cambridge: Harvard University Press, 1967): 175–83. Argues that Thoreau had quite early learned from Wordsworth the solution to "one of the major problems of the Romantic movement—for that portion of Romanticism preoccupied with the new interpretation of nature it was the major problem—of striking and maintaining the delicate balance between object and reflection" (177).

Mumford, Lewis. *The Brown Decades: A Study of the Arts in America*. New York: Dover, 1931. The chapter "Renewal of the Landscape" discusses Thoreau and his influence on later nature writers.

———. *Interpretations and Forecasts: 1922–1972*. New York: Harcourt Brace Jovanovich, 1944. Includes perceptive chapters on Audubon and Darwin.

Nicolson, Marjorie Hope. *Mountain Gloom and Mountain Glory: The Development of the Aesthetics of the Infinite*. Ithaca, N.Y.: Cornell University Press, 1959. Repr. New

York: Norton, 1963. Includes a lengthy analysis of Thomas Burnet's *Sacred Theory of the Earth.*

Pearson, L. E. "John Muir, Prophet-Naturalist." *Poet-Lore* 36 (Mar. 1925): 45–62. Admiring and wide-ranging discussion that includes interesting comparisons of Muir with Thoreau and Burroughs.

Peattie, Donald Culross. "The Business of Nature Writing." *Saturday Review of Literature* 23 (5 Apr. 1941): 3–4, 38–39. Analyzes the relations between nature writing and science.

———. *The Road of a Naturalist.* Boston: Houghton Mifflin, 1941. The chapter "Since Thoreau" expands upon the material excerpted in the *Saturday Review* as "The Business of Nature Writing."

Perry, Jennette Barbour. "Was Thoreau a Lover of Nature?" *Critic* 43 (Aug. 1903): 152. In this brief note, Perry questions Thoreau's relationship to nature, suggesting that "one who does not first love human nature is incapable of loving nature herself" (152).

"Poetry and Science." *Nation* 25 (25 Oct. 1877): 258–59. Critique of J. C. Shairp's *On the Poetic Interpretation of Nature.*

Reynolds, Myra. *The Treatment of Nature in English Poetry Between Pope and Wordsworth.* Chicago: University of Chicago Press, 1909. Repr. New York: Gordian Press, 1966. Traces in detail the transition from the neoclassical to the romantic view of nature.

Robinson, E. Arthur. "Conservation in Cooper's *The Pioneers.*" *PMLA* 82 (Dec. 1967): 564–78. Argues that virtually all the characters in *The Pioneers* can be grouped into three categories: "those who appear to believe that natural resources exist for their own benefit," those who believe in a utilitarian form of conservation aimed at insuring the continued availability of natural resources for future generations, and those who insist that nature be respected not because it can benefit humans but because it has intrinsic value.

Roosevelt, Theodore. *Literary Essays.* In *The Works of Theodore Roosevelt: National Edition,* vol. 12. New York: Scribner's, 1926. Includes a chapter, "Three Capital Books of the Wilderness," that was first published in the *Outlook* in 1912.

Schmitt, Peter J. *Back to Nature: The Arcadian Myth in Urban America.* New York: Oxford University Press, 1969. Includes a perceptive chapter, "The Wilderness Novel," that discusses the work of Jack London, Gene Stratton Porter, and many others.

Sedgwick, Henry D. "Bryant's Permanent Contribution to Literature." *Atlantic Monthly* 79 (Apr. 1897): 539–49. Early treatment of Bryant's poetic handling of nature.

Shaler, Nathaniel. *Domesticated Animals: Their Relation to Man and to His Advancement in Civilization.* New York: Charles Scribner's Sons, 1895. Includes an early, utilitarian appeal for the preservation of species, on the grounds that currently undomesticated animals might later prove useful. "[T]he problem of domestication shades into the question as to the preservation of the life which is now on the earth . . . from the swift destruction which our rude subjugation of the earth threatens to inflict. . . . [W]e must ask ourselves what limits are to be set to the displacement of the ancient order which is now going on" (251). The answer is what we would today term a bioregional preserve: "To attain this object we cannot trust to the share of this life which can be brought into zoological and botanical gardens, however extensive and well managed. The only way is to make certain reservations in various parts of the world, each containing an area and a variety of conditions great enough to afford a safe lodgment for a true sample of the life of an organic province" (255).

———. *The Interpretation of Nature*. Boston: Houghton Mifflin, 1893. A prolonged philosophical discussion of the "somewhat strained" "relations between natural science and religion" (iv).

———. "The Landscape as a Means of Culture." *Atlantic Monthly* 82 (Dec. 1898): 777–85. In an essay that may stem from the same impulse underlying today's familiar "nature interpretation"—as practiced, for example, by interpretive rangers in the national parks—Shaler proposes that the appreciation of landscape be taught as consciously and formally as we teach the appreciation of music and art.

Sharp, Dallas Lore. "Fifty Years of John Burroughs." *Atlantic Monthly* 106 (Nov. 1910): 631–41. Argues that Burroughs was "a good, but not a great naturalist," and that "[h]is claim . . . upon us is literary" (641).

Smallwood, William Martin, and Mabel Sarah Coon Smallwood. *Natural History and the American Mind*. New York: Columbia University Press, 1941. Detailed study of the effect of natural history on early American culture.

Spears, John. R. "Mr. Spears Finds Nature Books Useful." *New York Times Saturday Review of Books* (25 May 1907): 338. Brief evaluation of books by C. Hart Merriam, Mabel Osgood Wright, John Burroughs, Ernest Thompson Seton, and others.

———. "Mr. Spears on John Burroughs's Criticism of Thompson Seton." *New York Times Saturday Review of Books*, 25 Apr. 1903, 288. Defends Ernest Thompson Seton against John Burroughs's charge of "nature faking."

Stallknecht, Newton P. "Nature and Imagination in Wordsworth's Meditation Upon Mt. Snowdon." *Publications of the Modern Language Association of America* 52 (1937): 835–47. Invokes Whitehead and Spinoza while arguing that, for Wordsworth, nature was "an animate power" (843) with which our own minds could merge.

Stanley, H. M. "Burroughs as Prose Writer." *Dial* 32 (1 Jan. 1902): 7–8. Favorable critical evaluation of Burroughs's nature writing. Stanley argues that, despite Burroughs's claims to the contrary, "he affiliates more closely with Thoreau than any other author" (7).

Stillman, W. J. "The Philosophers' Camp: Emerson, Lowell, and Others in the Adirondacks." *Century Magazine* 46 (Aug. 1893): 598–606. Stillman reminisces, twenty-five years after the fact, about "a gathering unique in the history of vacations" (599)—the 1858 wilderness excursion memorialized by Emerson in his poem "The Adirondacs. A Journal."

"The Strength and the Weakness of John Burroughs." *Current Opinion* 71 (July 1921): 74–

75. Review of John L. Hervey's *All's Well*, which book praises Burroughs for his calmness and "clear vision" (74) and faults him for a lack of "real feeling" and for succumbing to "the prostration before science which modernity demands". (75).

Stubbs, M. Wilma. "Celia Thaxter, Poet of Nature." *Nature Magazine* 25 (June 1935): 297–98. Biographical sketch of the popular nature poet and frequent contributor to the *Atlantic.*

Templeman, William D. "Thoreau, Moralist of the Picturesque." *Publications of the Modern Language Association of America* 47 (1932): 864–89. Details William Gilpin's considerable influence on Thoreau.

Torrey, Bradford. "Thoreau's Attitude Toward Nature." *Atlantic Monthly* 84 (Nov. 1899): 706–10. Argues that Thoreau's nature description "expresses life, not theory, and calls for life on the part of the hearer" (707), and that what Thoreau sought—what "he required of ferns and clouds, of birds and swamps and deserted roads," was "that they should do something to redeem his life" (710).

West, Herbert Faulkner. *The Nature Writers: A Guide to Richer Reading.* Brattleboro, Vt.: Stephen Daye Press, 1939. West's introduction comprises a brief intellectual history of nature writing from ancient times to the twentieth century. Includes a foreword by Henry Beston.

Williams, Paul O. "The Influence of Thoreau on the American Nature Essay." *Thoreau Society Bulletin* 145 (Fall 1978): 1–5. Argues that nature essays are "written by people who feel that in the natural world there is, somehow, a hieroglyph which, if they can just read it, will turn out to be their own names," and that "Thoreau was such a person" (1).

Williams, Raymond. *Keywords: A Vocabulary of Culture and Society.* New York: Oxford University Press, 1976. This Marxist dictionary's six-page entry on "Nature"—"perhaps the most complex word in the language" (184)—should be required reading for ecocritics.

———. *Problems in Materialism and Culture.* London: Verso, 1980. More required reading, particularly the chapter "Ideas of Nature" (67–85), a searching critique of the constantly shifting political valence of an idea that is anything but "natural."

Wilson, [Mrs.] Eddie W. "The Wilderness in Literature." *Living Wilderness* 19 (1954): 1–4. A brief survey of the appearance of the wilderness theme in literature from Gilgamesh to Muir; offers plenty of quotes but no analysis.

Zahniser, Howard. "In April—John Burroughs." *Nature Magazine* 29 (Apr. 1937): 199. In July 1936 *Nature Magazine* began a one-year series of monthly essays, all written by Howard Zahniser, on prominent nature writers. Each essay is one to two pages long and offers a good introduction to the featured writer, albeit with little actual criticism. They're listed here individually and in alphabetical order.

———. "In August, Florence Merriam Bailey." *Nature Magazine* 28 (Aug. 1936): 71, 127.

———. "In December—Whittier." *Nature Magazine* 28 (Dec. 1936): 327.

———. "In February—William Bartram." *Nature Magazine* 29 (Feb. 1937): 71.

———. "In January—Thomas Nuttall." *Nature Magazine* 29 (Jan. 1937): 7.

———. "In July, Alexander Wilson." *Nature Magazine* 28 (July 1936): 7.

———. "In June—Dan Beard." *Nature Magazine* 29 (June 1937): 327.

———. "In May—Rowland E. Robinson." *Nature Magazine* 29 (May 1937): 263, 317.

———. "In November—A. C. Bent." *Nature Magazine* 28 (Nov. 1936): 263.

———. "In October—Frank Bolles." *Nature Magazine* 28 (Oct. 1936): 199.

———. "In September, Maurice Thompson." *Nature Magazine* 28 (Sept. 1936): 135.

Index